A TEXT BOOK OF

DATA COMMUNICATION

Semester – III

SECOND YEAR DEGREE COURSES IN COMPUTER SCIENCE & ENGINEERING

As Per New Revised Syllabus of Shivaji University, Kolhapur
(Effective from 2014)

R. C. JAISWAL
M. E. (E & TC)
Asst. Professor, E & TC Dept.
Pune Institute of Computer Technology
Katraj, Pune

G. R. PATIL
M. E. (Electronics)
Associate Professor, E & TC Dept.
Army Institute of Technology
Dighi, Pune.

NN SAKHARE
M. E. (Computer Network)
Lecturer, Comp. Engg. Dept.
Vishwakarma Institute of Information Technology (VIIT),
Kondhwa, Pune.

DATA COMMUNICATION (SE SEM - III COMPUTER - SU)　　　ISBN : 978-93-5164-240-4

First Edition : August 2014

©　　:

The text of this publication, or any part thereof, should not be reproduced or transmitted in any form or stored in any computer storage system or device for distribution including photocopy, recording, taping or information retrieval system or reproduced on any disc, tape, perforated media or other information storage device etc., without the written permission of Authors with whom the rights are reserved. Breach of this condition is liable for legal action.

Every effort has been made to avoid errors or omissions in this publication. In spite of this, errors may have crept in. Any mistake, error or discrepancy so noted and shall be brought to our notice shall be taken care of in the next edition. It is notified that neither the publisher nor the authors or seller shall be responsible for any damage or loss of action to any one, of any kind, in any manner, therefrom.

Published By :　　　　　　　　　　　　　　　　　　　　　　　　　　　**Printed at**
NIRALI PRAKASHAN　　　　　　　　　　　　　　　　　　　**Repro Knowledgecast Limited**
Abhyudaya Pragati, 1312, Shivaji Nagar,　　　　　　　　　　　　　　　　　　　　**India**
Off J.M. Road, PUNE – 411005
Tel - (020) 25512336/37/39, Fax - (020) 25511379
Email : niralipune@pragationline.com

DISTRIBUTION CENTRES
PUNE

Nirali Prakashan
119, Budhwar Peth, Jogeshwari Mandir Lane
Pune 411002, Maharashtra
Tel : (020) 2445 2044, 66022708, Fax : (020) 2445 1538
Email : bookorder@pragationline.com

Nirali Prakashan
S. No. 28/25, Dhyari,
Near Pari Company, Pune 411041
Tel : (022) 24690204 Fax : (020) 24690316
Email : dhyari@pragationline.com
bookorder@pragationline.com

MUMBAI
Nirali Prakashan
385, S.V.P. Road, Rasdhara Co-op. Hsg. Society Ltd.,
Girgaum, Mumbai 400004, Maharashtra
Tel : (022) 2385 6339 / 2386 9976, Fax : (022) 2386 9976
Email : niralimumbai@pragationline.com

DISTRIBUTION BRANCHES

NAGPUR
Pratibha Book Distributors
Above Maratha Mandir, Shop No. 3, First Floor,
Rani Jhanshi Square, Sitabuldi, Nagpur 440012,
Maharashtra, Tel : (0712) 254 7129

BENGALURU
Pragati Book House
House No. 1, Sanjeevappa Lane, Avenue Road Cross,
Opp. Rice Church, Bengaluru – 560002.
Tel : (080) 64513344, 64513355,
Mob : 9880582331, 9845021552
Email:bharatsavla@yahoo.com

JALGAON
Nirali Prakashan
34, V. V. Golani Market, Navi Peth, Jalgaon 425001,
Maharashtra, Tel : (0257) 222 0395
Mob : 94234 91860

KOLHAPUR
Nirali Prakashan
New Mahadvar Road,
Kedar Plaza, 1st Floor Opp. IDBI Bank
Kolhapur 416 012, Maharashtra. Mob : 9855046155

CHENNAI
Pragati Books
9/1, Montieth Road, Behind Taas Mahal, Egmore,
Chennai 600008 Tamil Nadu, Tel : (044) 6518 3535,
Mob : 94440 01782 / 98450 21552 / 98805 82331, Email : bharatsavla@yahoo.com

RETAIL OUTLETS
PUNE

Pragati Book Centre
157, Budhwar Peth, Opp. Ratan Talkies,
Pune 411002, Maharashtra
Tel : (020) 2445 8887 / 6602 2707, Fax : (020) 2445 8887

Pragati Book Centre
Amber Chamber, 28/A, Budhwar Peth,
Appa Balwant Chowk, Pune : 411002, Maharashtra,
Tel : (020) 20240335 / 66281669
Email : pbcpune@pragationline.com

Pragati Book Centre
676/B, Budhwar Peth, Opp. Jogeshwari Mandir,
Pune 411002, Maharashtra
Tel : (020) 6601 7784 / 6602 0855

PBC Book Sellers & Stationers
152, Budhwar Peth, Pune 411002, Maharashtra
Tel : (020) 2445 2254 / 6609 2463

MUMBAI
Pragati Book Corner
Indira Niwas, 111 - A, Bhavani Shankar Road, Dadar (W), Mumbai 400028, Maharashtra
Tel : (022) 2422 3526 / 6662 5254, Email : pbcmumbai@pragationline.com

PREFACE

In recent years communication has become an important part of our life. It has become essential to understand the basic concept of communication almost for every engineer. This text is designed to explain the basic concepts in Data Communication.

The book is written mainly for the second year students of Computer Science and Engineering course of Shivaji University, Kolhapur for the subject **"Data Communication"**. It is written as per the new revised syllabus (2014) of Shivaji University, Kolhapur.

The text includes information about basic concepts of Data Communication. Various building blocks of the data communication systems are explained in detail. Mathematical treatment of various concepts are given wherever necessary. Number of solved problems and exercises are given to strengthens the concepts. The working of communication system is explained with extensive waveforms, graphs and circuits to get an insight into the subject.

Our sincere hope is that the material presented in the book will be useful in understanding the subject as well as for attempting examination questions.

We take this opportunity to express our thanks to **Shri. Dineshbhai Furia** and **Shri. Jignesh Furia** and **Shri. M.P. Munde** for publishing this book in time.

We also take this opportunity to express our thank all the staff members of Nirali Prakashan namely Mrs. Anita Kulkarni, Mrs. Pratibha Bele, Mrs. Sarika Wagh and Miss Sarika Shinde for their tremendous dedication and hard work in bringing out this book in an excellent form.

We are also thankful to **Mr. Virdhaval Shinde**, Branch Manager, Kolhapur Offcie and **Mr. Ashok Nanaware**, Branch Manager, Sangli District for their valuable help and efforts for promotion of my book.

Our special thanks to our family members, students and all those who directly or indirectly supported me in this project.

The frontiers of knowledge are bondless and fathomless. Any suggestions and feedback shall be appreciated and acknowledged.

Pune   **Author**

August 2014

SYLLABUS

Unit 1 : Introduction

- Introduction : Data communications, Networks, Protocols & standards (3)
- Network Models : Layered Tasks, The OSI model, Layers in the OSI model, TCP/IP protocol suit, ATM reference model. (4)

Unit 2 : Communication Basics

- Data & Signals : Analog & Digital, Periodic analog signals, digital signals, Transmission Impairments, Data rate limits & Performance. (5)
- Digital Transmission : Line coding & line coding schemes (Unipolar, polar & bipolar) Transmission models. (3)

Unit 3 : Physical Layer

- Transmission media : Guided, Unguided media. (4)
- Network Hardware components : Transceivers & media converters, Repeaters, NIC & PC cards, Bridges, switches, Routers. (4)

Unit 4 : Data Link Layer

- Error detection & correction: Block coding, cyclic codes, checksum. (3)
- Data Link Control : Framming, Flow & error control, stop & wait protocol, sliding window protocol, HDLC protocol. (5)

Unit 5 : The Medium Access Control

- Channel allocation Problem, Multiple Access Protocols, ALHOA, CSMA, collision free protocols, Limited contention protocols. (7)

Unit 6 : IEEE Standards for LANS and MANS

- 802.3 Standard & Ethernet, (8)

  802.4 Standard & Token Bus,

  802.5 Standard & Token Ring,

  Comparison of 802.3, 802.4 and 802.5,

  802.6 standard (DQDB) and 802.2 logical link control.

CONTENTS

UNIT I

1. Networks and Models — 1.1 – 1.56

UNIT II

2. Signals and Data — 2.1 – 2.40
3. Digital Transmission System — 3.1 – 3.66

UNIT III

4. Transmission Media — 4.1 – 4.34
5. Network Hardware Components — 5.1 – 5.36

UNIT IV

6. Error Control and Data Link Layer — 6.1 – 6.80

UNIT V

7. Multiaccess Control — 7.1 – 7.46
8. IEEE Standards for LANS and MANS — 8.1 – 8.30

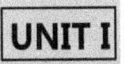

Chapter 1
NETWORKS AND MODELS

OBJECTIVES

After reading this chapter you will understand :

- Introduction to Networking, Advantages and Disadvantages of Installing Networks.
- Network Topologies like Bus, Star, Ring and Mesh.
- Network Classification, LAN, WAN, MAN, Internet and Other Types.
- Layered Task in Detail, Network Layered Architecture.
- Benefits and Downsides of Layered Design.
- Service primitives and relationship of service to protocols.
- Connection Oriented Vs. Connectionless Service.
- ISO-OSI Reference Model, Characteristics of the OSI Layers.
- Functions of each layer and Introduction to different Network Architectures.
- Introduction to TCP/IP and function of each layer.
- Comparison of OSI model and TCP/IP model.
- TCP/IP Protocol Architecture in detail.
- Addressing types like Specific Address, Port Address, IP Address and MAC Address (Hardware Address or Physical Address or Link Address).
- Understanding the Node to Node, Host to Host and Process to Process Delivery.

1.1 INTRODUCTION TO NETWORKING

A network involves a number of devices linked together to form a communication system for information and device sharing.

- Local Area Networks (LANs) are small, limited to about 500 meters, and are commonly deployed in corporate offices to facilitate low-cost, high-bandwidth information transfer within a company.
- Cities and other metropolitan regions can be connected via Metropolitan Area Networks or (MANs), and Wide Area Networks (WANs) involve systems communicating across large geographic regions such as states or countries.
- Globally, computers in networks interlink to form what we refer to as "the Internet."

1.2 ADVANTAGES OF INSTALLING A NETWORK

- **Speed :** Networks provide a very rapid method for sharing and transferring files. Without a network, files are shared by copying them to floppy disks, then carrying or sending the disks from one computer to another. This method of transferring files is very time-consuming.

- **Cost :** Networkable versions of many popular software programs are available at considerable savings when compared to buying individually licensed copies. Besides monetary savings, sharing a program on a network allows for easier upgrading of the program. The changes have to be done only once, on the file server, instead of on all the individual workstations.

- **Security :** Files and programs on a network can be designated as "copy inhibit," so that you do not have to worry about illegal copying of programs. Also, passwords can be established for specific directories to restrict access to authorized users.

- **Centralized Software Management :** One of the greatest benefits of installing a network is the fact that all of the software can be loaded on one computer (the file server). This eliminates the need to spend time and energy installing updates and tracking files on independent computers throughout the building.

- **Resource Sharing :** Sharing resources is another area in which a network exceeds stand-alone computers. Most institutes or companies cannot afford enough laser printers, fax machines, modems, scanners, and CD-ROM players for each computer. However, if these similar peripherals are added to a network, they can be shared by many users.

- **Electronic Mail :** The presence of a network provides the hardware necessary to install an e-mail system. E-mail aids in personal and professional communication for all personnel, and it facilitates the dissemination of general information to the entire users. Electronic mail on a LAN can enable users to communicate with others. If the LAN is connected to the Internet, user can communicate with others throughout the world.

- **Flexible Access :** Networks allow users to access their files from computers throughout the campus if it is a LAN. Users can begin an assignment in their LAN, save part of it on a public access area of the network, and then go to the media center after office hours to finish their work. Users can also work co-operatively through the network.

- **Workgroup Computing :** Workgroup software allows many users to work on a document or project concurrently.

1.3 DISADVANTAGES OF INSTALLING A NETWORK

- **Expensive to Install :** Although a network will generally save money over time, the initial cost of installation can be prohibitive. Cables, network cards, and software are expensive, and the installation may require the services of a technician.
- **Requires Administrative Time :** Proper maintenance of a network requires considerable time and expertise. Many companies have installed a network, only to find that they did not budget for the necessary administrative support.
- **File Server May Fail :** Although a file server is no more susceptible to failure than any other computer, when the files server "goes down," the entire network may come to a halt. When this happens, the entire company may lose access to necessary programs and files.
- **Cables May Break :** The Topology chapter presents information about the various configurations of cables. Some of the configurations are designed to minimize the inconvenience of a broken cable; with other configurations, one broken cable can stop the entire network.

1.4 NETWORK USAGE AND TYPIAL COMPUTER NETWORK

Networks are widely used in both the business and consumer landscapes.

- In the corporate environment, LANs are commonly used to share resources, including electronic files and devices such as printers.
- These LANs are generally connected to other networks via WANs and the Internet to facilitate global data access.
- In healthcare, LANs are used in the clinical environment to provide information such as patient's medical records and drug formularies for doctors and nurses.

Wireless networks provide the next step in utility and convenience for many industries, including health care.

- In general, wireless networks provide the power and freedom of mobility, with the setbacks of reduced speed and unpolished functions (as compared to wired networks).
- While wireless networks have existed for decades, only the recent boom of handheld and mobile devices has spurred the demand necessary to create robust networks.

If a home has more than one computer, then installing a computer network is a smart decision.

- Networks allow you to share an Internet connection and files among multiple PCs.

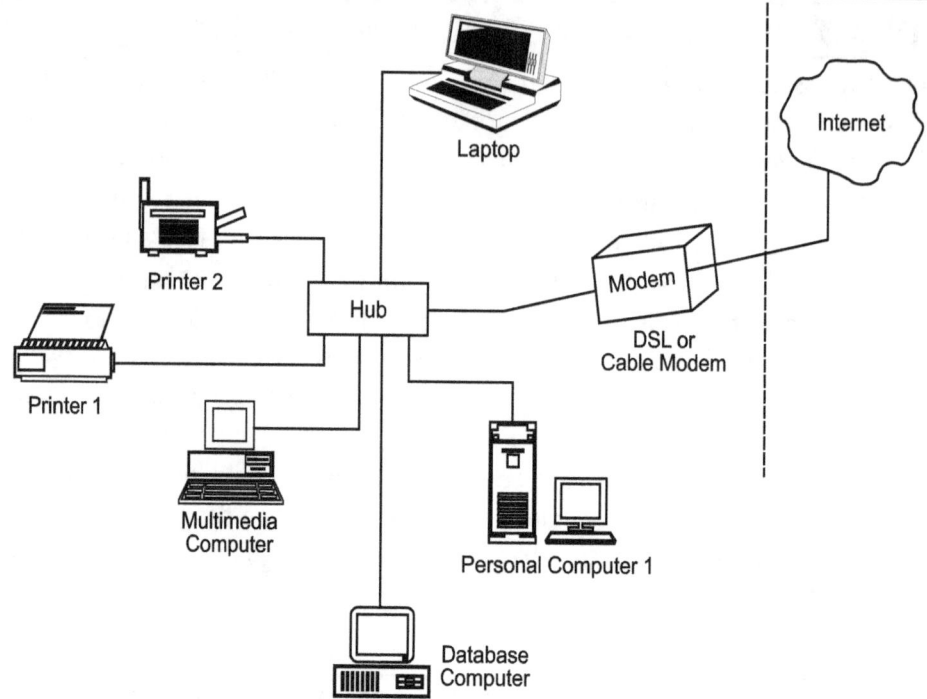

Fig. 1.1 : Typical Home Computer Network (Wired)

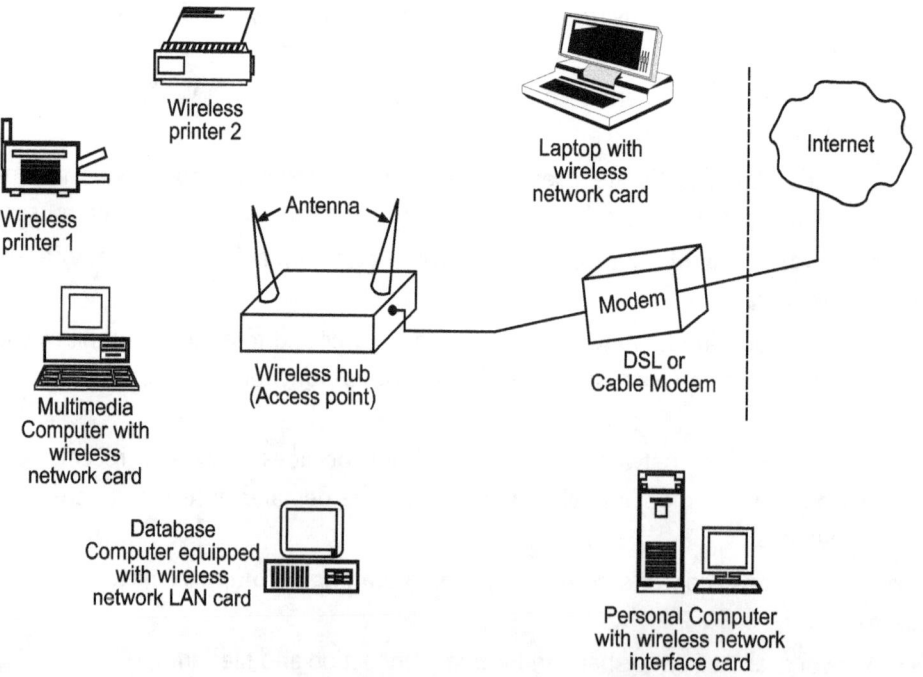

Fig. 1.2 : Typical Home Computer Network (Wireless)

- More importantly, they save time and money, and make using your computer equipment much more enjoyable for everyone in the office as well as in family.
- Lets consider the networking for the home, but all information given here applies to networking for a small business as well.
- Setting up a home network is the simplest way to get the most out of your computer equipment.
- And as your family grows or you add additional computers, expansion is no problem. Best of all, creating a network is easier than you might think.

The key benefits of networking a home include :
- Sharing a high-speed Internet connection - without anyone having to sign off, and without having another phone line installed.
- Playing games head-to-head on different computers from different rooms.
- Sharing an expensive resource like the colour photo printer in office without having to interrupt any office work.
- Everyone in the family can share files from every PC in the house - no need to put files onto floppy or zip discs and swap them.

To go wireless or wired ? That is the question. A wireless setup uses radio waves, while wired networks communicate through data cables. Both systems have their own advantages and disadvantages.

The following points decide whether to go for wired or wireless networks :
- **Range :** The range of the network is an important consideration while using a network.
- **Throughput :** The amount of data transferable using devices is important.
- **Integrity :** The network should have a stable form of communication. The robust designs of technology should provide data integrity performance equal to or better than other technologies.
- **Inter-operability :** Device should provide the ability to connect to wired or wireless LAN with ease.
- **Scalability :** Networks can be designed to be extremely simple or quite complex. Networks should support large number of nodes and/or large physical areas to boost or extend coverage.
- **Simplicity of installation and use :** Users should need very little new information to take advantage of LANs to be used. It should be simple and easy to install.
- **Security :** Because network technology has roots in military applications and banking applications, security has long been a design criterion for network technology.

- **Power requirement for networks :** End-user products should be designed to run with less power and accordingly the networking technique will be decided.
- **Safety :** The used technology should be safe for human and nature. Network must meet stringent government and industry regulations for safety.

Thus Network can be briefly explained as follows :
- A network is a group of two or more computers that are able to communicate with one another and share data (text, sound, images), files, programs, and operations.
- The computers are able to communicate and exchange information because they use software that observes the same set of parameters, or protocol.
- There are several different types of networks.
- All networks operate using the same basic principle : Whenever a computer on network sends information to another computer or peripheral, the information is in the form of a "packet." When the packet reaches the designated station, the information is transferred to the computer.
- The basic equipment you need to set up a network includes network cards, cables, and networking software. You also need a "hub" into which all the cables are connected.

1.5 NETWORK TOPOLOGY (PHYSICAL AND LOGICAL)

- The physical topology of a network refers to the configuration of cables, computers, and other peripherals.
- **Physical topology** should not be confused with **logical topology** which is the method used to pass information between workstations.
- Every LAN has a topology, or the way that the devices on a network are arranged and how they communicate with each other.
- The way that the workstations are connected to the network through the actual cables that transmit data, and the physical structure of the network is called the **physical topology**.
- The **logical topology** is also called as signal topology.
- The **logical topology** is the way that the signals act on the network media, or the way that the data passes through the network from one device to the next without regard to the physical interconnection of the devices.
- **Logical topologies** are bound to the network protocols that direct how the data moves across a network.
- The **Ethernet protocol** is a common **logical bus topology protocol**.

- **LocalTalk** is a common **logical bus or star topology protocol**. IBM's Token Ring is a common **logical ring topology protocol**.
- A network's **logical topology** is not necessarily the same as its physical topology. For example, twisted pair Ethernet is a **logical bus topology** in a physical star topology layout. While IBM's Token Ring is a logical ring topology, it is physically set up in a star topology.

1.6 NETWORK TOPOLOGY (PHYSICAL)

- The way, in which the connections are made, is called the topology of the network.
- Network topology specifically refers to the physical layout of the network, especially the locations of computers and how the cable is run between them.
- It is important to select the right topology.
- Each topology has its own strengths and weaknesses.
- The four most common topologies are :
    (a) Bus   (b) Star   (c) Ring   (d) Mesh

1.6.1 Bus Topology

Bus topology is often used when network installation is small.

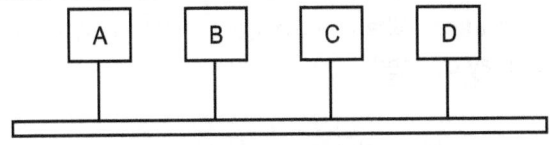

Fig. 1.3 : Bus Topology

Advantages :
- Simple and reliable in very small network, easy to use and understand.
- Least amount of cable required to connect computers, so it is less expensive.
- Extension of bus is easy by joining cable and using BNC connector. So more computers can be connected.
- A repeater can also be used to extend a bus, boost the signal and allow it to travel a longer distance.

Disadvantages :
- Heavy traffic (network traffic) can slow a bus considerably, because any computer can transmit data any time, uses entire B.W. and interrupts each other instead of communicating.
- Each barrel connector weakens the signal power.
- It is difficult to troubleshoot bus. A cable break or loose connector will also cause reflections and bring down the whole network and network activity stops.

1.6.2 Star Topology

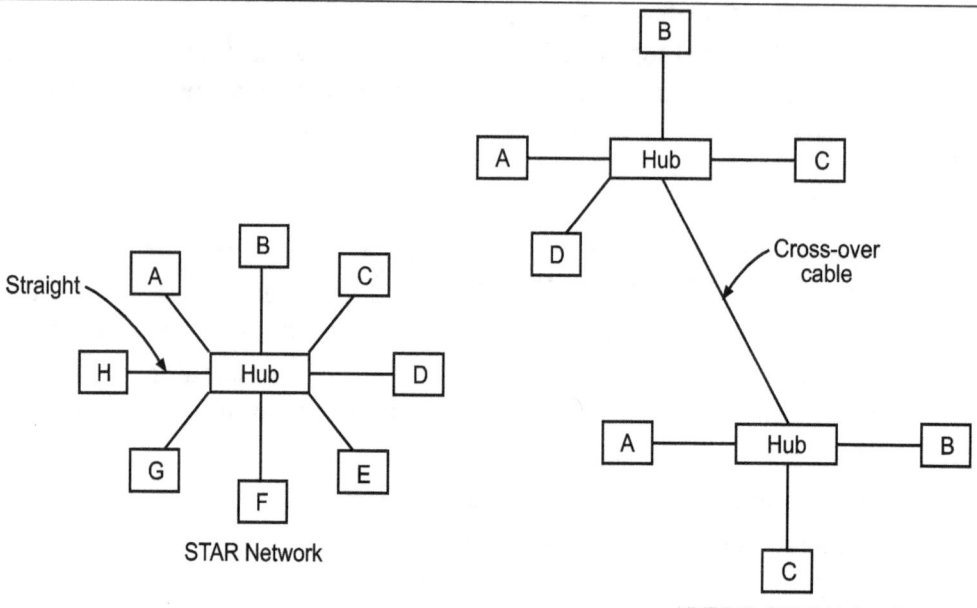

Fig. 1.4 : Star and Hybrid Star Topology

Star networks are used in concentrated networks, where the end-points are directly reachable from a central location. When network expansion is expected and when the greater reliability is needed, Hub may be used.

Advantages :
- It is very easy to modify and add new network without disturbing the rest of the network.
- Center of a star network is good place to diagnose network faults.
- Single computer failure do not bring down the whole network.
- With hub, you can use several cable types - UTP, STP, coaxial, fiber, etc.

Disadvantages :
- If central hub fails, the whole network fails to operate.
- Cost is more than bus network because network cables must be pulled to one central point. Thus cable requirement increases.

1.6.3 Ring Topology

- In ring network, each computer is connected to the next computer, with the last one connected to first.
- Messages flow around the ring in one direction.

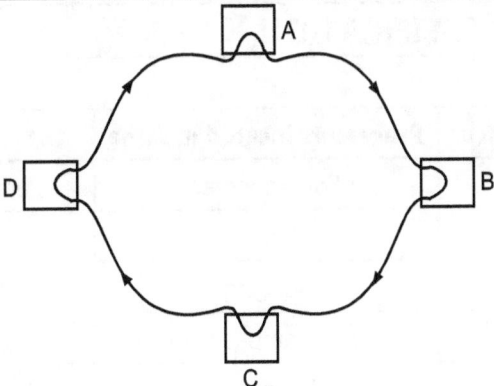

Fig. 1.5 : Ring Topology

- Since each computer retransmits what it receives, signal loss problems are there.
- There is no termination because there is no end to ring.

Advantage :
- When more users are added, systems slows but doesn't fail.

Disadvantages :
- Failure of one computer on the ring can affect the whole network.
- It is difficult to troubleshoot ring network.
- Adding or removing computers disturbs the entire network.

1.6.4 Mesh Topology

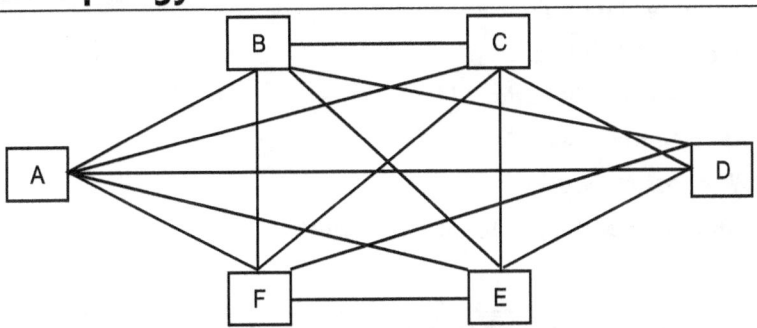

Fig. 1.6 : Mesh Topology

Each computer is connected to other with separate cable.

Advantages :
- Guaranteed communication.
- High channel capacity.

Disadvantages :
- Difficulty of installation and reconfiguration.
- Maintenance cost.

1.7 NETWORK CLASSIFICATION

Interprocessor Distance	Processors located in same	Example
1 m	Square meter	Personal Area Network
10 m	Room	Local Area Network
100 m	Building	Local Area Network
1 km	Campus	Local Area Network
10 km	City	Metropolitan Area Network
100 km	Country	Wide Area Network
1000 km	Continent	Wide Area Network
10,000 km	Planet	Internet

1. This is the classification of Networks depending upon the interprocessor distance. i.e. LAN, MAN, WAN and Internet, etc.
2. But other types of networks are also available depending upon their role in Network systems such as :
   - **Client-Server Network and Peer-to-Peer Network.**
   - **Voice Networks.**
   - **Satellite Networks.**
   - **Integrated Networks.**
   - **Centralized Networks.**
   - **Distributed Networks.**
   - **Wireless Networks.**
   - **Broadcast and point to point Networks.**

1.8 LOCAL AREA NETWORK (LAN)

- Networks used to interconnect computers in a single room, rooms within a building or buildings on one site are called Local Area Network (LAN).
- LAN transmits data with a speed of several megabits per second (10^6 bits per second). The transmission medium is normally *coaxial cables*.
- LAN links computers, i.e., software and hardware, in the same area for the purpose of sharing information.

- Usually LAN links computers within a limited geographical area because they must be connected by a cable, which is quite expensive.
- People working in LAN get more capabilities in data processing, work processing and other information exchange compared to *stand-alone computers*.
- Because of this information exchange, most of the business and government organizations are using LAN.

1.8.1 Major Characteristics of LAN

- Every computer has the potential to communicate with any other computers of the network.
- High degree of interconnection between computers.
- Easy physical connection of computers in a network.
- Inexpensive medium of data transmission.
- High data transmission rate.

1.8.2 Components of LAN

1. **Workstations :**
   - In LAN, a workstation refers to a machine that will allow users access to a LAN and its resources while providing intelligence on board allowing local execution of applications.
   - It may allow data to be stored locally or remotely on a file server.
   - Obviously, diskless workstations require all data to be stored remotely, including that data necessary for the diskless machine to boot up.
   - Executable files may reside locally or remotely as well, meaning a workstation can run its own programs or those copied off the LAN.

2. **Servers :**
   - A server is a computer that provides the data, software and hardware resources that are shared on the LAN.
   - A LAN can have more than one server; each has its unique name on the network and all LAN users identify the server by its name.
   - **Dedicated Server :** A server that functions only as a storage area for data and software and allows access to hardware resources is called a dedicated server. Dedicated servers need to be powerful computers.
   - **Non-Dedicated Server :** In many LANs, the server is just another work station. Thus, there is a user networking on the computer and using it as a workstation, but part of the computer also doubles up as a server. Such a server is called a non-dedicated server. Since, it is not completely dedicated to serving. LANs do not

require a dedicated server since resource sharing amongst a few workstations is proportionately on a smaller scale.

- **Other Types of Servers :** In large installations, which have hundreds of workstations sharing resource, a single computer is often not sufficient to function as a server.

Some of the other servers have been discussed here under :

- **File Server :** A file server stores files that workstations can access and it also decides on the rights and restrictions that the users need to have while accessing files on LAN.
- **Printer Server :** A Printer server takes care of the printing requirement of number of workstations.
- **Modem Server :** It allows LAN users to use the modem to transmit long distance messages. Server attached to one or two modems would serve the purpose.

3. **Clients :**
   - A client is any machine that requires something from a server.
   - In the more common definition of a client, the server supplies files and sometimes processing power to the smaller machines connected to it.
   - Each machine is a client.
   - Thus a typical ten PC local area network may have one large server with all the major files and databases on it and all the other machines connected as clients.
   - This type of terminology is common with TCP/IP networks, where no single machine is necessarily the central repository.

4. **Nodes :**
   - Small networks that comprise of a server and number of PCs.
   - Each PC on the network is called a node.
   - A node essentially means any device that is attached to the network. Because each machine has a unique name or number (so the rest of the network can identify it), you will hear the term node name or node number quite often.

5. **Network Interface Cards :**
   - The Network Interface card, or LAN adapter, functions as an interface between the computer and the network cabling, so it must serve two masters.
   - Inside the computer, it controls the flow of data to and from the Random-Access Memory (RAM).
   - Outside the computer, it controls the flow of data in and out of the network cable system.
   - An interface card has a specialized port that matches the electrical signaling standards used on the cable and the specific type of cable connector.

- One must select a network interface card that matches your computer's data bus and the network cable.
- Token ring LANs require token ring NICs, Ethernet LANs require Ethernet NICs, etc.
- The peripheral component interface bus (PCI) has emerged as a new standard for adapter card interfaces.
- It is advisable to use bus PCI-equipped computers and PCI LAN adapters wherever possible.
- Software is required to interface between a particular NIC and an operating system called as **Network Interface Card Driver**.

6. **Connectors :**
   - Connectors used with TP included RJ-11 and RJ-45 modular connectors in current used by phone companies.
   - Occasionally other special connectors, such as IBM's Data Connector, are used.
   - RJ-11 connectors accommodate 4 wires or 2 twisted pairs, while RJ-45 houses 8 wires or 4 twisted pairs.

7. **The Network Operating System :**
   - The Network Operating System software acts as the command center, enabling all of the network hardware and all other network software to function together as one cohesive, organized system.
   - In other words, the network operating system is the heart of the network.
   - It can be client-server or Peer-to-Peer Network Operating System.

1.8.3 Advantages of lan

- The reliability of network is high because the failure of one computer in the network does not effect the functioning for other computers.
- Addition of new computer to network is easy.
- High rate of data transmission is possible.
- Peripheral devices like magnetic disk and printer can be shared by other computers.

1.8.4 Uses of Lan

Followings are the major areas where LAN is normally used :
- File transfer and Access
- Word and text processing
- Electronic message handling
- Remote database access
- Personal computing

- Digital voice transmission and storage
- Office automation
- Factory automation
- Distributed Computing
- Fire and Security Systems
- Process Control
- Document Distribution.

1.9 WIDE AREA NETWORK (WAN)

- The term Wide Area Network (WAN) is used to describe a computer network spanning a regional, national or global area.
- For example, for a large company the head quarters might be at Delhi and regional branches at Mumbai, Chennai, Bangaluru and Kolkata.
- Here regional centers are connected to head quarters through WAN.
- The distance between computers connected to WAN is larger. Therefore the transmission medium used are normally telephone lines, microwaves and satellite links.

1.9.1 Characteristics of WAN

Following are the major characteristics of WAN.

1. **Communication Facility :**
   - For a big company spanning over different parts of the country, the employees can save long distance phone calls and it overcomes the time lag in overseas communications.
   - Computer conferencing is another use of WAN where users communicate with each other through their computer system.

2. **Remote Data Entry :**
   - Remote data entry is possible in WAN. It means sitting at any location you can enter data, update data and query other information of any computer attached to the WAN but located in other cities.
   - For example, suppose you are sitting at Chennai and want to see some data of a computer located at Delhi, you can do it through WAN.

3. **Centralized Information :**
   - In modern computerized environment you will find that big organizations go for centralized data storage.
   - This means if the organization is spread over many cities, they keep their important business data in a single place.
   - As the data are generated at different sites, WAN permits collection of this data from different sites and save at a single site.

1.10 DIFFERENCE BETWEEN LAN AND WAN

- LAN is restricted to limited geographical area of few kilometers. But WAN covers great distance and operate nationwide or even worldwide.
- In LAN, the computer terminals and peripheral devices are connected with wires and coaxial cables. In WAN there is no physical connection. Communication is done through telephone lines and satellite links.
- Cost of data transmission in LAN is less because the transmission medium is owned by a single organization. In case of WAN the cost of data transmission is very high because the transmission medium used are hired, either telephone lines or satellite links.
- The speed of data transmission is much higher in LAN than in WAN. The transmission speed in LAN varies from 0.1 to 100 megabits per second. In case of WAN the speed ranges from 1800 to 9600 bits per second (bps).
- Few data transmission errors occur in LAN compared to WAN. It is because in LAN the distance covered is negligible.

1.11 METROPOLITAN AREA NETWORK (MAN)

- A Metropolitan Area Network (MAN) is a bigger version of a Local Area Network (LAN) and usually uses similar technology.
- A MAN can cover a group of corporate offices or a town or city, and can be either privately or publicly owned. A MAN can support both data and voice, and may be related to the local cable television network (CATV).
- A MAN employs one or two cables, and does not contain switching elements, which simplifies the design.

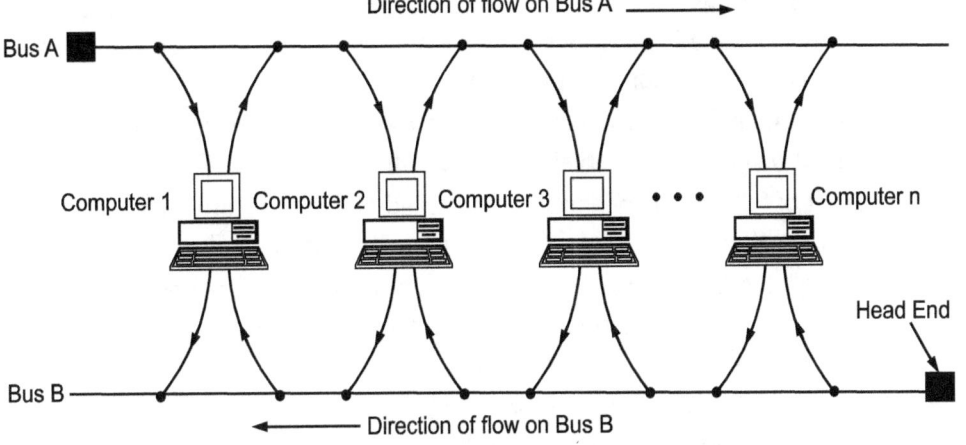

Fig. 1.7 : Typical MAN Network (also known as 802.6 DQDB network)

- A standard has been adopted for MANs called *Distributed Queue Dual Bus* (DQDB) and is defined by IEEE 802.6.
- DQDB consists of two unidirectional buses (cables) to which all of the computers on the network are connected.
- Each bus has a *head-end* that initiates transmission activity.
- In the following diagram, traffic that is intended for a computer to the right of the source computer uses the upper bus, while traffic intended for a computer to the left uses the lower bus.
- The network is based on fiber-optic cable in a dual-bus topology, and traffic on each bus is unidirectional, providing a fault-tolerant configuration.
- Bandwidth is allocated using time slots, and both synchronous and asynchronous modes are supported.

1.12 INTERNET

- Internet is the extensive, worldwide computer network available to the public. An internet is a more general term for any set of interconnected computer networks that are connected by internetworking.
- The Internet, or simply the Net, is the publicly available worldwide system of interconnected computer networks that transmit data by packet switching using a standardized Internet Protocol (IP) and many other protocols.
- It is made up of thousands of smaller commercial, academic, and government networks.
- It carries various information and services, such as electronic mail, on-line chat and the interlinked web pages and other documents of the World Wide Web.
- Hypertext is viewed using a program called a web browser which retrieves pieces of information, called "documents" or "web pages", from web servers and displays them, typically on a computer monitor.
- One can then follow hyperlinks on each page to other documents or even send information back to the server to interact with it.
- The act of following hyperlinks is often called "surfing" or "browsing" the web. Web pages are often arranged in collections of related material called "web sites."
- Although the English word *worldwide* is normally written as one word (without a space or hyphen), the proper name World Wide Web and abbreviation WWW are now well-established even in formal English.
- Typical network schematic is shown in Fig. 1.8.
- Function of webserver is to host website (web pages).

- Function of proxy server is to provide internet connectivity to the different machines with private IP addresses.

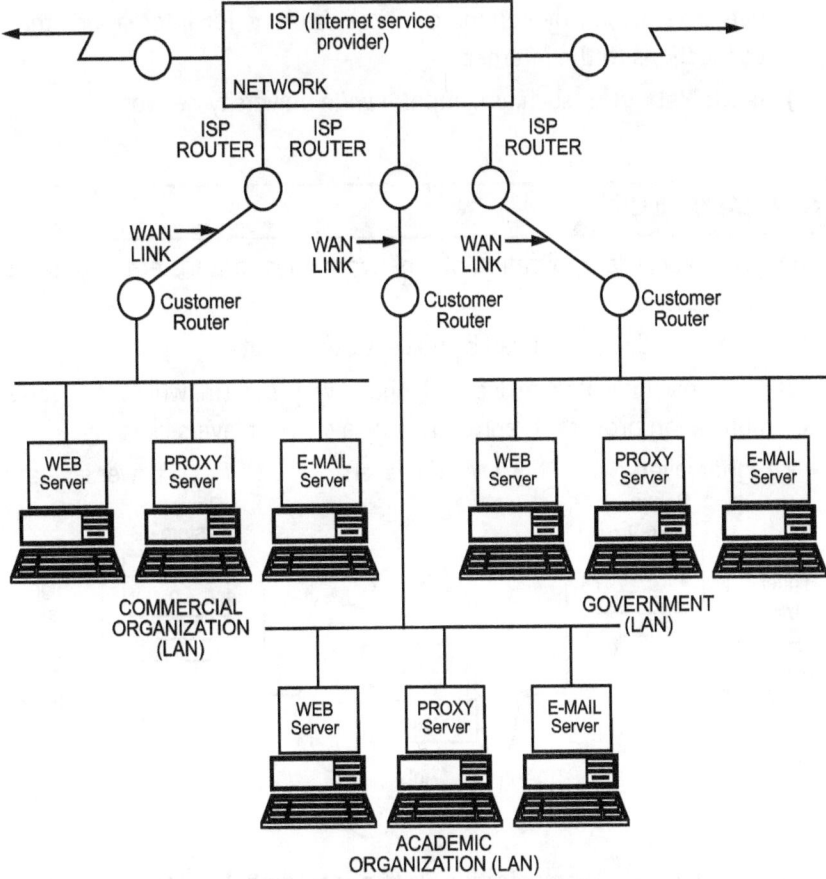

Fig. 1.8 : Typical Internet Connection Components

- E-mail server is used to provide different E-mail accounts for E-mail transactions.
- Thus, Routers are used to interconnect different LAN's to form Internet.
- Organization's **Router** and ISP's **ROUTER** are interconnected to form Internet.
- Customer router to ISP router link can be of –
    (1) Dial-up-line (2) Leased line (3) ISDN line, etc.
- LAN Technology can be of –
    (1) Ethernet (802.3 or CSMA/CD) Technology
    (2) Token Ring (802.5) Technology
    (3) Token Bus (802.4) Technology
- Thus, internet consists of the following groups of networks :
    (1) Backbones : Large networks that exist primarily to interconnect other networks.

(2) **Regional networks :** Connecting for example, universities and colleges.

(3) **Commercial Networks :** Providing access to the backbones to subscribers and networks owned by commercial organizations for internal use that also have connections to the Internet.

(4) **Local Networks**, such as campus – wide university networks.

1.13 LAYERED TASK

- The basic need/use/application of a networking is to transfer the data from system to another system.
- It is not always data, but it can be voice, video or data.
- This is simply indicated in Fig. 1.9, that every system which is involved in data communication process is represented by a stack of layers like :
  - Higher layers
  - Middle layers
  - Lower layers.

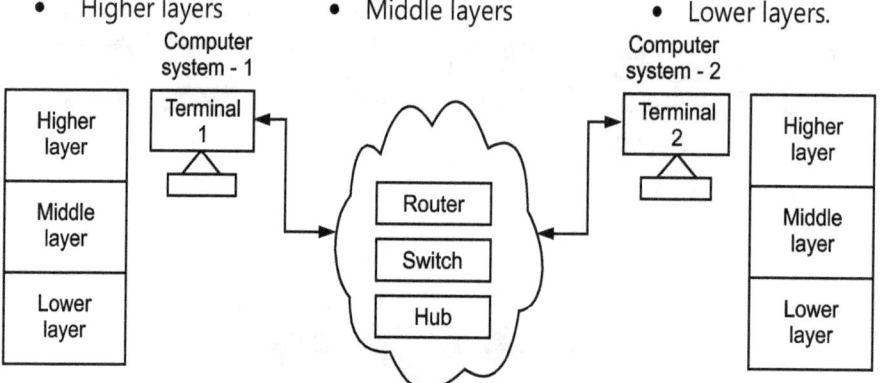

Fig. 1.9 : Network Communication System represented by Stack of Layers

- The significance of each layer and related tasks can be explained with the simple example of sending a letter by one person, which is being received by other person as shown in Fig. 1.10.
- Thus, transporting of letter from source to destination or between sender and receiver is done by carrier.
- Also each layer at the source (sender side) uses the services of the layer below it.
- The higher layer uses services of middle layer, middle layer uses the services of the lower layer and lower layer uses services of the carrier.
- Thus, in data communication system, each system is represented by the stack of different layers. This reduces the design complexity in the networks.
- This issue is discussed in detail, in following sections.

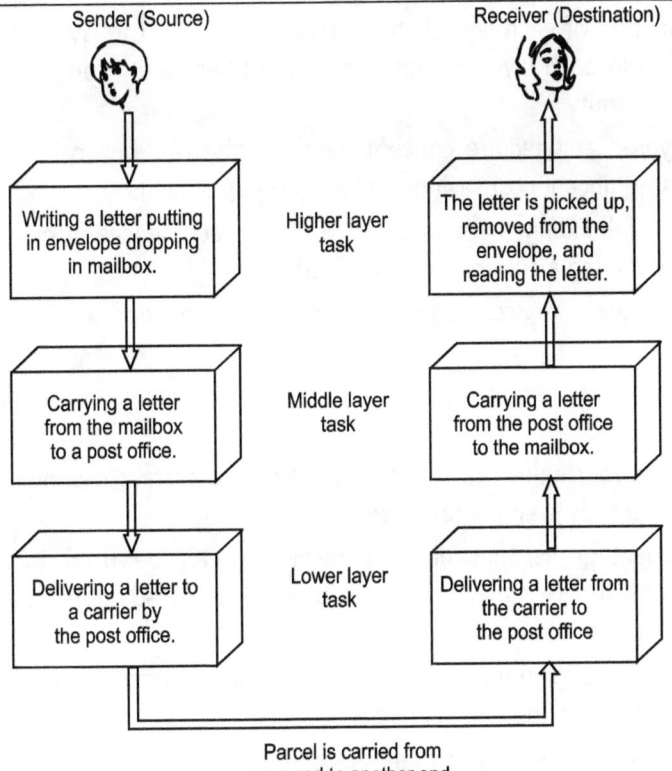

Fig. 1.10 : Tasks involved [Source to Destination] in Journey of Letter

1.14 NETWORK LAYERED ARCHITECTURE

- To reduce design complexity, most networks are organized as a series of layers or levels. Each one built upon the one below it.
- The number of layers, the name of each layer, the contents of each layer, and the function of each layer differs from network to network. However, in all networks, the purpose of each layer is to offer certain services to the higher layer.

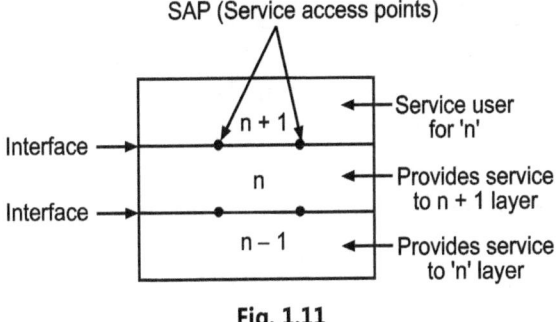

Fig. 1.11

- The function of each layer is to provide services to the layer above it. The active elements in each layer are often called entities. Entity can be software entity or hardware entity.
- The layered architecture concept redefines the way networks are conceived and creates significant cost savings and managerial benefits.
- Instead of building a separate network for each service, user can have multiple services sharing a common core network.
- Adding new services and managing the network infrastructure can be easy.
- That is why the layered architecture concept will become increasingly important for user.
- It offers opportunities to reduce capital and operating expenditure by offering a smooth step-by-step migration to IP.
- Key advantage is that network resources can be used more effectively in terms of simplicity and fewer equipment sites leading to lower total cost of ownership.
- Also, the need for transmission connections in the network can, in many cases, be reduced by more than 50 percent.

1.14.1 Benefits of Layered Designs

- Segmentation of high-level from low-level issues. Complex problems can be broken into smaller more manageable pieces.
- Since the specification of a layer says nothing about its implementation, the implementation details of a layer are hidden (abstracted) from other layers.
- Many upper layers can share the services of a lower layer. Thus layering allows us to reuse functionality.
- Development by teams is aided because of the logical segmentation.
- Easier exchange of parts at a later date.

1.14.2 Downsides of Layered Designs

- The trouble with layers of computer software is that sooner or later you loose touch with reality. Layers are abstraction boundaries, and the more they encapsulate their works the more one is unaware of the application's inner works.
- Layering is a form of information hiding. A "layering violation" occurs in situations where a layer uses knowledge of the implementation details of another layer in its own operations. At the limit this leads to changes to one layer resulting in changes to every other layer, which is an expensive and error prone proposition.

- Layering can lead to poor performance. To avoid this penalty, in situations where an upper layer can optimize its actions by knowing what a lower layer is doing, we can reveal information that would normally be hidden behind a layer boundary.
- The layers must be engineered at the outset, before the system is built.

1.15 PROTOCOL FUNDAMENTALS

- In computing, a **protocol** is a set of rules which is used by computers to communicate with each other across a network.
- A protocol is a convention or standard that controls or enables the connection, communication, and data transfer between computing endpoints. In its simplest form, a protocol can be defined as the rules governing the syntax, semantics, and synchronization of communication.
- Protocols may be implemented by hardware, software, or a combination of the two. At the lowest level, a protocol defines the behavior of a hardware connection.

Typical Properties :

Detection of the underlying physical connection (wired or wireless), or the existence of the other endpoint or node :

- Handshaking.
- Negotiation of various connection characteristics.
- How to start and end a message.
- Procedures on formatting a message.
- What to do with corrupted or improperly formatted messages (error correction).
- How to detect unexpected loss of the connection, and what to do next.
- Termination of the session and/or connection.

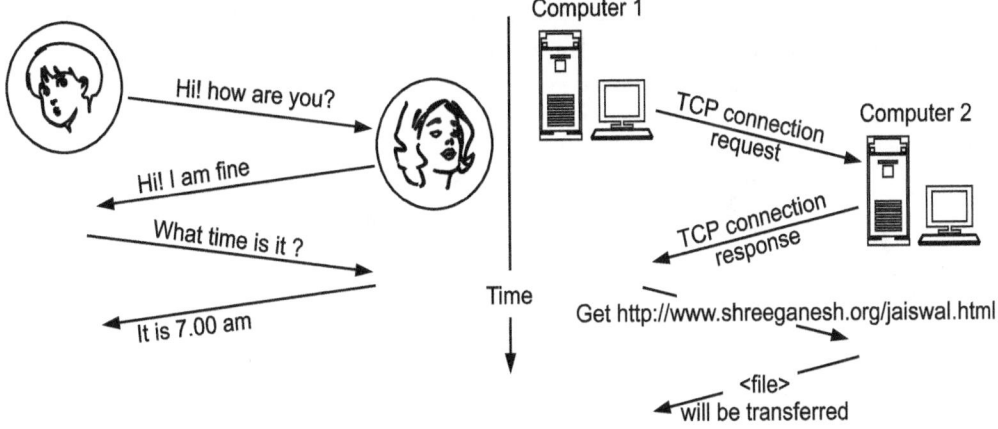

Fig. 1.12 : Human Protocol Vs Computer Network Protocol

Importance of Protocols :

The protocols in human communication are separate rules about appearance, speaking, listening and understanding. All these rules, also called *protocols of conversation*, represent different layers of communication. They work together to help people successfully communicate. The need for protocols also applies to network devices. Computers have no way of learning.

1.15.1 Terms and Definitions

1. **Protocol :** Protocol is agreement between the communication - communicating parties on how communication is to proceed.

   Or

2. **Protocol :** Protocol is strict procedure and sequence of actions to be followed in order to achieve orderly exchange of information among peer entities.

   Or

3. **Protocol :** Protocol is a set of rules governing the format and meaning of the frames, packets or messages that are exchanged by the peer entities within a layer.

4. **Protocol Stack :** A list of protocols used by a certain system, one protocol per layer is called a protocol stack.

5. **Interface :** Between each pair of adjacent layers, there is an interface. The interface defines which primitive operations and services the lower layers offers to the upper one.

6. **Network Architecture :** A set of layers and protocols is called as network architecture.

7. **Service :** Services and protocols are distinct concepts although they are frequently confused. Service is a set of primitives (operations) that a layer provides to the layer above it. The service defines what operations the layer is prepared to perform on behalf of its users, but it says nothing at all about how these operations are implemented. A service relates to an interface between two layers, with the lower layer being the service provider and the upper layer being the service user.

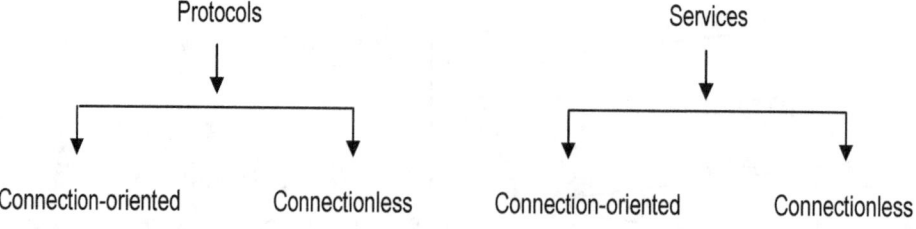

Layers can offer two different types of services to the layers above them.
- Connection-oriented and
- Connectionless.

1.16 SERVICE PRITIMITVES AND RELATIONSHIP OF SERVICE TO PROTOCOLS

- A service is formally specified by a set of primitives (operations) that define the service interface.
- The primitives differ for different services. As a simple example, a service may provide the following primitives :
  1. **LISTEN :** Listen for an incoming communication request.
  2. **CONNECT :** Make a communication request.
  3. **RECEIVE :** Receive data of a communication.
  4. **SEND :** Send data of a communication.
  5. **DISCONNECT :** Disconnect or discontinue a communication.

We will discuss service primitives in more detail in our transport layer chapter.

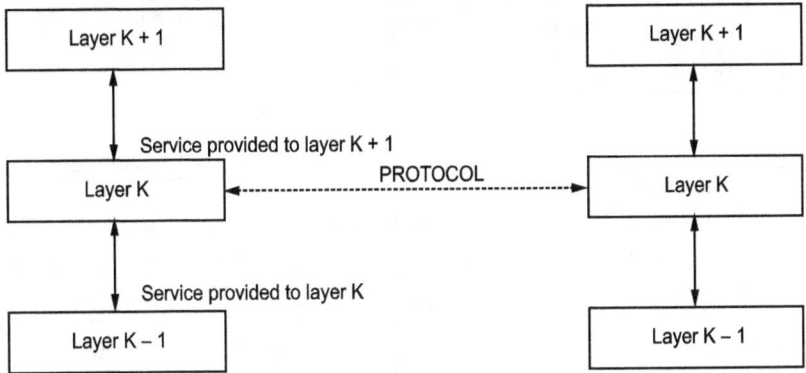

Fig. 1.13 : Depiction of peers at level (Relationship between service and a protocol)

- As discussed before, each layer has specific functions and offers certain services to the layer above it.
- A service is a set of primitives (operations) that a layer provides to the layer above it.
- In the definition of services, we do not specify their implementation.
- The implementation is only visible to the provider of the service.
- A protocol defines the implementation of the service and is not visible to the user of the service.
- A protocol is a set of rules governing the format and meaning of the frames, packets, or messages within a layer and can be changed at will by entities, provided that they do not change the service visible to their users.

1.17 CONNECTION-ORIENTED SERVICE VS. CONNECTINLESS SERVICE

	Connection-Oriented Service		Connectionless Service
1.	Idle-No Connection ↓ Connection Establishment ↓ Data Transfer ↓ Connection Release ↓ Idle - No Connection	1.	Idle - No connection | | ↓ Data Transfer | | ↓ Idle - No Connection
2.	Connection is established between sender and receiver before data transfer can commence.	2.	Connection is not established. Only data is transferred from source to destination with full source and destination address.
3.	It is like delivering the data strictly in the same order in which the data is put into the connection by the sender.	3.	When two messages are sent to the same destination one after another, it is possible that first one is delayed and second one arrives first.
4.	It has provision for acknowledgements, flow control and error recovery.	4.	Does not have such provisions.
5.	Connection-oriented service is modelled after telephone system.	5.	Connectionless service is modelled after postal service.
6.	Example is virtual circuit service like ATM network.	6.	Example is datagram service like INTERNET network.

1.18 ISO-OSI REFERENCE MODEL

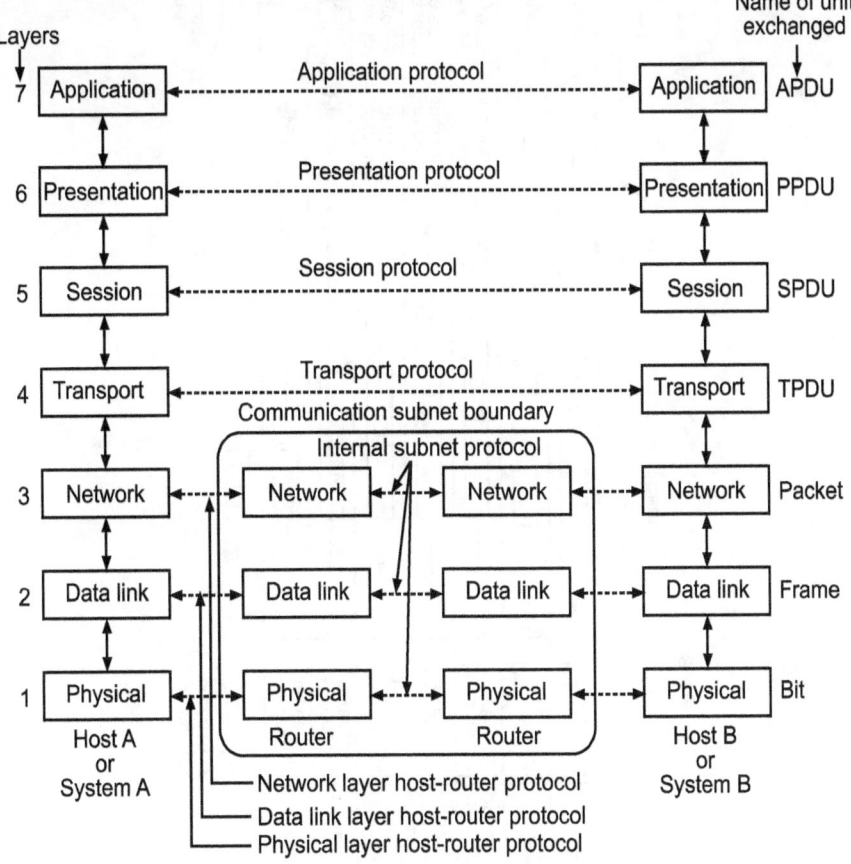

Fig. 1.14 : The OSI Reference Model

1. This model is based on a proposal developed by the International Standards Organization (ISO) as a first step towards International Standardization of Protocols used in various layers.
2. This model is called as ISO-OSI (Open Systems Interconnection) reference model because it deals with connecting open systems that is systems that are open for communication with other systems.
3. OSI model has seven layers. The OSI model defines a layered architecture as pictured. The protocols defined in each layer are responsible for following :
    - Communicating with the same peer protocol layer running in the opposite computer.
    - Providing services to the layer above it (except for the top-level application layer).
    - Peer layer communication provides a way for each layer to exchange messages or other data.

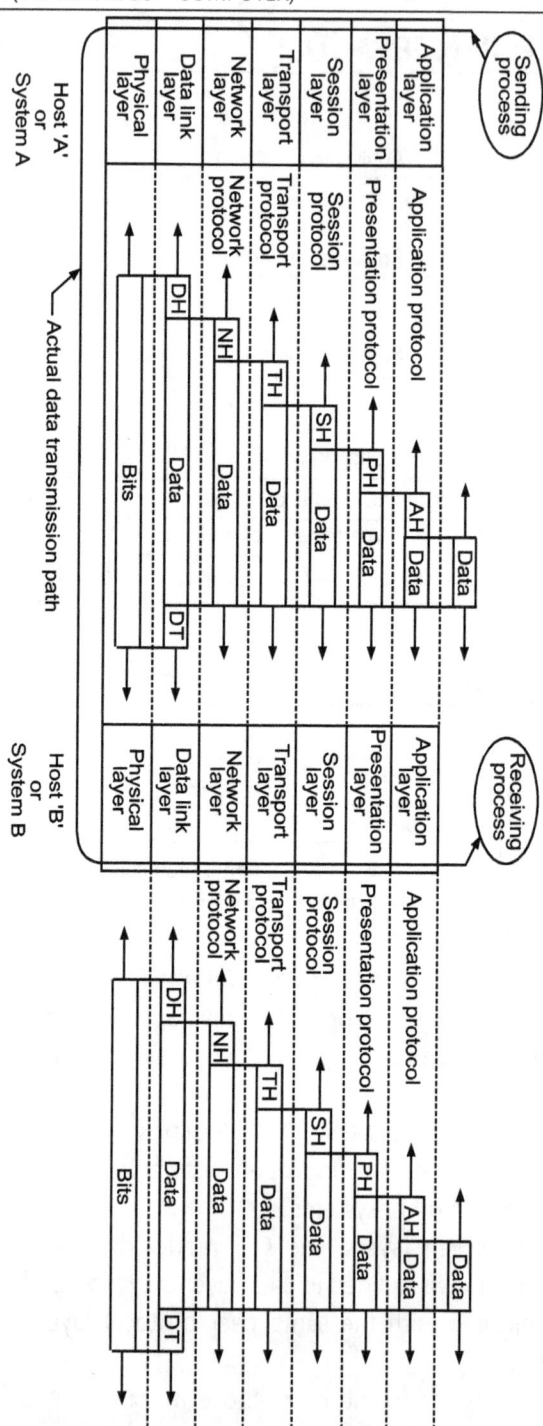

Fig. 1.15 : Data communication between two systems is shown by OSI reference model

4. **Obviously, each layer does not have a physical wire running between it and its peer layer in the opposite system.** To send a message, a protocol must put the message in a packet that passes down to the next lower layer. Thus lower layer provides a service to higher layers by taking their messages and passing them down the protocol stack to the lowest layer, where the messages are transferred across the physical link.

1.18.1 Characteristics of the OSI Layers

- The seven layers of the OSI reference model can be divided into two categories: upper layers and lower layers.
- The **upper layers** of the OSI model deal with application issues and generally are implemented only in software.
- The highest layer, the application layer, is closest to the end user. Both users and application layer processes interact with software applications that contain a communication component.
- The term upper layer is sometimes used to refer to any layer above another layer in the OSI model.
- The **lower layers** of the OSI model handle data transport issues. The physical layer and the data link layer are implemented in hardware and software.
- The lowest layer, the physical layer, is closest to the physical network medium (the network cabling, for example) and is responsible for actually placing information on the medium.

Fig. 1.16 illustrates the division between the upper and lower OSI layers.

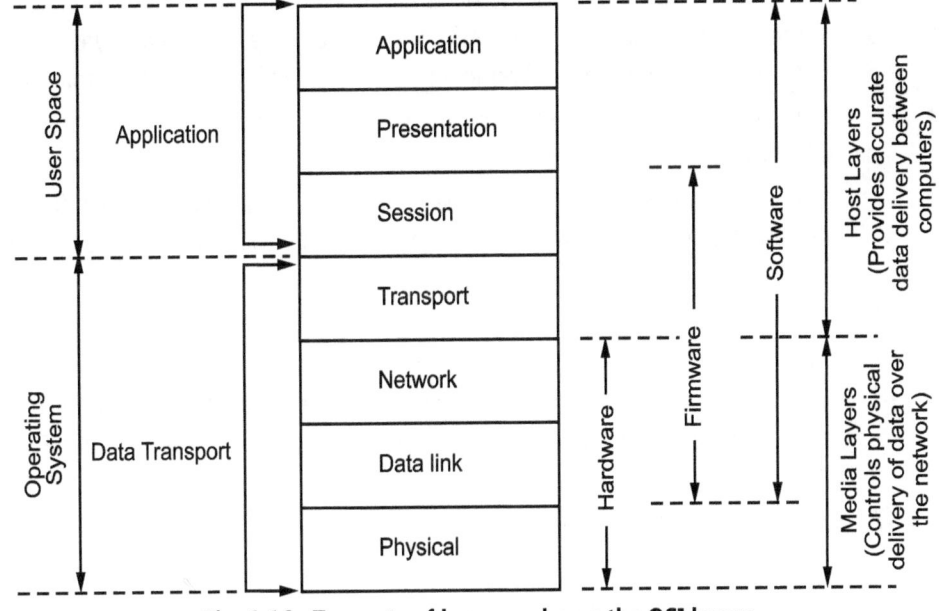

Fig. 1.16 : Two sets of layers make up the OSI layers

1.18.2 OSI Model Layers and Information Exchange

- The seven OSI layers use various forms of control information to communicate with their peer layers in other computer systems. This **control information** (headers) consists of specific requests and instructions that are exchanged between peer OSI layers.
- Control information typically takes one of two forms : headers and trailers.
- **Headers** are prepended to data that has been passed down from upper layers.
- **Trailers** are appended to data that has been passed down from upper layers.
- An OSI layer is not required to attach a header or a trailer to data from upper layers.
- Headers, trailers and data are relative concepts, depending on the layer that analyzes the information unit.
- At the network layer, for example, an information unit consists of a layer 3 header and data.
- At the data link layer, however, all the information is passed down by the network layer (the layer 3 header and the data) is treated as data.
- In other words, the data portion of an information unit at a given OSI layer potentially can contain headers, trailers and data from all the higher layers. This is known as **encapsulation.**

Information Exchange Process :

- The information exchange process occurs between peer OSI layers. Each layer in the source system adds control information to data, and each layer in the destination system analyzes and removes the control information from that data.
- If System **A** has data from a software application to send to System **B**, the data is passed to the application layer.
- The application layer in System **A** then communicates any control information required by the application layer in System **B** by prepending a header to the data.
- The resulting information unit (a header and the data) is passed to the presentation layer, which prepends its own header containing control information intended for the presentation layer in System **B**.
- The information unit grows in size as each layer prepends its own header (and, in some cases, a trailer) that contains control information to be used by its peer layer in System **B**.
- At the physical layer, the entire information unit is placed onto the network medium.
- The physical layer in System **B** receives the information unit and passes it to the data link layer.

- The data link layer in System **B** then reads the control information contained in the header prepended by the data link layer in System **A**.
- The header is then removed, and the remainder of the information unit is passed to the network layer.
- Each layer performs the same actions : The layer reads the header from its peer layer, strips it off, and passes the remaining information unit to the next highest layer.
- After the application layer performs these actions, the data is passed to the recipient software application in System **B**, in exactly the form in which it was transmitted by the application in System **A**.

1.18.3 OSI Layers in Detail

The following is a description of just what each layer does :

1. **The Physical layer** provides the electrical and mechanical interface to the network medium (the cable). This layer gives the data-link layer (layer 2) its ability to transport a stream of serial data bits between two communicating systems. It conveys the bits that move along the cable. It is responsible for making sure that the raw bits get from one place to another, no matter what shape they are in, and deals with the mechanical and electrical characteristics of the cable.

2. **The Data-Link layer** handles the physical transfer, framing (the assembly of data into a single unit or block), flow control and error-control functions (and retransmission in the event of an error) over a single transmission link; it is responsible for getting the data packaged and onto the network cable. The data link layer provides the network layer (layer 3) reliable information-transfer capabilities. The data-link layer is often subdivided into two parts – Logical Link Control (LLC) and Medium Access Control (MAC) depending on the implementation.

3. **The Network layer** establishes, maintains, and terminates logical and/or physical connections. The network layer is responsible for translating logical addresses or names into physical addresses. It provides network routing and flow-control functions across the computer-network interface.

4. **The Transport layer** ensures that data is successfully sent and received between the two computers. If data is sent incorrectly, this layer has the responsibility to ask for retransmission of the data. Specifically, it provides a network-independent, reliable message-independent, reliable message-interchange service to the top three application-oriented layers. This layer acts as an interface between the bottom and top three layers. By providing the session layer (layer 5) with a reliable message-transfer service, it hides the detailed operation of the underlying network from the session layer.

5. **The Session layer** decides when to turn communication on and off between two computers - it provides the mechanism that controls the data-exchange process and co-ordinates the interaction between them. It sets up and clears communication channels between two communicating components. Unlike the network layer (layer 3), it deals with the programs running in each machine to establish conversations between them.

6. **The Presentation layer** performs code conversion and data reformatting (syntax translation). It is the translator of the network, making sure that the data is in the correct form for the receiving application. Of course, both the sending and receiving applications must be able to use data subscribing to one of the available abstract data syntax forms.

7. **The Application layer** provides the user interface between the software running in the computer and the network. It provides functions to the user's software, including file transfer access, management and electronic mail.

Thus the OSI, or Open Systems Interconnection, model defines a networking frame-work for implementing protocols in seven layers. This can be summarized in Table 1.1.

Table 1.1

Application (Layer 7)	This layer supports application and end-user processes. Communication partners are identified, quality of service is identified, user authentication and privacy are considered, and any constraints on data syntax are identified. Everything at this layer is application-specific. This layer provides application services for file transfers, e-mail, and other network software services.
Presentation (Layer 6)	This layer provides independence from differences in data representation (e.g., encryption) by translating from application to network format, and vice versa. The presentation layer works to transform data into the form that the application layer can accept. This layer formats and encrypts data to be sent across a network, providing freedom from compatibility problems. It is sometimes called the **syntax layer.**
Session (Layer 5)	This layer establishes, manages and terminates connections between applications. The session layer sets up, co-ordinates, and terminates conversations, exchanges and dialogues between the applications at each end. It deals with session and connection co-ordination.
Transport (Layer 4)	This layer provides transparent transfer of data between end systems, or hosts, and is responsible for end-to-end error recovery and flow control. It ensures complete data transfer.

Network (Layer 3)	This layer provides switching and routing technologies, creating logical paths, known as virtual circuits, for transmitting data from node to node. Routing and forwarding are functions of this layer, as well as addressing, internetworking, error handling, congestion control and packet sequencing.
Data Link (Layer 2)	At this layer, data packets are encoded and decoded into bits. It furnishes transmission protocol knowledge and management and handles errors in the physical layer, flow control and frame synchronization. The data link layer is divided into two sublayers : The Media Access Control (MAC) layer and the Logical Link Control (LLC) layer. The MAC sublayer controls how a computer on the network gains access to the data and permission to transmit it. The LLC layer controls frame synchronization, flow control and error checking.
Physical (Layer 1)	This layer conveys the bit stream electrical impulse, light or radio signal through the network at the electrical and mechanical level. It provides the hardware means of sending and receiving data on a carrier, including defining cables, cards and physical aspects. Fast Ethernet, RS-232 and ATM are protocols with physical layer components.

Table 1.2 : Application Oriented Explanation

ISO-OSI REFERENCE MODEL LAYERS	FUNCTIONS
Application Layer (Layer 7)	• Computer Applications like Word processor, Presentation Graphics, Spreadsheet, Database. • Network Applications like Email, FTP, Remote Access, Client-Server, Peer-to-Peer, Network management. • Internetwork Applications like WWW, Data Exchange, Email Gateways, Finance transactions, Conferencing.
Presentation Layer (Layer 6)	• Provides data formats, translations and code conversion. • Data compression and Data encryption. • Text/data (ASCII or EBCDIC). • Sound/Video (MP3, Wave, Mpeg, Quick time). • Graphics/Images (JPEG, Gif, BMP).

Sessional Layer (Layer 5)	• Network file System (NFS), X-Windows System. • Re-establishment of connection in case of failure. • Connection Permission Half-Duplex, Full Duplex. • Dialog control. • Synchronization. • Process to process delivery.
Transport Layer (Layer 4)	• Establishes reliable End-to-End transport connection. • Flow control, error control, connection control. • Data error detection, recovery for end-to-end connection.
Network Layer (Layer 3)	• Routing Algorithm (Routing). • Logical addressing. • Congestion Control Algorithm. • Internetworking.
Data Link Layer (Layer 2)	• NIC (Network Interface Card) Driver has LLC (Logical Link Control)-Framing, Flow Control, Error Control, etc. • MAC (Media Access Control)-802.3, 802.4, 802.5, etc.
Physical Layer (Layer 1)	• Handles Voltages and Electrical Pulses. • Specifies Cables, Connectors and Media Interface Component.

1.19 NETWORK ARCHITECTURE

In computing, **network architecture** is the design of a computer network.

In telecommunication, the term **network architecture** has the following meanings :

1. The design principles, physical configuration, functional organization, operational procedures, and data formats used as the bases for the design, construction, modification, and operation of a communication network.

2. The structure of an existing communication network, including the physical configuration facilities, operational structure, operational procedures, and the data formats in use.

3. With the development of distributed computing, the term **network architecture** has also come to denote classifications and implementations of distributed computing architectures. For example, the application architecture of the telephone network PSTN has been termed the Advanced Intelligent Network.

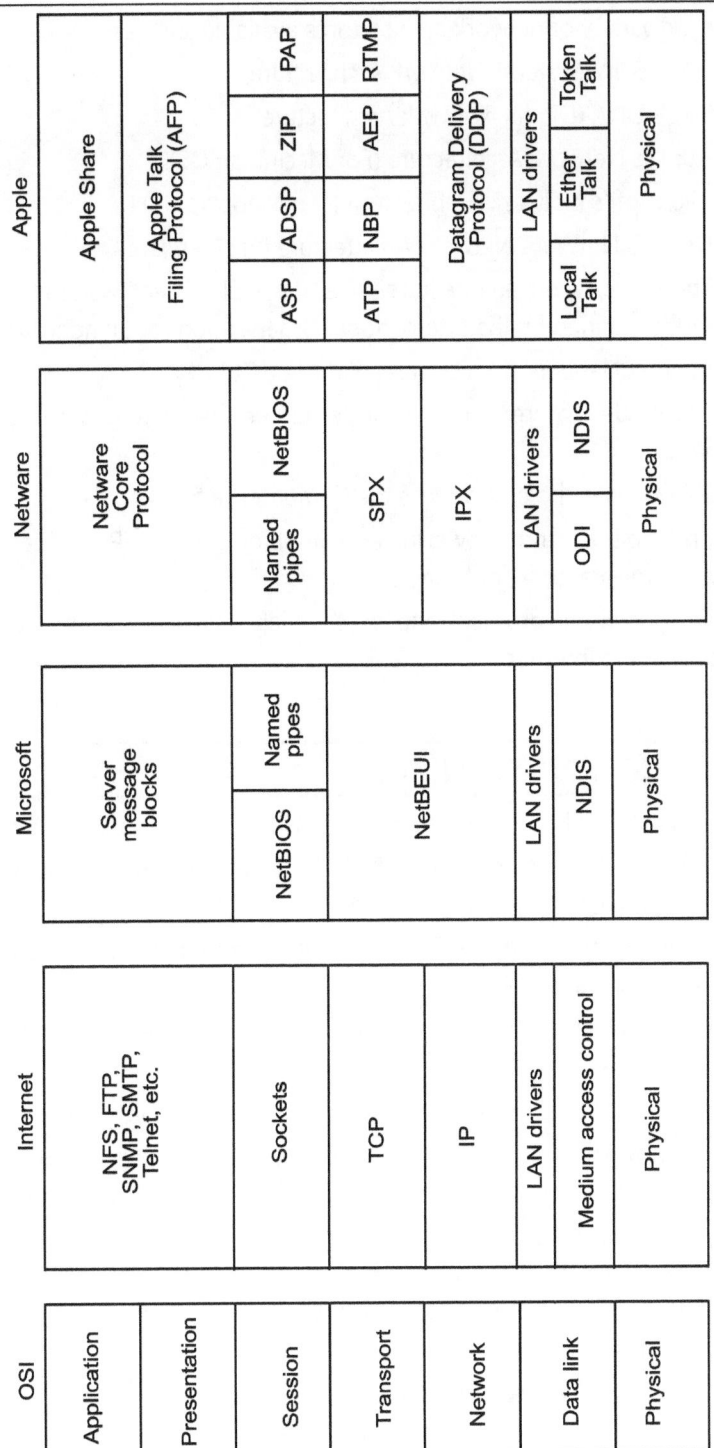

Fig. 1.17 : Different Network Architectures

4. There are variety of network architectures available such as :
   - IBM's SNA (Systems Network Architecture)
   - DEC's DNA (Digital Network Architecture)
   - Apple's Network Architecture (For Macintosh OS)
   - Microsoft's Network Architecture (For Windows OS)
   - Novell's NetWare Network Architecture (For Netware OS)
   - There are open architectures like the OSI (Open Systems Interconnection) model defined by the International Organization for Standardization.
   - Internet Network Architecture. (Based on TCP/IP).
5. The OSI model has remained a model rather than a fully accepted international standard.
6. ISO OSI Model is there to discuss the Computer networks.
7. OSI protocols are not powerful as compared to TCP/IP so they are not used anywhere for practical applications.
8. TCP/IP is powerful protocol and used widely that's why it is also known as the Protocol of the Internet.

1.20 INTRODUCTION TO TCP/IP

- TCP/IP is a suite of protocols, also known as the Internet Protocol Suite.
- It should not be confused with the OSI reference model, although elements of TCP/IP exist in OSI.
- The Transmission Control Protocol and the Internet Protocol are fundamental to the suite, hence the TCP/IP title.
- TCP/IP is a set of protocols developed to allow co-operating computers to share resources across a network.
- A community of researchers centered around the ARPANET developed this TCP/IP.
- The **Internet protocol suite** is the set of communication protocols that implement the protocol stack on which the internet and most commercial networks run.
- The internet protocol suite like many protocol suites can be viewed as a set of layers, each layer solves a set of problems involving the transmission of data, and provides a well-defined service to the upper layer protocols based on using services from some lower layers.
- Upper layers are logically closer to the user and deal with more abstract data, relying on lower layer protocols to translate data into forms that can eventually be physically transmitted.

- The Transmission Control Protocol/Internet Protocol (TCP/IP) protocol suite is the engine for the Internet and networks worldwide.
- Its simplicity and power has lead to its becoming the single network protocol of choice in the world today. In this chapter, we give an overview of the TCP/IP protocol suite.

Application Layer
Transport Layer
Network Layer (or Internet Layer)
Layer 1 and Layer 2 (or lower layers) (or Network Interface Layers)

Fig. 1.18 : Typical four-layer TCP/IP Model

OSI-ISO Reference Model

Application Layer (7)
Presentation Layer (6)
Session Layer (5)
Transport Layer (4)
Network Layer (3)
Data Link Layer (2)
Physical Layer (1)

TCP/IP Model

Application Layer
Transport Layer
Network Layer
Layer 1 and Layer 2

Fig. 1.19 : 7-Layer OSI Model and 4-Layer TCP/IP Model

Socket Application	← Application Layer
TCP and UDP	← Transport Layer
IP, ICMP, IGMP, ARP, RARP	← Network Layer
[LAN Technologies 802.3, 802.4, 802.5] and [WAN Technologies PPP, Frame relay, ATM]	← Lower layers

Fig. 1.20 : TCP/IP 4 layers and main protocols

11. The main design goal of TCP/IP was to build an interconnection of networks, referred to as an Internetwork, or Internet, that provided universal communication services over heterogeneous physical networks.
12. The clear benefit of such an internetwork is the enabling of communication between hosts on different networks, perhaps separated by a large geographical area.

1.20.1 Layers in the Internet Protocol Suite Stack

- The IP suite uses encapsulation to provide abstraction of protocols and services.
- Generally a protocol at a higher level uses a protocol at a lower level to help accomplish its aims.
- The internet protocol stack can be roughly fitted into the four fixed layers and are shown before.

Application Layer :
- This layer is broadly equivalent to the application, presentation and session layers of the OSI model.
- It gives an application access to the communication environment.
- Examples of protocols found at this layer are Telnet, FTP (File Transfer Protocol), SNMP (Simple Network Management Protocol), HTTP (Hyper Text Transfer Protocol) and SMTP (Simple Mail Transfer Protocol).
- An application is a user process co-operating with another process usually on a different host (there is also a benefit to application communication within a single host).
- The interface between the application and transport layers is defined by port numbers and sockets.

Transport Layer :
- The transport layer is similar to the OSI transport model, but with elements of the OSI session layer functionality.
- This layer provides an application layer delivery service.
- The two protocols found at the transport layer are **TCP (Transmission Control Protocol) and UDP (User Datagram Protocol)**.
- Either of these two protocols are used by the application layer process, the choice depends on the application's transmission reliability requirements.
- Transport layer provides the end-to-end data transfer by delivering data from an application to its remote peer.
- Multiple applications can be supported simultaneously.

- The most-used transport layer protocol is the Transmission Control Protocol (TCP), which provides connection-oriented reliable data delivery, duplicate data suppression, congestion control, and flow control.
- **TCP** is a **reliable, connection-oriented** protocol that provides error checking and flow control through a virtual link that it establishes and finally terminates.
- This gives a reliable service, therefore TCP would be utilized by FTP and SNMP File transfer and email delivery have to be accurate and error free.
- **UDP** is an **unreliable, connectionless** protocol that provides data transport with lower network traffic overheads than TCP. UDP does not error check or offer any flow control, this is left to the application process.
- SNMP uses UDP. SNMP is used to monitor network performance, so its operation must not contribute to congestion.

Network Layer or Internet Layer

- This layer is responsible for the routing and delivery of data across networks.
- It allows communication across networks of the same and different types and carries out translations to deal with dissimilar data addressing schemes.
- Internetwork layer, also called the *internet layer* or the *network layer*, provides the "virtual network" image of an internet (this layer shields the higher levels from the physical network architecture below it).
- Internet Protocol (IP) is the most important protocol in this layer.
- It is a connectionless protocol that doesn't assume reliability from lower layers.
- IP does *not* provide reliability, flow control, or error recovery.
- These functions must be provided at a higher level.
- A message unit in an IP network is called an *IP* datagram.
- This is the basic unit of information transmitted across TCP/IP networks.
- Other internetwork layer protocols are IP, ICMP, IGMP, ARP and RARP.
- With the advent of the concept of Internetworking, additional functionality was added to this layer, namely getting data from the source network to the destination network.
- This generally involves routing the packet across a network of networks, known as an internet.
- In the internet protocol suite, IP performs the basic task of getting packets of data from source to destination.
- IP can carry data for a number of different upper layer protocols; these protocols are each identified by a unique protocol number.
- ICMP and IGMP are protocols 1 and 2, respectively.

- Some of the protocols carried by IP, such as ICMP (used to transmit diagnostic information about IP transmission) and IGMP (used to manage multicast data) are layered on top of IP but perform internetwork layer functions, illustrating an incompatibility between the internet and the IP stack and OSI model.
- All routing protocols, such as BGP, OSPF, and RIP are also really part of the network layer, although they might seem to belong higher in the stack.

Layers 2 and 1 (Network Access Layers) :
- The combination of data link and physical layers deals with pure hardware (wires, satellite links, network interface cards, etc.) and access methods such as CSMA/CD (carrier sensed multiple access with collision detection).
- Ethernet exists at the network access layer - its hardware operates at the physical layer and its medium access control method (CSMA/CD) operates at the datalink layer.
- Network interface layer, also called the *link layer* or the *data-link layer*, is the interface to the actual network hardware.
- This interface may or may not provide reliable delivery, and may be packet or stream oriented.
- In fact, TCP/IP does not specify any protocol here, but can use almost any network interface available, which illustrates the flexibility of the IP layer.
- The link layer is not really part of the internet protocol suite, but is the method used to pass packets from the network layer on two different hosts.
- This process can be controlled both in the software device driver for the network card, as well as on firmware or specialist chipsets.
- These will perform data link functions such as adding a packet header to prepare it for transmission, then actually transmit the frame over a physical medium.
- The link layer can also be the layer where packets are intercepted to be sent over a virtual private network.
- When this is done, the link layer data is considered the application data and proceeds back down the IP stack for actual transmission.
- On the receiving end, the data goes up the IP stack twice (once for the VPN and the second time for routing).
- The physical layer is made up of the actual physical network components (hubs, repeaters, network cable, fiber optic cable, coaxial cable, network cards, Host Bus Adapter cards and the associated network connectors : RJ-45, BNC, etc).

1.21 TCP/IP AND OSI MODEL

1. This chapter gives a brief comparison between OSI and TCP/IP protocols with a special focus on the similarities and on how the protocols from both worlds map to each other.
2. The adoption of TCP/IP does not conflict with the OSI standards because the two protocol stacks were developed concurrently.
3. In some ways, TCP/IP contributed to OSI, and vice-versa.
4. Several important differences do exist, though, which arise from the basic requirements of TCP/IP which are :
   - A common set of applications
   - Dynamic routing
   - Connectionless protocols at the networking level
   - Universal connectivity
   - Packet-switching
5. The main differences between the OSI architecture and that of TCP/IP relate to the layers above the transport layer and those at the network layer.
6. OSI has both, the session layer and the presentation layer, whereas TCP/IP combines both into an application layer.
7. The requirement for a connectionless protocol also required TCP/IP to combine OSI's physical layer and data link layer into a network layer.

1.22 PROBLEMS WITH OSI

- OSI was a poor performer in implementation, and there are definite flaws in the protocols.
- Flow control is a problem at *every layer* and error control must be implemented to all layers as well.
- Network management is problematic and was actually omitted from the original OSI model.
- Semantic confusion about the Presentation and Application layers created so many major headaches that data security and encryption were eventually taken out altogether.

OSI was killed off because :
- Early slow and bug-filled, unusable implementations ruined its public image.
- OSI was thought to originate with the European Community and the U.S. federal government.

- Its probable market for use was proprietary. TCP/IP was bundled as part of Berkeley UNIX and was free.
- OSI is full of almost bureaucratic levels of unnecessary complexity.
- The seven-layer model was somewhat arbitrary, and was basically done in an attempt to wrest control away from IBM's 7-layer SNA protocol to a world standard controlled by a neutral organization (the ISO) rather than by a single corporation, not to simplify actually using the model.

1.23 PROBLEMS WITH TCP/IP

Far from blameless, TCP/IP has some problems as well, the primary one being that it speaks only its own language :

- It can't be used to intelligently describe another type of protocol stack (like SNA).
- Its network layer is more of an interface than a true layer of its own.
- There is no distinction between the Physical and Data Link layers. This is a poor choice from an engineering standpoint.
- Many of the *original* protocol implementations hack with very limited usefulness and arbitrary constraints based on hardware limitations or on simplifying the coding task.

1.24 SIMILARITIES BETWEEN OSI AND TCP/IP

Sr. No.	ISO OSI REFERENCE MODEL AND TCP/IP MODEL
1.	Based on a stack of independent protocols.
2.	Layers have roughly same functionality.
3.	Transport layer and below provide network-independent transport services.
4.	Layers above transport are application-oriented.

1.25 TCP/IP PROTOCOLS IN DETAIL

- ARP - Address Resolution Protocol (ARP) enables the packaging of IP data into Ethernet packages. It is the system and messaging protocol that is used to find the Ethernet (hardware) address from a specific IP number. Without this protocol, the

Ethernet package could not be generated from the IP package, because the Ethernet address could not be determined.

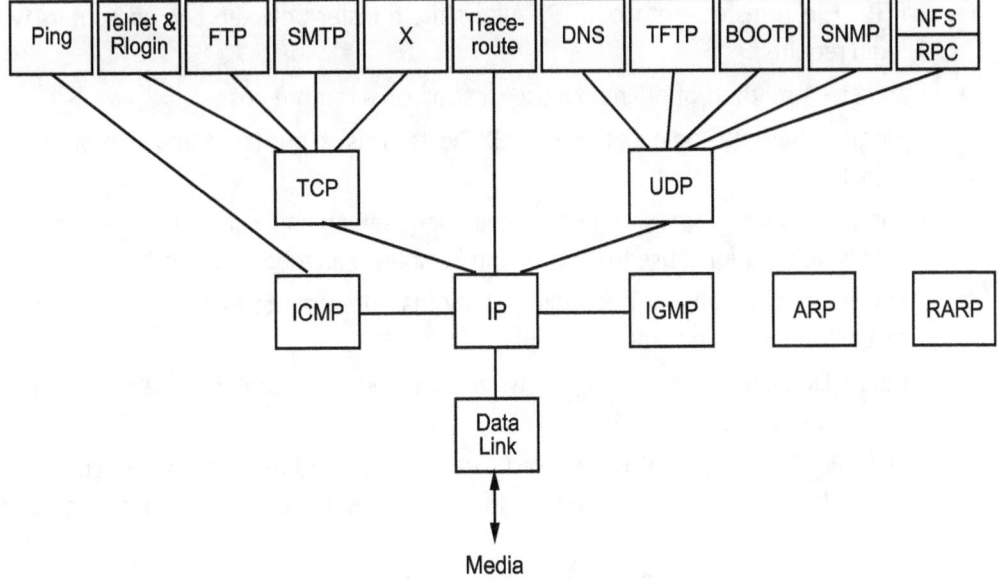

Fig. 1.21 : TCP/IP protocol suite in detail

- RARP - Reverse Address Resolution Protocol (RARP) is used to allow a computer without a local permanent data storage media to determine its IP address from its Ethernet address.
- IP - Internet Protocol (IP). Except for ARP and RARP all protocol's data packets will be packaged into an IP data packet. It provides the mechanism to use software to address and manage data packets being sent to computers.
- ICMP - Internet Control Message Protocol (ICMP) provides management and error reporting to help manage the process of sending data between computers.
- IGMP - Internet Group Management Protocol used to support multicasting.
- RIP - Routing Information Protocol (RIP), used to dynamically update router tables on WANs or the Internet.
- OSPF - Open Shortest Path First (OSPF) dynamic routing protocol.
- BGP - Border Gateway Protocol (BGP). A dynamic router protocol to communicate between routers on different systems.
- CIDR - Classless Inter Domain Routing (CIDR).
- TCP - A reliable connection oriented protocol used to control the management of application level services between computers.
- UDP - An unreliable connectionless protocol used to control the management of application level services between computers.

- Ping - A program that uses ICMP to send diagnostic messages to other computers to tell if they are reachable over the network.
- FTP - File Transfer Protocol (FTP). Allows file transfer between two computers with login required.
- Telnet - A method of opening a user session on a remote host.
- Rlogin - Remote login between UNIX hosts. This is outdated and is replaced by Telnet.
- The *X Window System*, or just X, is a client-server application that lets multiple clients (applications) use the bit-mapped display managed by a server.
- Traceroute is a network debugging utility that attempts to *trace* the path a packet takes through the network - its *route*.
- DNS - Domain Name Service, allows the network to determine IP addresses from names and vice versa.
- BOOTP - Bootstrap protocol is used to assign an IP address to diskless computers and tell it what server and file to load, which will provide it with an operating system.
- DHCP - Dynamic Host Configuration Protocol (DHCP) is a method of assigning and controlling the IP addresses of computers on a given network. It is a server based service that automatically assigns IP numbers when a computer boots. This way the IP address of a computer does not need to be assigned manually. This makes changing networks easier to manage. DHCP can perform all the functions of BOOTP.
- SNMP - Simple Network Management Protocol (SNMP). Used to manage all types of network elements based on various data sent and received.
- TFTP - Trivial File Transfer Protocol (TFTP). Allows file transfer between two computers with no login required. It is limited, and is intended for diskless stations.
- SMTP - Simple Mail Transfer Protocol (SMTP).
- NFS - Network File System (NFS). A protocol that allows UNIX and Linux systems remotely mount each other's file systems.

1.26 ISO PROTOCOLS IN DETAIL

- The Open Systems Interconnection (OSI) model is a reference model developed by ISO (International Organization for Standardization) in 1984 as a conceptual framework of standards for communication in the network across different equipment and applications by different vendors.
- It is now considered the primary architectural model for inter-computing and internetworking communications.

- Most of the network communication protocols used today have a structure based on the OSI model.
- The OSI model defines the communication process into 7 layers, dividing the tasks involved in moving information between networked computers into seven smaller, more manageable task groups. A task or group of tasks is then assigned to each of the seven OSI layers.
- Each layer is reasonably self-contained, so that the tasks assigned to each layer can be implemented independently. This enables the solutions offered by one layer to be updated without adversely affecting the other layers.
- **ISO defined a group of protocols for internetworking communications based on the OSI model, which are not being used in the network world because of effective and powerful TCP/IP Protocol.**
- ISO protocols are in the layers 3 to 7 and support almost any layer one and two protocols by various standard organizations and major vendors.

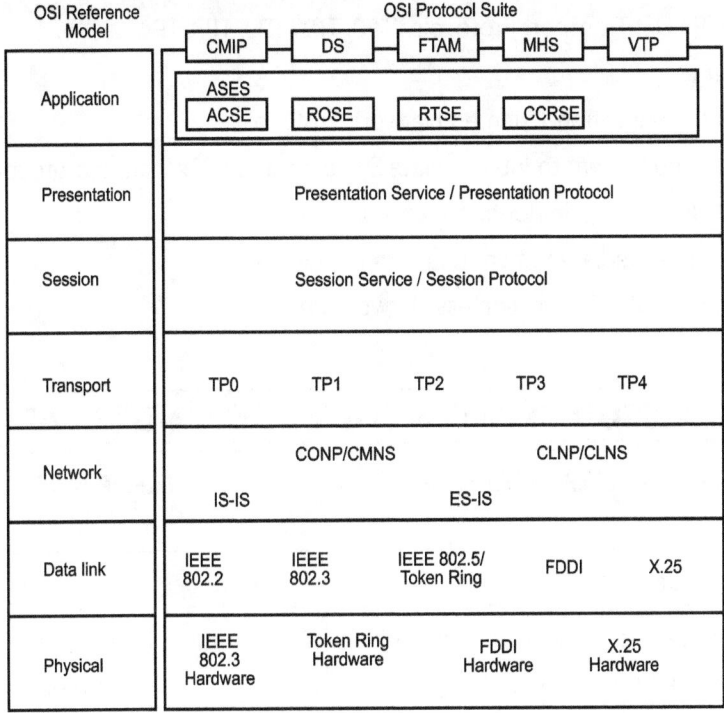

Fig. 1.21 : ISO Protocols in OSI 7 Layers Reference Model

Application Layer :
- ACSE : Association Control Service Element.
- ASN.1 : Abstract Syntax Notation One.
- CMIP : Common Management Information Protocol.

- CMIS : Common Management Information Service.
- CMOT : CMIP over TCP/IP.
- FTAM : File Transfer Access and Management.
- ROSE : Remote Operation Service Element.
- RTSE : Reliable Transfer Service Element Protocol.
- VTP : ISO Virtual Terminal Protocol.
- X.400 : Message Handling Service (ISO email transmission service) Protocols.
- X.500 : Directory Access Service Protocol (DAP).

Presentation Layer :
- ISO-PP : OSI Presentation Layer Protocol.

Session Layer :
- ISO-SP : OSI Session Layer Protocol.

Transport Layer :
- ISO-TP : OSI Transport Protocols : TP0, TP1, TP2, TP3, TP4

Network Layer :
- CONP : Connection-Oriented Network Protocol
- ES-IS : End System to Intermediate System Routing Exchange protocol
- IDRP : Inter-Domain Routing Protocol
- IS-IS : Intermediate System to Intermediate System
- ISO-IP : CLNP : Connectionless Network Protocol

1.27 COMPARISON BETWEEN OSI MODEL AND TCP/IP

Sr. No.	ISO OSI REFERENCE MODEL	TCP/IP MODEL
1.	7 layer model.	4 layer model.
2.	OSI model is useful in describing networks, but protocols are too general.	TCP/IP model is weak, but protocols are specific and widely used.
3.	Model was conceptual, designers didn't know what functionality to put in the layers.	Model is practical, designers know the functionality of each layer and used in real world network.
4.	Model is general, and easier to replace protocols.	Model is not general, and difficult to replace protocols.

(Contd.)

5.	Model had to adjust when networks didn't match the service specifications (wireless networks, internetworking).	Model need not require to adjust too much in this scenario.
6.	Model describe any type of network.	Model only describes TCP/IP which is not useful for describing any other networks (such as telephone networks)
7.	Network layer supports both connection-oriented and connection-less service.	Network layer supports only connectionless service.
8.	Transport layer supports only connection-oriented service.	Transport layer supports both connection oriented and connectionless service.
9.	OSI introduced concept of services, interface, Protocols.	These were force-fitted to TCP/IP later. It is not easy to replace protocols in TCP/IP.
10.	In OSI, reference model was done before protocols.	In TCP/IP, protocols were done before the model.
11.	OSI : Standardized first, build later.	TCP/IP : Build first, standardized later.
12.	OSI took too long to standardize.	TCP/IP was already in wide use by the time.
13.	OSI becomes too complex.	TCP/IP is not general it's Ad hoc.
14.	OSI Flaws • Bad Timing. • TCP/IP already well-established in academia. • Bad Technology. • Complicated, controversial model. • Unbalanced layers. • Repeating functions. • Designed for communications, not computing. • Bad implementations. • Complicated to understand and implement. • Bad politics. • Seen as biased toward European telecom, European Community and U.S. government.	TCP/IP Flaws • Blurred lines. • Doesn't clearly distinguish between services (what a layer does), interfaces (how the layer communicates) and protocols (how the layer does what it does). • Too specific. • Model is only suited to describe TCP/IP, not other networks. • Protocols can be very specific, inflexible. • No distinction between physical and data link layers. • No description of transmission media, nor frame delimiters.

1.28 ADDRESSING

1. In the data communication, like Internet communication following types of addresses are used.

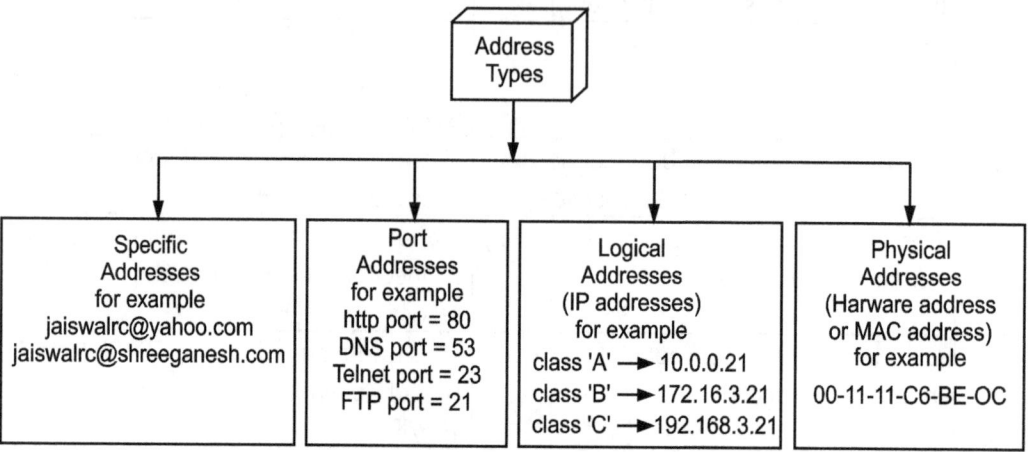

Fig. 1.23 (a) : Types of Addresses in Networking

2. These addresses are related to specific layer of the TCP/IP layered architecture.

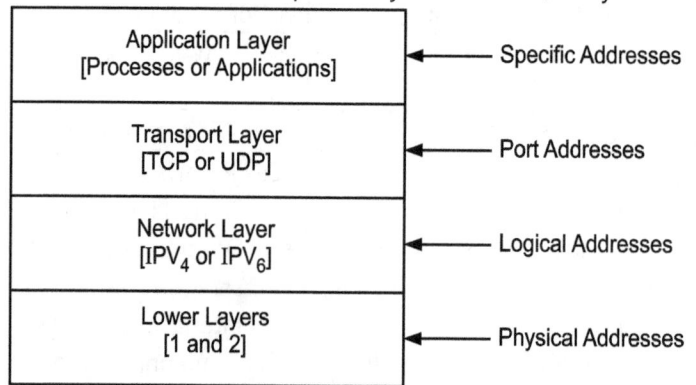

Fig. 1.23 (b) : Layer Specific Addresses are indicated

1.28.1 MAC Address

- The MAC address is a unique value associated with a network adapter. MAC addresses are also known as **hardware** addresses or **physical** addresses. They uniquely identify an adapter on a LAN.
- MAC addresses are 12-digit hexadecimal numbers (48 bits in length). By convention, MAC addresses are usually written in one of the following two formats :
    MM:MM:MM:SS:SS:SS
    MM-MM-MM-SS-SS-SS

- The first half of a MAC address contains the ID number of the adapter manufacturer. These IDs are regulated by an Internet standards body (see sidebar). The second half of a MAC address represents the serial number assigned to the adapter by the manufacturer.
- In the example,
    00:A0:C9:14:C8:29
  The prefix
    00A0C9
  indicates the manufacturer in Intel Corporation.
    00000C- For CISCO
    000011- for Tektronics
    00001B- For Novell
    000048- For Epson
    0000C6- For HP
    08003E- For Motorola
- MAC addresses allow computers to uniquely identify themselves on a network at relatively low level.
- Whereas MAC addressing works at the data link layer, IP addressing functions at the network layer (layer 3).
- It is a slight oversimplification, but one can think of IP addressing as supporting the software implementation and MAC addresses as supporting the hardware implementation of the network stack.
- The MAC address generally remains fixed and follows the network device, but the IP address changes as the network device moves from one network to another.
- IP networks maintain a mapping between the IP address of a device and its MAC address. This mapping is known as the **ARP cache** or **ARP table**.
- ARP, the Address Resolution Protocol, supports the logic for obtaining this mapping and keeping the cache up to date.
- DHCP also usually relies on MAC addresses to manage the unique assignment of IP addresses to devices.
- In Windows OS, At the command prompt, type 'ipconfig /all' without quotes and you can get MAC address of the LAN card or if using Windows XP, you can use the command 'getmac'.

1.28.2 IP Address

- Every machine on the Internet has a unique number assigned to it, called an IP address. Without an unique IP address on your machine, you will not be able to

- communicate with other devices, users, and computers on the Internet. You can look at your IP address as if it were a telephone number, each one being unique and used to identify a way to reach you and only you.
- An IP address always consists of 4 numbers separated by periods, with the numbers having a possible range of 0 through 255. An example of how an IP address appears is : **192.168.1.10**.
- This representation of an IP address is called decimal notation and is what is generally used by humans to refer to an IP address for readability purposes. With the ranges for each number being between 0 and 255 there are a total 4,294,967,296 possible IP addresses (4 Billions).
- Out of these addresses there are 3 special ranges that are reserved for special purposes. The first is the 0.0.0.0 address and refers to the default network and the 255.255.255.255 address which is called the broadcast address. These addresses are used for routing. The third address, 127.0.0.1, is the loopback address, and refers to your machine. Whenever you see, 127.0.0.1, you are actually referring to your own machine.
- There are some guidelines to how IP address can appear, though. The four numbers must be between 0 and 255, and the IP address of 0.0.0.0 and 255.255.255.255 are reserved, and are not considered usable IP addresses.
- IP addresses must be unique for each computer connected to a network. That means that if you have two computers on your network, each must have a different IP address to be able to communicate with each other. If by accident the same IP address is assigned to two computers, then those computers would have what is called an "IP Conflict" and not be able to communicate with each other.
- **IP address classes :** These IP addresses can further be broken down into classes. These classes are A, B, C, D, E and their possible ranges can be seen in table.

Class	Start address	Finish address
A	0.0.0.0	126.255.255.255
B	128.0.0.0	191.255.255.255
C	192.0.0.0	223.255.255.255
D	224.0.0.0	239.255.255.255
E	240.0.0.0	255.255.255.255

- If you look at the table you may notice something strange. The range of IP address from Class A to Class B skips the 127.0.0.0-127.255.255.255 range. That is because this range is reserved for the special addresses called Loopback addresses that have already been discussed above.

- The rest of classes are allocated to companies and organizations based upon the amount of IP addresses that they may need. Listed below are descriptions of the IP classes and the organizations that will typically receive that type of allocation.
- **Default Network :** The special network 0.0.0.0 is generally used for routing.
- **Class A :** From the table above you see that there are 126 class A networks. These networks consist of 16,777,214 possible IP addresses that can be assigned to devices and computers. This type of allocation is generally given to very large networks such as multi-national companies.
- **Loopback :** This is the special 127.0.0.0 network that is reserved as a loopback to your own computer. These addresses are used for testing and debugging of your programs or hardware.
- **Class B :** This class consists of 16,384 individual networks, each allocation consisting of 65,534 possible IP addresses. These blocks are generally allocated to Internet Service Providers and large networks, like a college or major hospital.
- **Class C :** There is a total of 2,097,152 Class C networks available, with each network consisting of 255 individual IP addresses. This type of class is generally given to small to mid-sized companies.
- **Class D :** The IP addresses in this class are reserved for a service called Multicast.
- **Class E :** The IP addresses in this class are reserved for experimental use.
- **Broadcast :** This is the special network of 255.255.255.255, and is used for broadcasting messages to the entire network that your computer resides on.

Private IP Addresses :
- There are also blocks of IP addresses that are set aside for internal private use for computers not directly connected to the Internet.
- These IP addresses are not supposed to be routed through the Internet, and most service providers will block the attempt to do so.
- These IP addresses are used for internal use by company or home networks that need to use TCP/IP but do not want to be directly visible on the Internet. These IP ranges are :

Class	Private Start Address	Private End Address
A	10.0.0.0	10.255.255.255
B	172.16.0.0	172.31.255.255
C	192.168.0.0	192.168.255.255

- If you are on a home/office private network and want to use TCP/IP, you should assign your computers/devices IP addresses from one of these three ranges. That way your router/firewall would be the only device with a true IP address which makes your network more secure.

1.28.3 Port Address

- In internet communication, the actual data communication is done between two processes of the system 1 and system 2.
- For example, web browser is communicating with webserver on the internet. Hence, on one computer system web-browsing process is running and on other computer system webserver process is running.
- Hence, at both ends the logical port numbers are assigned by operating system and TCP/IP protocol stack.
- IANA (Internet Assigned Number Authority) has divided port numbers into three angles as shown in Fig. 1.24.

Well - known ports	Registered ports	Dynamic ports
0000 to 1023	1024 to 49, 151	49, 151 to 65, 535

Fig. 1.24 : IANA Ports Address Range

- Thus, for web-browsing process port no. 1023 above numbers are used whereas for webserver process well known port – 80 is used.
- Well known port for webserver process is 80, for FTP is 21, Telnet – 23, DNS – 53 and for SMTP is 25.
- Port addresses used by computer systems can be checked using command **netstat – n – a** on command prompt.

1.28.4 Node to Node, Host to Host and Process to Process Delivery

- Thus, MAC address, IP address and port addresses are used by different layers like data link layer, network layer and transport layer respectively.
- This concept is easily explained in Fig. 1.25.
- The data link layer is responsible for delivery of frames between two neighbouring nodes over a link. This is called as Node-to-Node delivery.
- The network layer is responsible for delivery of datagrams between two hosts. This is called host to host delivery.
- Communication on the Internet is not defined as the exchange of data between two nodes or between two hosts. Real communication takes place between two **processes** or **application programs**. We need **process to process** delivery.
- The transport layer is responsible for process-to-process delivery. Two processes communicate in a client/server relationship.

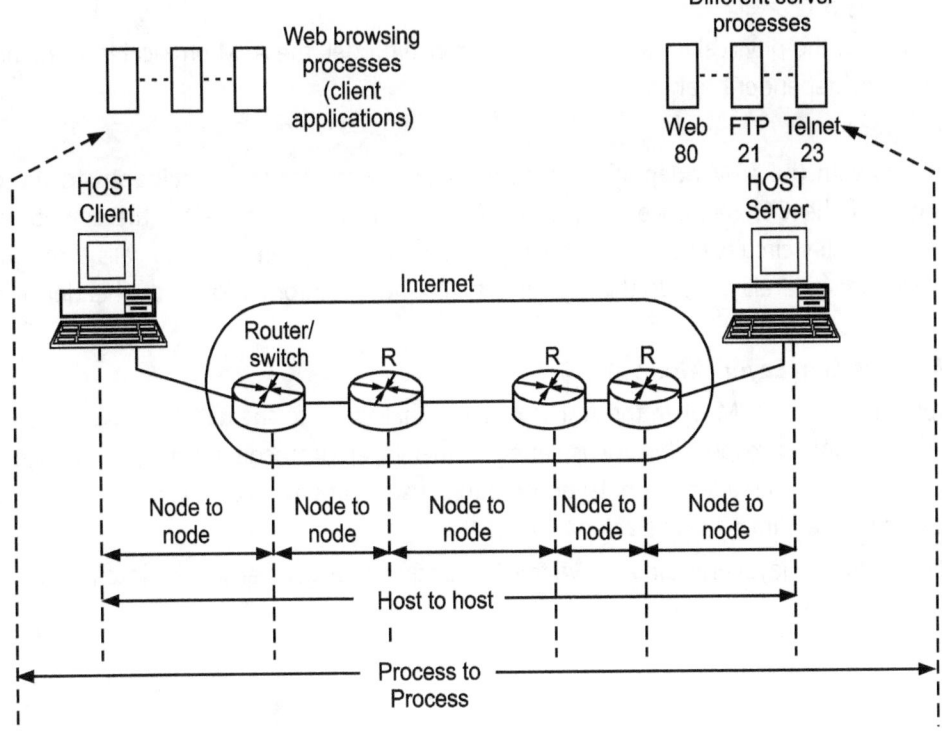

Node to Node : Data link layer.

Host to Host : Network layer.

Process to Process : Transport layer

Fig. 1.25 : Layers and Data Delivery

1.29 ATM REFERENCE MODEL

The ATM architecture uses a logical model to describe the functionality that it supports. ATM functionality corresponds to the physical layer and part of the data link layer of the OSI reference model.

The ATM reference model is composed of the following planes, which span all layers:

Control - This plane is responsible for generating and managing signaling requests.

User - This plane is responsible for managing the transfer of data.

Management - This plane contains two components:

Layer management manages layer-specific functions, such as the detection of failures and protocol problems.

Plane management manages and coordinates functions related to the complete system.

The ATM reference model is composed of the following ATM layers:

Physical Layer :

Analogous to the physical layer of the OSI reference model, the ATM physical layer manages the medium-dependent transmission.

ATM Layer :

Combined with the ATM adaptation layer, the ATM layer is roughly analogous to the data link layer of the OSI reference model. The ATM layer is responsible for the simultaneous sharing of virtual circuits over a physical link (cell multiplexing) and passing cells through the ATM network (cell relay). To do this, it uses the VPI and VCI information in the header of each ATM cell.

ATM Adaptation Layer (AAL) :

Combined with the ATM layer, the AAL is roughly analogous to the data link layer of the OSI model. The AAL is responsible for isolating higher-layer protocols from the details of the ATM processes. The adaptation layer prepares user data for conversion into cells and segments the data into 48-byte cell payloads.

Finally, the higher layers residing above the AAL accept user data, arrange it into packets, and hand it to the AAL.

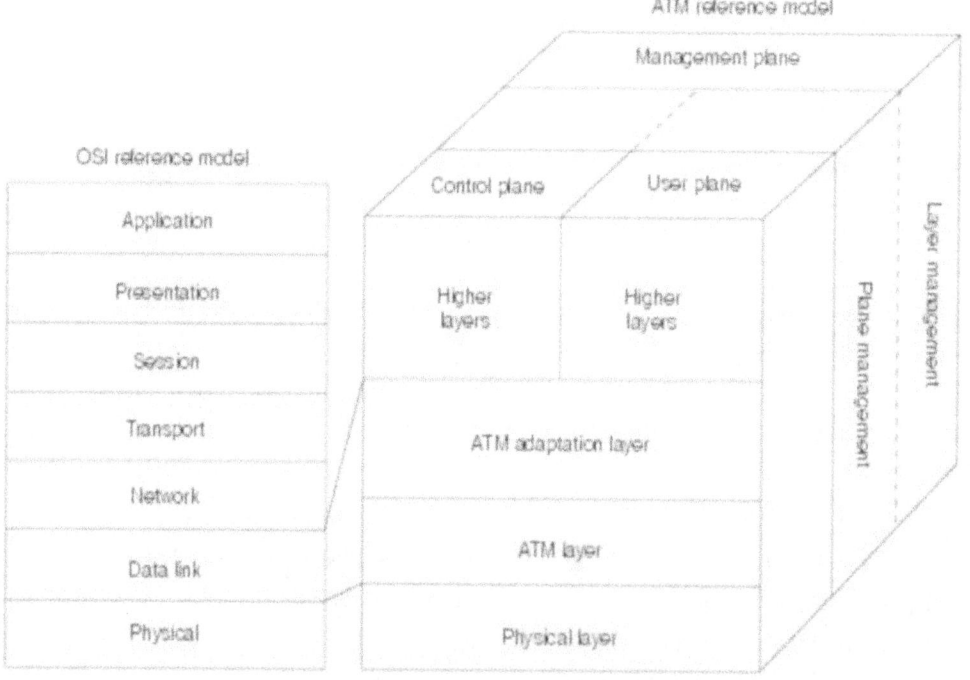

Fig. 1.26 : The ATM Reference Model Relates to the Lowest Two Layers of the OSI Reference Model

ATM Physical Layer :

The ATM physical layer has four functions: Cells are converted into a bitstream, the transmission and receipt of bits on the physical medium are controlled, ATM cell boundaries are tracked, and cells are packaged into the appropriate types of frames for the physical medium. The ATM physical layer is divided into two parts: the physical medium-dependent (PMD) sublayer and the transmission convergence (TC) sublayer.

The PMD sublayer provides two key functions. First, it synchronizes transmission and reception by sending and receiving a continuous flow of bits with associated timing information. Second, it specifies the physical media for the physical medium used, including connector types and cable Examples of physical medium standards for ATM include Synchronous Digital Hierarchy/Synchronous Optical Network (SDH/SONET).

The TC sublayer has four functions: cell delineation, header error control (HEC) sequence generation and verification, cell-rate decoupling, and transmission frame adaptation. The cell delineation function maintains ATM cell boundaries, allowing devices to locate cells within a stream of bits. HEC sequence generation and verification generates and checks the header error control code to ensure valid data. Cell-rate decoupling maintains synchronization and inserts or suppresses idle (unassigned) ATM cells to adapt the rate of valid ATM cells to the payload capacity of the transmission system. Transmission frame adaptation packages ATM cells into frames acceptable to the particular physical layer implementation.

ATM Adaptation Layer – AAL 1 :

AAL1, a connection-oriented service, is suitable for handling constant bit rate sources (CBR), such as voice and videoconferencing. ATM transports CBR traffic using circuit-emulation services. Circuit-emulation service also accommodates the attachment of equipment currently using leased lines to an ATM backbone network. AAL1 requires timing synchronization between the source and the destination. For this reason, AAL1 depends on a medium, such as SONET, that supports clocking.

ATM Adaptation Layer – AAL 2 :

Another traffic type has timing requirements like CBR but tends to be bursty in nature. This is called variable bit rate (VBR) traffic. This typically includes services characterized as packetized voice or video that do not have a constant data transmission speed but that do have requirements similar to constant bit rate services. AAL2 is suitable for VBR traffic. The AAL2 process uses 44 bytes of the cell payload for user data and reserves 4 bytes of the payload to support the AAL2 processes.

ATM Adaptation Layer – AAL 4 :

AAL3/4 supports both connection-oriented and connectionless data. It was designed for network service providers and is closely aligned with Switched Multimegabit Data Service (SMDS). AAL3/4 is used to transmit SMDS packets over an ATM network.

ATM Adaptation Layer – AAL 5 :

AAL5 is the primary AAL for data and supports both connection-oriented and connectionless data. It is used to transfer most non-SMDS data, such as classical IP over ATM and LAN Emulation (LANE). AAL5 also is known as the simple and efficient adaptation layer (SEAL) because the SAR sublayer simply accepts the CS-PDU and segments it into 48-octet SAR-PDUs without reserving any bytes in each cell.

1.29.1 Structure of an ATM Cell

An ATM cell consists of a 5-byte header and a 48-byte payload. The payload size of 48 bytes was chosen as described above. ATM defines two different cell formats: UNI (User-Network Interface) shown in Fig. 1.27 and NNI (Network-Network Interface) shown in Fig. 1.28. Most ATM links use UNI cell format.

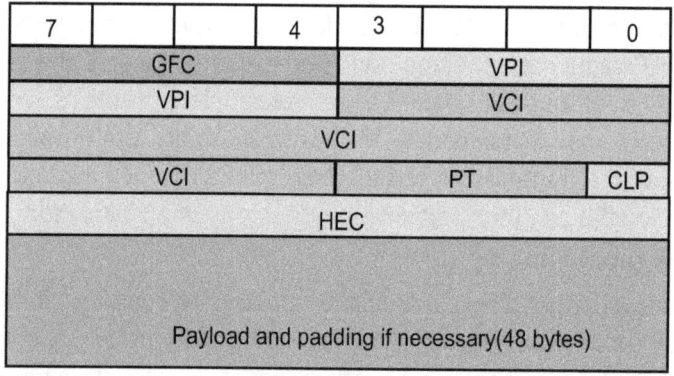

Fig. 1.27 : Diagram of the UNI – User Network Interface

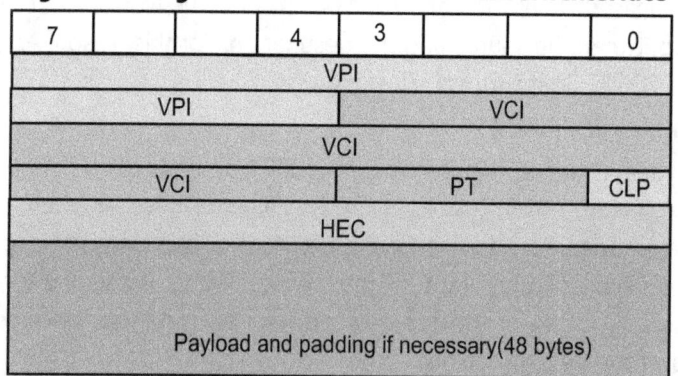

Fig. 1.28 : Diagram of the NNI – Network – Network Interface

GFC = Generic Flow Control (4 bits) (default:4-zero bits)
VPI = Virtual Path Identifier (8 bits UNI, or 12 bits NNI)
VCI = Virtual Channel identifier (16 bits)

PT = Payload Type (3 bits)

CLP = Cell Loss Priority (1-bit)

HEC = Header Error Control (8-bit CRC, polynomial = $X^8 + X^2 + X + 1$)

ATM uses the PT field to designate various special kinds of cells for operations, administration and management (OAM) purposes, and to delineate packet boundaries in some ATM adaptation layers (AAL).

Several ATM link protocols use the HEC field to drive a CRC-based framing algorithm, which allows locating the ATM cells with no overhead beyond what is otherwise needed for header protection. The 8-bit CRC is used to correct single-bit header errors and detect multi-bit header errors. When multi-bit header errors are detected, the current and subsequent cells are dropped until a cell with no header errors is found.

A UNI cell reserves the GFC field for a local flow control/submultiplexing system between users. This was intended to allow several terminals to share a single network connection, in the same way that two Integrated Services Digital Network (ISDN) phones can share a single basic rate ISDN connection. All four GFC bits must be zero by default.

The NNI cell format replicates the UNI format almost exactly, except that the 4-bit GFC field is re-allocated to the VPI field, extending the VPI to 12 bits. Thus, a single NNI ATM interconnection is capable of addressing almost 212 VPs of up to almost 216 VCs each (in practice some of the VP and VC numbers are reserved).

EXERCISES

1. What are the different advantages of installing a network ?
2. What are the different disadvantages of installing a network ?
3. Write a short note on network topology.
4. Compare all network topologies.
5. Classify the different networks.
6. Write a short note on :
   (a) LAN   (b) WAN
   (c) MAN   (d) Internet
7. What is Network Layered Architecture ?
8. What are the different benefits of layered design ?
9. What are service primitives and relationship of service to protocols ?
10. Compare connection oriented Vs. connectionless service.

11. Draw and explain ISO-OSI reference model.
12. Explain the function of each layer of OSI-ISO reference model.
13. List out the different network architectures.
14. Draw and explain TCP/IP network architecture.
15. Compare OSI model and TCP/IP model.
16. What is MAC address ?
17. What are the types of IP addresses ?
18. Explain private IP addresses.
19. Write a short note on port addresses.

UNIT II

Chapter 2
SIGNALS AND DATA

OBJECTIVES

After reading this chapter you will understand :

- Analog Signal/Data and Digital Signal/Data.
- Periodic Analog Signals (Simple and Composite).
- Sine Wave details (F, T, λ etc.), Other Signals like Square Wave, Pulse Wave, Triangular, RAMP (Positive and Negative), Audio Signal and Noise Signal.
- Time and Frequency Domain Representation of the Sine Wave, Square Wave, Non-periodic Wave Signal.
- Bandwidth of Composite Signal, Bandwidth of Periodic and Non-periodic Signal.
- Digital Signals (Two level and Four level), Bit Rate and Bit Length.
- Digital Signal as Composite Analog Signal.
- Baseband and Broadband Transmission of Digital Signals.
- Transmission Impairment like Attenuation, Distortion and Noise.
- Data Rate Limits, Nyquist Theorem and Shannon Capacity Theorem.
- QoS (Quality of Service) Parameters, Bandwidth, Throughput, Delay, Jitter, Bandwidth-delay Product etc.

2.1 ANALOG/DIGITAL, SIGNALS AND DATA

1. **Analog signal** has infinitely many levels of intensity over a period of time.
2. **Digital signal** can have only a limited number of discrete defined values (for example 0 and 1).
3. **Analog data** refers to information that is continuous in nature. Analog data takes continuous values.
4. **Digital data** refers to information that has discrete state values (for example 0 and 1).
5. Prototype examples for Analog signal, Digital signal, Analog data and Digital data are as shown in Fig. 2.1.

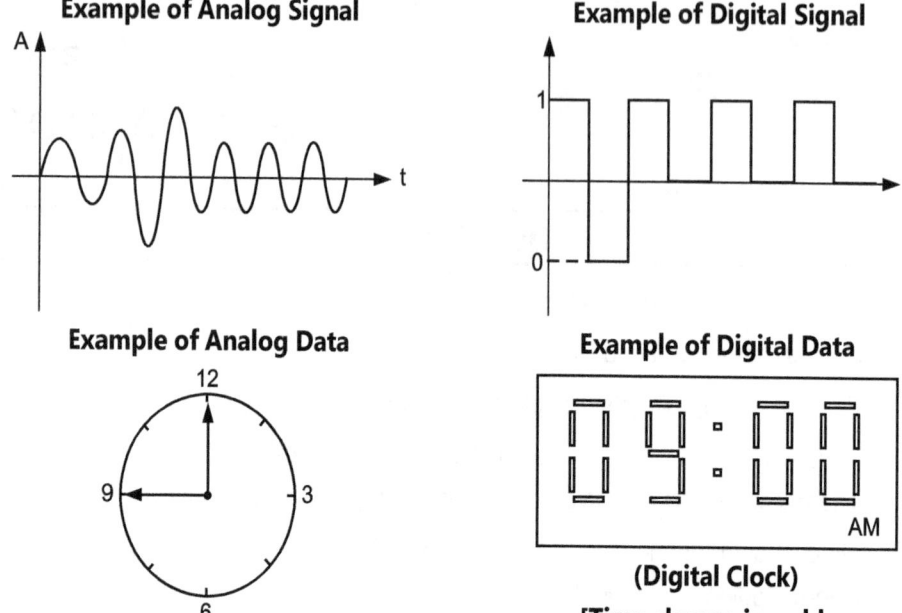

Fig. 2.1 : Analog/Digital Signals and Data Representation

2.2 PERIODIC ANALOG SIGNALS

1. Periodic analog signals are classified as :

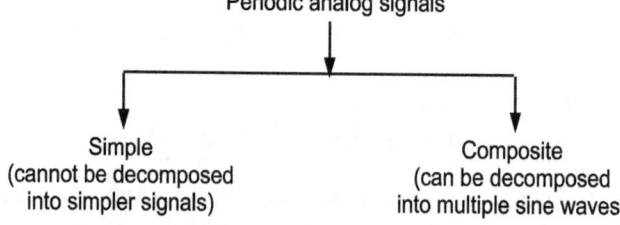

2. The example of **simple** periodic analog signals which cannot be decomposed into simpler signals is sine wave.

3. The examples of **composite** periodic analog signals which can be decomposed into multiple sine waves are :
   - Square wave (duty cycle = 50%).
   - Pulse wave (duty cycle ≠ 50%)
   - Triangular waveform.
   - RAMP waveform (positive or negative RAMP).

4. Let's see the characteristics of sine wave in detail.
5. Also we will discuss the remaining signal waveforms in brief.

2.2.1 Sine Wave Signal

- A sine wave has the same shape as the graph of the sine function used in trigonometry. Sine waves are produced by rotating electrical machines such as dynamos, power station turbines and electrical energy is transmitted to the consumer in this form.
- In electronics, sine waves are among the most useful of all signals in testing circuits and analyzing system performance.
- Sine wave in more detail is shown in Fig. 2.2.

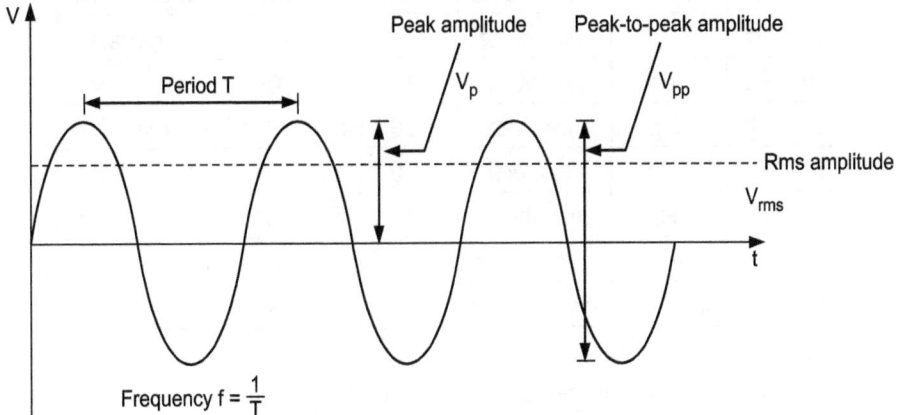

Fig. 2.2 : Periodic Sine Wave Signal

The terms defined below are needed to describe sine waves and other waveforms precisely :

1. **Period (T) :**
   - The period is the time taken for one complete cycle of a repeating waveform.
   - The period is often thought of as the time interval between peaks, but can be measured between any two corresponding points in successive cycles.

2. **Frequency (f) :**
   - Frequency is the number of cycles completed per second.
   - The measurement unit for frequency is the **hertz, Hz**. 1 Hz = 1 cycle per second.
   - If you know the period, the frequency of the signal can be calculated from

$$f = \frac{1}{T}$$

Conversely, the period is given by

$$T = \frac{1}{f}$$

- Signals you are likely to use vary in frequency from about 0.1 Hz, through values in **kilohertz, kHz** (thousands of cycles per second) to values in **megahertz, MHz** (millions of cycles per second).

Table 2.1 : SI Multiples for Hertz (Hz)

Submultiples			Multiples		
Value	Symbol	Name	Value	Symbol	Name
10^{-1} Hz	dHz	decihertz	10^1 Hz	daHz	decahertz
10^{-2} Hz	cHz	centihertz	10^2 Hz	hHz	hectohertz
10^{-3} Hz	**mHz**	**millihertz**	10^3 Hz	**kHz**	**kilohertz**
10^{-6} Hz	µHz	microhertz	10^6 Hz	**MHz**	**megahertz**
10^{-9} Hz	nHz	nanohertz	10^9 Hz	**GHz**	**gigahertz**
10^{-12} Hz	pHz	picohertz	10^{12} Hz	**THz**	**terahertz**
10^{-15} Hz	fHz	femtohertz	10^{15} Hz	PHz	petahertz
10^{-18} Hz	aHz	attohertz	10^{18} Hz	EHz	exahertz
10^{-21} Hz	zHz	zeptohertz	10^{21} Hz	ZHz	zettahertz
10^{-24} Hz	yHz	yoctohertz	10^{24} Hz	YHz	yottahertz
Common prefixed units are in bold face.					

- The **hertz** (symbol : **Hz**) is a unit of frequency.
- It is defined as the number of complete cycles per second. It is the basic unit of frequency in the International System of Units (SI). It is used worldwide in both general-purpose and scientific contexts.
- Hertz can be used to measure any periodic event; the most common uses of hertz are to describe radio and audio frequencies, more or less sinusoidal contexts in which case a frequency of 1 Hz is equal to one cycle per second.
- The unit hertz is defined by the International System of Units (SI).

3. **Amplitude :**
   - In electronics, the amplitude, or height, of a sine wave is measured in three different ways.
   - The **peak amplitude, V_p,** is measured from the X-axis, 0 V, to the top of a peak, or to the bottom of a trough. (In physics 'amplitude' usually refers to peak amplitude.)
   - The **peak-to-peak amplitude, V_{pp},** is measured between the maximum positive and negative values.
   - In practical terms, this is often the easier measurement to make. Its value is exactly twice V_p.
   - Although peak and peak-to-peak values are easily determined, it is often more useful to know the **root mean square**, or **rms amplitude** of the wave, where :

$$V_{rms} = \frac{V_p}{\sqrt{2}} \text{ or } V_{rms} = 0.7 \times V_p$$

and

$$V_p = \sqrt{2} \times V_{rms} \text{ or } V_p = 1.4 \times V_{rms}$$

4. **Phase :**
   - It is sometimes useful to divide a sine wave into degrees, °, as follows :
   - Remember that sine waves are generated by rotating electrical machines. A complete 360° turn of the voltage generator corresponds to one cycle of the sine wave.
   - Therefore 180° corresponds to a half turn, 90° to a quarter turn and so on. Using this method, any point on the sine wave graph can be identified by a particular number of degrees through the cycle.

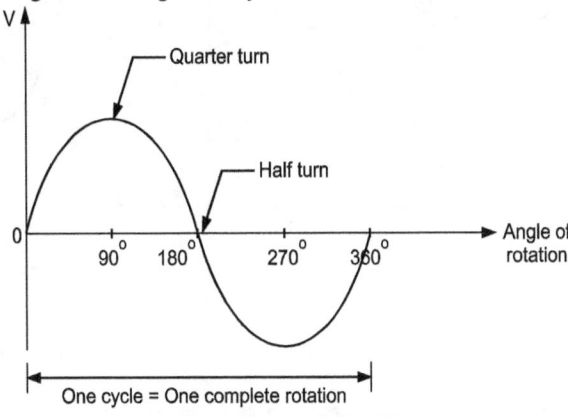

Fig. 2.3 : Phase of Sine Wave

   - If two sine waves have the same frequency and occur at the same time, they are said to be **in phase**.

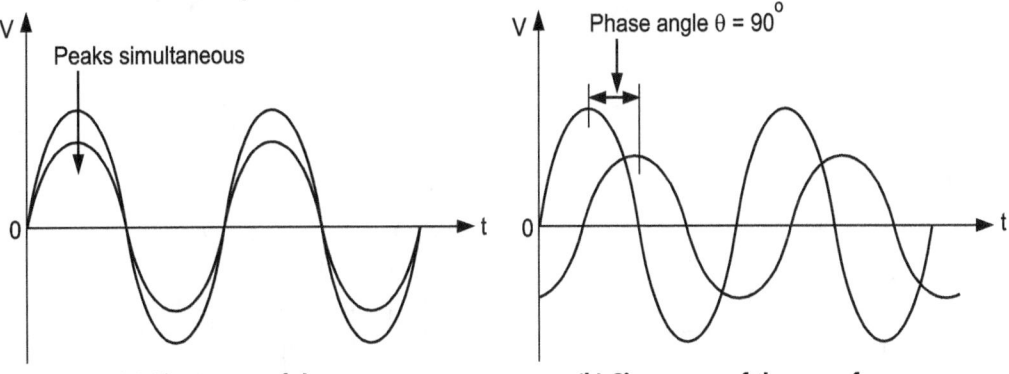

(a) Sine waves of the same frequency which are in phase

(b) Sine waves of the same frequency which are a quarter cycle (90°) out of phase

Fig. 2.4 : In Phase and Out of Phase Sine Waves

   - On the other hand, if the two waves occur at different times, they are said to be **out of phase**.

- When this happens, the difference in phase can be measured in degrees, and is called the **phase angle**, θ. As you can see, the two waves in part (b) are a quarter cycle out of phase, so the phase angle $\theta = 90°$.
- The graphs below show waveforms of different frequency and amplitude.

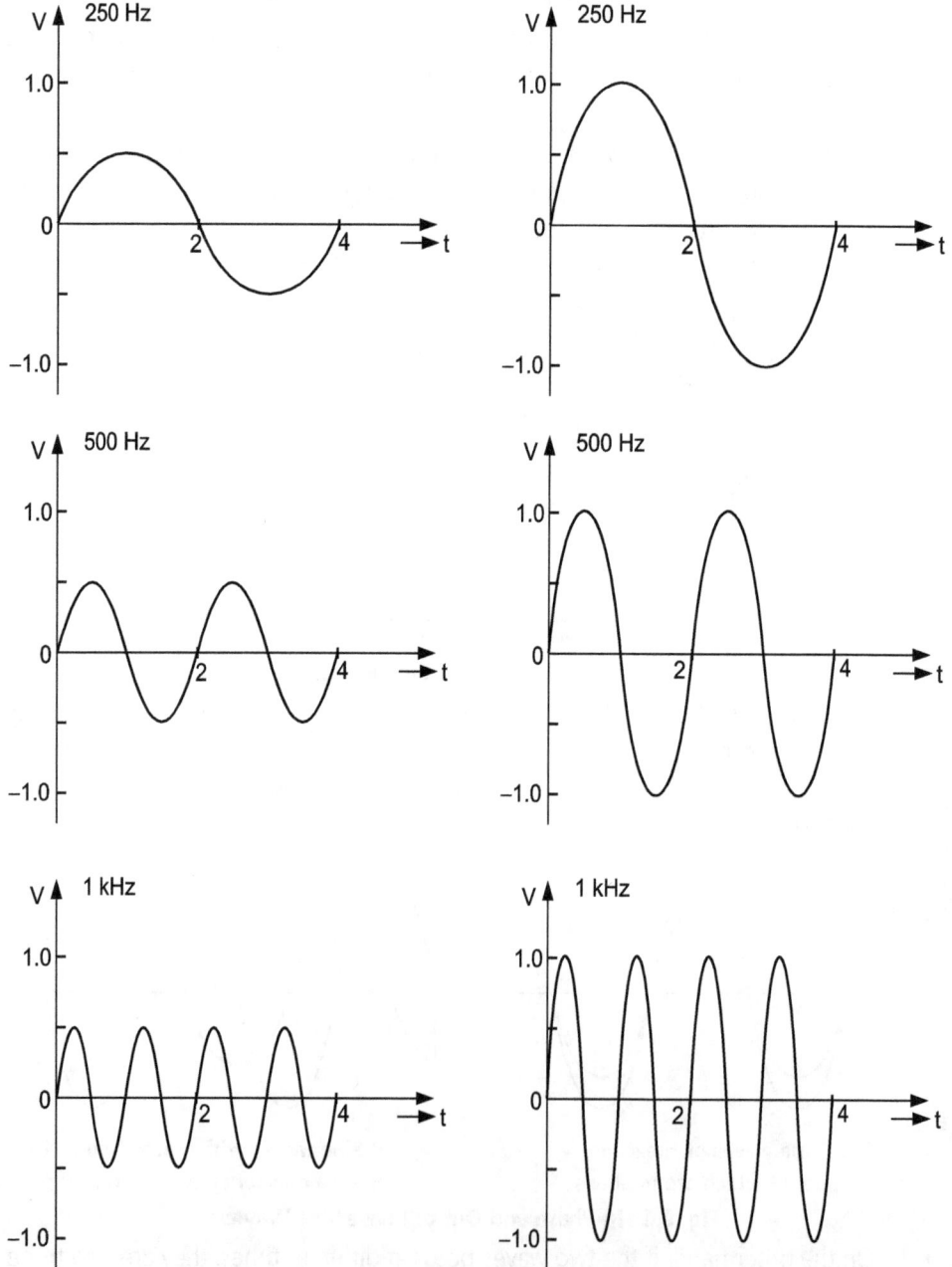

Fig. 2.5 : Sine Waves of 250 Hz, 500 Hz and 1 kHz with different amplitudes

5. Wavelength :

- Wavelength is the characteristic of sine wave which binds the period or the frequency of sine wave to the propagation speed of the medium.

$$\text{Wavelength} = \text{Propagation speed} \times \text{Period} = \frac{\text{Propagation speed}}{\text{Frequency}}$$

where, propagation speed of electromagnetic signal = 3×10^8 m/s.

Making of Waves :

- Sine waves can be mixed with DC signals, or with other sine waves to produce new waveforms. Here is one example of complex waveform.

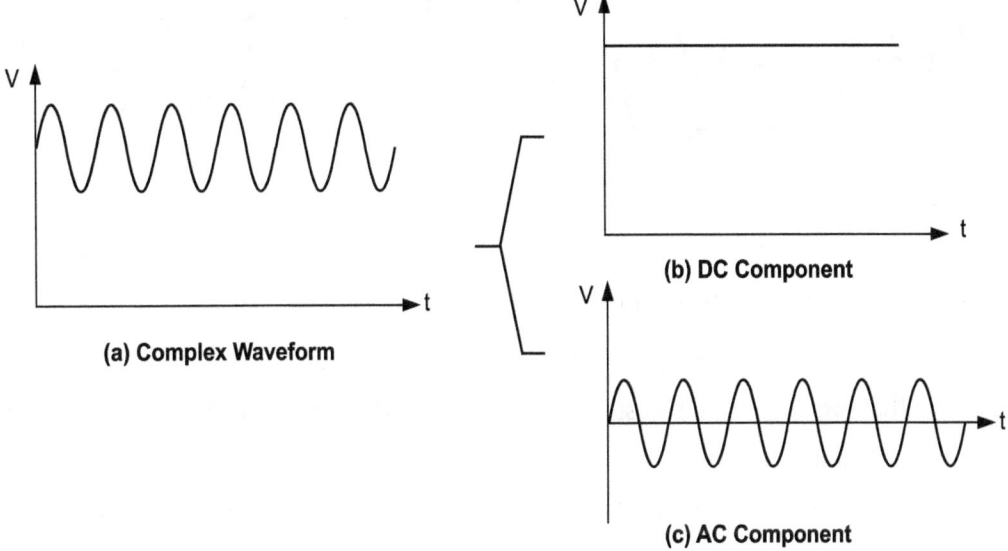

Fig. 2.6 : DC Component Superimposed with AC Component

- 'Complex' does not mean difficult to understand. A waveform like this can be thought of consisting of a DC component with a superimosed AC component. It is quite easy to separate these two components using a **capacitor.**
- More dramatic results are obtained by mixing a sine wave of a particular frequency with exact multiples of the same frequency, in other words, by adding **harmonics** to the **fundamental** frequency. The V/t graphs below show what happens when a sine wave is mixed with its 3rd harmonic (3 times the fundamental frequency) at reduced amplitude, and subsequently with its 5th, 7th and 9th harmonics.

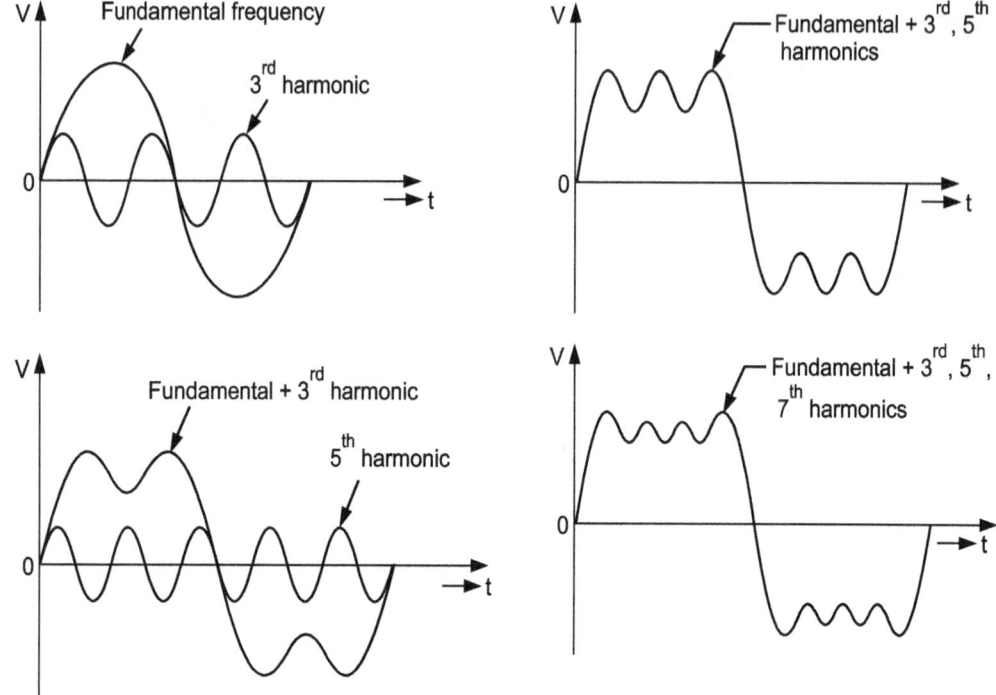

Fig. 2.7 : Fundamental and Harmonic Waveforms

- As you can see, as more odd harmonics are added, the waveform begins to look more and more like a square wave.
- This surprising result illustrates a general principle first formulated by the French mathematician Joseph Fourier, namely that *any* complex waveform can be built up from a pure sine wave plus particular harmonics of the fundamental frequency.
- Square waves, triangular waves and sawtooth waves can be produced in this way.

2.2.2 Other Signals

This part of section outlines the other types of signal you are going to meet. Circuits which generate these signals are versatile building blocks.

1. **Square waves :**

    - Like sine waves, square waves are described in terms of period, frequency and amplitude as shown in Fig. 2.8.

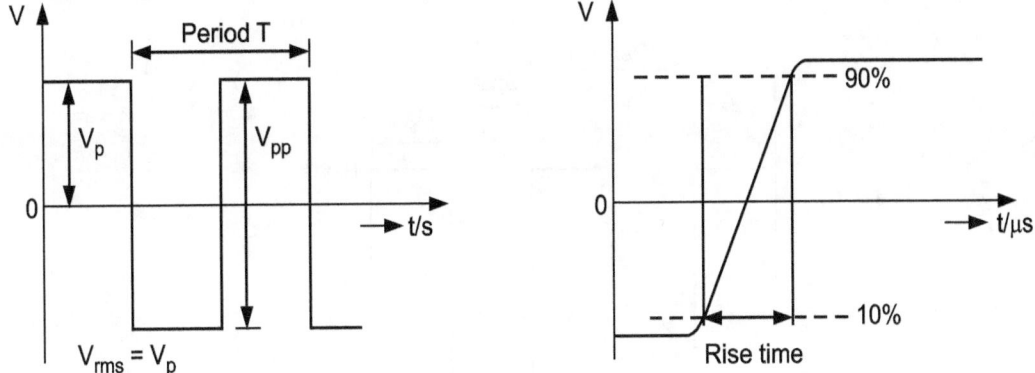

Fig. 2.8 : Square Waveform

- Peak amplitude, V_p, and peak-to-peak amplitude, V_{pp}, are measured as you might expect.
- However, the rms amplitude, V_{rms}, is greater than that of a sine wave.
- Remember that the rms amplitude is the DC voltage which will deliver the same power as the signal. If a square wave supply is connected across a lamp, the current flows first one way and then the other.
- The current switches direction but its *magnitude* remains the same.
- In other words, the square wave delivers its maximum power throughout the cycle so that V_{rms} is equal to V_p. (If this is confusing, don't worry, the rms amplitude of a square wave is not something you need to think about very often.)
- Although a square wave may change very rapidly from its minimum to maximum voltage, this change cannot be instantaneous.
- The **rise time** of the signal is defined as the time taken for the voltage to change from 10% to 90% of its maximum value. Rise times are usually very short, with durations measured in nanoseconds (1 ns = 10^{-9} s), or microseconds (1 μs = 10^{-6} s), as indicated in the graph.

2. **Pulse waveforms :**
   - Pulse waveforms look similar to square waves, except that all the action takes place above the X-axis.
   - At the beginning of a pulse, the voltage changes suddenly from a LOW level, close to the X-axis, to a HIGH level, usually close to the power supply voltage.

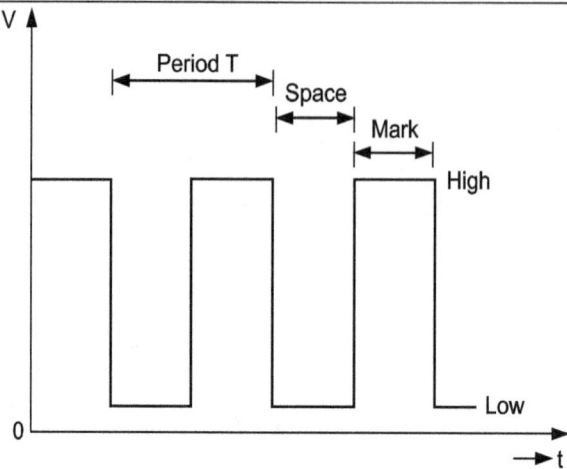

Fig. 2.9 : Pulse Waveform

- Sometimes, the 'frequency' of a pulse waveform is referred to as its **repetition rate**. This means the number of cycles per second, measured in hertz, Hz.
- The HIGH time of the pulse waveform is called the **mark**, while the LOW time is called the **space**. The mark and space do not need to be of equal duration. The **mark space ratio** is given by,

$$\text{Mark space ratio} = \frac{\text{HIGH time}}{\text{LOW time}}$$

- A mark space ratio = 1.0 means that the HIGH and LOW times are equal, while a mark space ratio = 0.5 indicates that the HIGH time is half as long as the LOW time.

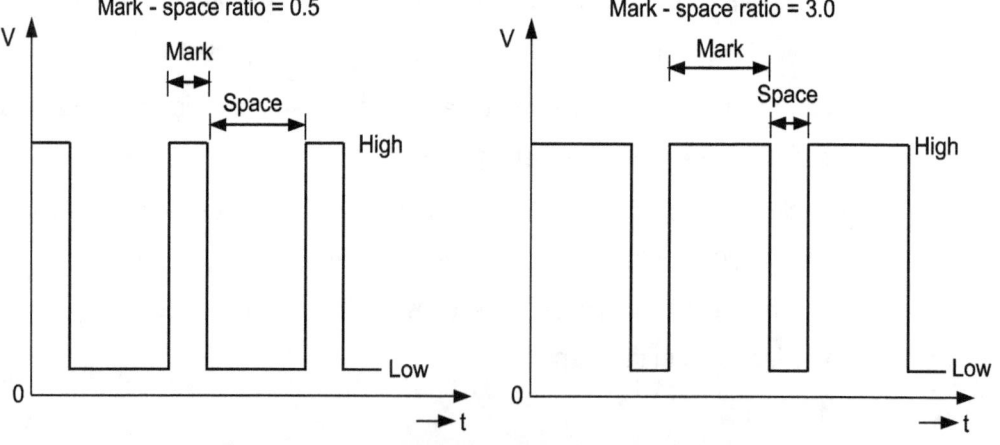

Fig. 2.10 : Pulse Waveforms with Different Duty Cycles

- A mark space ratio of 3.0 corresponds to a longer HIGH time, in this case, three times as long as the space.
- Another way of describing the same types of waveform uses the **duty cycle**, where,

$$\text{Duty cycle} = \frac{\text{HIGH time}}{\text{Period}} \times 100\%$$

- When the duty cycle is less than 50%, the HIGH time is shorter than the LOW time, and so on.

3. **Ramps :**

   - A voltage ramp is a steadily increasing or decreasing voltage, as shown in Fig. 2.11.

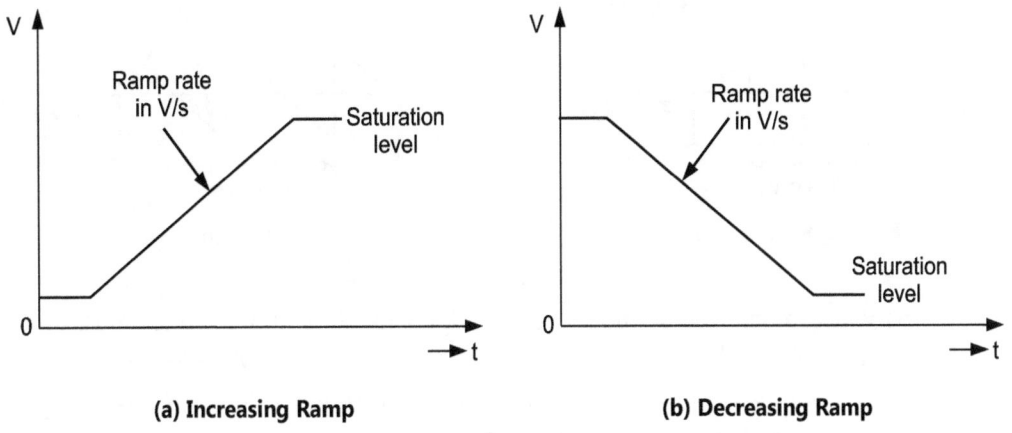

(a) Increasing Ramp (b) Decreasing Ramp

Fig. 2.11 : Ramp Waveforms (Increasing and Decreasing Ramp)

- The **ramp rate** is measured in units of volts per second, V/s. Such changes cannot continue indefinitely, but stop when the voltage reaches a **saturation level**, usually close to the power supply voltage.

4. **Triangular and sawtooth waves :**

   - These waveforms consist of alternate positive-going and negative-going ramps.
   - In a triangular wave, the rate of voltage change is equal during the two parts of each cycle, while in a sawtooth wave, the rates of change are unequal.
   - Sawtooth generator circuits are an essential building block in oscilloscope and television systems.

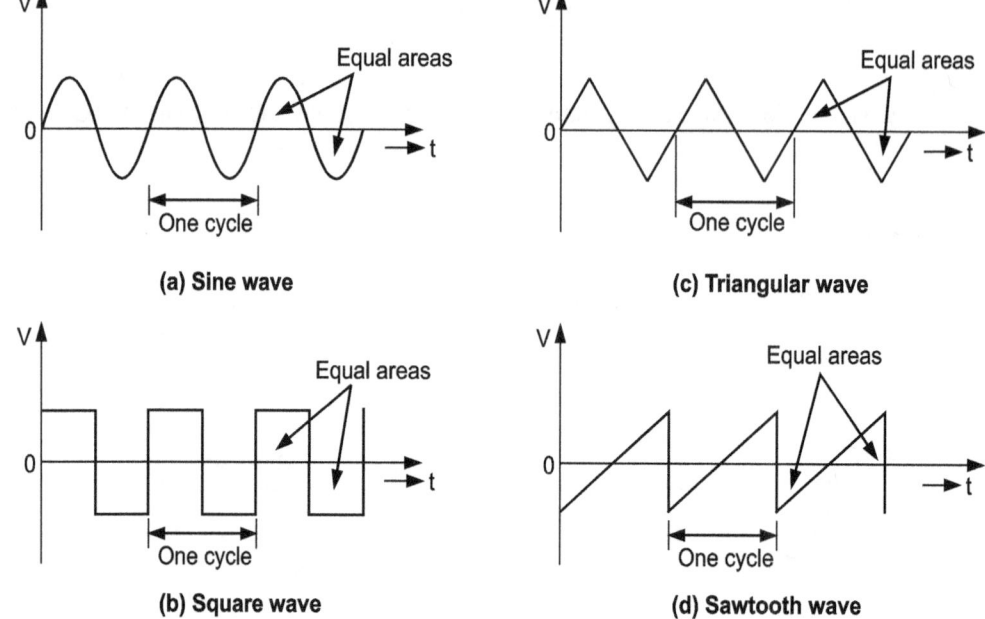

(a) Sine wave
(c) Triangular wave
(b) Square wave
(d) Sawtooth wave

Fig. 2.12 : Other Periodic Waves

- As you can see, the voltage levels change with time and are alternate between positive values (above the X-axis) and negative values (below the X-axis).
- Signals with repeated shapes are called **waveforms** and include **sine** waves, **square** waves, **triangular** waves and **sawtooth** waves.
- A distinguishing feature of alternating waves is that equal areas are enclosed above and below the X-axis.

5. **Audio signals :**

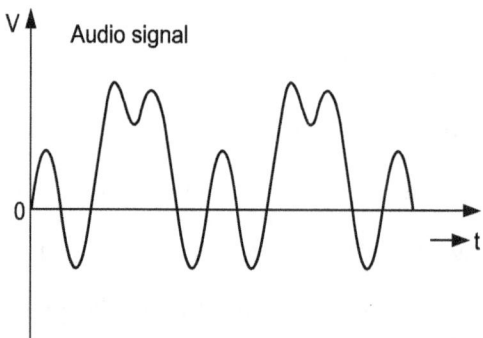

Fig. 2.13 : Audio Signal (20 Hz to 20 kHz) Waveform

- As already mentioned, sound frequencies which can be detected by the human ear vary from a lower limit of around 20 Hz to an upper limit of about 20 kHz.
- A sound wave amplified and played through a loudspeaker gives a pure audio tone.
- Audio signals like speech or music consist of many different frequencies.

- Sometimes it is possible to see a dominant frequency in the V/t graph of a musical signal, but it is clear that other frequencies are present.

6. **Noise :**
   - A noise signal consists of a mixture of frequencies with random amplitudes as shown in Fig. 2.14.

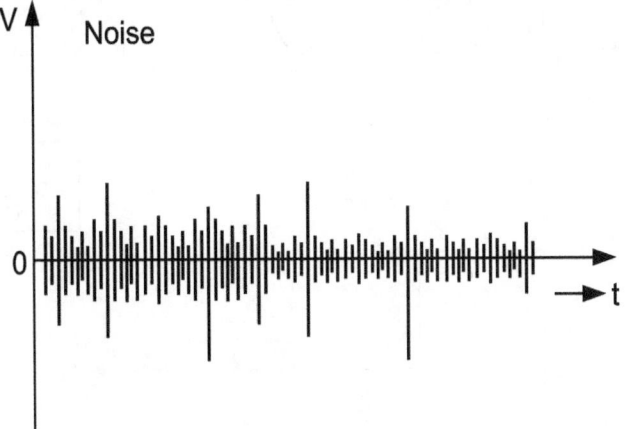

Fig. 2.14 : Noise Waveform Signal

   - Noise can originate in various ways.
   - For example, heat energy increases the random motion of electrons and results in the generation of **thermal noise** in all components, although some components are 'noisier' than others.
   - Additional sources of noise include radio signals, which are detected and amplified by many circuits, not just by radio receivers.
   - Interference is caused by the switching of mains appliances and 'spikes' and 'glitches' are caused by rapid changes in current and voltage elsewhere in an electronic system.

2.2.3 Time and Frequency Domain

- So far we have seen the amplitude, frequency and phase of the sine wave with respect to time axis, this is called as **time-domain** plot of sine wave.
- The plot between amplitude and frequency of a wave is called as **frequency-domain** plot of a wave.
- Thus, the complete sinewave of 3 Hz frequency in the time domain can be represented by one single spike in the frequency domain with (4 V peak amplitude).
- Frequency domain plot is extremely useful and compact when we are dealing with more than one sine waves.

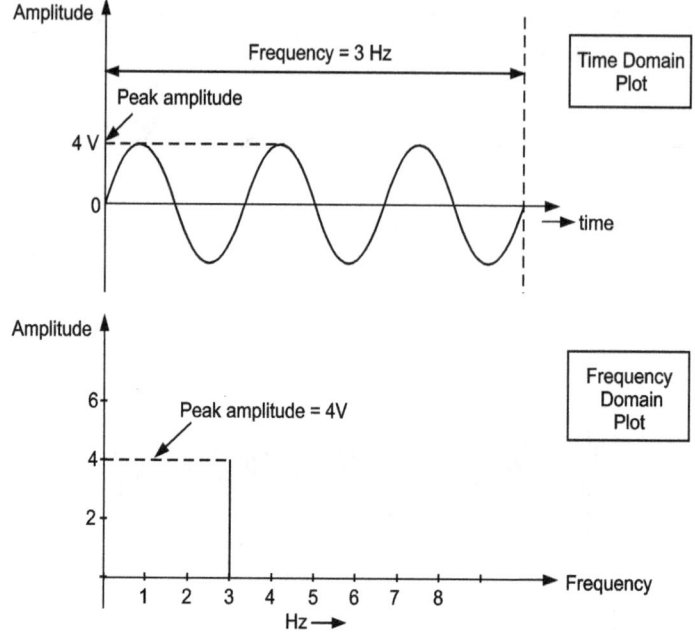

Fig. 2.15 : Time and Frequency Domain Plot of the Sine wave

- The time domain and frequency domain plot of 0 Hz, 4 Hz and 8 Hz sine waves are shown in Fig. 2.16.

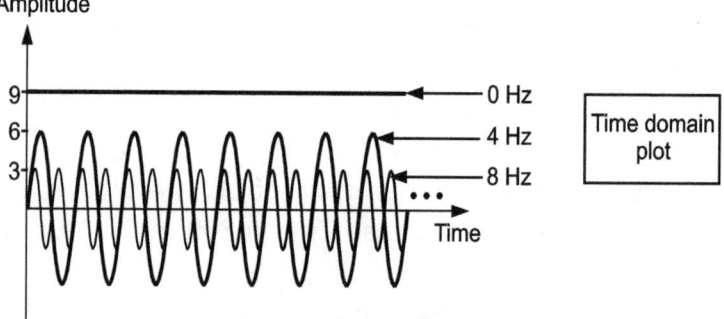

(a) Time-domain representation of three sine waves with frequencies 0, 4 and 8 Hz

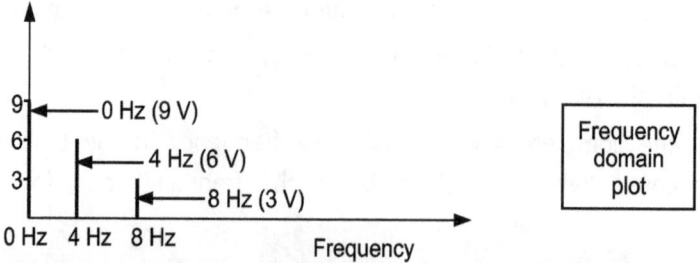

(b) Frequency-domain representation of the same three signals

Fig. 2.16 : Time Domain and Frequency Domain Plot of 0 Hz, 4 Hz and 8 Hz Sine waves

- If you consider the data communication application, we are required to deal with **composite signals** like square waveform signal.

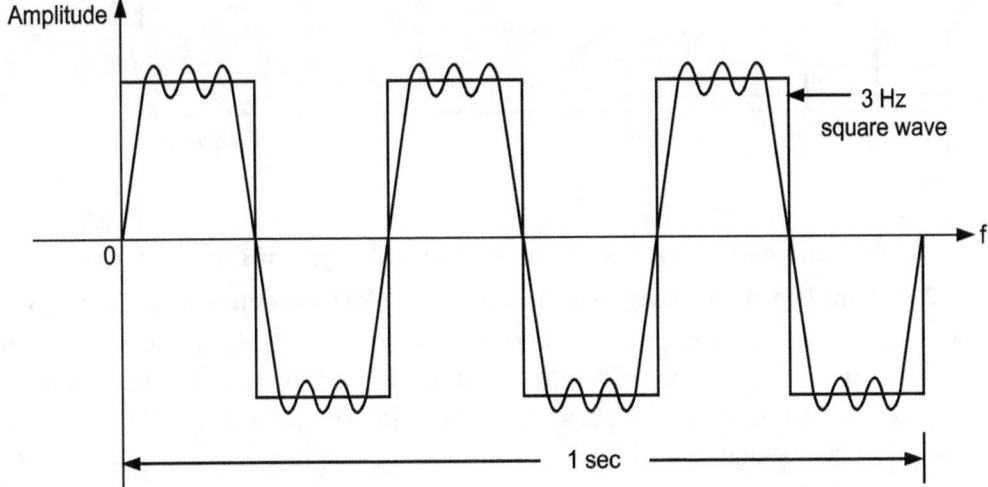

Fig. 2.17 : Square Waveform of 3 Hz (Composite and Periodic Wave is drawn)

- According to Fourier analysis, any composite signal is a combination of simple sine waves with different frequencies, amplitudes and phases.
- If the composite signal is periodic, then its decomposition gives a series of signals with discrete frequencies.
- If the composite signal is non-periodic then the decomposition gives a combination of sine waves with continuous frequencies.

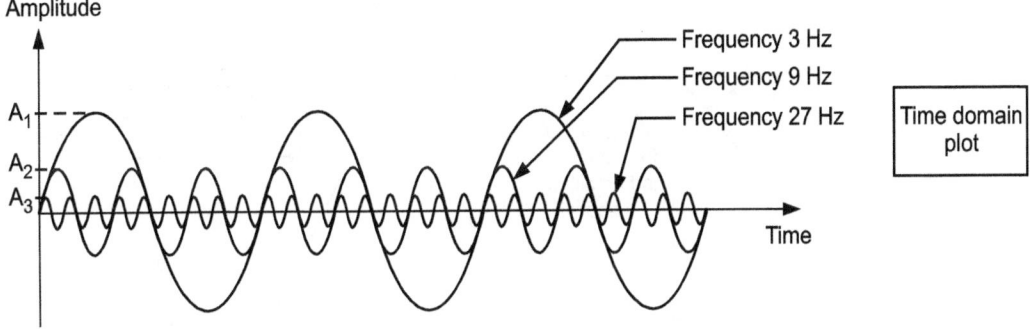

(a) Time-domain decomposition of a composite signal of 3 Hz square wave

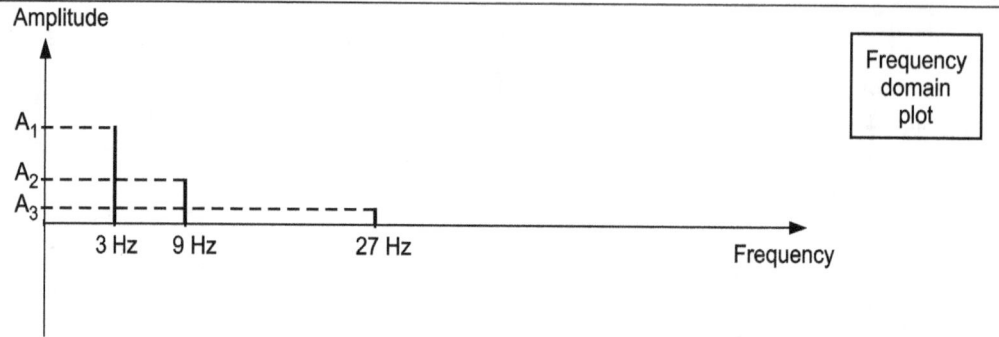

(b) Frequency-domain decomposition of a composite signal of 3 Hz square wave

Fig. 2.18 : Time Domain and Frequency Domain Plot of 3 Hz Composite Square Wave Signal

- Hence, we can say that, the square wave signal of 3 Hz is composed of the fundamental frequency = 3 Hz (or known as first harmonic), 3rd harmonic is of 9 Hz and 9th harmonic is of 27 Hz. Thus, it is integral multiple of 1, 3 and 9 but it is not float number multiple.

- Thus, for non-periodic signal, the time domain and frequency domain plots are as shown in Fig. 2.18 (c).

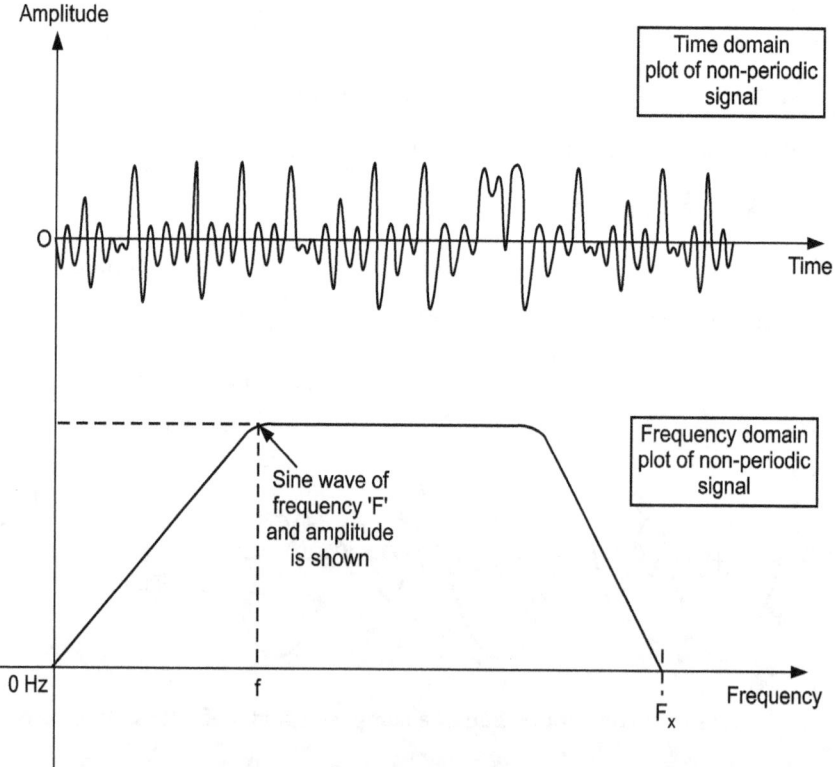

Fig. 2.18 (c) : Time Domain and Frequency Domain Plot of Non-periodic signal

- **The Bandwidth of Composite signal** can be given as the range of the frequencies contained in a composite signal.

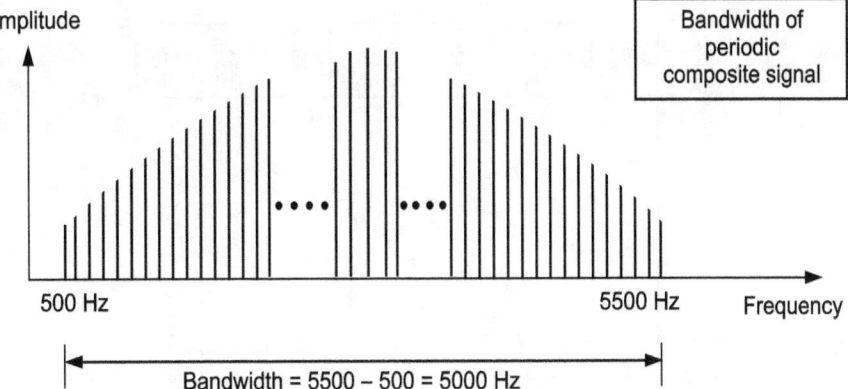

(a) Bandwidth of a periodic signal contains all integer frequencies between 500 Hz and 5500 Hz
[i.e. 500, 501, 502, 503, 504 ... 5500 etc.]

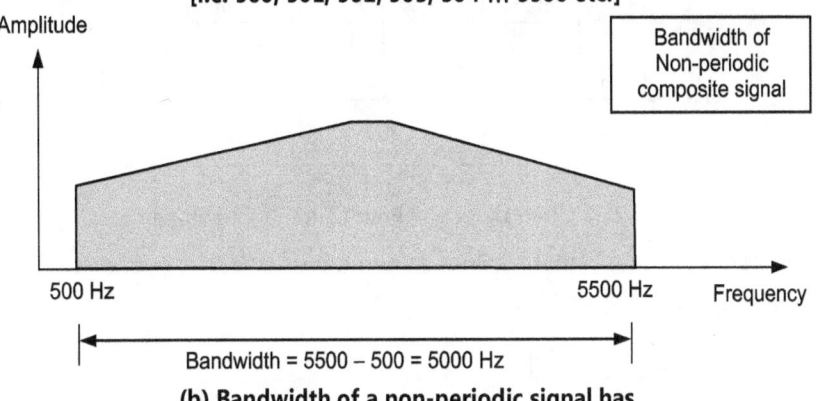

(b) Bandwidth of a non-periodic signal has
same range but the frequencies are continuous

Fig. 2.19 : Bandwidth of Periodic and Non-periodic Composite Signals

- Thus, the bandwidth of a periodic composite signal contains all integer frequencies between 500 Hz and 5500 Hz (i.e. 500 Hz, 501 Hz, 502 Hz, 503 Hz, 504 Hz ... 5500 Hz, etc.).
- Also the bandwidth of a non-periodic composite signal contains same range but the frequencies are continuous as shown in Fig. 2.19.

2.3 DIGITAL SIGNALS

1. We know that digital signals has discrete values.
2. Also digital signal can have more than two levels.
3. Two level and four level digital signals are shown in Fig. 2.20.

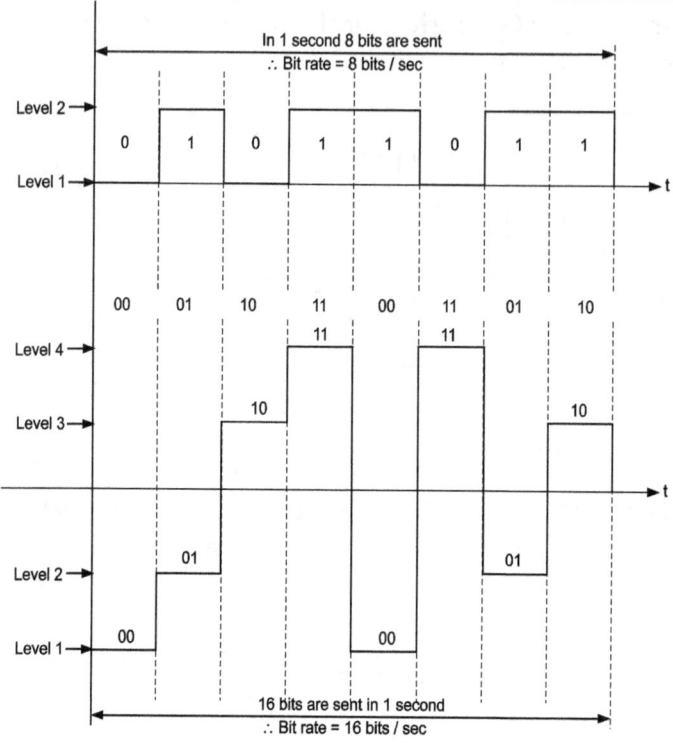

Fig. 2.20 : Two Level and Four Level Digital Signals

- **Bit Rate** of digital signal is given as number of bits sent in one second. Hence, bit rate is given in bps.

  ∴ Bit rate = Bits/sec

- **Bit Length** of digital signal is stated as the distance one bit occupies on the transmission medium and it is given as,

  Bit length = Propagation speed × Bit duration

2.3.1 Digital Signal as Composite Analog Signal

- We have already seen that fourier series analysis can be used to decompose a digital signal.
- If digital signal is periodic, decomposed signal has infinite bandwidth of discrete frequencies.
- If digital signal is non-periodic, decomposed signal has infinite bandwidth of continuous frequencies.
- The time domain and frequency domain analysis details are shown in Fig. 2.21.

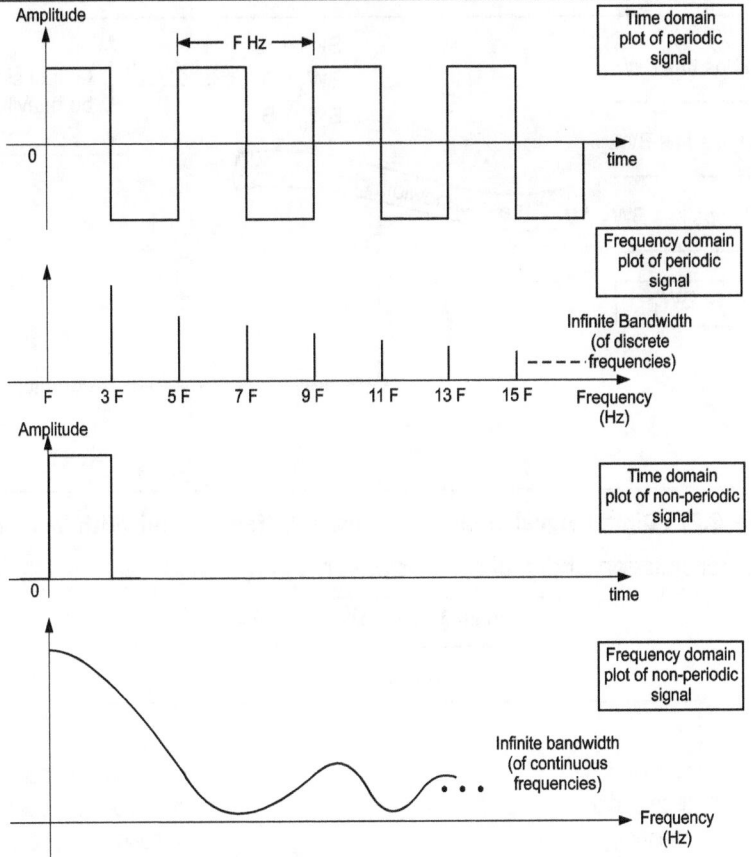

Fig. 2.21 : Time Domain/Frequency Domain Plot of Periodic Digital Signal and Non-periodic Digital Signal

2.3.2 Transmission of Digital Signals

Case 1 : Physical medium bandwidth is high :

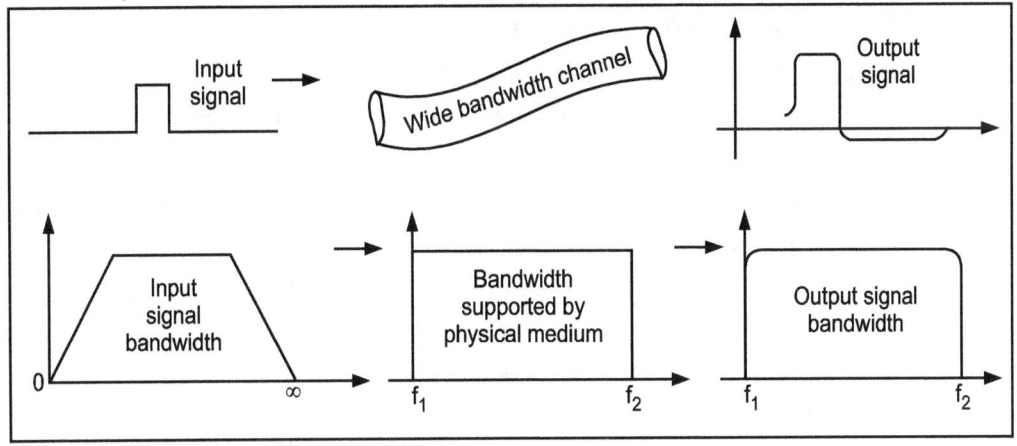

Case 2 : Physical medium bandwidth is low :

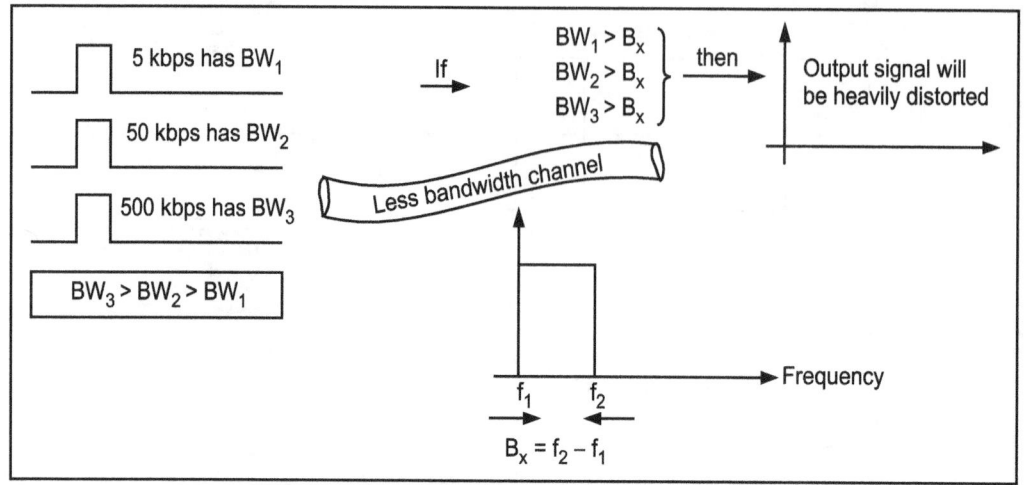

Fig. 2.22 : Digital Signal Transmission using Different Bandwidth Medium

- The transmission of digital signal is possible in two ways :

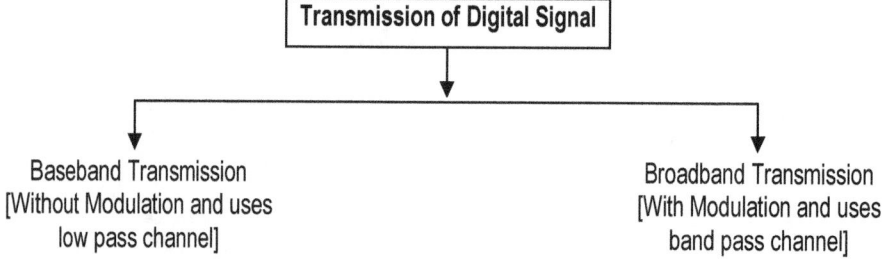

- In Fig. 2.22, we have considered the baseband transmission of the digital signal (which is always non-periodic in nature practically, in data communication).
- Here we have considered two cases :

  Case 1 : Wide bandwidth channel is used.

  Case 2 : Narrow bandwidth channel is used.
- In case 1, small amount of distortion takes place and output signal is less distorted as shown.
- Whereas in case 2, it is clearly shown that if bit rate of input baseband signal increases, then bandwidth requirement to transfer this data also increases.
- In such case 2, if the narrow bandwidth channel is used then output signal will be heavily distorted or may not be available at output.
- The bandwidth requirement for different data rates and for different harmonic values is as shown in Table 2.2.

Table 2.2 : Bandwidth requirement for different data rates and different harmonic values

Bit Rate (N)	Harmonic 1 and required BW = N/2	Harmonics 1 and 3 and required BW = 3N/2	Harmonics 1, 3 and 5 and required BW = 5N/2
N = 5 kbps	2.5 kHz	7.5 kHz	12.5 kHz
N = 50 kbps	25 kHz	75 kHz	125 kHz
N = 500 kbps	250 kHz	750 kHz	1250 kHz

- Thus, for proper digital signal transmission with more bit rate, the bandwidth requirement of medium channel increases and if not used, then signal may be heavily distorted or may even be lost.

- **Now second way of digital signal transmission is with modulation. [i.e. No baseband transmission]. It is known as broadband transmission.**

- Thus, Fig. 2.23 drawn is self explanatory.

- In this figure, we can see that modulation process allows us to use a bandpass channel (a channel with bandwidth which doesn't start from zero i.e. starts at f_1 and ends at f_2).

- Here, D to A conversion and A to D conversion are basically different concepts.

- D to A conversion is digital continuous wave modulation. For example, ASK (Amplitude Shift Keying), FSK (Frequency Shift Keying) or PSK (i.e. Phase Shift Keying).

- Due to this digital continuous wave modulation, which gives analog output in nature, has limited bandwidth = $f_2 - f_1$ and is less practical.

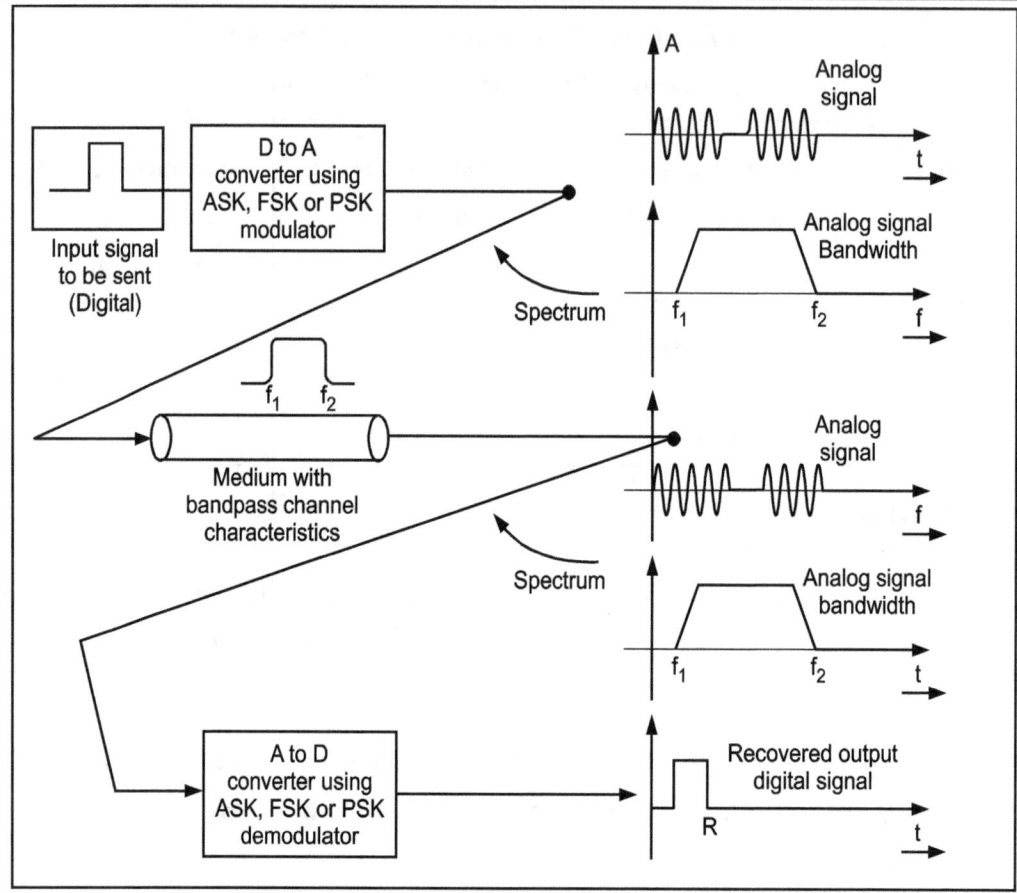

**Fig. 2.23 : Transmission and Reception of
Modulated Broadband Signal over Bandpass Channel Medium**

- This bandwidth of signal is easily passed through the medium with bandpass channel characteristics and has almost negligible distortion at medium (channel) output as shown.
- Thus, now this analog signal is given to A to D converter at receiver end to recover original unmodulated digital signal as shown.
- At receiver end, A to D converter is basically a ASK, FSK or PSK demodulator.
- This ASK, FSK or PSK modulator/demodulator will be studied in Unit 2 of this book, in detail.

2.4 TRANSMISSION IMPAIRMENT

- Transmission impairment means, due to imperfections of medium, signal sent from transmitter is not equal to signal received from receiver.

- There are three causes of impairment :
  - Attenuation
  - Distortion
  - Noise

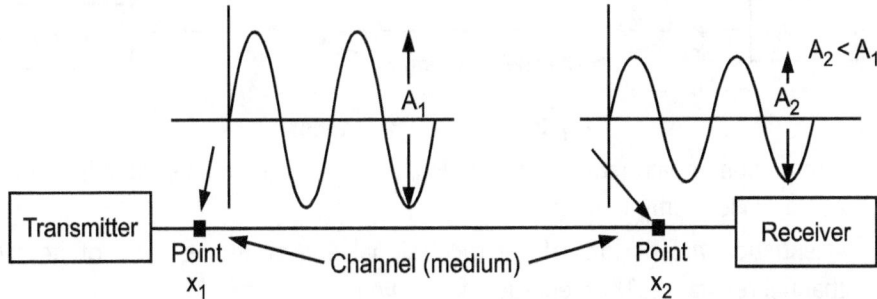

Fig. 2.24 : Attenuation Impairment

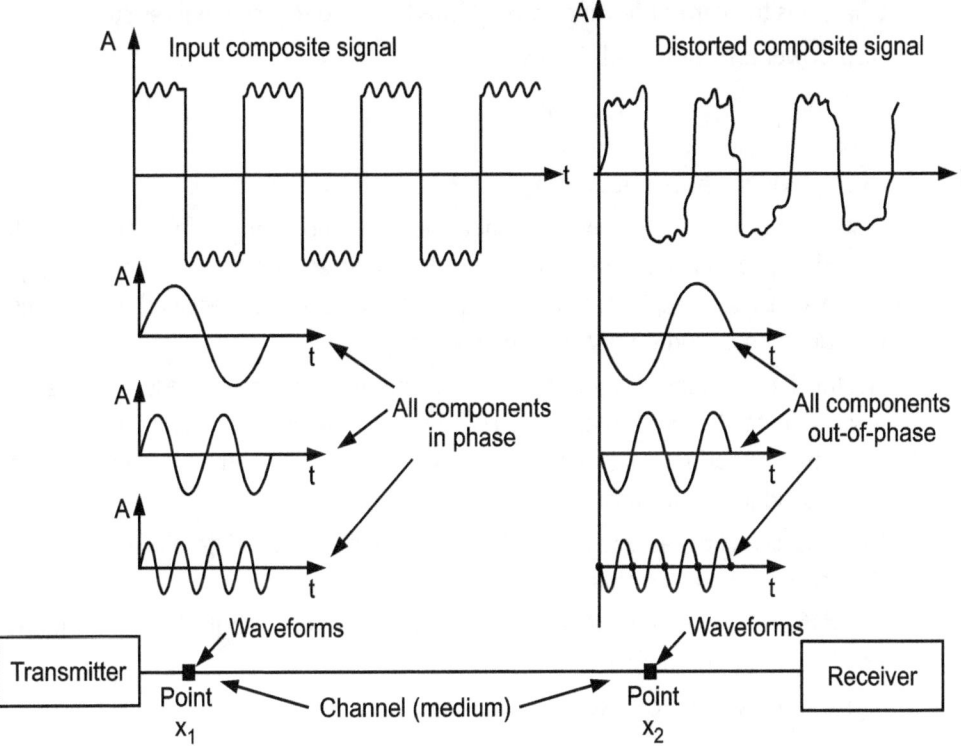

Fig. 2.25 : Distortion Impairment

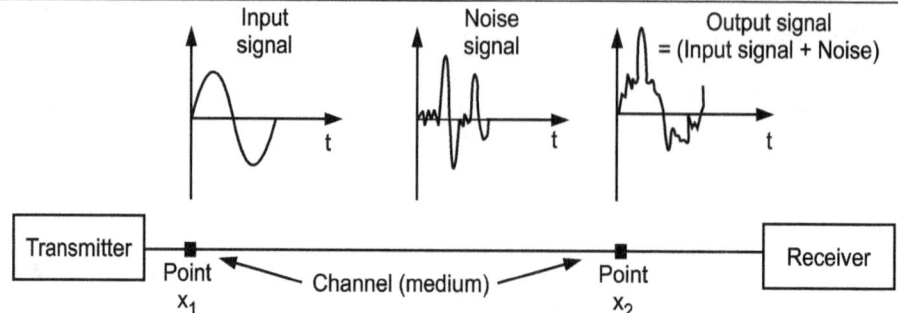

Fig. 2.26 : Noise Impairment

- Attenuation impairment is shown in Fig. 2.24. Distortion impairment is shown in Fig. 2.25 and Noise impairment is shown in Fig. 2.26.
- Attenuation means loss of electrical signal energy in the form of heat due to channel resistance. Thus, energy lost is given as,

$$E_L = I^2 (R)$$

where, I is the current flowing through medium and R = channel resistance.

Also power loss in decibels is given as,

$$P_L = \log_{10} \frac{P_2}{P_1}$$

where, P_2 is the power at point x_2 and P_1 is the power at point x_1.

- Distortion means the received signal at receiver end changes its shape or its form. This distortion is different in different frequencies due to different propagation speed of signal frequencies in medium. Thus, phases of received waveforms are changed and distortion occurs in received signal.
- Electrical disturbances interfere with the input signal and produce noise. Noise always limits the performance of communication system. In electrical terms, any unwanted introduction of energy tending to interfere with the proper reception and reproduction of transmitted signal.
- Noise is classified as external noise and internal noise. External noise is due to atmosphere, extraterrestrial noise or industrial noise.
- The different types of internal noises are thermal noise, shot noise, partition noise and low frequency or flicker noise.
- Signal to noise ratio of system is given by,

$$SNR = \frac{\text{Average signal power}}{\text{Average noise power}}$$

$$SNR_{dB} = 10 \log_{10} (SNR)$$

2.5 DATA RATE LIMITS

- In data communication system, the Data Rate depends upon three factors :
  - (a) Available bandwidth (of medium).
  - (b) Signal level (amplitude of signal).
  - (c) Quality of medium (channel) (Noise amplitude).
- There are two formulae to calculate the data rate.

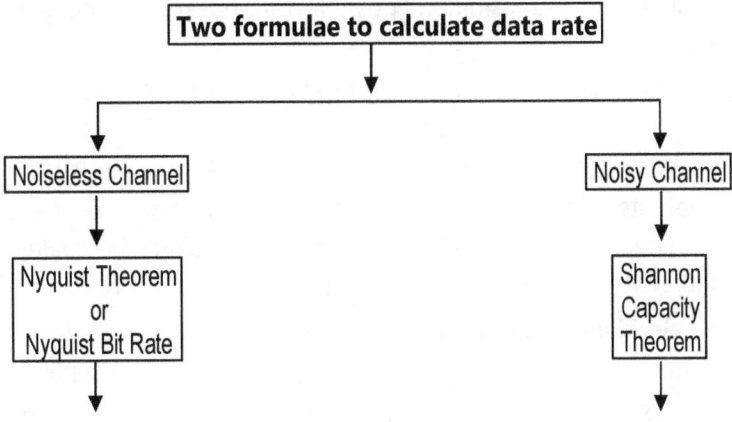

Bit rate = 2 × Bandwidth × Log_2 L

where, Bandwidth = Channel bandwidth and L = Signal levels used to represent data

Capacity = Bandwidth × Log_2 (1 + SNR)

where, Bandwidth = Channel bandwidth and SNR = Signal to Noise Ratio.

2.6 PERFORMANCE

In this section, we will discuss the following things :
- (a) QoS (Quality of Service).
- (b) Bandwidth.
- (c) Throughput.
- (d) Delay
- (e) Jitter.
- (f) Bandwidth-delay product.

2.6.1 Problems in Data Communication

- When the Internet was first deployed many years ago, it lacked the ability to provide Quality of Service guarantees due to limits in router computing power.
- It therefore ran at default QoS level, or "best effort".

- Many things can happen to packets as they travel from origin to destination, resulting in the following problems as seen from the point of view of the sender and receiver:
- **Dropped packets** : The routers might fail to deliver (**drop**) some packets if they arrive when their buffers are already full. Some, none, or all of the packets might be dropped, depending on the state of the network, and it is impossible to determine what will happen in advance. The receiving application must ask for this information to be retransmitted, possibly causing severe delays in the overall transmission.
- **Delay** : It might take a long time for a packet to reach its destination, because it gets held up in long queues, or takes a less direct route to avoid congestion. Alternatively, it might follow a fast, direct route. Thus delay is very unpredictable.
- **Jitter** : Packets from source will reach the destination with different delays. This variation in delay is known as jitter and can seriously affect the quality of streaming audio and/or video.
- **Out-of-order delivery** : When a collection of related packets is routed through the Internet, different packets may take different routes, each resulting in a different delay. The result is that the packets arrive in a different order to the one with which they were sent. This problem necessitates special additional protocols responsible for rearranging out-of-order packets to an isochronous state once they reach their destination. This is especially important for video and VoIP streams where quality is dramatically impacted by both latency or lack of isochronicity.
- **Error** : Sometimes packets are misdirected, or combined together, or corrupted, while enroute. The receiver has to detect this and, just as if the packet was dropped, ask the sender to repeat itself.

2.6.2 Applications Requiring QoS

A defined Quality of Service may be required for certain types of network traffic, for example:
- Streaming multimedia may require guaranteed throughput.
- IP telephony or Voice over IP (VoIP) may require strict limits on jitter and delay.
- Video Teleconferencing (VTC) requires low jitter.
- Alarm signalling (e.g. Burglar alarm).
- Dedicated link emulation requires both guaranteed throughput and imposes limits on maximum delay and jitter.
- A safety-critical application, such as remote surgery may require a guaranteed level of availability (this is also called *hard QoS*).

2.6.3 QoS Introduction

- Quality of Service (QoS) for networks is an industry-wide set of standards and mechanisms for ensuring high-quality performance for critical applications.
- By using QoS mechanisms, network administrators can use existing resources efficiently and ensure the required level of service without reactively expanding or over-provisioning their networks.
- Traditionally, the concept of quality in networks meant that all network traffic was treated equally.
- The result was that all network traffic received the network's best effort, with no guarantees for reliability, delay, variation in delay, or other performance characteristics.
- With best-effort delivery service, however, a single bandwidth-intensive application can result in poor or unacceptable performance for all applications.
- The QoS concept of quality is one in which the requirements of some applications and users are more critical than others, which means that some traffic needs preferential treatment.

2.6.4 Network Characteristics Managed by QoS

The goal of QoS is to provide preferential delivery service for the applications that need it by ensuring sufficient bandwidth, controlling latency and jitter, and reducing data loss. Table 2.3 describes these network characteristics.

Table 2.3 : Network characteristics managed by QoS

Network Characteristics	Description
Bandwidth	The rate at which traffic is carried by the network.
Latency	The delay in data transmission from source to destination.
Jitter	The variation in latency.
Reliability	The percentage of packets discarded by a router.

2.6.5 QoS Provides the Following Benefits

- Gives administrators control over network resources and allows them to manage the network from a business, rather than a technical perspective.
- Ensures that time-sensitive and mission-critical applications have the resources they require, while allowing other applications access to the network.
- Improves user experience.
- Reduces costs by using existing resources efficiently, thereby delaying or reducing the need for expansion or upgrades.

2.6.6 Bandwidth

Bandwidth is a central concept in many fields, including information theory, radio communications, signal processing and Telecom Networks.

Definition 1 :

Bandwidth is a measure of frequency range, measured in hertz.

Example : The range of frequencies within which the performance of the antenna, with respect to some characteristics, conforms to a specified standard. (2.4-2.5 GHz antenna has 100 MHz bandwidth).

As an example, the 3 dB bandwidth of the function depicted in Fig. 2.27 is $f_2 - f_1$, whereas other definitions of bandwidth would yield a different answer.

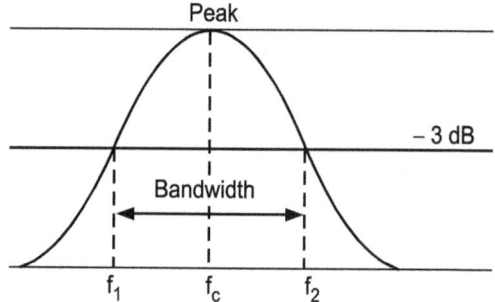

Fig. 2.27 : 3 dB Bandwidth in Analog System

Definition 2 :

Bandwidth is the amount of data that can be transmitted in a fixed amount of time, expressed in bits per second (bps) or bytes per second.

Example : A V.90 modem supports a maximum theoretical bandwidth of 56 kbps. Fast Ethernet supports a maximum theoretical bandwidth of 100 Mbps.

Bit Rates in Multimedia Communications :

(1) Audio (MP3) :
- 32 kbits/s – MW (AM) quality.
- 96 kbits/s – FM quality.
- 128-160 kbits/s – Decent quality, difference can sometimes be obvious.
- 192 kbits/s – Good quality, difference can only be heard by a few.
- 224-320 kbits/s – High quality, nearly lossless quality.

(2) Other Audio :
- 4 kbits/s – Minimum necessary for recognizable speech (using special-purpose speech codec).
- 8 kbits/s – Telephone quality (using speech codec).

- 500 kbits/s – 1 Mbits/s – Lossless audio as used in formats such as FLAC (free lossless audio codec), WavPack or Monkey's Audio.
- 1411 kbits/s – PCM (WAV) sound format of Compact Disc Digital Audio.

(3) Video (MPEG2):
- 16 kbits/s – Videophone quality (minimum necessary for a consumer-acceptable "talking head" picture).
- 128-384 kbits/s – Business-oriented videoconferencing system quality.
- 1 Mbits/s – VHS quality.
- 5 Mbits/s – DVD quality.
- 15 Mbits/s – HDTV quality.

2.6.7 Throughput

- In Data communication networks, **throughput** is the amount of digital data per unit time that is delivered to a certain terminal in a network, from a network node, or from one node to another, for example via a communication link.
- The throughput is usually measured in bit per second (bit/s or bps).
- The **system throughput** or **aggregate throughput** is the sum of the data rates that are delivered to all terminals in a network.
- Often **maximum throughput** is implied by the term **throughput**. The maximum **throughput** of a node or communication link is synonym to its **capacity**.
- The **maximum throughput** is defined as the **asymptotic throughput** when the load (the amount of incoming data) is very large.
- In packet switched systems where the load and throughput are equal (where there are no packet drops), the maximum throughput may be defined as the load in bit/s when the delivery time (the latency) asymptotically reaches infinity.
- The concept is applicable for all Telecom Networks.

2.6.8 Delay (Latency)

- The flow of a compressed voice circuit is shown in Fig. 2.28.
- The analog signal from the telephone is digitized into pulse code modulation (PCM) signals by the voice coder-decoder (codec).
- The PCM samples are then passed to the compression algorithm, which compresses the voice into a packet format for transmission across the WAN.
- On the far side of the cloud the exact same functions are performed in reverse order. The entire flow is shown in Fig. 2.28.

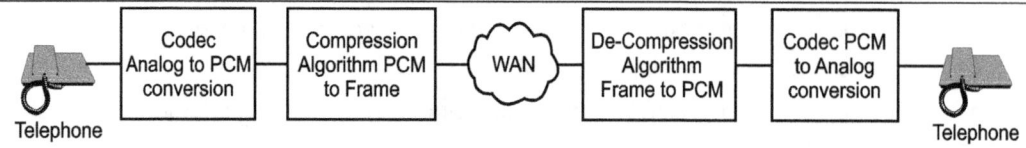

Fig. 2.28 : End-to-End Voice Flow

- Based on how the network is configured, the router/gateway can perform both the codec and compression functions or only one of them.
- **Fixed delay components** add directly to the overall delay on the connection.
- **Variable delays arise** from queuing delays in the egress trunk buffers on the serial port connected to the WAN.
- **Different Delays are :**
    1. Coder (Processing) Delay
    2. Algorithmic Delay
    3. Packetization Delay
    4. Serialization Delay
    5. Queuing/Buffering Delay
    6. Network Switching Delay
    7. De-Jitter Delay
- **Thus, Latency(Delay)** = Propagation time + Transmission Time + Queuing time + Processing delay

    Where propagation time = Distance / Propagation speed.
- Transmission time = Message Size / Bandwidth.

2.6.9 Jitter

- Simply stated, *jitter* is the variation of packet interarrival time.
- Jitter is one issue that exists only in packet-based networks.
- While in a packet voice environment, the sender is expected to reliably transmit voice packets at a regular interval (for example, send one frame every 20 ms).
- These voice packets can be delayed throughout the packet network and not arrive at that same regular interval at the receiving station (for example, they might not be received every 20 ms; see Fig. 2.29).
- The difference between the time at which the packet is expected and the time at which it is actually received is *jitter*.
- In Fig. 2.29, you can see that the amount of time it takes for packets A and B to send and receive is equal ($D_1 = D_2$).
- Packet C encounters delay in the network, however, it is received *after* it is expected.

- This is why a *jitter buffer*, which conceals interarrival packet delay variation, is necessary.
- Voice packets in IP networks have highly variable packet-interarrival intervals.

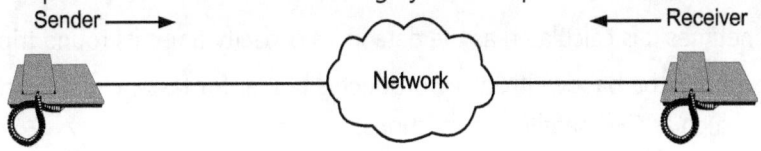

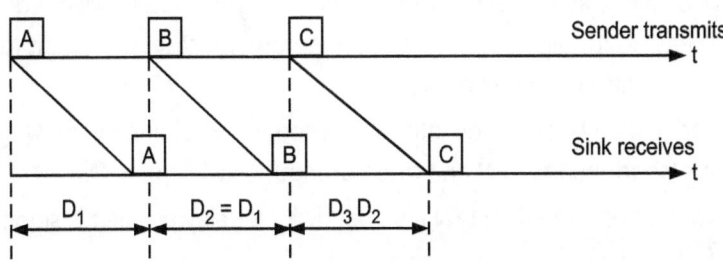

Fig. 2.29 : Variation of Packet Arrival Time (Jitter)

- Recommended practice is to count the number of packets that arrive late and create a ratio of these packets to the number of packets that are successfully processed.
- You can then use this ratio to adjust the jitter buffer to target a predetermined, allowable late-packet ratio. This adaptation of jitter buffer sizing is effective in compensation of delays.
- Note that jitter and total delay are *not* the same thing, although having plenty of jitter in a packet network can increase the amount of total delay in the network.
- This is because the more jitter you have, the larger jitter buffers are needed to compensate for the unpredictable nature of the packet network.
- Most Digital Signal Processors do not have infinite jitter buffers to handle excessive network delays.
- Sometimes it is better to just drop packets or have fixed-length buffers instead of creating unwanted delays in the jitter buffers.
- If your data network is engineered well and you take the proper precautions, jitter is usually not a major problem and the jitter buffer does not significantly contribute to the total end-to-end delay.

2.6.10 Bandwidth-Delay Product

- In data communications, **bandwidth-delay product** refers to the product of a data link's capacity (in bits per second) and its end-to-end delay (in seconds).

- The result, an amount of data measured in bits (or bytes), is equivalent to the maximum amount of data on the network circuit at any given time, i.e. data that has been transmitted but not yet received.
- Sometimes it is calculated as the data link's capacity times its round trip time.
- Obviously, the bandwidth-delay product is higher for faster circuits with long-delay links such as GEO satellite connections.
- The product is particularly important for protocols such as TCP that guarantee reliable delivery, as it describes the amount of yet-unacknowledged data that the sender has to duplicate in a buffer memory in case the client requires it to retransmit a garbled or lost packet.
- A network with a large bandwidth-delay product is commonly known as a **long fat network** (shortened to **LFN** and often pronounced "elephant").
- A network is considered an LFN if its bandwidth-delay product is significantly larger than 10^5 bits (~12 kB).

Examples :
- Customer on a DSL link, 1 Mbit/s, 200 ms one-way delay : 200 kbit = 25 kB.
- High-speed terrestrial network : 100 Mbit/s, 100 ms : 10 Mbit = 1.25 MB.
- Server on a long-distance 1 Gbit/s link, average one-way delay 300 ms = 300 Mbit = 37.5 MB total required for buffering.

SOLVED EXAMPLES

Example 2.1 :

Calculate the time periods of following frequency components.

(a) 50 Hz (b) 60 Hz
(c) 1 kHz (d) 10 MHz

Solution :

(a) $T = \dfrac{1}{50 \text{ Hz}} = 0.02 \text{ s} = 20 \text{ ms}$

(b) $T = \dfrac{1}{60 \text{ Hz}} = 0.016 \text{ s} = 16.66 \text{ ms}$

(c) $T = \dfrac{1}{1 \text{ kHz}} = 1 \times 10^{-3} \text{ s} = 1 \text{ ms}$

(d) $T = \dfrac{1}{10 \text{ MHz}} = 1 \times 10^{-6} \text{ s} = 1 \text{ μsec}$.

Example 2.2 :
Calculate the wavelength of the following signals.
- (a) Audio signal = 5 kHz
- (b) Bass frequency signal = 300 Hz
- (c) Speech signal = 3400 Hz
- (d) Ultrasonic signal = 30 kHz
- (e) Video signal = 5.5 MHz
- (f) Microwave signal = 1 GHz
- (g) Violet colour signal = 790 THz = 790×10^{12} Hz
- (h) Red colour signal = 405 THz = 405×10^{12} Hz.

Solution :

(a) Audio signal wavelength $\lambda = \dfrac{3 \times 10^8}{f} = \dfrac{3 \times 10^8}{5 \text{ kHz}}$

$= 60 \times 10^3$ meters

(b) Bass frequency signal $\lambda = \dfrac{3 \times 10^8}{300} = 1 \times 10^6$ meters

(c) Speech signal $\lambda = \dfrac{3 \times 10^8}{3400} = 88.235 \times 10^3$ meters

(d) Ultrasonic signal $\lambda = \dfrac{3 \times 10^8}{30 \times 10^3} = 10{,}000$ meters

(e) Video signal $\lambda = \dfrac{3 \times 10^8}{5.5 \times 10^6} = 54.54$ meters

(f) Microwave signal $\lambda = \dfrac{3 \times 10^8}{1 \times 10^9} = 0.3$ meters

(g) Violet colour signal $\lambda = \dfrac{3 \times 10^8}{790 \times 10^{12}} \cong 380$ nanometers = 380 nm

(h) Red colour signal $\lambda = \dfrac{3 \times 10^8}{405 \times 10^{12}} = 740$ nm

Example 2.3 :
A periodic signal is decomposed into five sine waves with frequencies of 50, 150, 250, 350, 450 Hz. What is the bandwidth ? Draw the spectrum, assuming all components have a maximum amplitude of 21 V.

Solution :

$$B.W = f_H - f_L$$

Bandwidth = 450 Hz − 50 Hz = 400 Hz

∴ B.W. = 400 Hz

∵ Spectrum is as given.

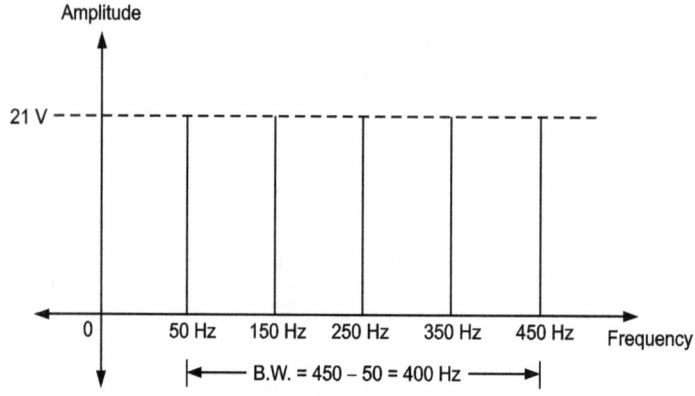

Fig. 2.30 : Frequency Spectrum for Example 2.3

Example 2.4 :

A periodic signal has a B.W. of 30 Hz. The highest frequency is 90 Hz. What is the lowest frequency ? Draw the spectrum if the signal contains all frequencies of the amplitude = 21 volts.

Solution :

$$B.W. = f_H - f_L$$
$$30 = 90 - f_L$$
$$f_L = 90 - 30 = 60 \text{ Hz}$$

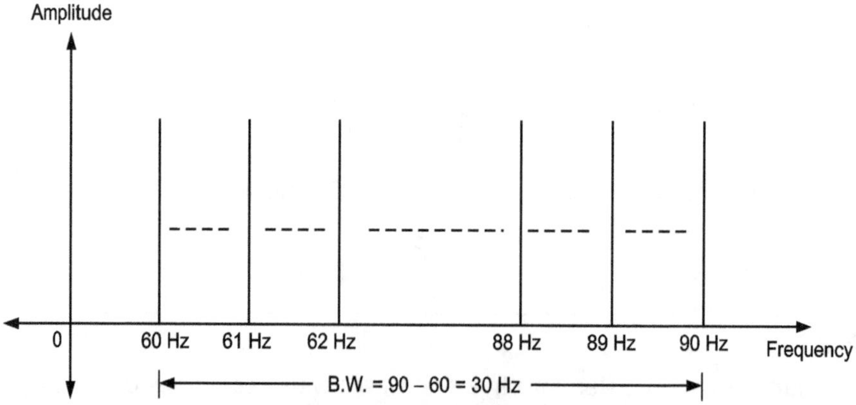

Fig. 2.31 : Spectrum for Example 2.4

Example 2.5 :

A non-periodic composite signal has a B.W. = 200 MHz, with a middle frequency of 200 MHz and peak amplitude of 40 V. The two extreme frequencies have an amplitude of 0 V. Draw the frequency spectrum of a given signal specification.

Solution :

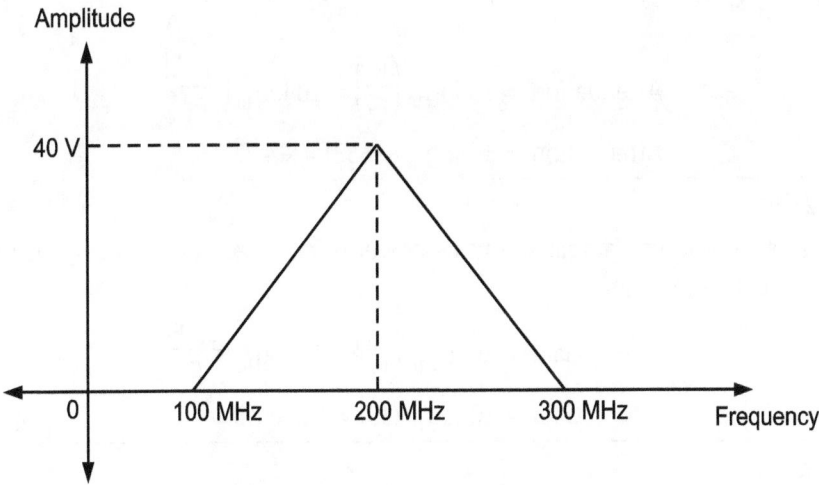

Fig. 2.32 : Spectrum for Example 2.5

Example 2.6 :
A digital signal has 16 levels. How many bits are needed per level ?

Solution :
$$\text{Number of bits/level} = \log_2 (16) = 4.$$

Example 2.7 :
A digital signal has 256 levels. How many bits are needed per level ?

Solution :
$$\text{Number of bits/level} = \log_2 (256)$$
$$= \frac{\log_{10} (256)}{\log_{10} (2)} = 8$$

Example 2.8 :
We have a low pass channel with bandwidth = 200 kHz. What is the maximum bit rate of this channel ?

Solution :
1st harmonic of 200 kHz = 200 kHz

∴ Bit rate = 2×1st harmonic

Bit rate = 2×200 kHz = 400 kbps

Example 2.9 :
Suppose a signal travels through a transmission medium and its power is reduced to one-third i.e. $P_2 = \frac{1}{3} P_1$. Calculate attenuation.

Solution :

$$\text{Attenuation} = 10 \log_{10}\left(\frac{P_2}{P_1}\right) = 10 \log_{10}\left(\frac{\frac{1}{3}P_1}{P_1}\right)$$

$$\text{Attenuation} = 10 \log_{10}(0.333) = -4.77 \text{ dB}.$$

Example 2.10 :
A signal travels through an amplifier and its power is increased to 15 times. This means that $P_2 = 15 P_1$. Calculate the gain.

Solution :

$$\text{Gain} = 10 \log_{10}\left(\frac{P_2}{P_1}\right) = 10 \log_{10}\left(\frac{15 P_1}{P_1}\right)$$

$$\text{Gain} = 10 \log_{10}(15) = 11.76 \text{ dB}.$$

Example 2.11 :
Convert the -60 dB$_m$ power in watts.

$$dB_m = 10 \log_{10}(P_m)$$

$$-60 = 10 \log_{10}(P_m)$$

$$\log^{-1}\left[\frac{-60}{10}\right] = P_m$$

$$\boxed{P_m = 1 \times 10^{-6} \text{ watts}}$$

Example 2.12 :
The power of a signal is 100 mW and the power of the noise is 10 µW. Calculate SNR and SNR$_{dB}$.

Solution :

$$\text{SNR} = \frac{S}{N} = \frac{100 \times 10^{-3}}{10 \times 10^{-6}} = 10000$$

$$\text{SNR}_{dB} = 10 \log_{10}(\text{SNR}) = 10 \log_{10}(10000)$$

$$\text{SNR}_{dB} = 40 \text{ dB}$$

$$\therefore \boxed{\begin{array}{c} \text{SNR} = 10000 \\ \text{SNR}_{dB} = 40 \text{ dB} \end{array}}$$

Example 2.13 :
Consider a noiseless channel with a B.W. of 4000 Hz transmitting a signal with two signal levels. Calculate maximum bit rate. Also calculate the bit rate if 6 signal levels are decided.

Solution :

Bit rate for 2 signal levels = $2 \times 4000 \times \log_2 2$ = 8000 bps.
Bit rate for 6 signal levels = $2 \times 4000 \times \log_2 6$ = 20679.7 bps.

Example 2.14 :

Calculate the theoretical highest bit rate of a telephone line if bandwidth assigned for data communication is 3400 Hz and SNR = 3200.

Solution :

$$B = 3400$$
$$SNR = 3200$$
$$\text{Bit rate} = B \log_2 (1 + SNR)$$
$$= 3400 \times \log_2 (1 + 3200)$$
$$= 3400 \times \frac{\log 3201}{\log 2}$$
$$= 3400 \times 11.64430$$

$$\boxed{\text{Bit rate} = 39590.644 \text{ bps}}$$

Example 2.15 :

Calculate bit rate for above example if $SNR_{dB} = 30$ dB, $SNR_{dB} = 40$ dB.

Solution :

$$SNR_{dB} = 30 \text{ dB} = 10 \log_{10} (SNR)$$
$$\therefore SNR = 1000$$
$$SNR_{dB} = 40 \text{ dB} = 10 \log_{10} (SNR)$$
$$\therefore SNR = 10,000$$
$$\therefore \text{Bit rate for } SNR = 1000 \text{ is} = 3400 \log_2 (1 + 1000)$$

$$\boxed{\text{Bit rate} = 33888.56 \text{ bps}}$$

Bit rate for SNR = 10,000

$$\therefore \text{Bit rate} = 3400 \log_2 (1 + 10000)$$

$$\boxed{\text{Bit rate} = 45178.713 \text{ bps}}$$

Example 2.16 :

Calculate the bit rate if bandwidth assigned for telephone line is = 1 MHz and $SNR_{dB} = 40$ dB.

Solution :

$$\text{Bit rate} = B \cdot \log_2 (1 + SNR), B = 1 \times 10^6 \text{ Hz}$$
$$\therefore SNR_{dB} = 10 \log_{10} (SNR)$$
$$40 \text{ dB} = 10 \log_{10} (SNR)$$
$$\therefore \boxed{SNR = 10000}$$
$$\therefore \text{Bit rate} = 1 \times 10^6 \times \log_2 (1 + SNR)$$

$$= 1 \times 10^6 \times \log_2 (1 + 10000)$$

$$\text{Bit rate} = 13.28 \times 10^6 \text{ bits/sec.}$$

$$\boxed{\text{Bit rate} = 13.28 \text{ Mbps}}$$

Example 2.17 :

Calculate the maximum data rate by Shannon formula and required levels using Nyquist formula for a data communication link for B.W. = 1.2 MHz and SNR = 64.

Solution :

Shannon formula $\qquad \boxed{C = B \log_2 (1 + SNR)}$

$$= 1.2 \times 10^6 \log_2 (1 + 64)$$

$\boxed{C = 7.226 \text{ Mbps}}$, $\boxed{C = 2 B \log_2 L}$ is Nyquist formula

$$7.226 \times 10^6 = 2 \times 1.2 \times 10^6 \cdot \log_2 (L)$$

$$\frac{7.225 \times 10^6}{2 \times 1.2 \times 10^6} = \log_2 (L)$$

$$L = 8.06$$

$$\boxed{L = 8 \text{ levels}}$$

Example 2.18 :

A network with B.W. of 12 Mbps can pass only an average of 14,000 frames per minute with each frame carrying an average of 12,000 bits. What is the throughput of this network ?

Solution : $\qquad$ 1 minute = 60 sec.

$$\text{Throughput} = \frac{14000 \times 12000}{60 \text{ sec}} = 2.8 \text{ Mbps}$$

Example 2.19 :

What is the propagation time if the distance between the two points is 14,000 km ? Assume the propagation speed to be 2.4×10^8 m/s in cable.

Solution :

$$14000 \text{ km} = 14000 \times 1000 = 14 \times 10^6 \text{ meters}$$

$$\text{Propagation time} = \frac{14000 \times 1000}{2.4 \times 10^8} = 58.33 \text{ msec.}$$

$$\boxed{\text{Propagation time} = 58.33 \text{ msec.}}$$

Example 2.20 :

What are the propagation time and the transmission time for a 3.5 kbyte message sent by an email, if the B.W. of the network is 2 Gbps ? Assume that the distance between the transmitter and receiver is 14000 km and that light travels at 2.4×10^8 m/s.

Solution :

$$3.5 \text{ kbyte} = 3.5 \times 10^3 \times 8 = 28000 \text{ bits}$$
$$14000 \text{ km} = 14000 \times 1000 = \text{meters}$$

∴ $\quad$ Propagation time $= \dfrac{14000 \times 1000}{2.4 \times 10^8} = 58.33$ msec

∴ $\quad$ Transmission time $= \dfrac{3500 \times 8}{2 \times 10^9} = 0.014$ msec.

Example 2.21 :

What are the propagation time and the transmission time for a 6 Mbyte message sent by an email if the B.W. of network is 1.2 Mbps ? Assume that the distance between the sender and the receiver is 14000 km and that light travels at 2.4×10^8 m/sec.

Solution :

$$6 \text{ Mbyte} = 6 \times 10^6 \times 8 = 48 \times 10^6 \text{ bits}$$
$$\text{Distance} = 14000 \text{ km} = 14000 \times 1000 = 14 \times 10^6 \text{ meters}$$

∴ $\quad$ Propagation time $= \dfrac{14000 \times 1000}{2.4 \times 10^8} = 58.33$ msec.

∴ $\quad$ Transmission time $= \dfrac{6 \times 10^6 \times 8}{1.2 \times 10^6} = 40$ sec.

> Propagation time = 58.33 msec.
> Transmission time = 40 sec

EXERCISES

1. Define the following :
   (a) Analog signal
   (b) Digital signal
   (c) Analog data
   (d) Digital data
2. Draw and explain the periodic analog signal.
3. What is composite signal ?
4. What is duty cycle of square waveform and pulse waveform ?
5. Draw and explain the time domain and frequency domain representation of sine wave signal.

6. Draw and explain the time domain and frequency domain representation of the composite signal.
7. Draw time and frequency domain plot of non-periodic signal.
8. Comment on bandwidth of composite signal with suitable example.
9. Write short notes on :
   (a) Digital signals
   (b) Digital signal as composite analog signal
10. Explain the limitation of transmitting baseband digital signal over the channel.
11. Write a short note on transmission impairment.
12. What factors are responsible for limiting data rates in data communication system ?
13. Explain Nyquist bit rate and Shannon capacity theorem.
14. What is QoS (Quality of Service) ?
15. Write short notes on :
   (a) Bandwidth   (b) Throughput
   (c) Delay   (d) Jitter
   (e) Bandwidth-delay product

Chapter 3
DIGITAL TRANSMISSION SYSTEM

OBJECTIVES

After reading this chapter, you will understand :

- Line Coding Fundamental Theory.
- Elimination of DC Component and Line Codes Format Selection Criteria.
- Data Element, Signal Element and Signalling Rate.
- Concept of Baseline Wandering, DC Component Effect and Self Synchronization.
- Classification and Types of Line Coding such as Unipolar (NRZ), Polar [NRZ, RZ, Biphase (Manchester and Differential Manchester)], Bipolar (AMI and Pseudoternary).
- Multilevel Codes like (2B/1Q, 8B/6T and 4D-PAM5) etc.
- Multitransition Coding like MLT-3.
- Comparison between NRZ-L and NRZ-I, Bipolar Method and Polar NRZ.
- 2B1Q Coding Rules, 8B6T Coding Rules and MLT-3 Coding Rules.
- Comparison between all Line Codes.
- Concept of Block Coding, Block Codes like 4B/5B Block Coding and 8B/10B Block Coding etc.
- Detail Application Areas of 8B/10B Block Codes.
- Running Disparity and Rules for Running Disparity.
- Scrambling Techniques and Different Types like B8ZS and HDB3 etc.
- A to D Conversion Systems like PCM and DM in detail.
- In PCM, Sampling, Quantizing and Encoding is covered.
- Linear DM and Adaptive DM Techniques Discussion.
- Data Transmission Modes like Parallel Mode and Serial Mode of Communication.
- Asynchronous, Synchronous and Isochronous Serial Modes of Transmission.

INTRODUCTION

The basic classification of various conversions is as follows:

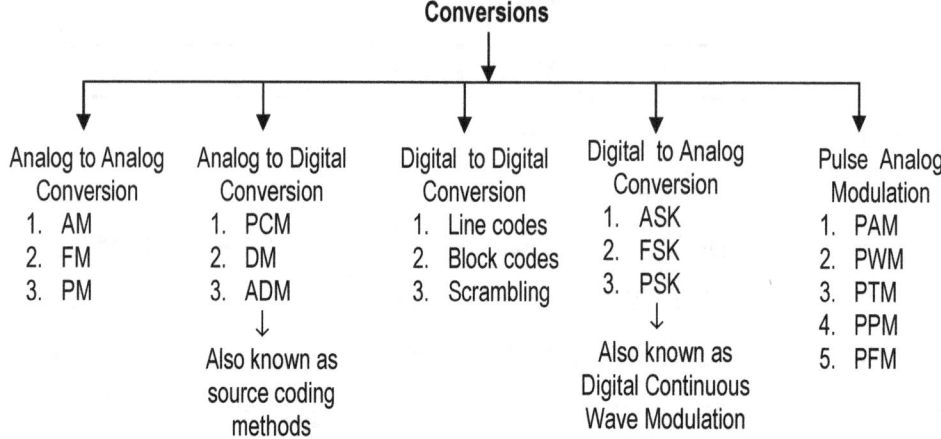

3.1 DIGITAL TO DIGITAL CONVERSION

In Data Communication, a line code (also called digital baseband modulation) is a code chosen for use within a communication system for baseband transmission purposes. Line coding is often used for digital data transport. Here in this section we can represent the digital data by using digital signals. **The conversion involves three techniques like Line coding, block coding and scrambling**.

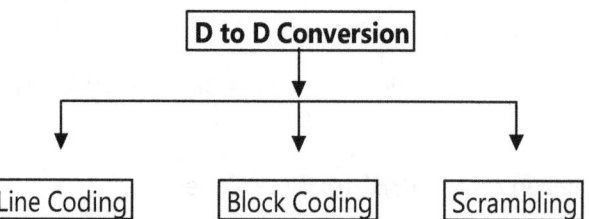

3.2 LINE CODING FUNDAMENTAL THEORY

- Line coding consists of representing the digital signal to be transported by an amplitude and time-discrete signal that is optimally tuned for the specific properties of the physical channel (and of the receiving equipment). The waveform pattern of voltage or current used to represent the 1s and 0s of a digital signal on a transmission link is called *line encoding*. The common types of line encoding are unipolar, polar, bipolar and Manchester encoding.
- For reliable clock recovery at the receiver, one usually imposes a maximum runlength constraint on the generated channel sequence, i.e. the maximum number of consecutive ones or zeros is bounded to a reasonable number. A clock period is recovered by observing transitions in the received sequence, so that a maximum

runlength guarantees such clock recovery, while sequences without such a constraint could seriously hamper the detection quality.
- After line coding, the signal is put through a "physical channel", either a "transmission medium" or "data storage medium". Sometimes the characteristics of two very different-seeming channels are similar enough that the same line code is used for them. The most common physical channels are :
  - The line-coded signal can directly be put on a transmission line, in the form of variations of the voltage or current (often using differential signalling).
  - The line-coded signal (the "baseband signal") undergoes further pulse shaping (to reduce its frequency bandwidth) and then modulated (to shift its frequency bandwidth) to create the "RF signal" that can be sent through free space.
  - The line-coded signal can be used to turn on and off a light in Free Space Optics, most commonly infrared remote control.
  - The line-coded signal can be printed on paper to create a bar-code.
  - The line-coded signal can be converted to magnetized spots on a hard drive or tape drive.
  - The line-coded signal can be converted to pits on optical disc.
- Unfortunately, most long-distance communication channels cannot transport a DC component. The DC component is also called the disparity, the bias, or the DC coefficient. The simplest possible line code is called unipolar because it has an unbounded DC component which gives too many errors on such systems.
- Most line codes eliminate the DC components such codes are called DC balanced, zero-DC, zero-bias or DC equalized etc. There are two ways of eliminating the DC component :
  - **Use a constant-weight code :** In other words, design each transmitted code word such that every code word that contains some positive or negative levels also contain enough of the opposite levels, such that the average level over each code word is zero. For example, Manchester code and Interleaved 2 of 5.
  - **Use a paired disparity code :** In other words, design the receiver such that every code word that averages to a negative level is paired with another code word that averages to a positive level. Design the receiver so that either code word of the pair decodes to the same data bits. Design the transmitter to keep track of the running DC buildup, and always pick the code word that pushes the DC level back towards zero. For example, AMI, 8B10B, 4B3T, etc.
- Line coding should make it possible for the receiver to synchronize itself to the phase of the received signal. If the synchronization is not ideal, then the signal to be decoded will not have optimal differences (in amplitude) between the various digits or symbols used in the line code. This will increase the error probability in the received data.

- It is also preferred for the line code to have a structure that will enable error detection.
- Note that the line-coded signal and a signal produced at a terminal may differ, thus requiring translation.
- A line code will typically reflect technical requirements of the transmission medium, such as optical fiber or shielded twisted pair. These requirements are unique for each medium, because each one has different behaviour related to interference, distortion, capacitance and loss of amplitude.
- Each of the various line formats has a particular advantage and disadvantage. It is not possible to select one, which will meet all needs. The format may be selected to meet one or more of the following criteria :
  - Minimize transmission hardware
  - Facilitate synchronization
  - Ease error detection and correction
  - Minimize spectral content
  - Eliminate a DC component.

3.3 LINE CODING TECHNICAL THEORY

- Digital data is converted into digital signal in line coding.
- Digital data can be voice, video, image, text or numbers which are stored as a bit sequence in digital storage.
- Typical line coding and line decoding mechanism is as shown in Fig. 3.1.
- **Thus, the block schematics clearly explain that data elements are being carried and signal elements are the carriers.**
- The ratio r_{ds} is given as, $r_{ds} = \dfrac{\text{Data elements}}{\text{Signal elements}}$
- Thus, for different values of r_{ds}, Fig. 3.2 clearly indicates the waveform.
- The different values of r_{ds} are :

$$r_{ds} = 1,\ r_{ds} = \frac{1}{2},\ r_{ds} = 2,\ r_{ds} = \frac{3}{4}\ \text{and}\ r_{ds} = \frac{4}{3}.$$

Fig. 3.1 : Data Elements and Signal Elements in Line Encoding and Line Decoding Mechanism

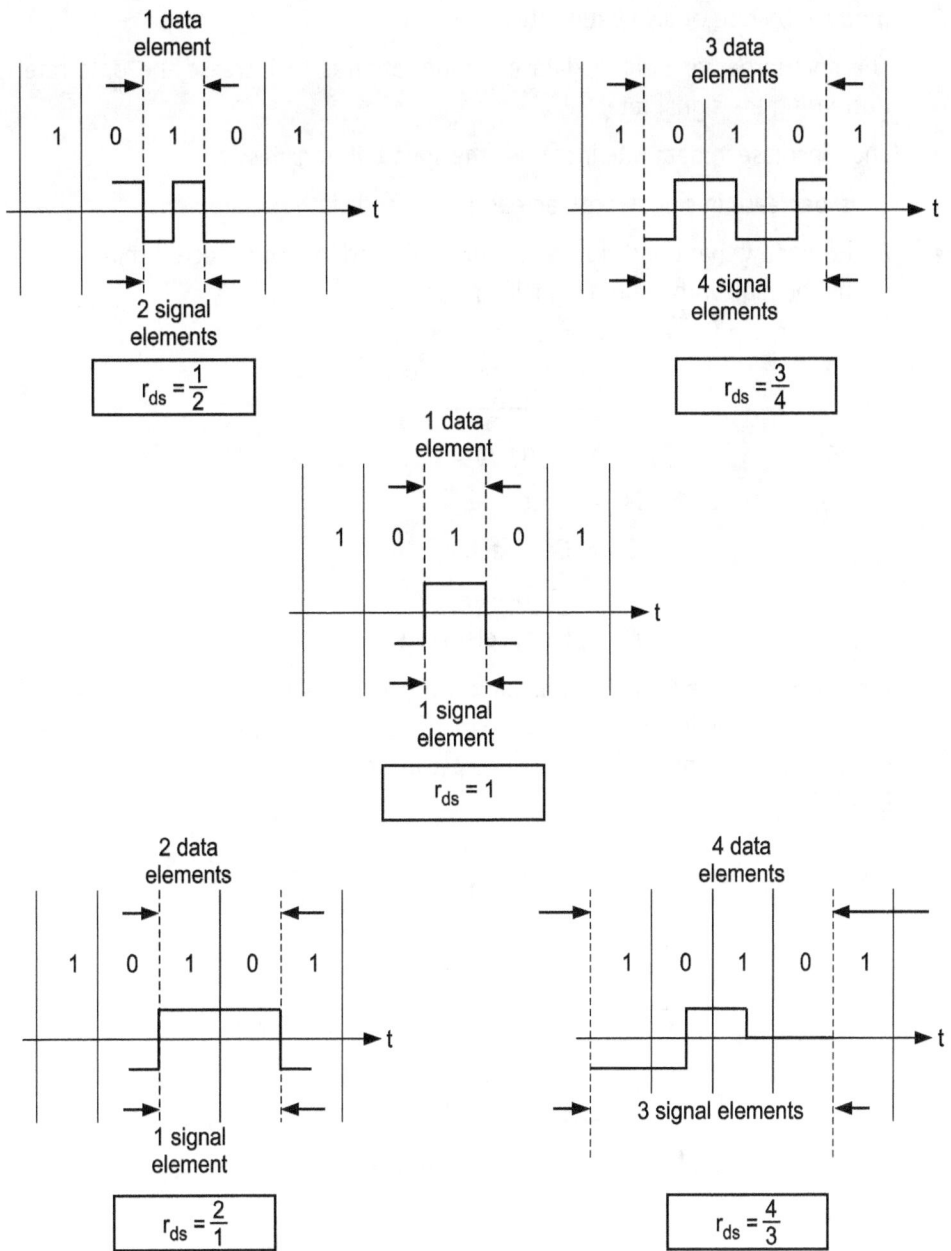

Fig. 3.2 : Ratio of Data Elements to Signal Elements and Related Waveforms

- Thus, data rate can be defined as, the number of data elements sent in 1s. The unit of data rate is bps.

- Signal rate can be defined as, the number of signal elements sent in 1s. The unit of signal rate is baud.

- Sometimes data rate is called as bit rate and signal rate is called as pulse rate or modulation rate or also baud rate.
- The final target or goal in data communication is to increase the data rate while decreasing the signal rate.
- Thus, increase in data rate increases the speed of transmission.
- Thus, decrease in signal rate decreases the bandwidth requirement.
- And we know that bandwidth spectrum is limited, hence expected thing is data rate should be high with limited signalling rate.

$$\boxed{S = \frac{C}{r_{ds}} \times N \text{ bauds}}$$

where,
S = Signal rate
N = Data rate
C = Case factor
$r_{ds} = \dfrac{\text{Data elements}}{\text{Signal elements}}$

- We have also seen that actual bandwidth of a digital signal is infinite, but the effective bandwidth is finite (Thus, in effective bandwidth, the upper frequency component with negligible amplitudes can be ignored. Hence, called as effective bandwidth).
- Thus, Bandwidth $= C \times N \times \dfrac{1}{r_{ds}}$

$$\therefore \boxed{B_{min} = C \times N \times \frac{1}{r_{ds}}}$$

$$\therefore \boxed{N_{max} = \frac{1}{C} \times B \times r_{ds}}$$

- Finally, compare this N_{max} with Nyquist formula.

$$\therefore \boxed{N_{max} = \frac{1}{C} \times B \times r_{ds} = 2B \times \log_2(L)}$$

- **Baseline wandering** : Receiver calculates average received signal power while decoding the line codes. This average is known as baseline. If '0' and '1' string is long then drifting in baseline is possible, which is called as **baseline wandering**. Due to which decoding becomes difficult and incorrect. Good line codes should prevent the baseline wandering.

- **DC component :** Telephone lines cannot pass frequencies below 210 Hz, so in line codes, if digital level '0' or '1' is constant for long time, which generates low frequencies around zero. This DC component saturate the core of coupling transformers in communication path.
- **Self synchronization :** Transmitter and receiver clock should be matched otherwise, data error occurs or misinterpreting of data is possible. In self synchronization the timing information is added alongwith data.
- Thus, good line codes must have built-in error detection and correction capabilities. Also, it should have good immunity to noise and interference. But more level line code is complex in nature and it is costly.

3.4 TYPES OF LINE CODING

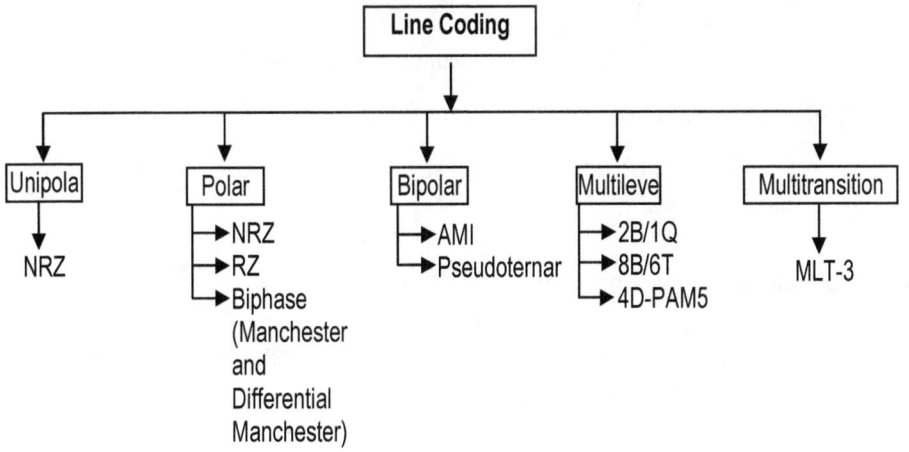

3.5 LINE CODING IN DETAIL

As we have seen there are basically five categories of studying line coding like :
- Unipolar
- Polar
- Bipolar
- Multilevel

- Multitransition.

Let's study one by one in detail.

3.5.1 Unipolar Scheme / NRZ (Non-Return-to-Zero)

- In unipolar line coding scheme, all voltage levels or signal levels are on one side of the time axis. The signal level can be below or above of time axis.

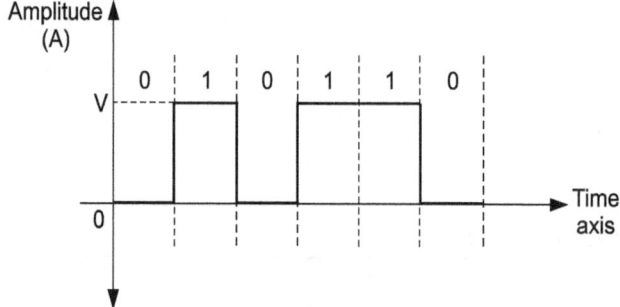

Fig. 3.3 : NRZ (unipolar) Waveform

- Positive voltage defines bit '1' and zero voltage defines bit '0'.
- Here signal does not return to zero at the middle of the bit, hence called as NRZ (Non-Return-to-Zero).
- Normalized power is given as $\frac{1}{2}(V)^2 + \frac{1}{2}(0)^2 = \frac{1}{2}V^2$

   i.e. Normalized power required to send 1 bit/unit line resistance is double as compared to polar NRZ. Hence NRZ unipolar scheme is costly.

3.5.2 Polar Schemes [NRZ-L, NRZ-I, RZ]

- Polar NRZ (NRZ-L and NRZ-I) uses two levels of voltage amplitude.
- NRZ-L stands for NRZ-level and NRZ-I stands for NRZ-Invert.
- In NRZ-L, the level of voltage determines the value of the bit.
- In NRZ-I, the change or lack of change in the level of voltage determines the value of bit, if there is no change the bit is '0' and if there is change the bit is '1'.

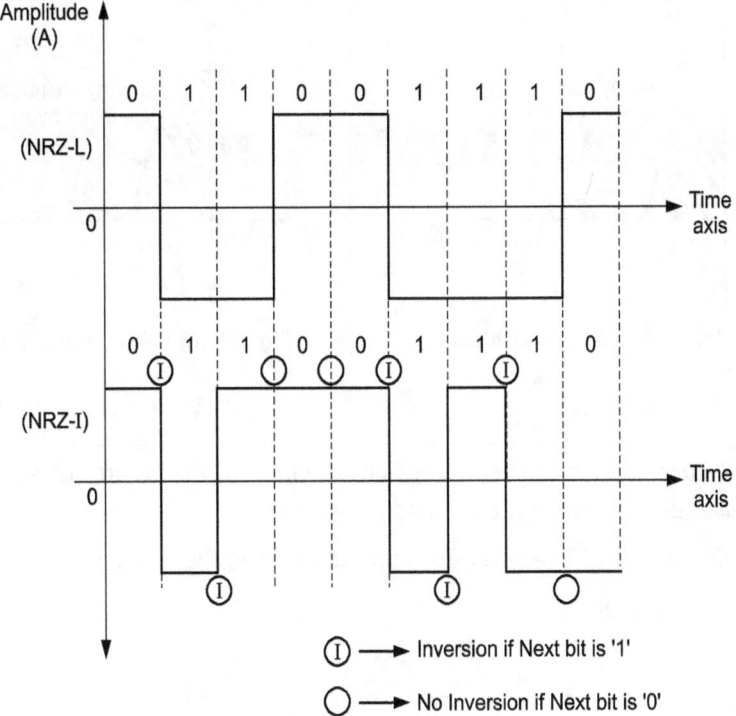

Fig. 3.4 : NRZ-L and NRZ-I Waveforms

- The NRZ-L and NRZ-I comparison is as given :

NRZ-L	NRZ-I
1. Baseline wandering problem is severe in NRZ-L.	1. It is less as compared to NRZ-L.
2. The average signal power is less if long sequence of '0' or '1' is present.	2. This problem occurs only for a long sequence of '0'.
3. Synchronization problem exists and it is severe in NRZ-L.	3. Synchronization problem exists and it is less as compared to NRZ-L.
4. NRZ-L gives more problem if there is a sudden change of polarity in the system.	4. NRZ-I does not have this problem.
5. Average signal rate $(S_{avg}) = \frac{N}{2}$ bauds.	5. Average signal rate $(S_{avg}) = \frac{N}{2}$ bauds.
6. DC component carrying high level of energy, gives DC component problem.	6. DC component carrying high level of energy, gives DC component problem.
7. Normalized bandwidth graph is as shown below :	7. Normalized bandwidth graph is as shown below :

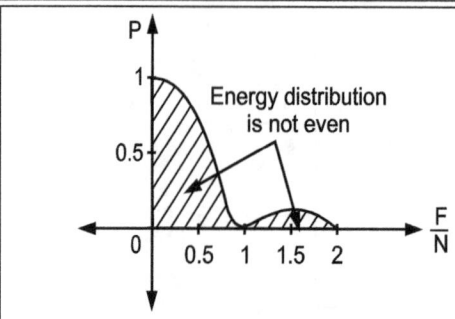
Fig. 3.5 (a) : NRZ-L bandwidth curve

for $\left[r = 1, S_{avg} = \dfrac{N}{2} \right]$

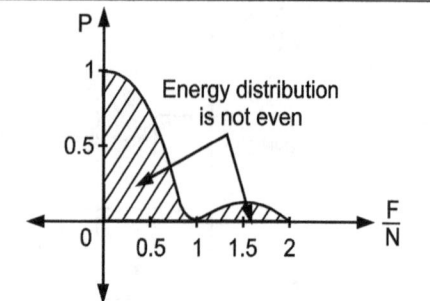
Fig. 3.5 (b) : NRZ-I bandwidth curve

for $\left[r = 1, S_{avg} = \dfrac{N}{2} \right]$

- **RZ (Return to Zero) Scheme :** Synchronization problems are solved in RZ scheme. Receiver understands start and end of next bit.
- In NRZ-L and NRZ-I, receiver does not understand the start and end of next bit.
- RZ uses three values :
  - Positive
  - Zero
  - Negative.
- **In RZ, the signal does not change between the bits but it changes during the bits.**

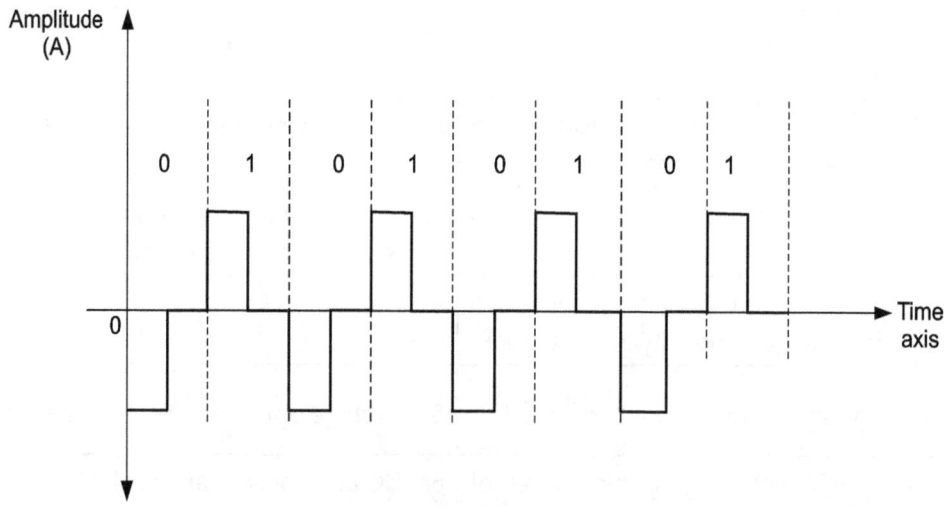

Fig. 3.6 : RZ Waveform

- Thus, in RZ, signal goes to zero in the middle of each bit. It does not change until the beginning of the next bit (0 or 1 bit).

- In RZ, it occupies two signal changes to encode a bit and hence has more signalling rate and hence occupies more bandwidth as shown in Fig. 3.7.

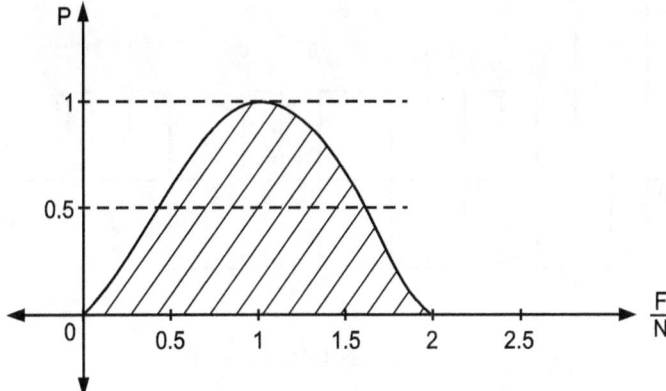

Fig. 3.7 : Normalized bandwidth of RZ $\left[\text{for } r = \frac{1}{2}, S_{avg} = N \right]$

- Also RZ gives more problem if there is sudden change of polarity in the system (i.e. '0' will be accepted as '1' and vice versa).
- In RZ, there is no DC component problem.
- RZ system is complex because three levels are used.
- Thus, due to all these problems, RZ is not used as it is.
- **To overcome these problems, RZ has been replaced by the Manchester and differential Manchester methods.**
- Manchester and differential Manchester methods are also known as **Biphase line coding techniques**.
- **Manchester scheme = RZ scheme + NRZ (L) scheme :**
  The idea of transition at the middle of the bit in RZ and NRZ (L) are combined to give Manchester line coding technique.
- **Differential Manchester scheme = RZ scheme + NRZ (I) scheme :**
  The transition at the middle of the bit in RZ and NRZ (I) idea are combined to give differential Manchester line coding technique.
- Manchester and differential Manchester line coding waveforms are shown in Fig. 3.8.
- Manchester method overcomes the problem of NRZ-L and differential Manchester method overcomes the problem of NRZ-I line coding techniques.
- Advantages of Manchester and differential Manchester method :
  - No baseline wandering.
  - Absence of DC component (each bit has positive and negative voltage contribution).

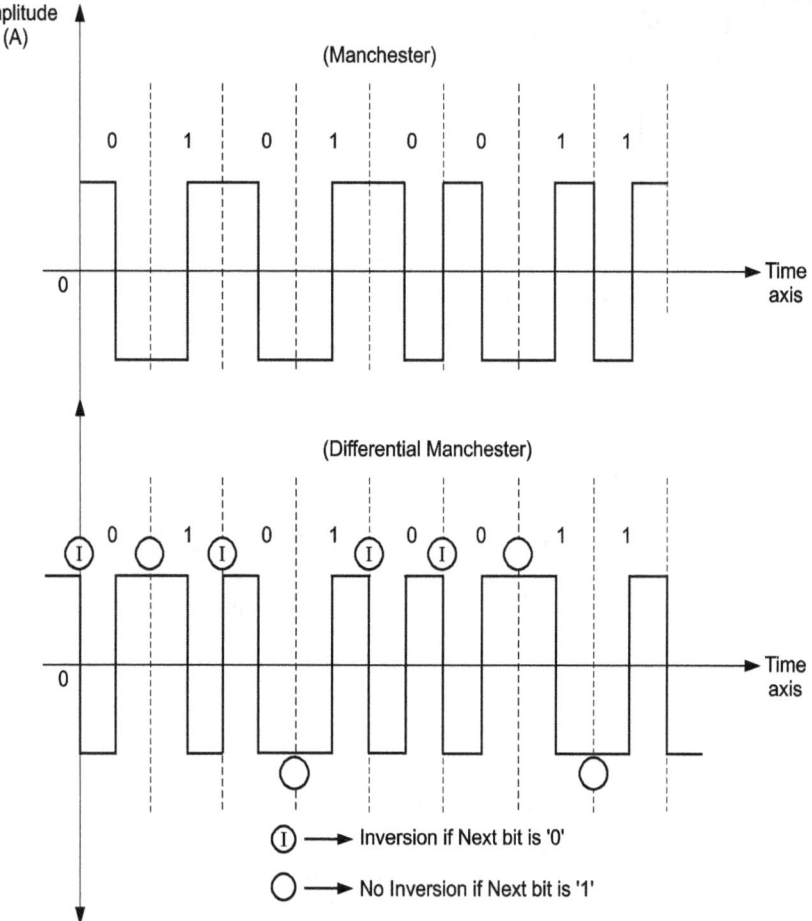

Fig. 3.8 : Manchester and Differential Manchester Line Coding

- Disadvantage of Manchester and differential Manchester method :
  Bandwidth required = 2 × NRZ bandwidth.

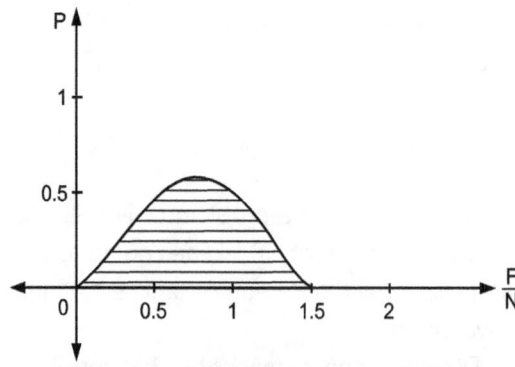

Fig. 3.9 : Normalized Bandwidth of Manchester and Differential Manchester Line Coding Techniques $\left[\text{for } r = \frac{1}{2}, S_{avg} = N\right]$

3.5.3 Bipolar Line Coding (AMI and Pseudoternary)

- **AMI stands** for Alternate Mark Inversion.

  Binary '0' → Zero volts (Neutral).

  Binary '1' → Alternate positive and negative voltages.

- In Pseudoternary,

  Binary '1' → Zero volts (Neutral).

  Binary '0' → Alternate positive and negative voltages.

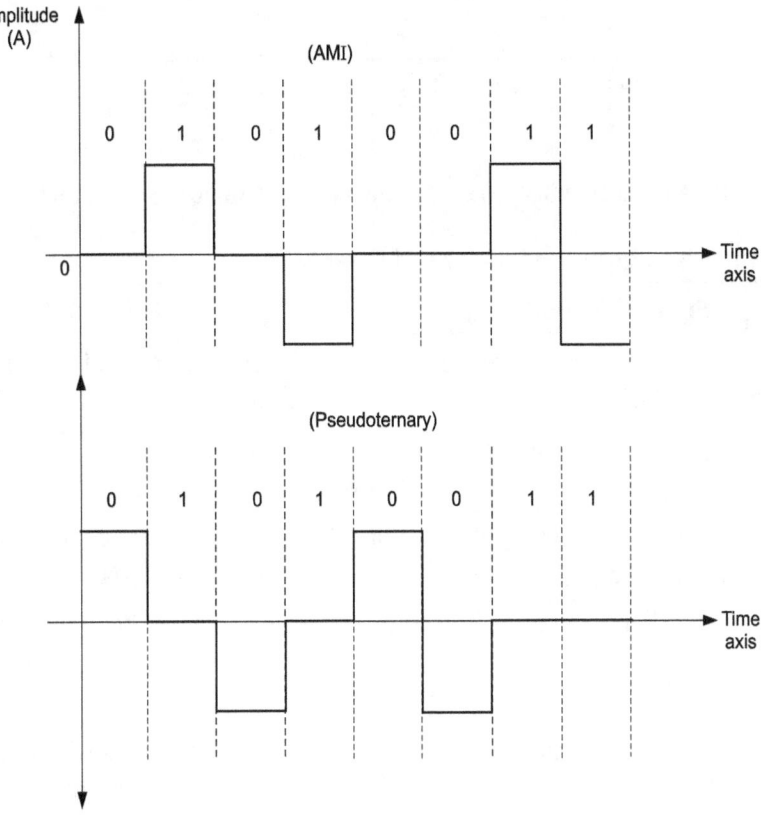

Fig. 3.10 : AMI and Pseudoternary Line Coding Techniques

- Typical normalized bandwidth curve for bipolar line coding method is shown in Fig. 3.11.
- In AMI, long stream of '0' and in Pseudoternary, long stream of '1' cannot produce DC components because these are neutral zero voltages, which cannot create DC components.
- **AMI is commonly used in long-distance communication applications**.
- AMI has synchronization problems in communication.

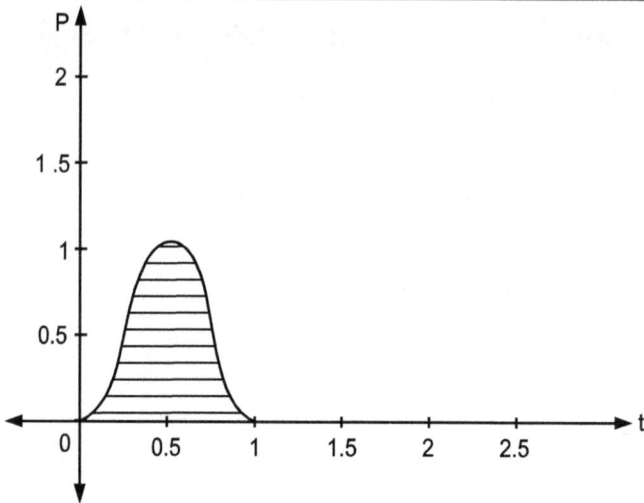

Fig. 3.11 : Normalized Bandwidth for Bipolar Line Coding $\left[\text{for } r = 1 \text{ and } S_{avg} = \frac{N}{2}\right]$

- **Comparison between Bipolar and Polar NRZ :**

Bipolar Method	Polar NRZ
1. Bipolar method was developed as alternative to NRZ.	1. Polar NRZ method was developed as alternative to unipolar NRZ.
2. Bipolar signal rate = Polar NRZ signal rate.	2. Same as Bipolar.
3. It has no DC component problem for long '0' and '1' data.	3. It has DC component problem for long '0' and '1' data.
4. Bipolar methods has most of its energy concentrated around frequency = $\frac{N}{2}$.	4. NRZ method has most of its energy concentrated near zero frequency, so unsuitable for transmission.
5. Normalized bandwidth curve is as shown in Fig. 3.12 (a).	5. Normalized bandwidth curve is as shown in Fig. 3.12 (b).

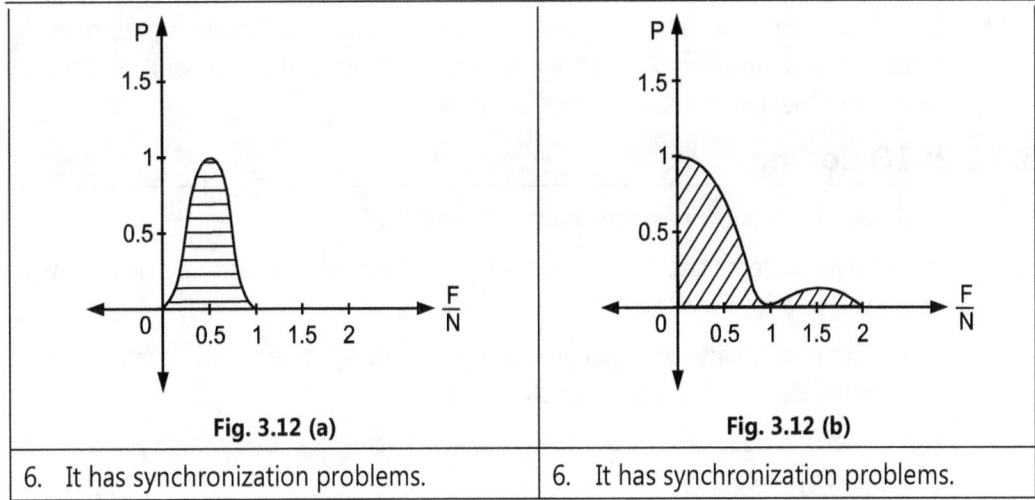

Fig. 3.12 (a)	Fig. 3.12 (b)
6. It has synchronization problems.	6. It has synchronization problems.

3.6 MULTILEVEL LINE CODING [2B/1Q, 8B.6T, 4D-PAM5]

- Multilevel line coding techniques has following advantages :
  - Increase in data speed or decrease in required bandwidth.
  - Prevents baseline wandering to provide synchronization.
  - Error detection possible.
- For this coding the designers have classified these types as **mBnL**.

  where,
  m = Length of binary pattern
  B = Binary data
  n = Length of the signal pattern
  L = Number of levels in signalling
  　　L = 2 → Binary
  　　L = 3 → Ternary
  　　L = 4 → Quaternary

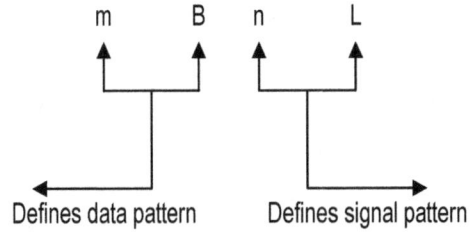

- In **mBnL** method, a pattern of 'm' data elements is encoded as a pattern of 'n' signal elements in which $2^m < L^n$. Because data encoding is not possible if $2^m > L^n$, as some of the data patterns cannot be encoded.

3.6.1 2B1Q Coding

- 2B1Q stands for two binary, one quaternary method.
- It uses data patterns size = 2 and encodes the 2 bit patterns as one signal element belonging to a four-level signal.
- The 2B1Q (two binary, one quaternary) line encoding scheme was intended to be used by the ISDN DSL and SDSL applications.
- This code is a four-level line code in which two binary bits (2B) represent one quaternary symbol (1Q).
- The 2B1Q line coding was seen as a major enhancement over the original T1 line coding, because 2B1Q encoded two bits per signal change instead of just one per change.

2B1Q Coding Rules :

- 2B1Q is a 4-level code. It takes two 2-level bits and converts them into one 4-level baud (quat) as indicated in Table 3.1.
- This conversion effectively doubles the period of the symbol. Since the period is inversely proportional to frequency (i.e., f=1/T) the frequency on the line is reduced. With every advantage there is always drawback and the 2B1Q is no exception.
- A 4-level code results in reduced distance between decision levels, thus increasing the required SNR for a given performance level (BER). However, the baud rate reduction and narrower bandwidth result in performance gains which outweigh this drawback.
- The important elements of the transmit quat are its sign, and its amplitude. The values assigned to the levels are set so that there is equal spacing between the four levels.
- Levels can be chosen to be +1, +0.33, -0.33 and -1. In order to eliminate the decimals, we will choose the four levels to be +3, +1, -1, and -3. The 2B1Q conversion table is shown in Table 3.1.
- The first bit of the dibit is called the "sign-bit". If it is 0, the output quat will have a negative sign. If the first bit is 1, then the output quat will have a positive sign.
- The second bit of the dibit is called the amplitude bit, and it determines the magnitude of the output quat. If it is 0, then the output level has an amplitude of 3.

- If the second bit of the dibit is 1, then the output amplitude is 1. This provides for a very simple means of encoding a binary bit stream into a 4-level code. An example of 2B1Q coding is shown in Fig. 3.13.

Table 3.1 : 2B1Q Coding Rules

Dibit	Output Quat
10	+3
11	+1
01	−1
00	−3

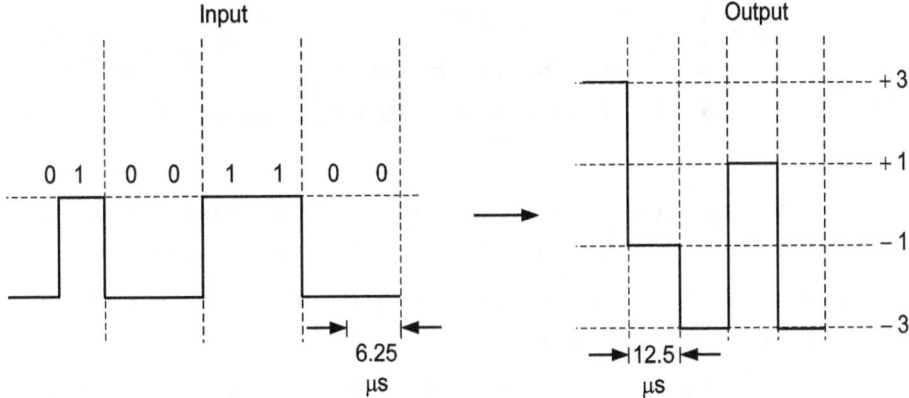

2-Level, Binary Data, 160 kbit/s   4-Level, Quaternary Data, 80 kbaud/s

Fig. 3.13 : 2B1Q Line Coding Example, 2 Binary, 1 Quaternary

Performance :

- The transmit baud rate of the 2B1Q system is one half the rate of linear codes (80 kbaud/s vs 160 kbaud/s). This puts the bandwidth of the 2B1Q system in a lower frequency region of the Power Spectral Density (PSD) graph. It also produces a bandwidth which is much narrower than that for Biphase.
- Fig. 3.14 shows comparison of filtered PSD plots. Telephone transmission lines act as a low pass filter with attenuation varying directly with frequency. Lower bandwidth codes will experience less attenuation, thus achieving greater reach.
- A limiting factor to most linear line codes is the performance in the presence of Near End Crosstalk (NEXT). NEXT is generated onto a transmission line from the adjoining twisted pairs that are found in a bundle of cable.
- The signal on the adjoining pair will induce a signal on the line. The magnitude of the induced signal will increase proportionally with frequency. Therefore, if you

lower a signal bandwidth (i.e., lower frequency content) you reduce the effect of NEXT.

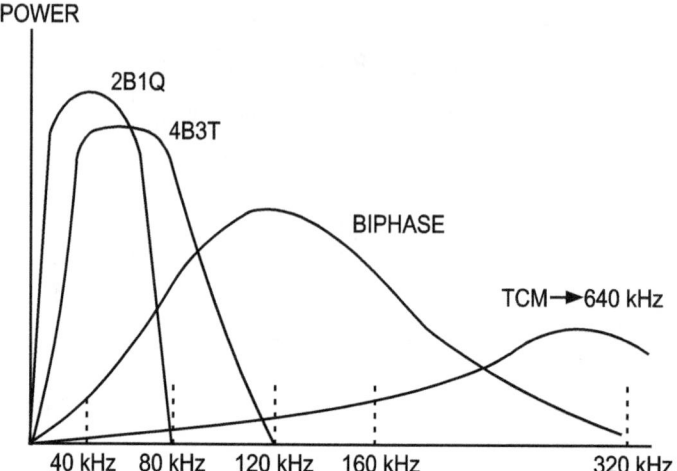

Fig. 3.14 : 2B1Q Power Spectral Density Comparison

Complexity :

- One drawback of low frequency transmission is that the pulse output on the line tend to develop long "tails", or pulse responses caused by excessive group delay.
- Several consecutive pulses will tend to have effect on its neighbours, resulting in Inter Symbol Interference (ISI).
- This ISI must be compensated in order to ensure valid data recovery. Decision Feedback Equalization (DFE) is a technique which can be used to remove the effect of ISI.
- A DFE is simply a finite impulse response filter which performs convolution of the loop impulse response with the received data.
- This convolution will provide an estimate of the effects of ISI which can be removed from the received signal.

3.6.2 8B6T Coding

- Some Encoding schemes for Ethernets are :
  - 10Mbps Ethernet (*Manchester encoding*).
  - 100baseTX (*MLT-3*, 2 pair cat5, 4B5B).
  - 100BaseFX (*NRZ-I*, 2 pair fiber, 4B5B).
  - 100BaseT4 (3 level 1V, 0V, & -1V, 4 pair cat 3, *8B/6T*).
  - Token Ring (*Differential Manchester*).

- 100Base-T4 is designed to produce a 100 Mbps data rate over lower-quality voice grade, or Category 3, cable. The advantage of this is that in many existing buildings, there is an abundance of voice-grade cabling and very little else. Thus, if this cabling can be used, installation costs are minimized.
- With present technology, a data rate of 100 Mbps over one or two Category 3 pairs is impractical. Instead, 100Base-T4 specifies that the data stream to be transmitted is divided into three separate data streams. Four twisted pairs are used.
- Data are transmitted using three pairs and received using three pairs. Thus, two of the pairs must be configured for bidirectional transmission.
- As with 100Base-X, a simple NRZ encoding scheme is not used for 100Base-T4. This would require a signalling rate of 33 Mbps on each twisted pair and does not provide synchronization.
- Instead, a ternary signalling scheme known as 8B6T is used. With ternary signalling, each signal element can take on one of three values-positive voltage, negative voltage, or zero voltage.
- A pure ternary code is one in which the full information-carrying capacity of the ternary signal is exploited. However, pure ternary is not attractive for the same reason for which pure binary (NRZ) code is rejected the lack of synchronization.
- The 8B6T code is designed to approach the efficiency of ternary and overcome this disadvantage.
- With 8B6T, the data to be transmitted is handled in 8-bit blocks. Each block of 8 bits is mapped into a code group of 6 ternary symbols. The stream of code groups is then transmitted in round-robin fashion across the three output channels.
- In 8B6T line encoding technique,
  - The data to be transmitted are handled in 8-bit blocks.
  - Each block of 8 bits is mapped into a code group of 6 ternary symbols.
  - The stream of code groups is then transmitted in round-robin fashion across the three output channels.
  - Thus, the ternary transmission rate on each output channel is $(6/8) \times 33.333 = 25$ Mbaud.

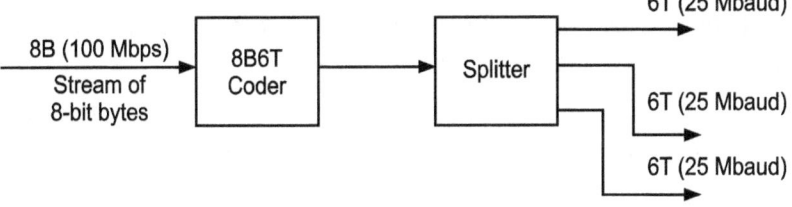

Fig. 3.15 : Transmission Scheme

Table 3.2 : Portion of 8B6T Code Table

Data octet	6T code group	Data octet	6T code group	Data octet	6T code group	Data octet	6T code group
00	+ - 0 0 + -	10	+ 0 + - - 0	20	0 0 - + + -	30	+ - 0 0 - +
01	0 + - + - 0	11	+ + 0 - 0 -	21	- - + 0 0 +	31	0 + - - + 0
02	+ - 0 + - 0	12	+ 0 + - 0 -	22	+ + - 0 + -	32	+ - 0 - + 0
03	- 0 + + - 0	13	0 + + - 0 -	23	+ + - 0 - +	33	- 0 + - + 0
04	- 0 + 0 + -	14	0 + + - - 0	24	0 0 + 0 - +	34	- 0 + 0 - +
05	0 + - - 0 +	15	+ + 0 0 - -	25	0 0 + 0 + -	35	0 + - + 0 -
06	+ - 0 - 0 +	16	+ 0 + 0 - -	26	0 0 - 0 0 +	36	+ - 0 + 0 -
07	- 0 + - 0 +	17	0 + + 0 - -	27	- - + + +	37	- 0 + + 0 -
08	- + 0 0 + -	18	0 + - 0 + -	28	-	38	- + 0 0 - +
09	0 - + + - 0	19	0 + - 0 - +	29	- 0 - + + 0	39	0 - + - + 0
0A	- + 0 + - 0	1A	0 + - + + -	2A	- - 0 + 0 +	3A	- + 0 - + 0
0B	+ 0 - + - 0	1B	0 + - 0 0 +	2B	- 0 - + 0 +	3B	+ 0 - - + 0
0C	+ 0 - 0 + -	1C	0 - + 0 0 +	2C	0 - - + 0 +	3C	+ 0 - 0 - +
0D	0 - + - 0 +	1D	0 - + + + -	2D	0 - - + + 0	3D	0 - + + 0 -
0E	- + 0 - 0 +	1E	0 - + 0 - +	2E	- - 0 0 + +	3E	- + 0 + 0 -
0F	+ 0 - - 0 +	1F	0 - + 0 + -	2F	- 0 - 0 + +	3F	+ 0 - + 0 -
					0 - - 0 + +		

- Table 3.2 shows a portion of the 8B6T code table; the full table maps all possible 8-bit patterns into a unique code group of 6 ternary symbols. The mapping was chosen with two requirements in mind :

    synchronization and DC balance

- For synchronization, the codes were chosen to maximize the average number of transitions per code group. The second requirement is to maintain DC balance, so that the average voltage on the line is zero.

- For this purpose, all of the selected code groups either have an equal number of positive and negative symbols or an excess of one positive symbol. To maintain balance, a DC balancing algorithm is used.

- In essence, this algorithm monitors the cumulative weight of all code groups transmitted on a single pair. Each code group has a weight of 0 or 1.

- To maintain balance, the algorithm may negate a transmitted code group by changing all plus symbols to minus symbols and all minus symbols to plus symbols so that the cumulative weight at the conclusion of each code group is always either 0 or 1.

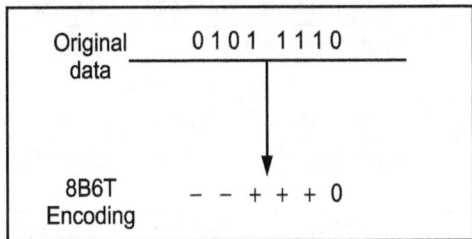

Fig. 3.16 : 8 bits of Data Encoded into a Sequence of Six Ternary Codes

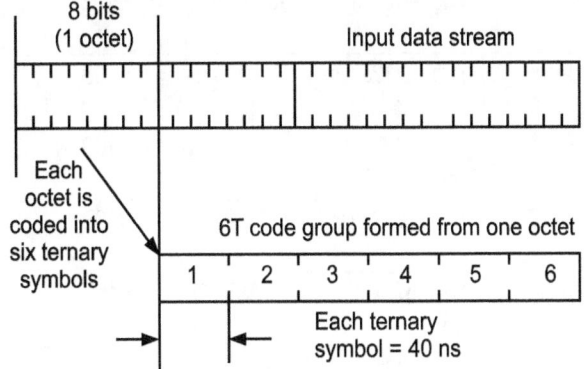

Fig. 3.17 : 8B6T Coding

- 8B6T coding, as used with 100BASE-T4 signalling, maps data octets into ternary symbols. Each octet is mapped to a pattern of 6 ternary symbols, called a 6T code group. The 6T code groups are fanned out to three independent serial channels. The effective data rate carried on each pair is one third of 100 Mbps, which is 33.333... Mbps. The ternary symbol transmission rate on each pair is 6/8 times 33.33 Mbps, or precisely 25.000 MHz.

- Also for different Ethernet, different line coding techniques used are as follows :

Standard	Name	Media Type	Encoding	Line	Network Size
10GEthernet IEEE 802.3ae	10GBASE-SR	Two 50/125 μm MMF, 850 nm	64B/66B	NRZ	2/550 m
	10GBASE-SW	Two 62.5/125 μm MMF, 850 nm	64B/66B	NRZ	2/33 m
	10GBASE-LX4	Two 50/125 μm MMF, 4xDWM signal	8B/10B	NRZ	300 m

	10GBASE-LX4	Two 62.5/125 µm MMF, 4xDWM signal	8B/10B	NRZ	300 m
	10GBASE-LX4	Two 8-10 µm SMF, 1310 nm, 4xDWM signal	8B/10B	NRZ	10 km
	10GBASE-LR	Two 8-10 µm SMF, 1310 nm	64B/66B	NRZ	10 km
	10GBASE-LW	Two 8-10 µm SMF, 1310 nm	64B/66B	NRZ	10 km
	10GBASE-ER	Two 8-10 µm SMF, 1550 nm	64B/66B	NRZ	2/40 km
	10GBASE-EW	Two 8-10 µm SMF, 1550 nm	64B/66B	NRZ	2/40 km
Gigabit Ethernet IEEE 802.3z/ab	1000BASE-ZX	Two 8-10 µm SMF, 1310 nm	8B/10B	NRZ	80 km
	1000BASE-LX	Two 8-10 µm SMF, 1310 nm	8B/10B	NRZ	5 km
	1000BASE-LX	Two 50/125 µm MMF, 1310 nm	8B/10B	NRZ	550/2000 m
	1000BASE-LX	Two 62.5/125 µm MMF, 1310 nm	8B/10B	NRZ	550/1000 m
	1000BASE-SX	Two 50/125 µm MMF, 850 nm	8B/10B	NRZ	500/750 m
	1000BASE-SX	Two 62.5/125 µm MMF, 850 nm	8B/10B	NRZ	220/400 m
	1000BASE-CX	Two pairs 150 Ohm STP (twinax)	8B/10B	NRZ	25 m
	1000BASE-T	Four pair UTP 5 (or better)	4D-PAM5	PAM5	<100 m
Fast Ethernet IEEE 802.3u	100BASE-Fx	Two optical 50/125 µm SMF	4B/5B	NRZI	40 km
	100BASE-Fx	Two optical 62.5/125 µm MMF	4B/5B	NRZI	2 km
	100BASE-Tx	Two pairs of STP cables	4B/5B	MLT3	200 m
	100BASE-Tx	Two pairs of UTP 5 (or better)	4B/5B	MLT3	<100 m
	100BASE-T4	Four pairs of UTP 3 (or better)	8B/6T	MLT3	<100 m
	100BASE-T2	Two pairs of UTP 3 (or better)	PAM5x5	PAM5	<100 m
Ethernet IEEE 802.3a-t	10BASE-FB	Two optical 62.5 /125 µm MMF sync hub	4B/5B	Manchester	<2000 m
	10BASE-FP	Two optical 62.5/125 µm MMF passive hub	4B/5B	Manchester	<1000 m
	10BASE-FL	Two optical 62.5/125 µm MMF asyn hub	4B/5B	Manchester	2000 m
	10BASE-T	Two pairs of UTP 3 (or better)	4B/5B	Manchester	<100 m
	10Broad36	One 75 Ohm coaxial (CATV)	4B/5B	Manchester	<3600 m
	10BASE-2	One 50 Ohm thin coaxial cable	4B/5B	Manchester	<185 m
	10BASE-5	One 50 Ohm thick coaxial cable	4B/5B	Manchester	<500 m

3.6.3 The 4D-PAM5 Line Coding

- 4D-PAM5 **encoding** is a four-dimensional, five-level pulse amplitude modulation.
- This is a way of encoding bits on copper wires to get a 1 GB per second transfer rate when the maximum rate of a single wire is 125 MHz. This is done by employing a multilevel amplitude signal.
- A five-level signal, called pulse amplitude modulation 5, is used.
- This works in a similar manner to MLT-3 except the levels are −2V, −1V, 0V and 2V. The transmitted signal on each wire is a five-level pulse modulation symbol.
- Four symbols transmitted simultaneously on the four pairs of wire forms the 4D-PAM5 code group that represents an 8-bit frame octet.
- The symbols to be transmitted are selected from a four-dimensional (4D) code group of five-level symbols.
- Because there are four separate pairs being used for transmission and reception of data, there are 625 possible codes to choose from when using all four pairs. Therefore, all 8 bits can be transferred using only one 4D-PAM5 symbol.
- The data signals have distinct and measurable amplitude and phases, allowing more data bits per cycle.
- This type of encoding is used by Gigabit Ethernet, whereby 1000 Mbps is squeezed into 125 MHz signals.
- The electronics are more complex and the technology is more susceptible to noise.
- Actually, only four levels are used for data; the 0V level is used to recover the transmitted signal from high noise. This fifth level of coding is used for error detection and correction.

1000Base-T Architecture :

- A twisted-pair version was introduced by the IEEE in 1999 under the name IEEE 802.3ab. The physical layer was specified as UTP Cat. 5 cabling in order to guarantee easy integration with existing 10BASE-T and 100BASE-T networks.
- 1000BASE-T over UTP is usually the preferred option for horizontal cabling and desktop connection. This is an alternative to 1000BASE-CX, which is rarely used in practice.
- The physical layer is split into the Physical Coding Sublayer (PCS) which controls logic functions, and the Physical Medium Attachment (PMA) sublayer which performs analogue-digital mixed signal functions.

Physical Coding Sublayer (PCS):

1000BASE-T operates over Cat. 5 (or better) cabling systems by using all four pairs, sending and receiving a 250 Mbps data stream over each of the four pairs (4 × 250 Mbps = 1 Gbps) simultaneously (See Fig. 3.18).

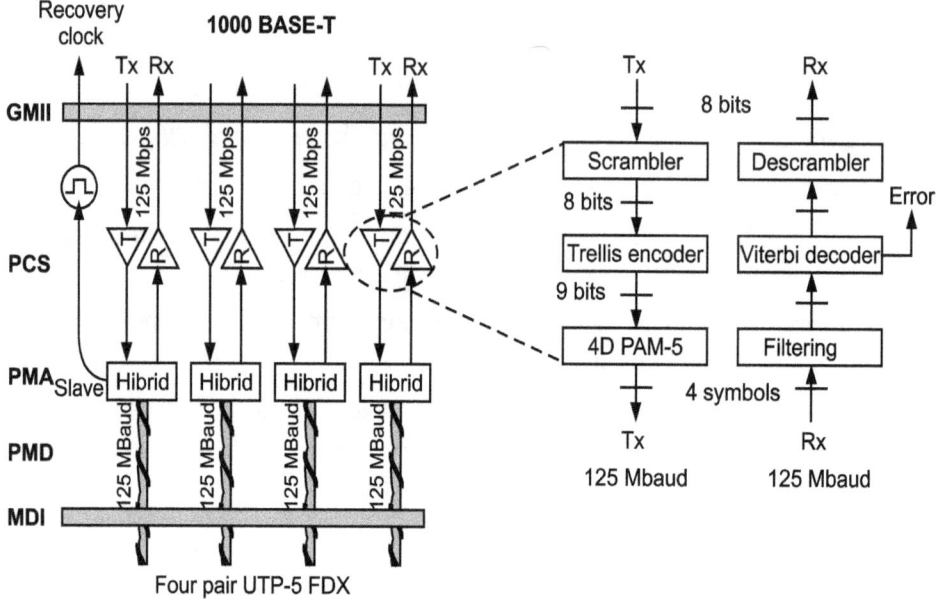

Fig. 3.18 : 1000BASE-T Link Topology including Loop Timing Configuration

It is the combination of the signal level on all four twisted-pairs that defines a symbol. Each pair carries the equivalent of 125 MBaud (symbol/s), hence 250 Mbps.

In Fig. 3.19, each 8 bit byte is mapped into 4 level PAM5 symbols which consists of one signal level (−2, −1, 0, 1, 2) on each of the four twisted pairs (A, B, C, D). There are 625 possible symbols, leaving 512 patterns for data and 113 are for control codes such as idle, start of packet, end of packet. The PCS sublayer performs the generation and processing of continuous code-groups to be transmitted or received over four channels. The process of converting data bits to code groups is called 4D-PAM5, (see Fig. 3.19). This modulation technique means:

- The four data lines (4 UTP wires) are used simultaneously to transmit/receive.
- Each byte is mapped into 4 pulse amplitude modulation (PAM) symbols.
  Five symbols form the PAM constellation being used {+2, +1, 0, −1, −2}.
- Data encoding needs only four levels (two bits per symbol), the fifth is used as forward error correction (FEC) coding.
- In the absence of data, IDLE symbols (restricted to {+2, 0, −2}) are used to keep the synchronization.
- 125 MBaud (1 Baud = 1 symbol/s) on each of the pairs.

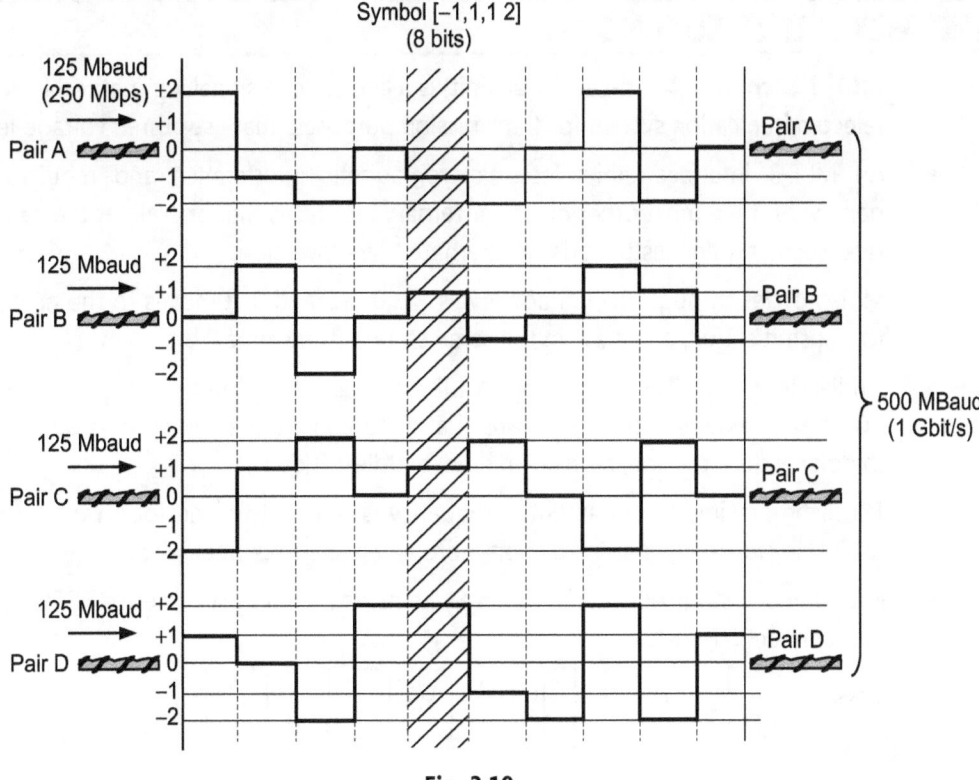

Fig. 3.19

As a result, each wire pair achieves 250 Mbps throughput using baseband signalling at 125 Mbaud - achieving 1 Gbps at a spectral power density similar to that of 100BASE-TX (See Fig. 3.20).

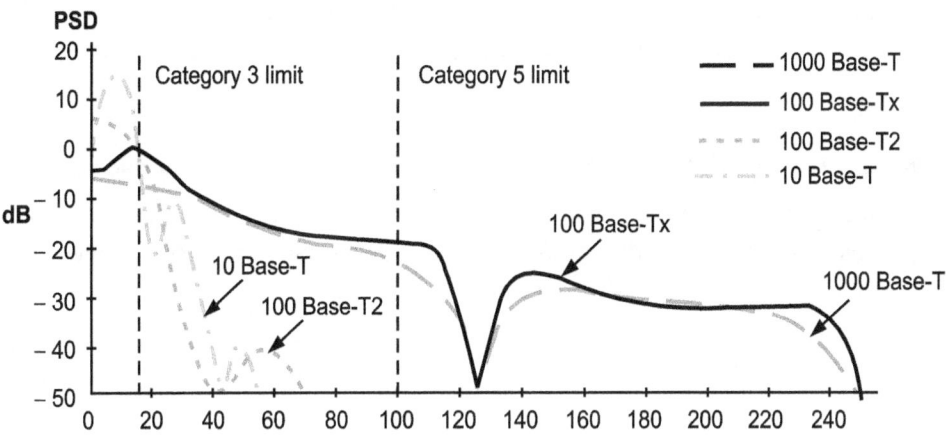

Fig. 3.20 : Power Spectral Density (PSD) for 10/100/1000BASE-T Electrical Technologies

3.7 MLT-3 LINE CODING

- **MLT-3 encoding** (Multi-Level Transmit) is a line code (a signalling method used in a telecommunication system for transmission purposes) that uses three voltage levels.
- An MLT-3 interface emits less electromagnetic interference and requires less bandwidth than most other binary or ternary interfaces that operate at the same bit rate, such as Manchester code or Alternate Mark Inversion.
- MLT-3 cycles through the voltage levels −1, 0, +1, and 0. It moves to the next state to transmit a 1 bit, and stays in the same state to transmit a 0 bit.
- Similar to simple NRZ encoding, MLT-3 has a coding efficiency of 1 bit/baud, however it requires four transitions (baud) to complete a full cycle (from low-to-middle, middle-to-high, high-to-middle, middle-to-low).
- Thus, the maximum fundamental frequency is reduced to one fourth of the baud rate. This makes signal transmission more amenable to copper wires.
- MLT-3 was first introduced by Cisco Systems as a coding scheme for FDDI copper interconnect (TP-PMD).

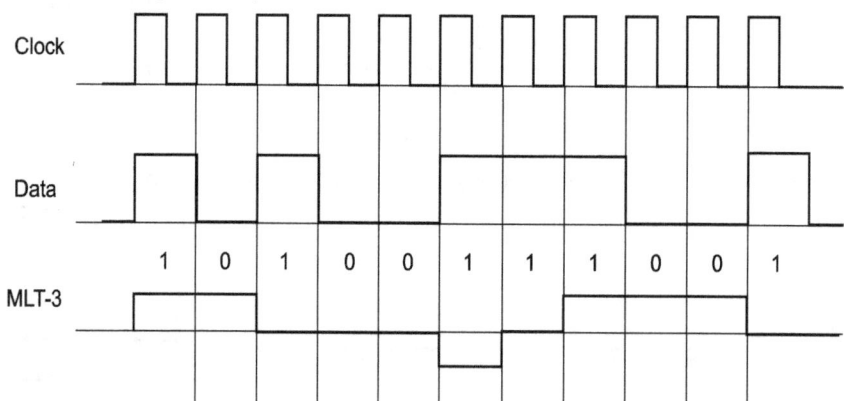

Fig. 3.21 : Example of MLT-3 Encoding (Light-colored lines indicate two previous states)

- Ethernet LANs use digital signals to share data among network devices. 10Base-T uses Manchester encoding to transmit the signal : transition occurs in the middle of each bit period. Two levels represent one bit.
- A low to high transition in the middle of the bit represents a '1'. A high to low transition in the middle of the bit represents a '0'. There is no DC component. It uses positive/negative voltages.
- 100-BaseTX uses 4B/5B encoding, where each 4-bit nibbles is being transferred, encoded as 5-bit symbols. The signaling model is a three level multi-level technique called MLT-3.

Table 3.3 : Ethernet Encoding and Signaling

	10Base-T	100Base-TX
Data rate	10 Mbps	100 Mbps
Encoding	Manchester	4B/5B
Signaling	5V, differential	MLT-3
Cable	Cat. 3 UTP	Cat. 5 UTP

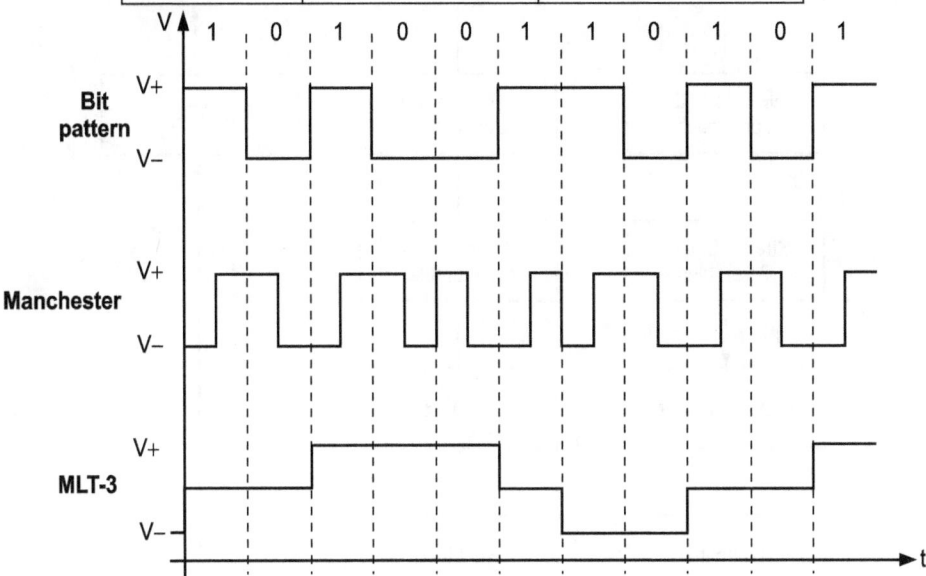

Fig. 3.22 : Ethernet Encoding Schemes

- It is also used by FDDI and TP-PMD to obtain 100 Mbps out of a 31.25 MHz signal. Where TP-PMD stands for Twisted Pair-Physical layer, Medium Dependent (TP-PMD) and FDDI stands for Fiber Distributed Data Interface backbone network.
- The mechanism chosen to overcome signaling rate issues is Multi-Level Transmit 3 (MLT-3). This is a tri-polar encoding mechanism based on three different signal levels. Its purpose within TP-PMD is to encode the data in such a manner that the signaling rate is reduced with the emissions that radiate from the cable.
- MLT-3 encoding is essentially very simple, operating with a positive signal level, a negative one and a zero level. It does however require a binary input rather than the normal NRZI encoded signal normally passed from the PHY.
- Therefore, an NRZI decoder is placed within the PMD to produce a binary output suitable for MLT-3.

- The transition between levels is what differentiates between a binary 1_2 and 0_2. In addition to the ability to transition between three signal levels, a counter is required.
- This can be a single bit counter as it is only necessary to determine between odd and even.

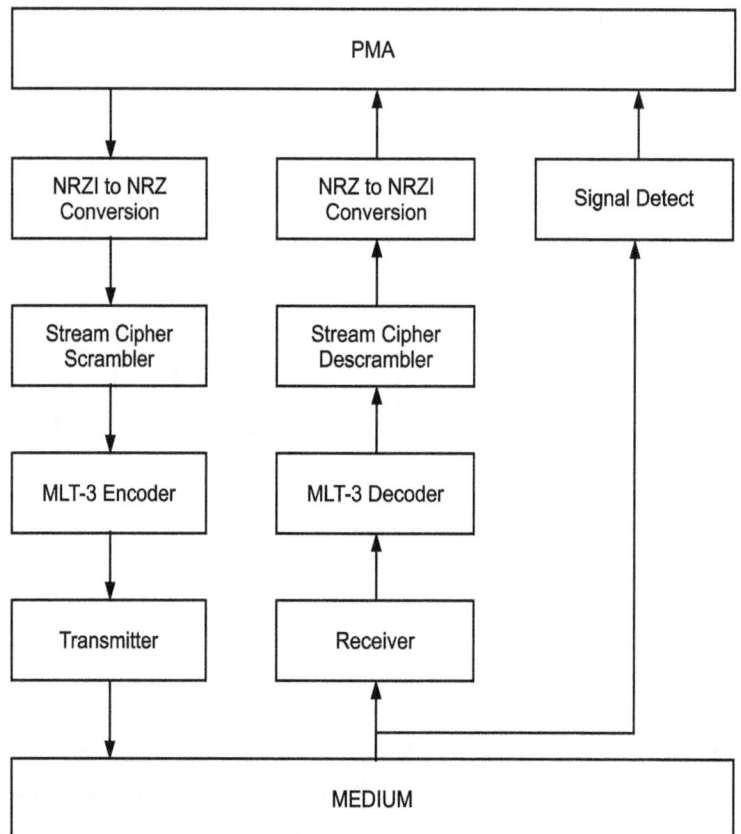

Fig. 3.23 : TP-PMD Block Diagram (PMA : Physical Medium Attachment)

- The rules for encoding are :
- The transmitter can only transition between adjacent signal states i.e. from positive to zero, zero to negative, zero to positive. A transition from negative to positive is not allowed.
- A transition only takes place when a 1_2 is transmitted. No transition takes place when a 0_2 is transmitted.
- If a 1_2 is transmitted, the signal will transition from its current state to an adjacent state, i.e. from positive to zero, negative to zero.
- If the current state is zero and a transition is required then it will be positive if the counter is even or negative if the counter is odd.
- The counter is incremented when the zero state is left.

- These rules are demonstrated in Fig. 3.24, which shows a example of MLT-3 encoding. The receiver function is opposite to that described above, with the decoded MLT-3 signal being passed through an NRZI encoder before being handed to the PHY.

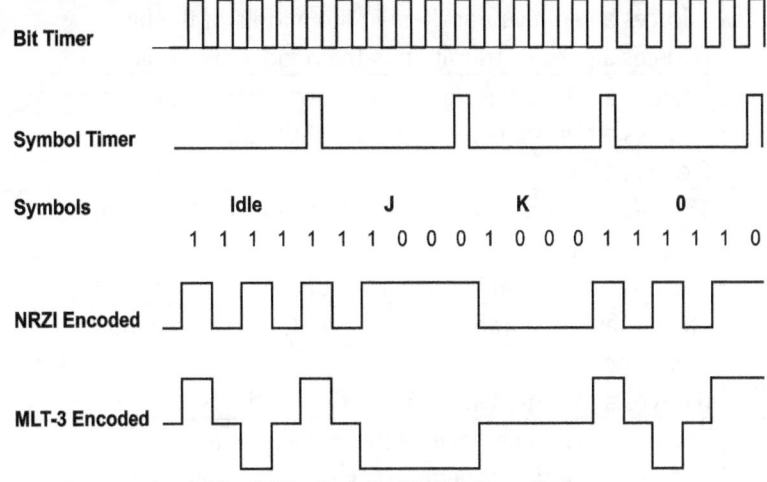

Fig. 3.24 : Sample MLT-3 Encoding

- The benefit produced by this system is the much reduced signaling rate, down from 125 MHz on fiber to 31.25 MHz over copper.
- This produces much lower radiated emissions allowing the technology to stay well within published guidelines.

3.8 SUMMARY OF LINE CODING

Common Line Codes :

Signal	Comments
NRZ-L	Non-return to zero level. This is the standard positive logic signal format used in digital circuits. 1 forces a high level 0 forces a low level
NRZ-M	Non-return to zero mark. 1 forces a transition 0 does nothing
NRZ-S	Non-return to zero space. 1 does nothing 0 forces a transition
RZ	Return to zero. 1 goes high for half the bit period 0 does nothing

Common Line Codes :

Signal	Comments
Biphase-L	Manchester. Two consecutive bits of the same type force a transition at the beginning of a bit period. 1 forces a negative transition in the middle of the bit 0 forces a positive transition in the middle of the bit
Biphase-M	There is always a transition at the beginning of a bit period. 1 forces a transition in the middle of the bit. 0 does nothing.
Biphase-S	There is always a transition at the beginning of a bit period. 1 does nothing 0 forces a transition in the middle of the bit.
Differential Manchester	There is always a transition in the middle of a bit period. 1 does nothing 0 forces a transition at the beginning of the bit
Bipolar	The positive and negative pulses are alternate. 1 forces a positive or negative pulse for half the bit period. 0 does nothing.

Common Line Codes :

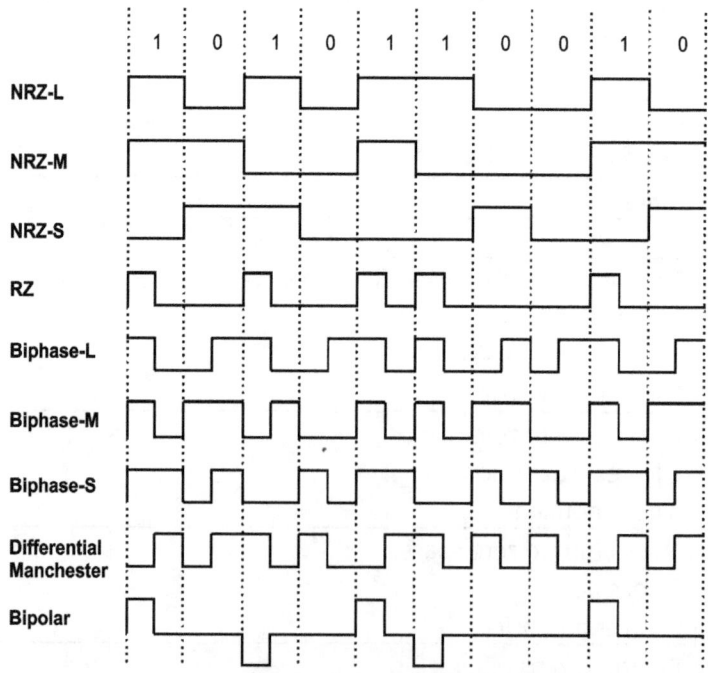

Fig. 3.25 : Common Line Codes at a Glance

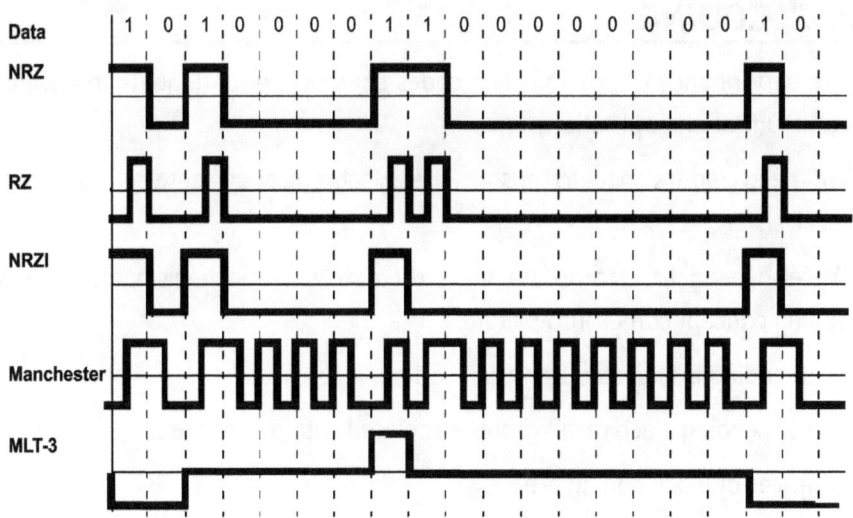

Fig. 3.26 : Symbol Encoding Schemes used in Ethernet

3.8.1 Comparison of Line Coding Techniques

Sr. No.	Main Technique	Type	Average Bandwidth $B_{avg} =$	Characteristics
1.	Unipolar Line coding	NRZ	N/2	DC component effect present. No self synchronization for long 0 & 1 bit streams. Implementation is costly.
2.	Polar Line coding	NRZ-L	N/2	DC component effect present. No self synchronization for long 0 & 1 bit streams.
		NRZ-I	N/2	DC component effect present. No self synchronization for long 0 bit streams.
		Biphase	N	DC component effect absent. Self synchronization is achieved.
3.	Bipolar Line coding	AMI	N/2	DC component effect present. No self synchronization for long 0 bit streams.
4.	Multilevel Line coding	2B1Q	N/4	No self synchronization for long same double bits.
		8B6T	3N/4	DC component effect absent. Self synchronization is achieved.
		4D-PAM5	N/8	DC component effect absent. Self synchronization is achieved.
5.	Multiline Line coding	MLT-3	N/3	DC component effect absent. No self synchronization for long 0 bit streams.

3.9 BLOCK CODING

- The performance of previous line codes studied is not adequate in advanced data communication applications.
- We need redundancy to ensure the synchronization between transmitter and receiver.
- We also need to incorporate the error detection mechanism, hence, new block coding concept comes into picture.
- Block coding is indicated as mB/nB coding.
- In block coding, each m-bit group is replaced with n-bit group.
- Examples of block coding are :
  - 4B/5B.
  - 8B/10B.
- In 4B/5B, (/) slash indicates block coding, whereas 8B6T is example of multilevel coding.
- Block coding includes the following three steps.
  - Division step.
  - Substitution step.
  - Combination step.
- In the division step, sequence of bits are divided into the groups of m-bits in block encoding.
- For example in 4B/5B, the bit sequence is divided into 4-bit groups, in block encoding.
- In the substitution step, we substitute m-bit group for n-bit group, in block encoding.
- For example, in 4B/5B, we substitute 4-bit code for a 5-bit group in block encoding.
- In last or final step i.e. combination step, n-bit groups are combined together to form a block encoded stream output.

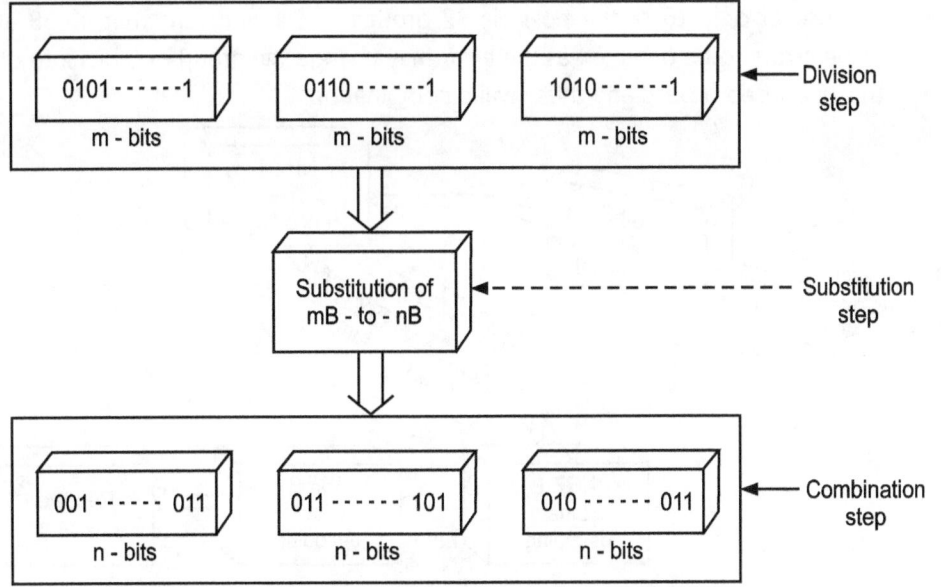

Fig. 3.27 : Basic Block Encoding Steps

3.9.1 4B/5B Block Coding

- This 4B/5B technique was designed to be used in combination with NRZ-I line coding technique.
- In NRZ-I, there are two problems :
  - DC component effect.
  - Self synchronization problem for long stream of '0's.
- Also in NRZ, average bandwidth $B_{avg} = \frac{N}{2}$, i.e. it has good signalling rate (i.e. $\frac{1}{2}$ of Biphase coding).
- The solution over self-synchronization problem for long stream of '0's is to change the bit stream prior to encoding with NRZ-I, so that long bit stream of '0's will be cancelled.
- Thus, maximum number of consecutive '0's will be three only.
- Depending on the standard or specification of interest, there may be several 4B/5B characters left unused.
- The presence of any of the "unused" characters in the data stream can be used as an indication that there is a fault somewhere in the link.
- Therefore, the unused characters can actually be used to detect errors in the data stream.

- The use of only 16 of the possible 32 groups of 5 bits means that 4B/5B allows some errors to be detected as the error may change the group of 5 bits into one of the 16 unused groups and thus invalid combinations.

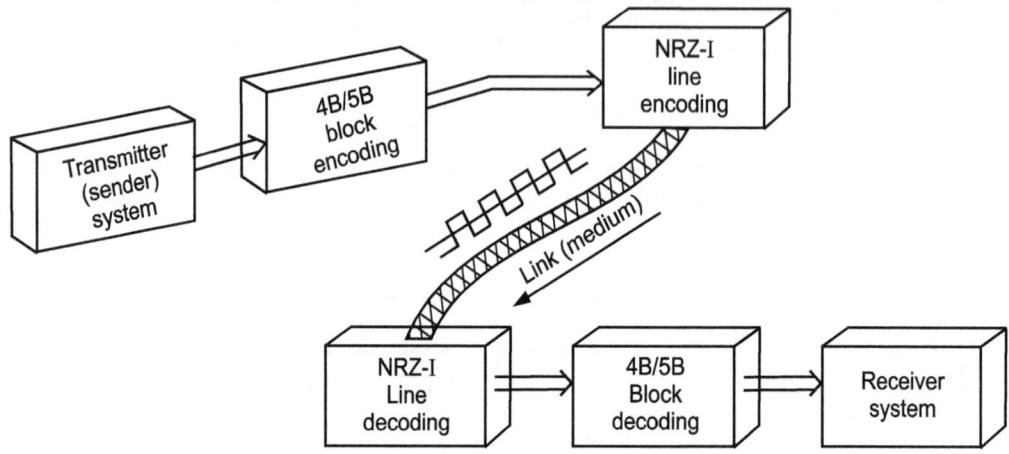

Fig. 3.28 : 4B/5B Block Coding + NRZ-I Line Coding to improve Self-Synchronization and DC Component Effect

- 4B/5B is used in the following standards :
    - 100BASE-TX standard defined by IEEE 802.3u in 1995.
    - MADI (Multichannel Audio Digital Interface)
- Note that normal data symbols begin with at most one 0 bit and end with at most two, so there can be most three 0 bits in a row.
- Control symbols used in combinations that also preserve this rule. Thus, 4B/5B encoding is a (0,3) RLL code.
- FDDI and 100BASE-TX begin frames with a JK pair. FDDI ends frames with a TT pair, while 100BASE-TX uses a TR pair.

Table 3.4 : Encoding table of 4B/5B

Name	4B	5B	Description
0	0000	11110	hex data 0
1	0001	01001	hex data 1
2	0010	10100	hex data 2
3	0011	10101	hex data 3
4	0100	01010	hex data 4
5	0101	01011	hex data 5
6	0110	01110	hex data 6

(Contd.)

Name	4B	5B	Description
7	0111	01111	hex data 7
8	1000	10010	hex data 8
9	1001	10011	hex data 9
A	1010	10110	hex data A
B	1011	10111	hex data B
C	1100	11010	hex data C
D	1101	11011	hex data D
E	1110	11100	hex data E
F	1111	11101	hex data F
Q	-NONE-	00000	Quiet (signal lost)
I	-NONE-	11111	Idle
J	-NONE-	11000	Start #1
K	-NONE-	10001	Start #2
T	-NONE-	01101	End
R	-NONE-	00111	Reset
S	-NONE-	11001	Set
H	-NONE-	00100	Halt

- The following character sets are sometimes referred to as command characters.

Table 3.5 : Control characters

Control Character	5B symbols	Purpose
JK	11000 10001	Sync, Start delimiter
II	11111 11111	Not Used
TT	01101 01101	FDDI end delimiter
TS	01101 11001	Not Used
IH	11111 00100	SAL
TR	01101 00111	100BASE-TX end delimiter
SR	11001 00111	Not Used
SS	11001 11001	Not Used
HH	00100 00100	HDLC0
HI	00100 11111	HDLC1
HQ	00100 00000	HDLC2
RR	00111 00111	HDLC3
RS	00111 11001	HDLC4
QH	00000 00100	HDLC5
QI	00000 11111	HDLC6
QQ	00000 00000	HDLC7

(HDLC = High-Level Data Link Control)   (FDDI = Fiber Distributed Data Interface)

- Despite this 4B/5B does not guarantee at least one transition for each bit period, however there are enough transitions to allow the clock signal to be recovered.
- Unfortunately the use of 5 bits to represent 4 bits does mean that the bandwidth needed to transmit the data is increased by 25%.
- Substitution in 4B/5B block coding is as shown in Fig. 3.29.

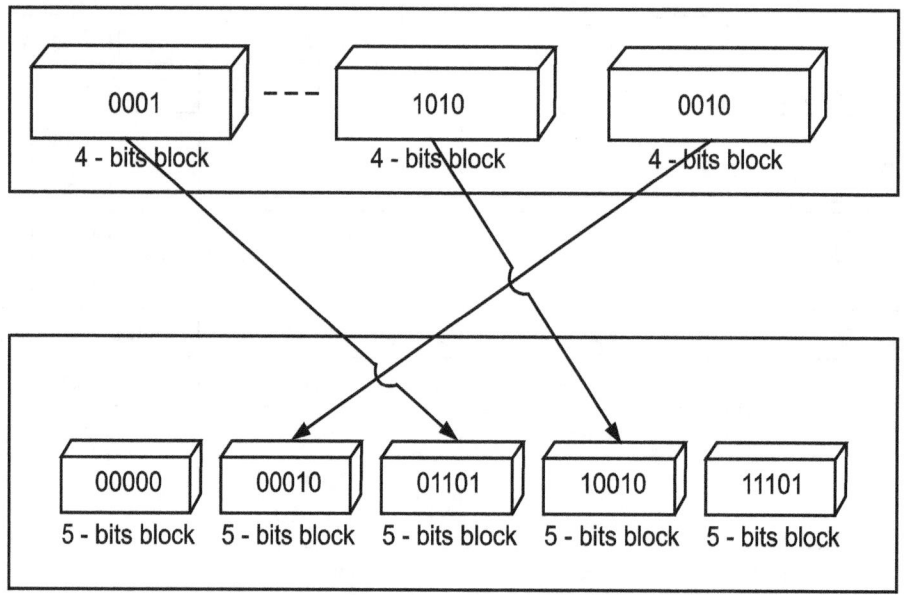

Fig. 3.29 : 4B/5B Substitution Process

3.9.2 The 8B/10B Block Coding

- The 8B/10B code is known as 8-Binary/10-Binary block coding technique.
- The 4B/5B is similar to 8B/10B, except that a group of 8 bits of data is substituted by a 10 bit code.
- It has greater error detection capability than 4B/5B block coding technique.
- The 8B/10B is combination of 5B/6B and 3B/4B.
- Disparity controller section minimizes/removes DC component effect due to long streams of consecutive '0' or '1's.
- Thus, 8B/10B encoding also has better self-synchronization capacity as compared to 4B/5B block encoding.

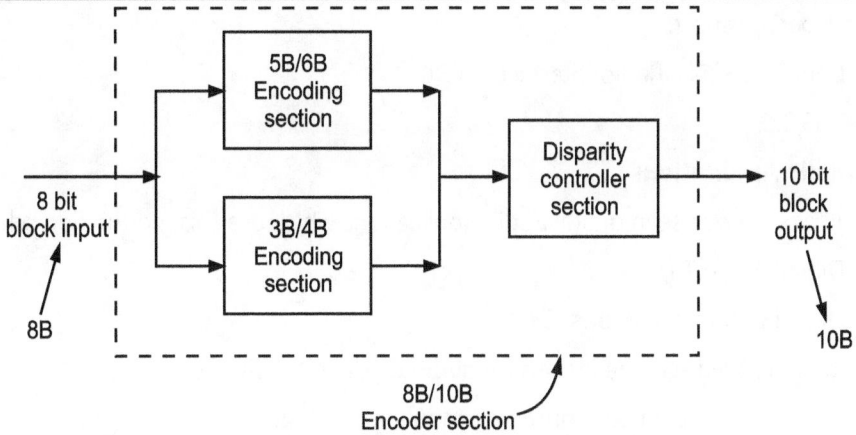

Fig. 3.30 : The 8B/10B Block Coding Method

Technologies that use 8B/10B :

Following are the areas in which 8B/10B encoding finds application :

- PCI Express (Peripheral Component Interconnect Express).
- IEEE 1394b.
- Serial ATA (The serial ATA, or SATA computer bus, is a storage interface).
- SAS (Serial Attached SCSI) (Small Computer System Interface).
- Fibre Channel.
- SSA (Serial Storage Architecture).
- Gigabit Ethernet (except for the twisted pair based 1000Base-T).
- InfiniBand (InfiniBand is a switched fabric communication link primarily used in high-performance computing).
- XAUI (XAUI is a standard for extending the XGMII (10 Gigabit Media Independent Interface) between the MAC and PHY layer of 10 Gigabit Ethernet (10GbE). XAUI is pronounced "zowie", a concatenation of the roman numeral X, meaning ten, and the initials of "Attachment Unit Interface".
- Serial RapidIO (The RapidIO architecture is a high-performance packet-switched, interconnect technology for interconnecting chips on a circuit board, and also circuit boards to each other using a backplane.)
- DVI (Digital Visual Interface) and HDMI (Transition Minimized Differential Signaling) (High-Definition Multimedia Interface).
- DVB (Asynchronous Serial Interface (ASI)) (Digital Video Broadcasting).
- DisplayPort Main Link.

- HyperTransport.
- Common Public Radio Interface (CPRI).
- USB 3.0.

Digital Audio Applications :

Encoding has a heavy use in digital audio applications which use this modulation scheme :
- Digital Audio Tape.
- Digital Compact Cassette (DCC).

A differing but related scheme is used for audio CDs and CD-ROMs :
- Compact Disc Eight-to-Fourteen Modulation.

Exceptions :
- For 10 Gigabit Ethernet's 10GBASE-R Physical Medium Dependent (PMD) interfaces, 64B/66B encoding is used.
- This scheme is considerably different in design to 8B/10B encoding, but was created with similar considerations of DC balance, maximum run length, transition density and electromagnetic emission minimization.
- Note that 8B/10B is the encoding scheme, not a specific code. While many applications do use the same code, there exist some incompatible implementations; for example, Transition Minimized Differential Signalling, which also expands 8 bits to 10 bits, has some subtle differences.

Encoding Tables :
- Note that in the following tables, "A" and "a" are the least significant bit. The bits are sent low to high : a → b → c → d → e → i → f → g → h → j (i.e. the 5B/6B code followed by the 3B/4B code). With that the uniqueness of the special bit sequence in the comma codes is ensured.
- The residual effect on the stream to the number of zero and one bits transmitted is maintained as the Running Disparity (RD) and the effect of slew is balanced by the choice of encoding for following symbols.
- Each 6 or 4 bit code word has either equal numbers of '0' and '1' bits (a disparity of 0), or comes in a pair of forms, one with two more '1' bits than '0' bits (four '1' bits and two '0' bits, or three '1' bits and one '0' bit, respectively) and one with two less.
- When a 6 or 4 bit code is used that has a non-zero disparity (count of '1' bits minus count of '0' bits, i.e. −2 or +2), the choice of positive or negative disparity encodings must be the one that toggles the running disparity. i.e. the non-zero disparity codes are alternate.

- This encoding is used by Fibre Channel, Gigabit Ethernet, 10 Gigabit Ethernet, and ATM (Asynchronous Transfer Mode) transmission interfaces. Example format :

Table 3.6 : Data Encoding

-	Data Byte	8B/10B	5B/6B	3B/4B
00	0000 0000	011000 1011	011000	0100
01	0000 0001	100010 1011	100010	1001
02	0000 0010	010010 1011	010010	0101
04	0000 0101	001010 1011	001010	0010
07	0000 0111	000111 0100	000111	0001
08	0000 1000	000110 1011	000110	--
0F	0000 1111	101000 1011	101000	--
F0	1111 0000	100100 1110	--	--
FF	1111 1111	010100 1110	--	--

Running Disparity :

- Running Disparity is a concept used in the 8B/10B encoding to keep the number of 1s and 0s that are transmitted "down the wire" roughly equal.
- This scheme only needs two states for Running Disparity of +1 and −1. It starts at −1.
- For each 5B/6B and 3B/4B code with an unequal number of 1s and 0s, there are two bit patterns that can be used to transmit it. One with two more 1 bits and one with all bits inverted and thus two more 0s.
- Depending on the current running disparity of the signal, the encoding engine selects which of the two possible 6 or 4 bit sequences to send for the given data. (Obviously, if the 6 or 4 bit code has equal numbers of 1s and 0s, there is no choice to make, as the disparity would be unchanged.)

Table 3.7 : Rules for Running Disparity

Previous RD	Disparity of 6 or 4 Bit Code	Disparity chosen	Next RD
−1	0	0	−1
−1	±2	+2	+1
+1	0	0	+1
+1	±2	−2	−1

3.10 SCRAMBLING

- Properties of Biphase line codes are :
  - No DC component.
  - Self-synchronization capacity.
  - High bandwidth requirement.
- Biphase technique can be used in LAN environment of short distance communication.
- It cannot be used for long distance communication because of their wide bandwidth requirement.
- DC component problem does not allow combination of block coding + NRZ coding. Also synchronization problems for long stream of '0' occur.
- To avoid synchronization problems, we can use Bipolar AMI for long distance.
- But scrambling can give you synchronization that substitutes long '0' level pulses with a combination of other levels.
- Thus, part of AMI can be modified to include scrambling as shown in Fig. 3.31.
- There are two scrambling techniques :
  (i) B8ZS.
  (ii) HDB3.

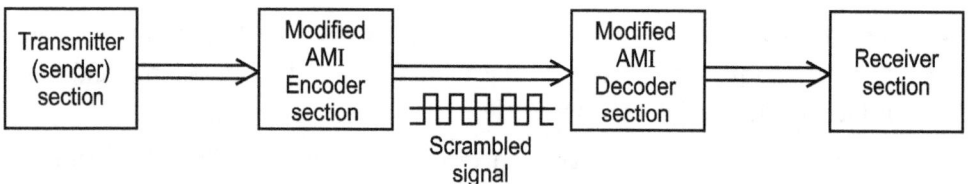

Fig. 3.31 : Modified AMI – Scrambling Technique

3.10.1 Bipolar with 8-zeros Substitution (B8ZS) Signal Encoding

The bipolar-AMI encoding supplemented with a scrambling scheme, which uses two code violations to ensure synchronization in runs of 0's.

- Replace '00000000' with '000+−0−+', if the preceding voltage pulse was positive.
- Replace '00000000' with '000−+0+−', if the preceding voltage pulse was not positive.
- The amount of data remains unchanged.

- The spectrum graph shows that there is no DC component, with most of the energy concentrating in a relative sharp spectrum, making the encoding suitable for high-rate transmissions.
- Used mainly in North America.

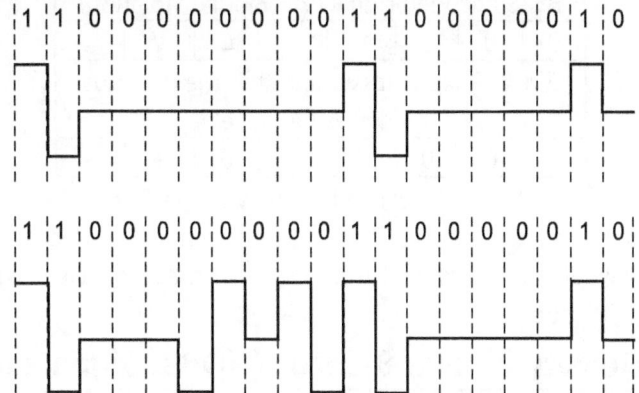

Fig. 3.32 : Bipolar with 8-zeros Substitution (B8ZS) Signal Encoding

Following data for B8ZS encoding is very important

- **B8ZS** is an abbreviation for bipolar with eight-zeros substitution, which is a method of line coding used in the T-carrier system which allows full 64 kbps per channel, though it does not allow for Clear Channel Capability (CCC - 64 kbps) in and of itself.
- The service would still have to be point-to-point (P2P) and not switched throughout digital switching network.
- The standard is to use B8ZS as the line encoding option when providing P2P circuits and services.
- The older AMI scheme was implemented in channel cards that always robbed a bit for signalling regardless if the service on that channel was switched or P2P. B8ZS cards can be optioned not to rob that bit.
- On a T1, ones are sent by applying voltage to the wire, where a zero is sent by having no voltage on the wire. Sending excessive zeros in a row could cause receiving equipment to lose synchronization with sending equipment, so it is important that such a pattern is not sent.
- The original standard of line coding, Alternate Mark Inversion, specifies that there are three states of the line, no voltage is a zero, positive voltage is a one (or mark), and negative voltage is also a one (or mark).
- Because of the inversion of the voltage for each "mark," or one, sent, the receiving equipment can easily determine the data rate of the line and not lose synchronization.

- B8ZS builds upon this, by using violations of this rule to replace a pattern of eight zeros in a row.

Original signal :							
0	0	0	0	0	0	0	0
B8ZS encoded signal (V = Bipolar violation)							
0	0	0	V	1	0	V	1
Signal Polarity (assuming that the previous mark was negative)							
0	0	0	−	+	0	+	−

- B8ZS is used in the North American hierarchy at the T1 rate. When European E1 was developed much later than T1, it was then common knowledge that forcing 'ones' into a DS0 would corrupt data. E1 uses another method called High Density Bipolar Three (HDB3) code.

3.10.2 High-Density Bipolar 3-Zeros (HDB3) Signal Encoding

The bipolar-AMI encoding is supplemented with the following substitution scheme for '0000' runs.

- Used in Europe and Japan.
- Successive violations are of alternate polarity to avoid dc component.

Polarity of preceding pulse	Number of bipolar pulses (ones) since last substitution	
	odd	even
−	000−	+00+
+	000+	−00−

The HDB3 signal encoding is shown in Fig. 3.33.

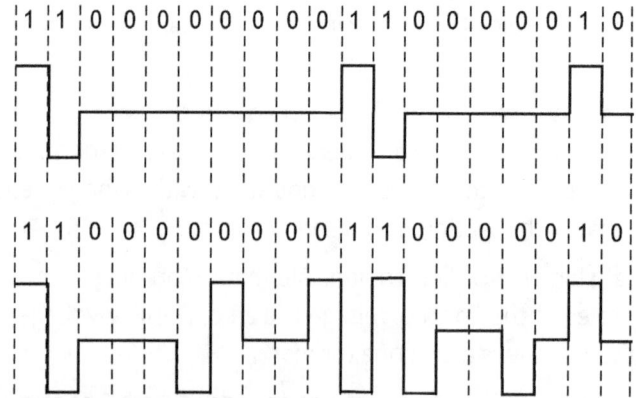

Fig. 3.33 : High-Density Bipolar 3-Zeros (HDB3) Signal Encoding

Based on the AMI code (alternating the levels of voltage when transmitting "1"), this limits the maximum number of consecutive zeros transmitted to three. The basic idea consists of replacing series of four bits that are equal to "0" with a code word "000V" or "B00V", where "V" is a pulse that violates the AMI law of alternate polarity and is rectangular or some other shape. The rules for using "000V" or "B00V" are as follows :

- "B00V" is used when up to the previous pulse, the coded signal presents a DC component that is not null (the number of positive pulses is not compensated for by the number of negative pulses).
- "000V" is used under the same conditions as above when up to the previous pulse the DC component is null.
- The pulse "B" ("B" for balancing), which respects the AMI alternancy rule, has positive or negative polarity, ensuring that two successive V pulses will have different polarity.

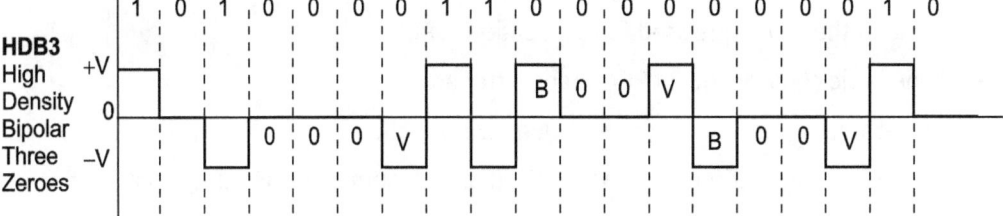

Fig. 3.34 : The HDB3 Coding Waveforms

The HDB3 code has the following characteristics :

- The timing information is preserved by embedding it in the line signal even when long sequences of zeros are transmitted, which allows the clock to be recovered properly on reception.
- The DC component of a signal that is coded in HDB3 is null.

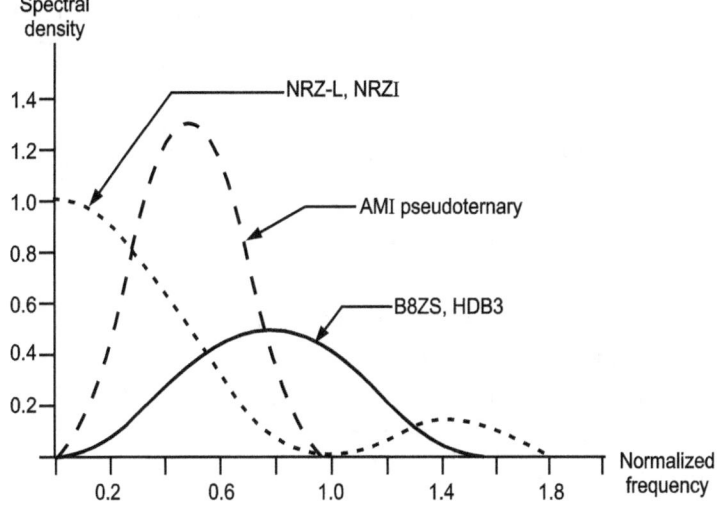

Fig. 3.35 : Spectral Density of Codes

3.11 ANALOG-TO-DIGITAL CONVERSION

- Digital signals has superior quality as compared to analog signals.
- As we have already seen the classification of different conversions i.e. Analog to Analog conversion, Analog to Digital conversion, Digital to Analog conversion and Digital to Digital conversion etc.
- The different techniques to convert analog signals into digital are as follows :
  (a) PCM (b) DM

3.12 PCM (PULSE CODE MODULATION) TRANSMITTER

- The process of converting analog signals into digital data is called as Digitization.
- One of the technique used for digitization is PCM.
- The basic components of PCM transmitter are :
  - Sampling section.
  - Quantizing section.
  - Encoding section.
  - PISO (Parallel Input-Serial Output) Converter.
- The block diagram of PCM transmitter is as shown in Fig. 3.36.

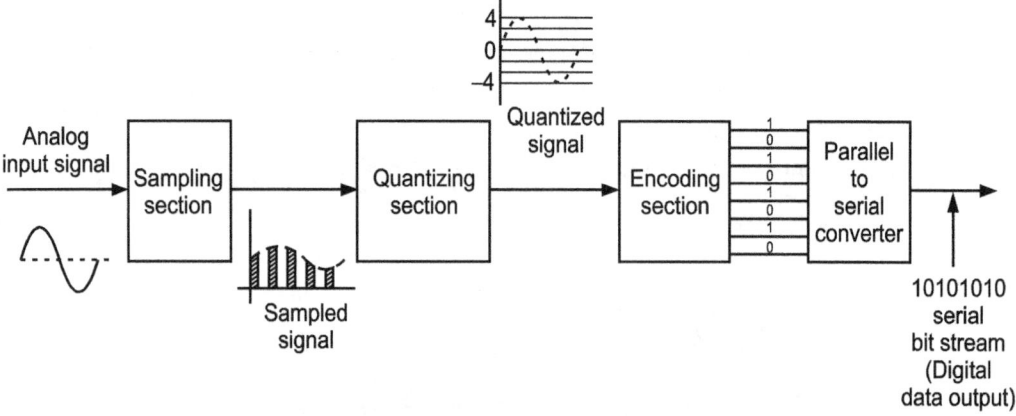

Fig. 3.36 : PCM Transmitter Section

- Following processes are done in PCM transmitter section :
  - Analog signal is sampled using sampling section.
  - Sampled signal is quantized using quantizing section.
  - Quantized signal is converted into parallel bit stream using encoding section.
  - Parallel bit stream converted into serial bit stream using PISO (Parallel Input Serial Output) converter section and finally Digital data is available at output.

3.12.1 Sampling

- The analog input signal is sampled every T_s seconds, where T_s is the sample interval or period.

- Sampling frequency $f_s = \dfrac{1}{T_s}$ Hz.

- There are three types of sampling :
  - (a) Ideal sampling
  - (b) Natural sampling
  - (c) Flat-top sampling.

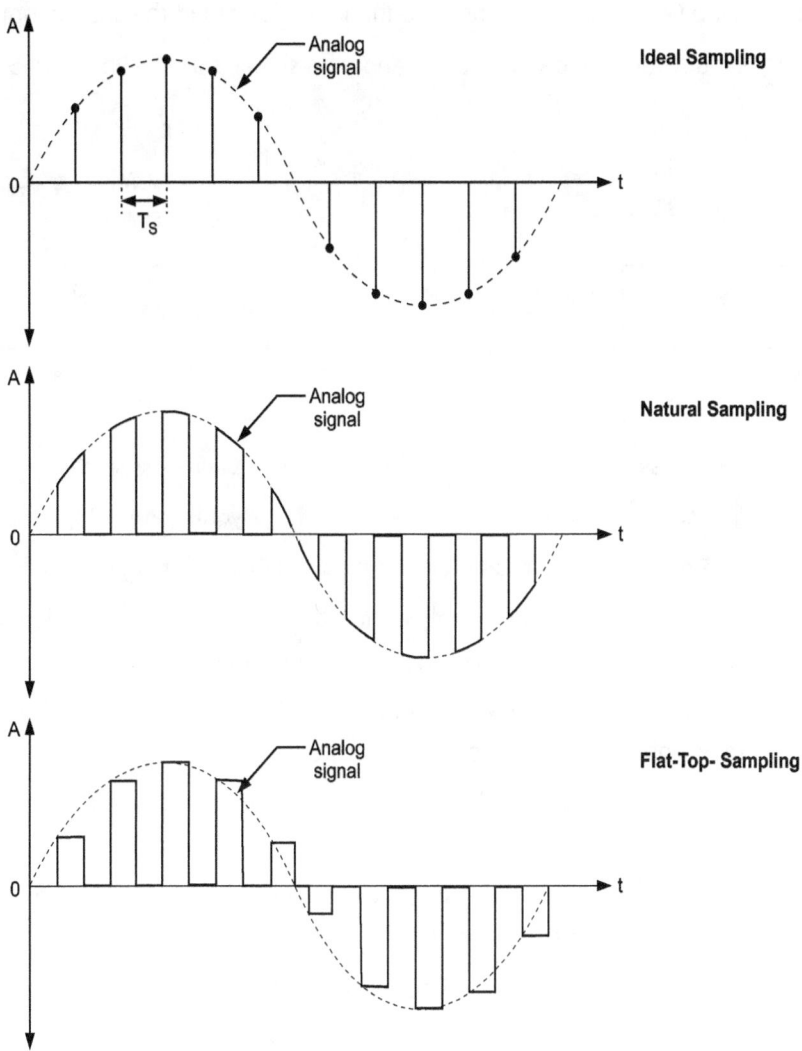

Fig. 3.37 : Sampling Methods for PCM System

- In ideal sampling, the pulses from the analog signal are sampled and is difficult to implement.
- In natural sampling method, high speed switch is tuned on for small period of time when sampling is applied.
- In flat-top-sampling method, sampled level is held using capacitor-based switching circuit. This is widely used sampling method.
- The process of sampling is also called as PAM (Pulse Amplitude Modulation).
- **Nyquist theorem :** To recover original signal with minimum distortion, sampling rate must be ≥ 2 times the highest frequency contained in the analog input signal.
- Thus, Nyquist rate for low-pass and band pass signal is as shown in Fig. 3.38.

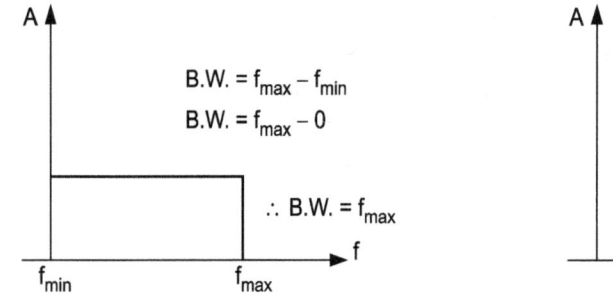
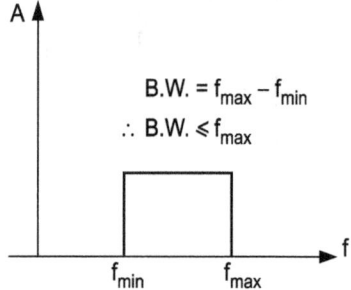

Low-pass signal
Nyquist rate = 2 f_{max}

Band-pass signal
Nyquist rate = 2 f_{max}

Fig. 3.38 : Nyquist Rate for Low-pass and Band-pass Signal

- Thus, we can sample the signal only if the signal is band limited i.e. signal of infinite bandwidth cannot be sampled. Thus, requirement is $f_s \geq 2\, f_{max}$.
- Also, if input sine wave signal is sampled with the sampling frequency $f_s = f$, then recovered signal at receiver end gives distorted output.
- If $f_s = 2f$, then recovered signal at receiver end gives good output (i.e. with minimum distortion).
- If $f_s = 4f$, then recovered signal at receiver end will be exact replica of input signal i.e. it gives best output at receiver end.
- These input signals and recovered signals are as shown in Fig. 3.39.

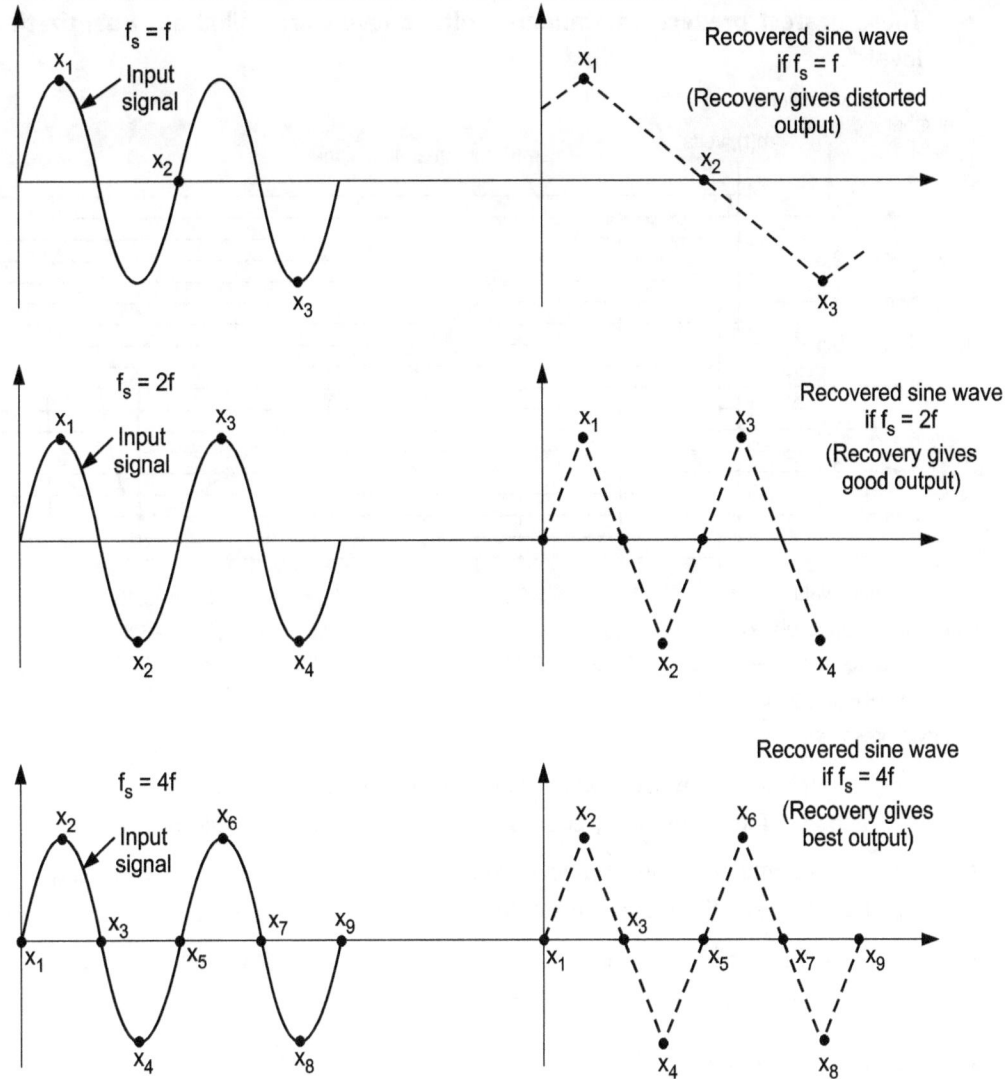

Fig. 3.39 : Different Sine Wave Analog Signals are Sampled at $f_s = f$, $f_s = 2f$ and $f_s = 4f$. Also Recovered Signals at Receiver End are Shown

3.12.2 Quantization

- Quantization is basically a process of approximation. This is also like rounding off procedure i.e., if the sampled voltage level is 3.45 then rounding off value = 3.5. If sampled voltage level is 5.78 then rounding off value = 5.8.
- Thus, quantizer converts the sampled signal level into an approximated quantized voltage level, which is nearest to the predecided standard voltage level.

- **These nearest predecided standard voltage levels are called as "quantization levels".**

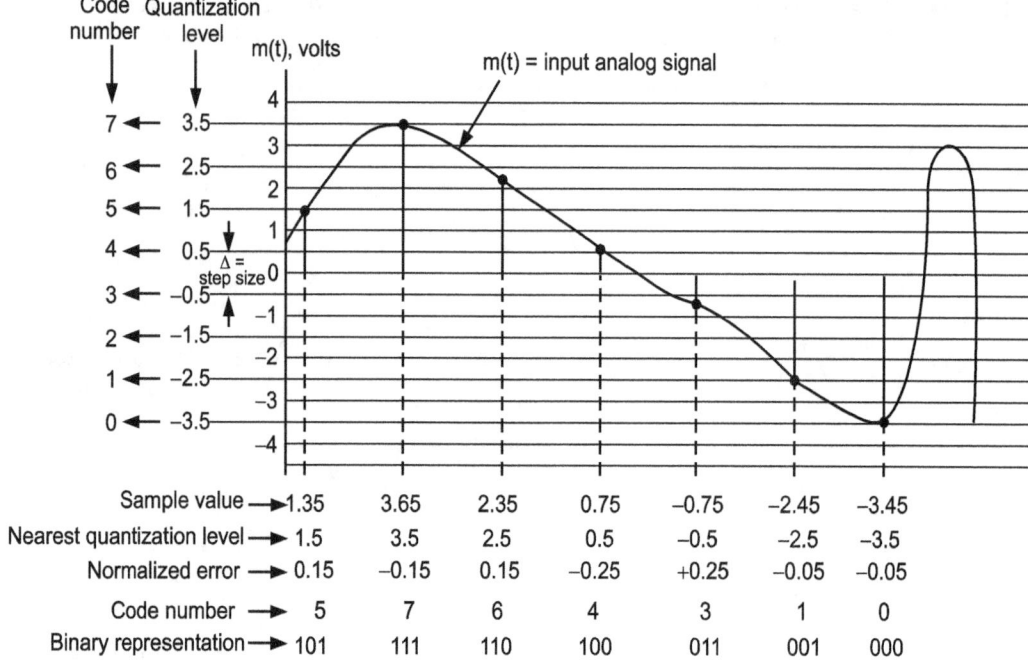

Fig. 3.40 : Sampled value, Quantized level, Normalized error, Code number and Binary code representation for the given signal

- Here we assume that the original analog signal has amplitudes between E_{min} and E_{max}. Here the signal voltage is instantaneous.
- In Fig. 3.40, $E_{max} = 4$ V and $E_{min} = -4$ V. This entire range has been divided into 'L' equal intervals each having equal size = Δ.
- Hence, step size = $\Delta = \dfrac{E_{max} - E_{min}}{L}$

  Here, in Fig. 3.40,   L = 8

  E_{max} = 4V

  E_{min} = −4V

- At the centre of these steps the quantization levels are located as shown.
- The difference between quantized level and sampled value is known as :
  - Normalized error.
  - or Quantization error.
  - or Quantization noise.

- Quantization error should be as small as possible. Thus, maximum quantization error Q_E is always $-\Delta/2 \leq Q_E \leq \Delta/2$.
- Thus, to minimize the quantization error, we must reduce step size.
- Step size can be reduced by increasing the number of quantization levels.
- Thus, if we use 3 bit PCM, then quantization levels will be $2^N = 2^3 = 8 = L =$ Levels.
- If N = 4 bit i.e., 4 bit PCM, then

    Quantization levels $= L = 2^N = 2^4 = 16$ levels.
- To increase quantization levels, number of bits are increased and hence bit rate in PCM increases, hence bandwidth requirement of the channel increases.
- In audio communication, normally we use 8-bit PCM, hence $2^8 = 256$ levels. In video communication, the number of levels are in thousands.
- Thus, if number of levels are more then bandwidth required increases.

    If number of levels are less then quantization error increases.
- Hence, compromise is done always, while selecting number of levels.
- Signal to noise ratio is given as,

$$\boxed{SNR_{dB} = 6.02 \times N_b + 1.76 \text{ dB}}$$

    where, N_b = Number of bits/sample
- There are two types of quantizers :
    (i) Uniform quantizer.
    (ii) Non-uniform quantizer.
- In uniform quantizer the representation levels or quantized levels are uniformly spaced.
- In non-uniform quantizer the representation levels or quantized levels are spaced non-uniformly.
- Also the quantizer characteristics are categorized in two forms as follows :
    (i) Midtread type quantizer.
    (ii) Midrise type quantizer.

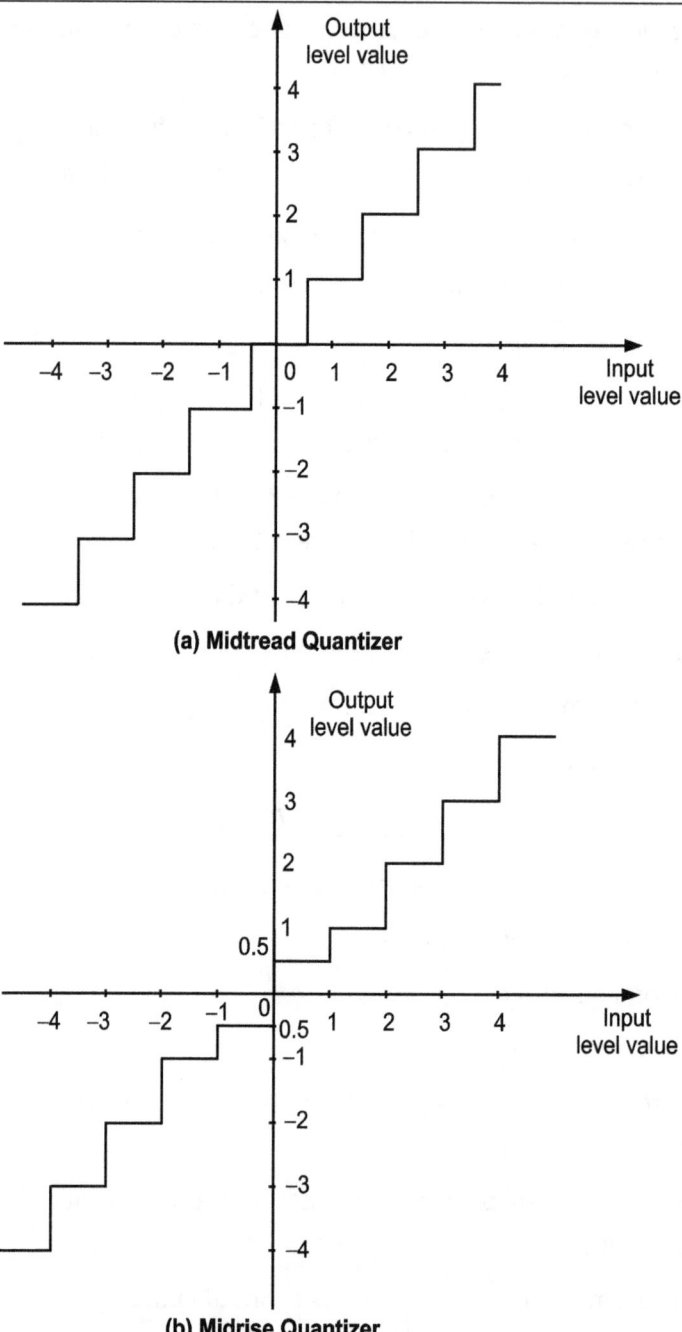

(a) Midtread Quantizer

(b) Midrise Quantizer

Fig. 3.41 : Midtread and Midrise Quantizers

3.12.3 Encoding and Parallel to Serial Converter

- In PCM sampling → quantizing is the previous step which we have seen in detail.
- Each quantized level is given a separate code number. For example, code 0, 1, 2, 3, 4, 5, 6, 7, etc.
- Thus, in encoding process each code number is represented by the digital code or binary code.

Table 3.8 : Code number represented in Binary code

Code Number	Binary Code
0	000
1	001
2	010
3	011
4	100
5	101
6	110
7	111

- Thus, available binary code is in parallel bits form.
- This parallel bit stream is converted into serial bit stream using parallel to serial converter.
- Thus, output bit rate is given by,

$$\text{Bit rate} = \text{Sampling rate} \times \text{Number of bits/sample}$$
$$= f_s \times N_b$$

3.13 PCM RECEIVER

- The PCM transmitter and PCM receiver block diagram is given in Fig. 3.42 and Fig. 3.43 respectively.
- The PCM receiver consists of the following blocks :
  - Regeneration block.
  - Serial to parallel converter.
  - Decoder section.
  - Sample and hold section.
  - Reconstruction LPF section.

- Regeneration block removes the noise from incoming PCM signal and gives noisefree PCM to serial to parallel converter of DAC section.
- Parallel bit streams are given to decoder section and then to sample and hold section, which is used to make and connect samples.
- Thus, decoder + sample and hold section convert the codewords into a pulse that holds the amplitude until the next pulse.

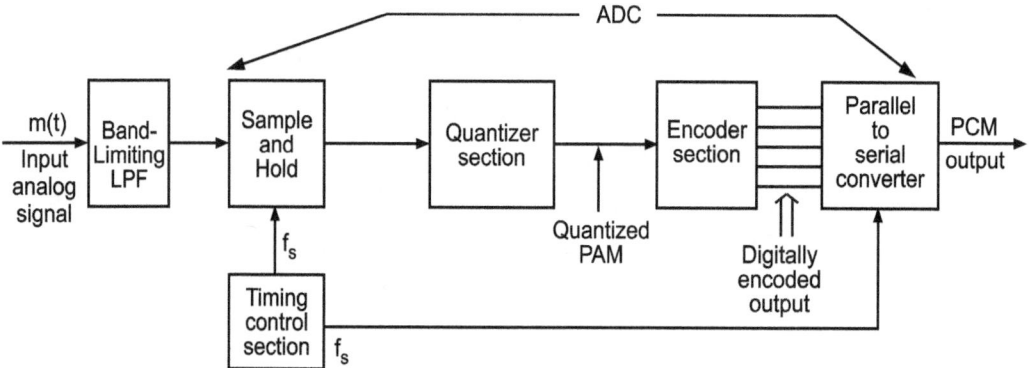

Fig. 3.42 : PCM Transmitter (Generalized Block Diagram)

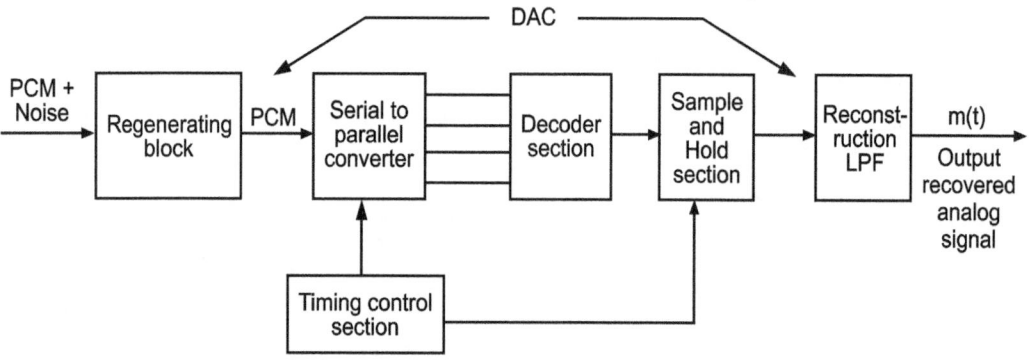

Fig. 3.43 : PCM Receiver (Generalized Block Diagram)

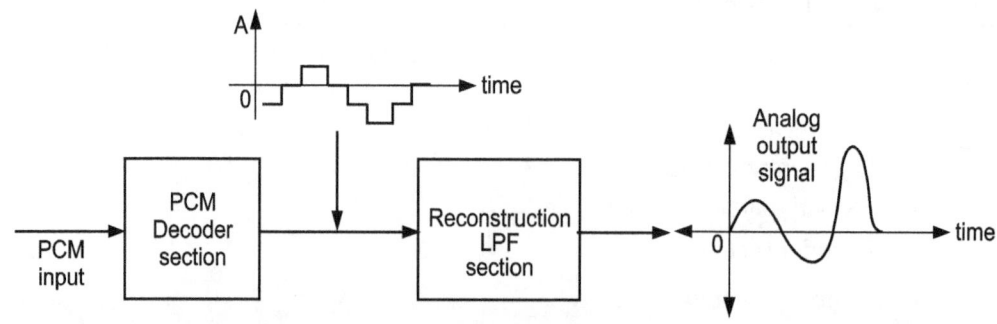

Fig. 3.44 : Typical Staircase Waveform converted into Smooth Analog Output Signal

- Finally, after the staircase signal is completed, it is passed through a LPF section to smooth the staircase signal into a required original analog signal.
- The reconstruction filter has cut-off frequency equal to ($\cong$) signal frequency sent by transmitter.
- **PCM Bandwidth** is given by,

$$\boxed{B_{min} = N_b \times B_{analog}}$$

- Also **Maximum Data Rate of a channel** is given by,

$$\boxed{D_{R_{max}} = 2 \times B \times \log_2(L)} \text{ in bits/sec}$$

where, $D_{R_{max}}$ = Maximum data rate of channel

B = Signal bandwidth

L = Number of levels

This is stated by Nyquist theorem for data rate calculation.

- Also **Minimum Required Bandwidth** is given by,

$$\boxed{B_{min} = \frac{D_R}{2 \times \log_2(L)}} \text{ in Hz}$$

3.14 DELTA MODULATION

- The basic disadvantage of the PCM system is complexity. Transmitter as well as Receiver has complex processing steps in PCM system. Another A to D conversion techniques are :
  - DM (Delta Modulation).
  - ADM (Adaptive Delta Modulation).
- In PCM, every sampled value is quantized and every quantized level gives you binary bit stream output whereas, in DM, instead of code words or bit stream, bits are sent one after the another.
- The **DM modulator** block diagram is as shown in Fig. 3.45.

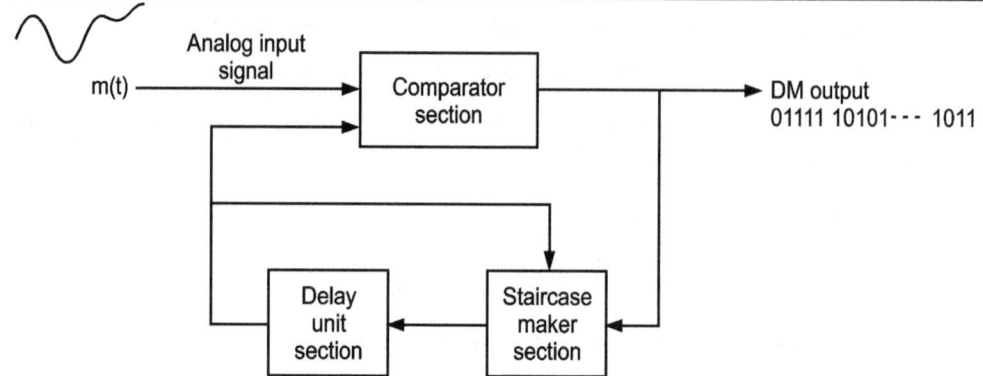

Fig. 3.45 : DM Modulator Block Diagram

- The **DM Demodulator** block diagram is as shown in Fig. 3.46.

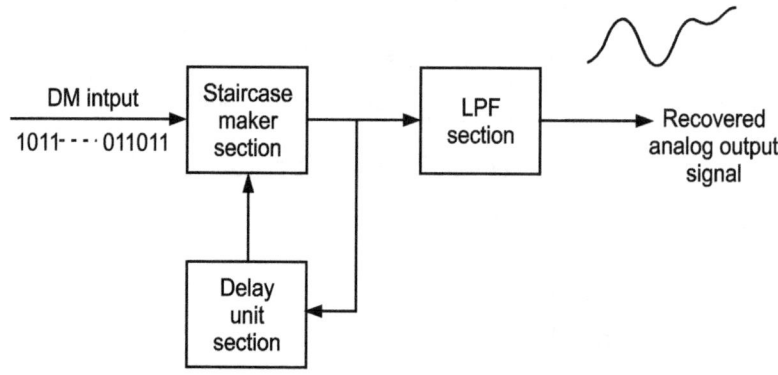

Fig. 3.46 : DM Demodulator Block Diagram

- In delta modulation process, it checks and records the small negative and positive changes known as 'δ'.
- Input signal m(t) is approximated to step signal by the delta modulator system, represented as D(t).
- This step size is always fixed. The negative changes are $-\delta$ and +ve changes are known as 'δ'.
- The difference between m(t) and D(t) is positive then, approximate or D(t) signal is increased by one step i.e., 'δ' and thus, '1' is transmitted.
- The difference between m(t) and D(t) is negative then, approximate or D(t) signal is decreased by one step i.e. 'δ' and thus '0' is transmitted.

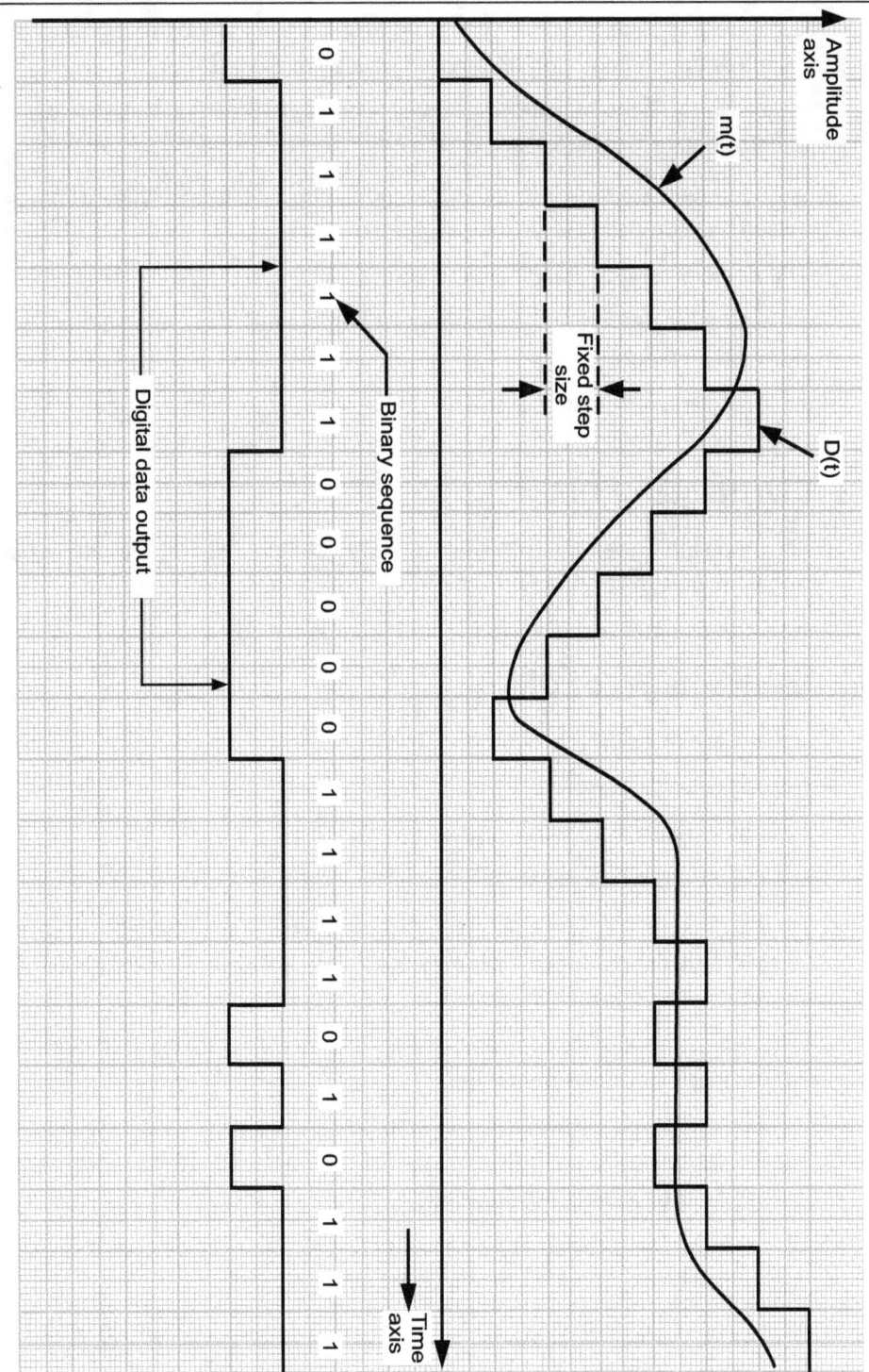

Fig. 3.47 : DM (Delta Modulation), Analog Input and Digital Output Waveform

- Thus, in delta modulation, for every sample, only one binary bit i.e. either '1' or '0' is transmitted depending upon difference between m(t) and D(t).
- In other words, if the amplitude of the analog signal is larger, then the next bit in the digital data is '1', otherwise it is '0'.
- Also, delay unit section is required to hold the staircase function for a period between two comparisons we have discussed.
- In DM demodulator, digital data bit stream is applied to staircase maker section.
- Staircase maker section and Delay unit section creates the analog signal, which is not smooth in nature.
- Thus, final required analog signal which is smooth in nature, is available at the output of low-pass-filter section.

3.14.1 Advantages of DM

- Delta modulator gives only one bit for every sample. Hence, bit rate as well as channel bandwidth requirement is less.
- Simplest transmitter and receiver circuitry reduces the cost.

3.14.2 Disadvantages of DM

- There are two distortions occurring in DM.
    - Slope overload distortion.
    - Granular noise distortion (Hunting effect).
- These distortions are as shown in Fig. 3.48.
- If the rise rate of input signal m(t) is high, then staircase signal can not approximate it or predict it because step size 'δ' is fixed and small for staircase signal D(t) to follow the analog signal m(t).
- Due to which there is large error between m(t) and D(t) signal. This large error is known as **slope overload distortion.**
- To reduce this **slope overload error**, step size should be increased when slope or rising rate of analog signal m(t) is high. This can be achieved with new technique known as **Adaptive Delta Modulation.**
- Thus, in ADM (Adaptive Delta Modulation), the value of step size 'δ' changes according to the amplitude of the input analog signal m(t).
- If analog input signal m(t) is flat in nature and step size of D(t) is having high 'δ' (step size), then staircase signal D(t) keeps on oscillating by $\pm \delta$ around the signal. This difference or error between m(t) and D(t) is known as **granular noise** and this effect of oscillating by $\pm \delta$ around the signal is known as **hunting effect.**

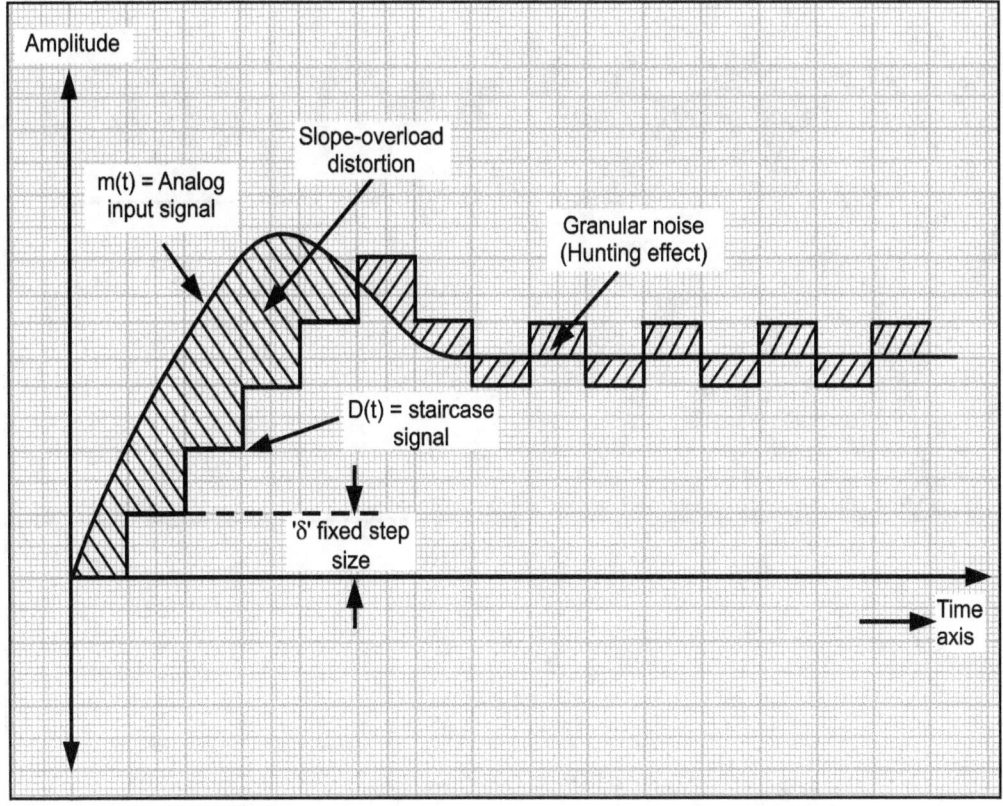

Fig. 3.48 : Slope Overload and Granular Noise Distortions in DM

- To reduce the granular noise, ADM (Adaptive Delta Modulation) technique is used, which reduces step size 'δ' when signal m(t) becomes flat in nature.
- Finally, ADM technique uses variable step size to overcome slope-overload noise and granular noise.
- The waveform of ADM technique to reduce slope-overload noise and granular noise is as shown in Fig. 3.49.
- Thus, following are the advantages of ADM :
  - SNR is better than DM.
  - Bandwidth utilization is better than DM.
  - Dynamic range is better than DM.

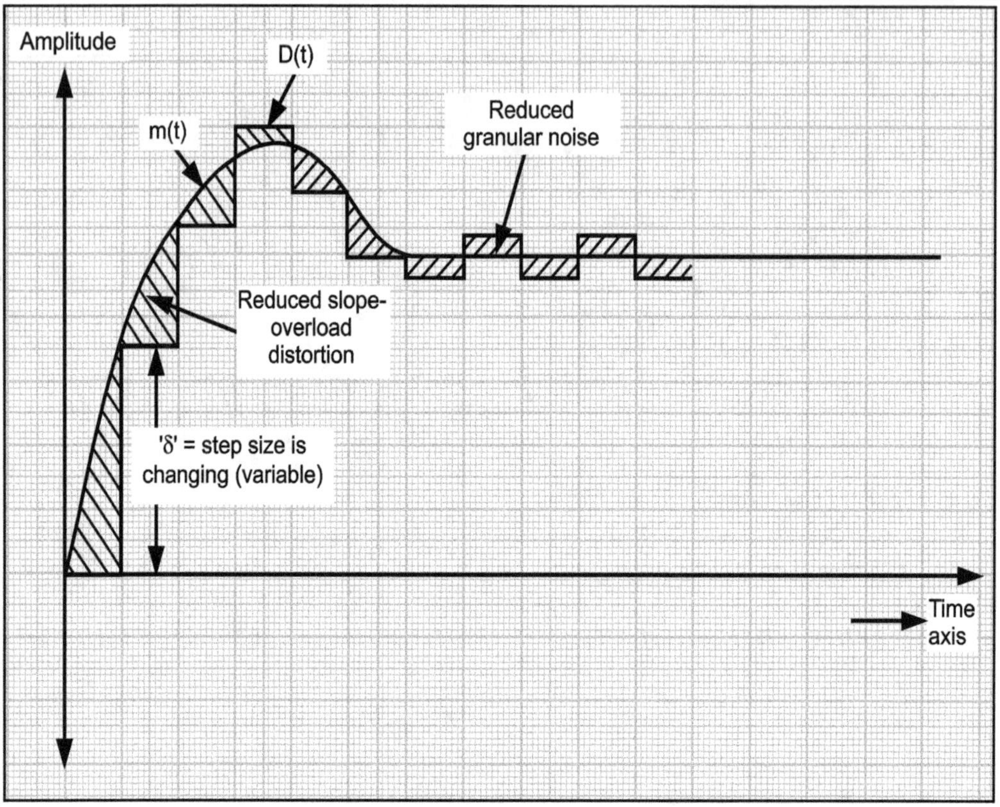

Fig. 3.49 : ADM (Reduced Slope-Overload Noise and Granular Noise)

3.15 TRANSMISSION MODES

- Transmission modes are classified as :

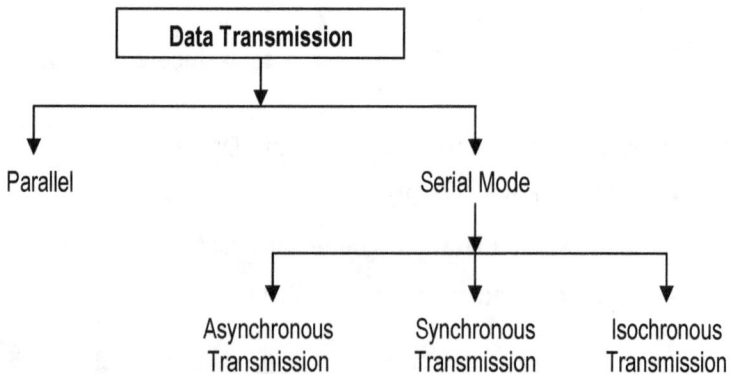

- **Parallel mode of transmission :** In parallel mode, a group of 'n' bits are formed and simultaneously send from one device to other. This is called as parallel data transmission.

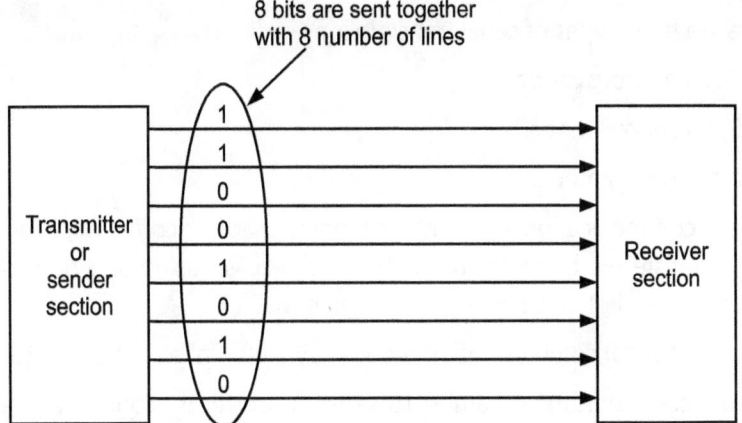

Fig. 3.50 : Parallel Transmission Mode

- 'n' wires are used to send 'n' number of bits at a time.
- Thus, on 'n' wires, 'n' bits are ready and with one clock transition 'n' bits will be transferred from transmitter and will be received by receiver.
- In parallel transmission mode 'n' wires or here 8 wires are bundled in a cable with connector at each end.

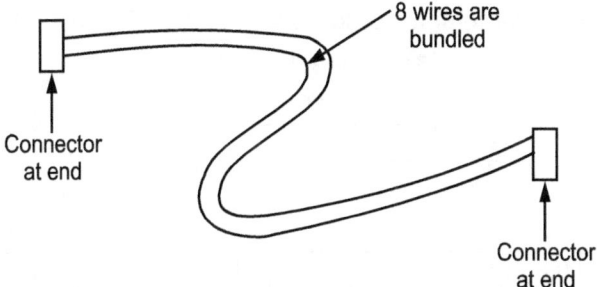

Fig. 3.51 : Wires are Bundled in Parallel Transmission

- Advantages of parallel transmission mode :
  - Speed is high.
  - Simple method.
- Disadvantages of parallel transmission mode :
  - Cost increases because of 'n' number of wires.
  - Complexity increases if 'n' increases and maintenance becomes difficult.

- Due to expensive and complex property, it is used for small distance communication.
- **Serial mode of transmission :**

  There are three types of serial transmission :
  - Asynchronous mode.
  - Synchronous mode.
  - Isochronous mode.
- In serial communication, only one channel is used for communication. Thus, digital data is transferred between transmitter and receiver using only one communication channel instead of 'n' channels in parallel mode.
- The cost of serial communication reduces by factor 'n' as compared to parallel one.
- In serial communication, parallel to serial converter is required at transmitter end and serial to parallel converter is required at receiver end.

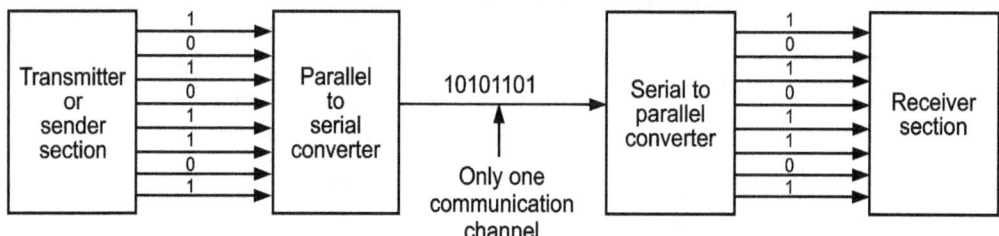

Fig. 3.52 : Serial Mode of Transmission

- Asynchronous serial communication is as shown in Fig. 3.53.

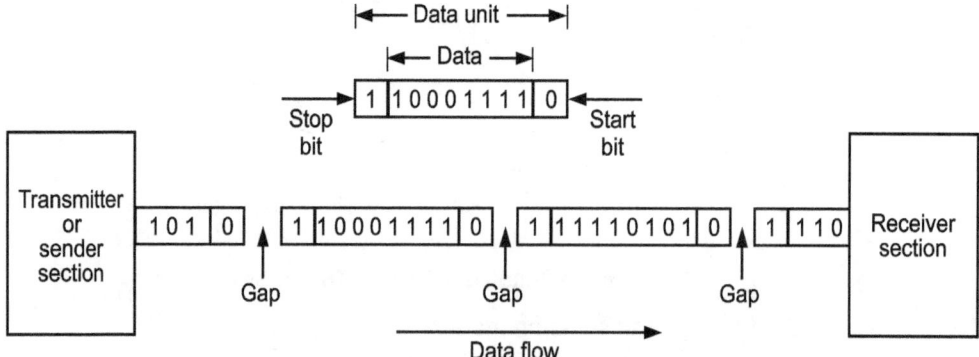

Fig. 3.53 : Asynchronous Serial Communication

- Typical synchronous serial communication is as shown in Fig. 3.54.

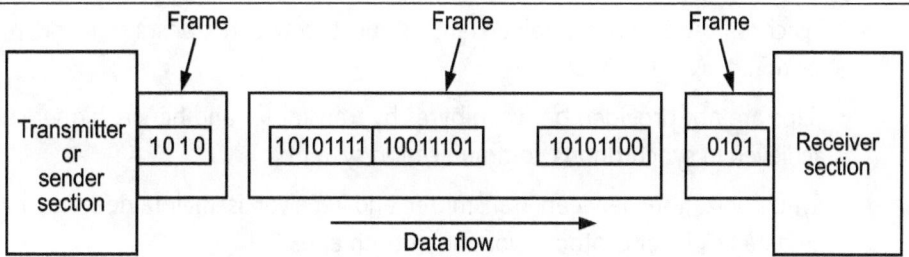

Fig. 3.54 : Synchronous Serial Communication

- In asynchronous communication system :
    - Importance is not given to timing of signal.
    - Grouping of bit stream is done i.e. 1 byte = 8 bits group.
    - Extra start bit is added at the beginning of each byte for synchronization.
    - Extra stop bit is added at the end of each byte for synchronization.
    - Start bit alerts receiver that the byte has arrived.
    - Stop bit informs receiver that the byte has finished.
    - Varying gap is maintained between two bytes.
    - Gap is either stream of additional stop bits or idle channel.
    - Here the asynchronous effect is present at byte level but the bits are fully synchronized.
    - Presence of gaps between two bytes reduces speed of communication.
    - Keyboard to computer CPU is an example of asynchronous communication.

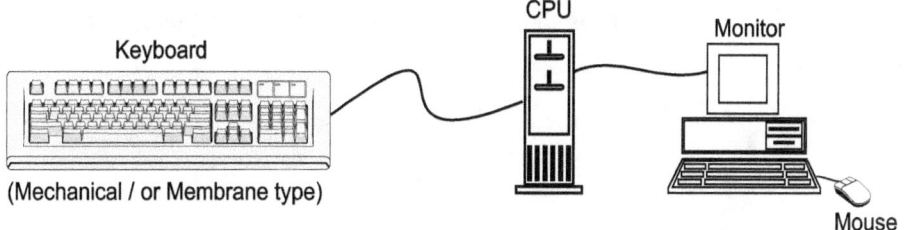

Fig. 3.55 : Example of Asynchronous Communication

- In synchronous communication system :
    - Multiple bytes are combined into longer frames.
    - Data bits are transmitted as an unbroken stream of '1' and '0'.
    - Receiver performs the separation of bit stream, converting into bytes for decoding purpose.
    - Start and stop bits are not added in synchronous communication.

- Synchronization is maintained and is must between transmitter and receiver section.
- Gaps are not provided between bytes by transmitter and hence, higher speed is achieved in synchronous communication system.
- Synchronization between transmitter and receiver is maintained and handled by data link layer protocol working at both ends.
- Gaps are absent between individual bits, but there can be gaps between two frames.
- This synchronous communication system fails when uneven delays between frames are not acceptable.
- For example, in TV broadcast of PAL system, 25 frames of each picture or 25 images/second are required to be transmitted and viewed at the same rate. Then and then only picture can be displayed without loss or distortion in TV receiver display. This is not possible because of uneven gaps present between different frames.
- In isochronous communication system,
    - It is used in real time audio, video and multimedia applications.
    - Data arrival at fixed rate is guaranteed and delays between frames are absent.

SOLVED EXAMPLES

Example 3.1 :

A signal is carrying data in which one data element is encoded as one signal element (r_{ds} = 1). If the bit rate is 200 kbps, what is the average value of the baud rate if C = 0.5 ?

Solution :

$r_{ds} = 1$

$N = 2,00,000 \text{ bps} = 200 \text{ kbps} = 200 \times 10^3$

$C = 0.5$

$S = ?$

$\therefore \quad S = C \times N \times \dfrac{1}{r_{ds}}$

$= 0.5 \times 200 \times 10^3 \times \dfrac{1}{1}$

$= 100 \times 10^3 \text{ baud}$

$\boxed{S = 100 \text{ kbaud}}$

DATA COMMUNICATION (S.E. SEM. III SU – COMPUTER) DIGITAL TRANSMISSION SYSTEM

Example 3.2 :

In a digital transmission, the receiver clock is 0.2% faster than the sender clock. How many extra bits per second does the receiver receive if the data rate is 2 kbps ? How many if the data rate is 2 Mbps ?

Solution :

$$C_1 = 2 \text{ kbps} = 2000 \text{ bps}$$
$$C_2 = 2 \text{ Mbps} = 20{,}00{,}000 \text{ bps}$$

(a)
$$100 - 0.2\%$$
$$2000 - ?$$

$$\therefore \quad \frac{2000 \times 0.2}{100} = 4 \text{ bits extra received}$$

(b)
$$100 - 0.2$$
$$20{,}00{,}000 - ?$$

$$\therefore \quad \frac{20{,}00{,}000 \times 0.2}{100} = 4000 \text{ bits extra received}$$

∴ Hence for 200 kbps data rate = 2,00,000 + 4 = 200004 bits received.

Hence for 2 Mbps data rate = 20,00,000 + 4,000 = 2004000 bits received.

Example 3.3 :

A system is using NRZ-I to transfer 2 Mbps data. What are the average signal rate and minimum B.W. ?

Solution :

$$\text{Average signal rate } S = \frac{N}{2} = \frac{2 \times 10^6}{2} = 1 \text{ Mbaud.}$$

$$B_{min} = S = 1 \text{ MHz.}$$

Example 3.4 :

Calculate the SNR_{dB} for the following system :

    (a) PCM with 8 levels
    (b) PCM with 32 levels
    (c) PCM with 64 levels

Solution :

$$SNR_{dB} = 6.02 \cdot N_b + 1.76 \text{ dB}$$

(a) $\quad SNR_{dB} = 6.02 \times 8 + 1.76 = 49.92 \text{ dB}$

(b) $\quad SNR_{dB} = 6.02 \times 32 + 1.76 = 194.4 \text{ dB}$

(c) $\quad SNR_{dB} = 6.02 \times 64 + 1.76 = 387.04 \text{ dB}$

DATA COMMUNICATION (S.E. SEM. III SU – COMPUTER)   DIGITAL TRANSMISSION SYSTEM

Example 3.5 :

Calculate the minimum number of bits per sample for the PSTN line having following different SNR_{dB}.

   (a)   PSTN line with SNR_{dB} = 35 dB
   (b)   PSTN line with SNR_{dB} = 38 dB
   (c)   PSTN line with SNR_{dB} = 48 dB

Solution :

$$SNR_{dB} = 6.02 \cdot N_b + 1.76 \text{ dB}$$

(a) $35 = 6.02 \times N_b + 1.76$

$$\boxed{N_b = 5.52 \text{ i.e. use 6 bits}}$$

(b) $38 = 6.02 \times N_b + 1.76$

$$\boxed{N_b = 6.019 = \text{use 7 bits}}$$

(c) $48 = 6.02 \times N_b + 1.76$

$$\boxed{N_b = 7.68 = \text{use 8 bits}}$$

Example 3.6 :

Calculate the sampling rate and bit rate for the 8 bit PCM system, if voice signal to be sampled is of 4 kHz.

Solution :

∴   Sampling rate = 2 × 4 kHz = 8000 samples/sec
∴   Bit rate = Sampling rate × 8 bits/sample
              = 8000 × 8
       Bit rate = 64000 bps
∴ $\boxed{\text{Bit rate} = 64 \text{ kbps}}$

Example 3.7 :

Calculate the minimum B.W. of 8 bit PCM system, if we have audio input frequency of 3800 Hz.

Solution :

         B.W. = ?
         N_b = 8
         B_{analog} = 3800 Hz
∴ $BW_{minimum} = N_b \times B_{analog}$
∴ $\boxed{BW_{min} = 8 \times 3800 = 30400 \text{ Hz}}$

EXERCISES

1. Classify the different conversion systems for signal and data.
2. Explain the applications of line codes.
3. How to eliminate DC components in line coding ?
4. List the different line coding format selection criteria.
5. What is the difference between data element and signal element.
6. What is the concept of data element/signal element ratio ?
7. Explain the term signalling rate in communication.
8. Explain the following terms in detail :
   (a) Baseline wandering.
   (b) DC component.
   (c) Self synchronization.
9. Classify the different line coding techniques.
10. Write short notes on :
    (a) Unipolar (NRZ) line code
    (b) Polar line codes (NRZ, RZ and Biphase)
    (c) Bipolar (AMI and Pseudoternary) code
    (d) Multilevel code (2B/1Q, 8B/6T and 4D-PAM5)
    (e) Multitransition line codes.
11. Compare NRZ-L Vs. NRZ-I.
12. Compare Bipolar method Vs. Polar NRZ.
13. Explain 2B1Q coding rules.
14. Write short notes on following :
    (a) Block coding
    (b) 4B/5B block coding
    (c) 8B/10B block coding.
15. What are the different technologies that use 8B/10B coding ?
16. What is running disparity ? What are the rules for running disparity ?

17. What is scrambling ? Explain the following scrambling techniques in detail :
    (a) B8ZS
    (b) HDB3
18. Draw and explain the block diagram of PCM transmitter and receiver.
19. Write short notes on following :
    (a) Sampling
    (b) Quantizing
20. Draw and explain block diagram of DM transmitter and DM receiver.
21. What are the different advantages and disadvantages of DM system ?
22. What is the advantage of variable step size in adaptive DM ? Explain with typical waveform.
23. Write short notes on :
    (a) Parallel mode of transmission
    (b) Serial mode of transmission
24. What are the different types of serial communication ? Explain each technique in detail.

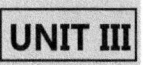

Chapter 4
TRANSMISSION MEDIA

OBJECTIVES

After reading this chapter you will understand :

- Important factors in determining Media, Classification of Transmission Media.
- Guided Media like Twisted Pair Cable (UTP & STP), Coaxial Cable (Thin and Thick Ethernet Cable) and Fiber Optic Cable.
- Cat 1 to Cat 7 Cables detail, Advantages and Disadvantages of UTP Cable.
- Coaxial Cable Advantages and Disadvantages.
- Fiber Optic Cable Construction and Cross-section Study.
- Fiber Optic Classification based on Material and Principle of Operation.
- Single Mode, Multimode and Graded Index Fiber, Advantages and Disadvantages of Fiber Optic Cable.
- Coaxial Cable Vs. Fiber Optic Cable.
- Unguided Media like Radio, Microwave and Infrared System.
- Electromagnetic Spectrum in detail.
- Radio Transmission System in detail.
- Microwave Transmission System, Terrestrial and Satellite Microwave Transmission System.
- Infrared Transmission and Applications of IR System.

4.1 PHYSICAL MEDIA

- In computers, media refers to whatever medium is used to communicate data.
- Media is usually the copper or fiber optic glass cables but data can also be sent through the air via electromagnetic frequencies such as infrared, micro waves or radio waves.
- Media is important because it is often half the cost of the network.
- **Important factors in determining media include :**
    - Required speed.

- Distance.
- Ease of installation and maintenance access.
- Technical expertise required to install and utilize.
- Resistance to internal EMI (Electromagnetic Interference) inside the cable, especially the cross talk of parallel wires.
- Resistance to external EMI outside the cable.
- Resistance to other environmental hazards such as workers carelessly drilling into walls, fire and the weather.
- *Bandwidth* : The range of frequencies that the cable can accommodate. LANs generally carry data rates of 1 to 100 megabits per second and require moderately high bandwidth.
- *Attenuation* characteristics : Attenuation describes how cables reduce the strength of a signal with distance. Resistance is one factor that contributes to signal attenuation.
- Cost.

- When data is sent across the network it is converted into electrical signals.
- These signals are generated as electromagnetic waves (analog signaling) or as a sequence of voltage pulses (digital signaling).
- To be sent from one location to another, a signal must travel along a physical path.
- The physical path that is used to carry a signal between a signal transmitter and a signal receiver is called the **transmission medium**.
- **There are two types of transmission media : guided and unguided.**

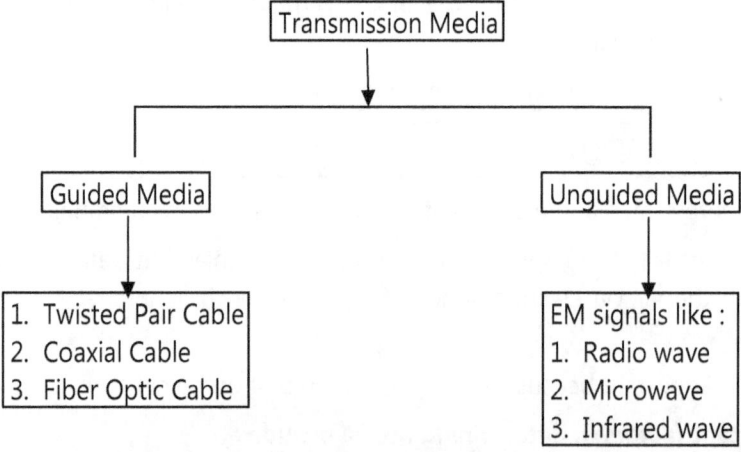

Fig. 4.1 : Classification of Transmission Media

4.2 GUIDED MEDIA

- Guided media are manufactured so that signals will be confined to a narrow path and will behave predictably.
- The three most commonly used types of guided media are twisted-pair wiring, coaxial cable, and optical fiber cable.
- Each type is suited to specific applications and network topologies.

4.2.1 Unshielded Twisted Pair (UTP) Cable and Shielded Twisted Pair (STP) Cable

Unshielded Twisted Pair (UTP) Cable :

- Twisted pair has become the most popular network cabling media today.
- Twisted pair cabling is used in a star or star tree topology for Ethernet networks.
- Maximum number of network devices is 1,024, with a maximum cable length of 100 meters for individual devices and a total distance of 500 meters of cabling between the farthest two devices, including links between data closets.
- The signal from a network hub can be repeated three times, giving you a maximum of four data closets.
- The distance between closets can be extended by switching to a star bus topology and using fiber optic cable for links between closets.
- **Twisted pair copper cable** is perhaps the oldest and certainly still the most commonly used transmission medium.
- A twisted pair consists of two insulated copper cables, typically about 1 mm in diameter, twisted together to reduce electrical interference between adjacent pairs of wires (two pairs of parallel wires can act as a crude antenna).

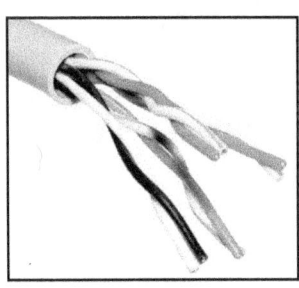

Fig. 4.2 : Unshielded Twisted Pair cable

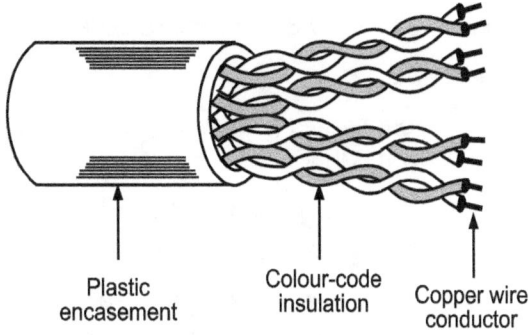

Fig. 4.3 : Four pair UTP cable used in LAN (Local Area Network)

- Twisted pair cable is still used in the public telephone system, specifically in the subscriber loop, the link from a domestic or business telephone subscriber to the local telephone exchange.
- These links are good for several kilometers without amplification, but longer runs need repeaters.
- The local subscriber loop is essentially an analogue transmission medium, but twisted pair cables can also be used for digital transmission.
- The data rate (or *bandwidth*) for twisted pair depends on factors such as the diameter of wire used and the length of the transmission line, but several megabits per second (Mbps) can be achieved over a few kilometers.
- Low cost and ease of installation have kept twisted pair in widespread use both in the telephone system and in Local Area Networks (LANs).
- The type of twisted pair cables used in LANs fall into two main categories.
- **Category 3** twisted pair cable is the type you will normally find connected to your domestic telephone outlet and consists of two insulated wires twisted gently twisted together. Typically, four pairs are grouped together within a plastic sheath which serves both as protection and to keep the eight wires together.
- **Category 5** twisted pairs, introduced in the late eighties, are similar to category 3 twisted pair but with more twists per centimeter and Teflon-based insulation.
- This results in a further reduction in crosstalk and a better quality signal over long distances, which makes them more suitable for high-speed data communication.
- Both types are referred to as *Unshielded Twisted Pair* (UTP). A summary of the twisted pair categories is given below.

Category 1 : Used for traditional telephone voice communication (but not data) - most telephone cable used before 1983 were category 1.

Category 2 : Four twisted pairs - suitable for data rates of up to 4 Mbps.

Category 3 :

- Four twisted pairs with three twists per foot - suitable for data rates of up to 10 Mbps.
- In the beginning of twisted pair technology, some networks were set up utilizing spare pairs on existing phone systems or cabled with Category 3.
- These networks are only capable of 10Base-T (10 megabits per second) data transfer, and most of them set up on spare pairs of existing phone wiring run for slower than that.

- These networks have been obsolete for some time and cannot match the network speeds of today. New Category 3 should only be installed for phone systems.

Category 4 : Supports data transmission of up to 20 Mbps.

Category 5 :
- Four twisted pairs with a higher number of twists per foot than previous categories and Teflon based outer coating.
- Category 5 is generally accepted as the cable to install because of its higher transmission rate and better noise immunity.
- Testing of these cables assumes that only two pairs will be used - one to transmit (T_X) and one to receive (R_X).
- Falling costs in recent years have made category 5 twisted pair a more cost-effective option.
- The predominant type of twisted pair installed in the majority of commercial buildings is unshielded Category 5.
- It is most commonly used for 100 Base T Ethernet networks, giving data transfer rates of 100 megabits per second.
- In addition, the IEEE has approved a network standard for 1000 BASE T Ethernet networks (data transfer of 1,000 megabits per second) which can utilize most existing Category 5 cabling when it has been properly installed and certified.
- In addition to unshielded Category 5, there is also a shielded version, which provides some protection against electromagnetic interference.
- A typical application might be for a heavy manufacturing plant where interference from large electric motors could present a problem.
- For the vast majority of existing offices and smaller industrial plants, unshielded Category 5 is the most commonly found cable.

Category 5e :
- **Enhanced category 5** - more comprehensive testing is carried out on all four pairs to measure the effect of transmitting data, particularly with regard to crosstalk.
- This category is primarily intended for use in Gigabit Ethernet networks.
- Over the last several years, Category 5e has become the replacement for Category 5.

- There are two main types, known as "Little e" and "Big E", capable of 155 and 350-megabit transmission respectively.
- Although there are no network standards to support these speeds, the increased bandwidth does enhance this cable's ability to run gigabit Ethernet.
- With the price drop of Category 5e over the last few years, it has become the most common choice for new network installation.

Category 6:

- A proposed standard for cable having a transmission frequency of 200 MHz, with all components coming from one manufacturer (i.e. no "mixing").
- With the ever increasing speed of networks today, Category 6 is becoming more common in new office installations that demand reliable gigabit network speed.
- It is a viable choice today for a new network installation in a commercial space where the tenants plan to stay for an extended length of time.
- In addition, gigabit switches and network cards are also beginning to drop in price, so the cost of the hardware necessary to set up a true gigabit network is becoming less expensive as well.

Category 7:

A proposed standard for cable having a transmission frequency of 600 MHz using fully shielded cables, i.e. shielding is to be provided for both individual pairs and for the grouped pairs. A new connection type is also proposed.

- The maximum recommended cable run for unshielded twisted pair is 100 meters.
- UTP cables are terminated with RJ45 connectors, similar in design to the connectors used to connect telephones into a wall socket outlet (RJ11).
- Twisted pair cables are most commonly used to connect workstations to hubs or MAUs.
- The standard connector for unshielded twisted pair cabling is RJ-45 connector.
- This is a plastic connector that looks like a large telephone-style connector.
- A slot allows the RJ-45 to be inserted only one way.
- RJ stands for Registered Jack, implying that the connector follows a standard borrowed from the telephone industry.
- This standard designates which wire goes with each pin inside the connector.

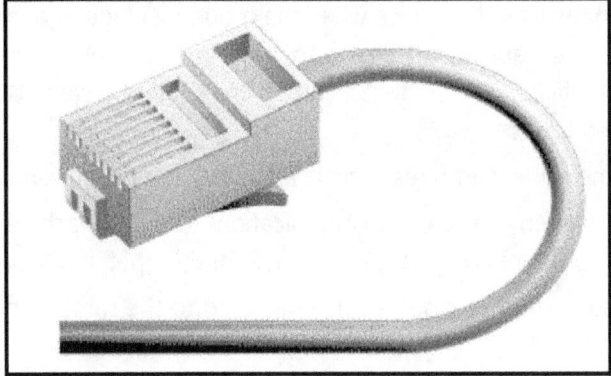

Fig. 4.4 : RJ-45 Connector and UTP Cable

Shielded Twisted Pair Cable :

- *Shielded Twisted Pair* (STP) cable was introduced in the 1980s by IBM as the recommended medium for their Token Ring network technology, and has a characteristic impedance of 150 ohms.

- Each cable consists of two pairs, with each pair individually foil shielded, and an overall braided shield.

- Because STP was specified by IBM, many users thought that it was required for reliable data transfer.

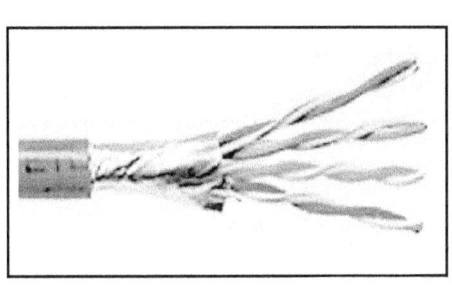   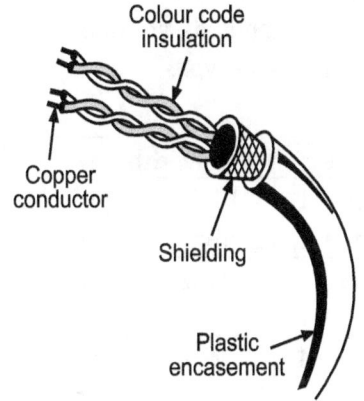

Fig. 4.5 : Shielded Twisted Pair Cable   Fig. 4.6 : Typical two pair Shielded Twisted Pair Cable (STP Cable)

4. Since this is not in fact the case its popularity has declined due to :
   - The high cost of the cable and connectors (much more complex than UTP).
   - The increased bulk of cable and connectors compared to UTP.
   - The increased time required for installation compared to UTP.

- **Ground loops** - These arise when the ground voltage at each end of a cable run is different, causing a current to flow in the cable's shield and creating a magnetic field, which induces, current (noise) in the same cable the shielding is designed to protect.
- The same cable length restrictions apply (100 meters maximum) as for UTP.
- STP is limited for data communication to IBM machines and Token Ring networks - there is no standard for STP for Ethernet, ISDN or analog telephones.
- Shielded twisted pair is now manufactured to the same standard as Unshielded Twisted Pair.

Thus following points summarize the features of STP cable :
- Speed and throughput—10 to 100 Mbps
- Average cost per node—Moderately expensive
- Media and connector size—Medium to large
- Maximum cable length—100 m (short)

When comparing UTP and STP, keep the following points in mind :
- The speed of both types of cable is usually satisfactory for local-area distances.
- These are the least-expensive media for data communication. UTP is less expensive than STP.
- Because most buildings are already wired with UTP, many transmission standards are adapted to use it, to avoid costly rewiring with an alternative cable type.

Table 4.1 : Categories of Unshielded Twisted Pair

Type	Bandwidth	Use
Category 1	< 1 MHz	Voice Only (Telephone Wire).
Category 2	1 MHz	Data to 4 Mbps (Local Talk) and Telephone, T_1 lines etc.
Category 3	16 MHz	Data to 10 Mbps (Ethernet), Telephone, 10Base-T, Token Ring, LAN applications.
Category 4	20 MHz	Data to 20 Mbps (16 Mbps Token Ring), 10Base-T, LAN application.
Category 5	100 MHz	Data to 100 Mbps (Fast Ethernet), 10Base-T, 100Base-T, LAN applications.
Category 5e	350 MHz	125 Mbps, Data Networks.
Category 6	550 MHz	Proposed standard for cable having a data rate of 200 Mbps, LAN applications.
Category 7	600 MHz	Proposed standard for cable having a data rate of 600 Mbps using fully shielded cables, LAN applications.

Some advantages of twisted pair wiring are as follows :
- Reasonable cost.
- High speed.
- Easy to add additional network devices.
- Supports large number of network devices.
- Telephone cable standards are mature and well established. Materials are plentiful, and a wide variety of cable installers are familiar with the installation requirements.
- It may be possible to use in-place telephone wiring if it is of sufficiently high quality.
- UTP represents the lowest cost cabling. The cost for STP is higher and is comparable to the cost of coaxial cable.

Some disadvantages of twisted pair are as follows :
- High attenuation (signal loss) limits individual runs to 100 meters.
- Susceptible to EMI/RFI (except shielded type).
- STP can be expensive and difficult to work with.
- Compared to fiber optic cable, all Twisted Pair cable is more sensitive to EMI. UTP especially may be unsuitable for use in high-EMI environments.
- Twisted Pair cables are regarded as being less suitable for high-speed transmissions than coaxial cable or fiber optic. Technology advances, however, are pushing upward the data rates possible with Twisted Pair. Cable segment lengths are also more limited with Twisted Pair.

4.2.2 Coaxial Cable

- A coaxial cable consists of a central copper wire core, which is surrounded by an insulating material.
- The insulator is surrounded by braided metal shielding which helps to absorb external electronic signals (noise) and prevents it from interfering with the data signal.
- A plastic sheath protects the outer conductor. A durable plastic or Teflon jacket coats the cable to prevent damage. Fig. 4.7 diagram illustrates the basic construction of a coaxial cable.

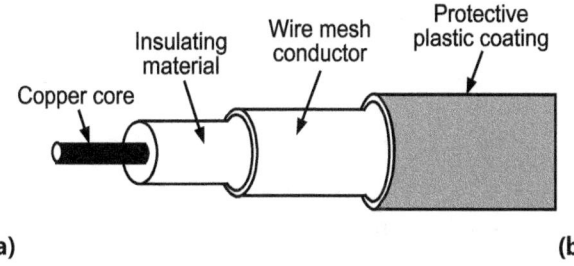

(a)   (b)

Fig. 4.7 : Coaxial cable construction

- The construction and shielding of coaxial cable provides a high degree of immunity to noise, and coaxial cable can be used over longer distances (upto 500 meters) than twisted pair cable.
- Coaxial cable runs are used to provide the network backbone cable segments in networks having a **bus topology**, and require a terminating resistor at each end of the cable in order to prevent interference due to signal reflection.
- Coaxial cable has many desirable characteristics. It is highly resistant to EMI and can support high *bandwidths*.
- Some types of coaxial cable have heavy shields and center conductors to enhance these characteristics and to extend the distances, so that signals can be transmitted reliably.
- A wide variety of coaxial cable cable is available. You must use cable that exactly matches the requirements of a particular type of network.
- Coaxial cable cables vary in a measurement known as the *impedance* (measured in a unit called the ohm), which is an indication of the cable's resistance to current flow.
- The specifications of a given cabling standard indicate the required impedance of the cable.
- Two types of coaxial cable can be used in computer networks :
    - **Thinnet or Cheapernet (also known as Baseband Coax - RG-58)**
    - **Thicknet**

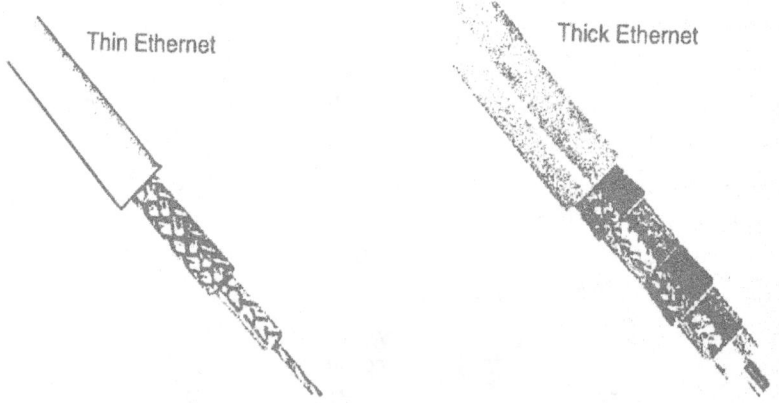

Fig. 4.8 : Thin Ethernet and Thick Ethernet

- Thinnet (10Base2) is so called because of the thin, inexpensive coaxial cabling it uses, and is fairly flexible, being 0.25 inches in diameter.

- 13.The IEEE specification refers to this type of cable as 10Base2, referring to its main specifications of 10 Mbps data rate, baseband transmission type, and 185 (nearly 200) meter maximum segment length.
- The cable between computers must be at least 0.5 meters (20 inches) long.
- An IEEE standard for Thinnet doesn't allow a drop cable to be used from the bus T-connector to a workstation.
- Instead, the T-connector fits directly onto the network adapter card using a BNC connector.
- **A Thinnet network** can support a maximum of 30 nodes per cable segment, and up to five segments can be connected using repeaters, of which three segments may be populated, allowing up to 90 nodes to be supported (based on the IEEE 802.3 specification).
- 18.**Thicknet cable** (also known as **Standard Ethernet**) is relatively rigid, being 0.5 inches in diameter.
- **The IEEE specification refers to this type of cable as 10Base5, referring to its main specifications of 10 Mbps data rate, baseband transmission type, and 500-metre maximum segment length.**
- Thicknet is generally used to provide the network backbone and can support up to 100 nodes per backbone segment.
- The minimum cable length between connections (or taps) on a Thicknet cable segment is 2.5 meters (about 8 feet).
- Thicknet cable has a data rate of 10 Mbps and can carry a signal for 500 meters before a repeater is required.
- The grade of coaxial cable used will depend on where it is used.
- Normal PVC coaxial cable is flexible, easy to work with, and may be used in exposed areas of offices, but because it gives of poisonous fumes when it burns, it is against the fire regulations in many countries for it to be installed in floor and ceiling voids which are also used to allow air to circulate around the building.
- Thick coax was the transmission medium originally used by Xerox for their Ethernet network, although it was later superceded by thin coax.
- Although still used in many networks, coaxial cable is gradually being replaced by fiber optic and UTP cable - fiber optic is normally used for the network backbone, with UTP being used to connect workstations to hubs or MAUs.
- Here are some common examples of coaxial cables used in LANs, along with their impedances, and the LAN standards with which they are associated :

- RG-8 and RG-11 are 50-ohm cables required for thick wire Ethernet. (10Base5 - ThikNet).
- RG-58 is a smaller 50-ohm cable required for use with thin wire Ethernet. (10Base2 – ThinNet).
- RG-59 is a 75-ohm cable most familiar when used to wire cable TV. RG-59 is also used to cable broadband 802.3 Ethernet.
- RG-62 is a 93-ohm cable used for ARCnet. It is also commonly employed to wire terminals in an IBM SNA network.

Some advantages of coaxial cable are as follows :
- Low cost due to less total footage of cable, hubs not needed.
- Lower attenuation than twisted pair.
- Good immunity to EMI/RFI / Highly insensitive to EMI.
- Supports high bandwidths.
- Heavier types of coax are sturdy and can withstand harsh environments.
- Represents a mature technology that is well understood and consistently applied among vendors.

Coaxial cable also has some disadvantages including the following :
- Limited in network speed.
- Limited in size of network.
- One bad connector can take down entire network.
- Although fairly insensitive to EMI, coax remains vulnerable to EMI in harsh conditions such as factories.
- Coax can be bulky.
- Coax is among the most expensive types of wire cables.

4.2.3 Fiber Optic Cable

- Data transmission over optical fiber has greatly increased over the last few years, although fiber to the desktop has not really caught on as expected.
- However, fiber optic plays an important role in many networks.
- In addition, it has some outstanding advantages over copper cabling for certain applications.
- There are a number of network topologies and standards based on fiber optic, such as 10 BASE FL and FDDI, which apply mainly to the backbone cabling of very large facilities and campus environments.

- The discussion will be limited here to the uses of fiber optic in star bus Ethernet network topologies.
- When used as a link in a star bus topology, multi-mode fiber optic cable can transmit a maximum distance of 2,000 meters between all data closets, using a less expensive LED light source.
- While single mode fiber can transmit up to 3,000 meters, it requires a more expensive laser light source.
- By using fiber optic to link closets, it is possible to greatly extend the distance limitations in Ethernet networks using twisted pair only.
- Fiber optic is an outstanding choice for linking buildings together.
- In addition to the much greater distances possible, it is completely immune to over currents from lightning strikes and ground potential problems.
- There is literally nothing metallic in a fiber optic cable to conduct current. It is an excellent choice for heavy manufacturing environments, such as a foundry, due to its immunity to EMI/RFI.
- Finally, it is the best choice where data of a highly sensitive nature is being transmitted.
- Fiber optic cable radiates no electrical signal at all, and the cable would be down for quite some time if someone tried to splice into it.

Construction of Optical Fiber :

- Optical fiber cable carries light signals instead of electric signal.
- Each fiber has inner core of either plastic or glass that carries light.
- The inner core is surrounded by cladding, a layer of plastic or glass that reflects the light back into core.
- Fiber optic cable can have single fiber or bundle of fibers at the centre of the cable. The refractive index of the core is relatively high.
- Refractive index is low. Cladding material is lossy.
- This entire optical core-cladding assembly is then coated with protective inner jacket and outer plastic jacket as shown in Fig. 4.9.

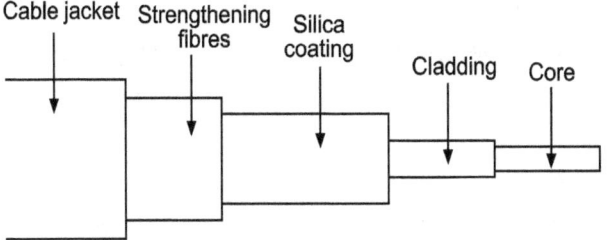

Fig. 4.9 : Construction of Fiber Optic Cable

The cross-section of a fiber illustrating the different layers is as shown in Fig. 4.10.

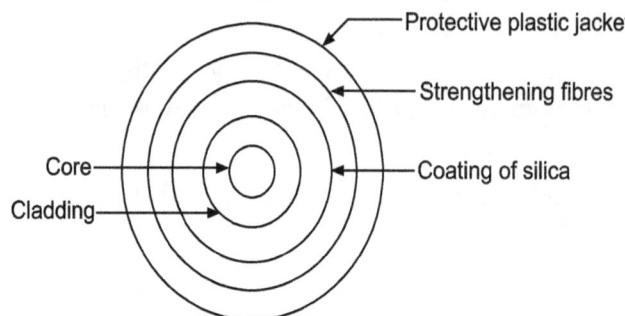

Fig. 4.10 : A Cross-Section of a Fiber illustrating the Different Layers

The core is surrounded by cladding surface and entire thing is coated with silicon oil and organic material with silica. External plastic jacket is to provide mechanical strength and optical fiber is protected from mechanical wear and tear.

Typical optical fiber communication is shown in Fig. 4.11.

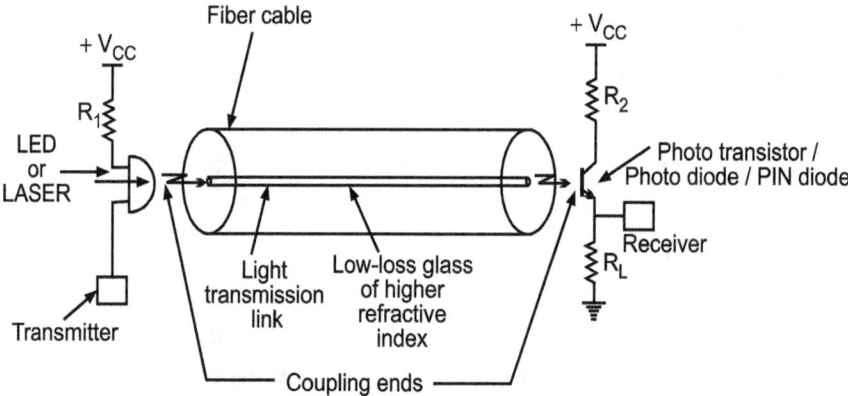

Fig. 4.11 : Typical Fiber Optic Communication System

The basic point-to-point fiber optic communication system consists of three basic units.

1. Optical transmitter unit
2. Fiber optic cable unit
3. Optical receiver unit.

Optical Transmitter Unit :

The transmitter converts applied electrical, analog or digital signal into a corresponding light signal. The source of the light signal can be either a light emitting diode, or a solid-state laser diode.

Fiber Optic Cable Unit :

Converted signal travels in the form of light from one end of fiber to other end of fiber. This is also called as light transmission link. If the distance between transmitter and receiver is in kilometers, then two or more fiber optic cables can be joined together.

Optical Receiver :

The receiver converts the optical signal into the original electrical signal. This optical receiver uses the photodetectors like avalanche type photodiode or PIN type of photodiode (P type-Intrinsic-N type material is used).

Optical fibers can be classified in two ways as shown.

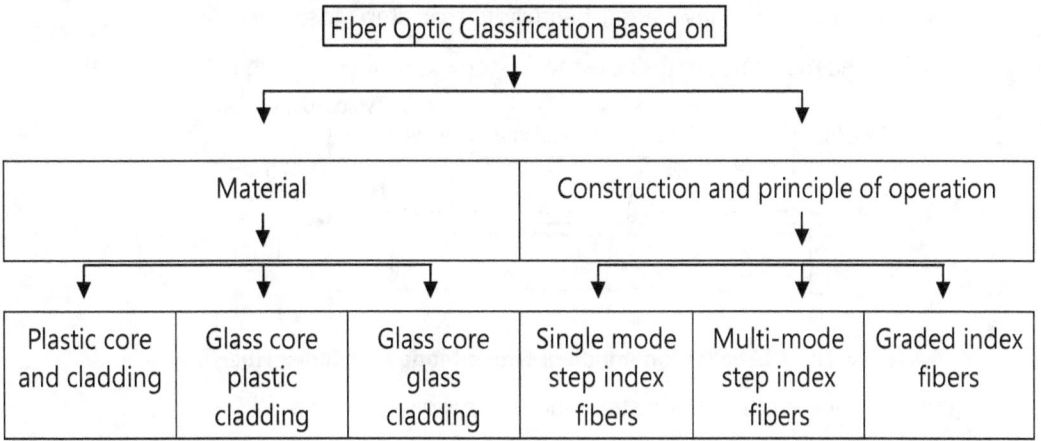

Plastic Core and Cladding :

These type of fibers are more rugged than glass. They are less expensive. They provide high attenuation characteristics and can be used within a single building or a building complex. Less attenuation when exposed to external radiation.

Glass Core with Plastic Cladding :

These type of fibers are more effectively used in military applications.

Glass Core and Glass Cladding :

These type of fibers are least rugged and are more susceptible to increase in attenuation when exposed to external radiation compared to above both optical fibers.

Single Mode step index fiber has following Properties :

- Support only one mode of operation.
- Use of LASER is must, makes power launching difficult.
- Fiber coupling is difficult due to less diameter size of core which is approximately ≈ 8 to 12 µm.

Multi-mode step index fiber has following properties :

- Supports hundreds of modes of propagation.
- LED can be used as optical transmitter, so power launching becomes easy.
- Fiber coupling is easy because moderate core diameter which is approximately ≈ 50 to 200 µm.

- In this fiber the pulse which is sent at transmitter end spreads in time, when it is received at receiver end. This pulse distortion is called as intermodal dispersion.

Graded index fiber :

- The intermodal dispersion of pulse is reduced in the graded index fiber due to its construction itself.
- Graded index fibers have larger bandwidth than step index fibers.

Construction of the monomode or single mode step index fiber is given in Fig. 4.12 (a).

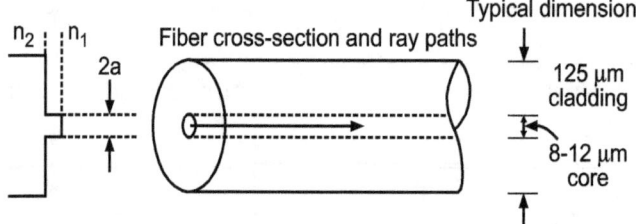

Fig. 4.12 (a) : Monomode or Single Mode Step Index Fiber

Construction of the multi-mode step index fiber is given in Fig. 4.12 (b).

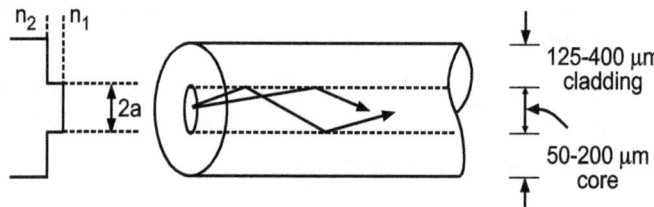

Fig. 4.12 (b) : Multi-mode Step Index Fiber

Construction of the graded index fiber is given in Fig. 4.12 (c).

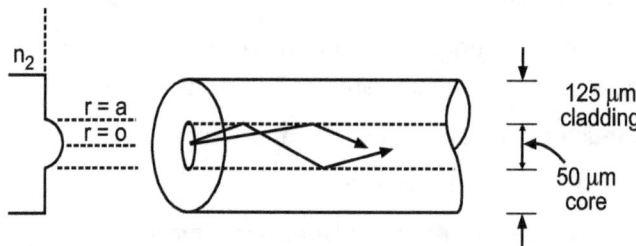

Fig. 4.12 (c) : Graded Index Fiber

Thus fiber optic transmission line confines light energy within its surface and guides the light in a direction parallel to its axis.

In previous figures,

n_1 = refractive index of the core

n_2 = refractive index of cladding

Main advantages of fiber optic cable :

- High data rate and wide bandwidth.
- Immunity to EMI/RFI and lightning damage.
- No ground loops.
- Low attenuation (Low data loss).
- Longer distance - 2 and 5 km with multi-mode fiber and over 25 km with single mode fiber.
- Small cable diameter fits anywhere.
- Light weight.
- No sparks if cut.
- No shock hazard.
- Secure communication.
- Safe and easy installation.
- Low system cost.
- Longer life expectancy than copper or coaxial cable.
- Cabling of the future.

Main disadvantages of fiber optic cable are as follows :

Cost :

Despite the fact that the raw material for making optical fibers is abundant and cheap, optial fibers are still more expensive per meter than copper.

Special Skills :

Optical fibers cannot be joined together as easily as copper. It requires additional training for person. Expensive precision splicing and measurement equipment are also required.

Installation and Maintenance Cost :

Initial installation of the fiber optic system is more and maintenance is expensive.

- Thus choosing the correct type of cabling depends on what type of network you have or intend to have, the number of network devices used, expected future growth, the speed requirements of your applications and the physical layout of your facility.
- Make this decision with the assistance of a professional, licensed and insured network cabling company and a good information technology consultant.

Table 4.2 : Summary of Cable Characteristics

Cable Type	Cable Cost	Installation Cost	EMI Sensitivity	Data Bandwidth
UTP	Lowest	Lowest	Highest	Lowest
STP	Medium	Moderate	Low	Moderate
Coax	Medium	Moderate	Low	High
Fiber Optic	Highest	Highest	None	Very high

Table 4.3 : Characteristic comparison of guided media

	Twisted Pair	Coaxial Cable	Fiber Optic Cable
1.	It uses electrical signal for transmission.	It uses electrical signal for transmission.	It uses optical signal for transmission.
2.	Affected by EMI and noise.	Less affected by EMI and noise.	Not affected by EMI and noise.
3.	Bandwidth is low which is 3 to 4 MHz.	Bandwidth is high which is 300 to 400 MHz.	Bandwidth is very high which is 2 to 3 GHz.
4.	Used for analog and digital transmission.	Used for analog and digital transmission.	Used for analog and digital transmission.
5.	Supports low data rates upto 4 Mbps.	Supports high data rates upto 400 to 500 Mbps.	Supports very high data rates upto 3 Gbps.
6.	Cost is very less.	Cost is moderate.	More costly.
7.	For long distance communication, repeaters are required after every 2 km distance.	For long distance communication, repeaters are required after every 1 km distance.	For long distance communication, repeaters are required after every 10 km distance.
8.	Signal attenuation is more.	Signal attenuation is moderate.	Signal attenuation is least.
9.	Installation is easiest.	Installation is easy.	Installation is difficult.
10.	Signal to noise ratio is less.	Signal to noise ratio is moderate.	Signal to noise ratio is very high.
11.	Crosstalk is more.	Crosstalk is moderate.	No crosstalk is present.
12.	Losses like copper losses and radiation losses are present.	Losses like copper losses and radiation losses are present.	Losses like microbending and macrobending losses are present.

4.3 UNGUIDED MEDIA

4.3.1 Introduction

- Unguided media are natural parts of the earth's environment that can be used as physical paths to carry electrical signals.
- The atmosphere and outer space are examples of unguided media that are commonly used to carry signals.
- **These media can carry such electromagnetic signals as microwaves, infrared light waves, and radio waves.**
- Network signals are transmitted through all transmission media as a type of waveform.
- When transmitted through wire and cable, the signal is an electrical waveform.
- When transmitted through fiber-optic cable, the signal is a light wave : either visible or infrared light.
- When transmitted through earth's atmosphere or outer space, the signal can take the form of waves in the radio spectrum, including VHF and microwaves, or it can be light waves, including infrared or visible light (for example, lasers).
- Recent advances in radio hardware technology have produced significant advancements in wireless networking devices : the cellular telephone, wireless modems, and wireless LANs.
- These devices use technology that in some cases has been around for decades but until recently was too impractical or expensive for widespread consumer use.
- The next few sections explain technologies unique to unguided media that are especially of concern to networking.
- There are a variety of wireless network media, each of which uses a different transmission protocol. Typically, a wireless network uses infrared light or radio transmissions to distribute data.
- **Infrared networks** communicate by using beams of infrared light. They have a maximum range of 100 meters. Theoretically, they can transmit at 10 Mbps, but 1-3 Mbps is more typical.
- **Narrow band radio networks** can cover an area up to 5,000 square meters at up to 4.8 Mbps. Their disadvantage is that they offer little security.
- **Spread-spectrum radio networks** use multiple frequencies. These multiple channels provide network security. They can transmit data at up to 1 Mbps at a range of 800 feet indoors, though 300 kbps is more typical.

- Some common applications of wireless data communication include the following :
  - Accessing the Internet using a cellular phone.
  - Establishing a home or business Internet connection over satellite.
  - Beaming data between two hand-held computing devices.
  - Using a wireless keyboard and mouse for the PC.

4.3.2 The Electromagnetic Spectrum

- All electromagnetic waves travel at the speed of light (300,000,000 metres per second) in a vacuum, whatever their frequency (in copper or fibre), the speed drops to approximately two thirds of this value, and is slightly frequency dependent.
- The relationship between frequency, wavelength and the speed of light (C) in a vacuum is given by :

$$F\lambda = C$$

- Since C is a constant, if wavelength is known, then frequency can be calculated and vice versa.
- Thus, a frequency of 1 MHz would give a wavelength of approximately 300 meters, and a 1 cm wavelength would give a frequency of approximately 30 GHz. The Electromagnetic Spectrum is shown in Fig. 4.13.

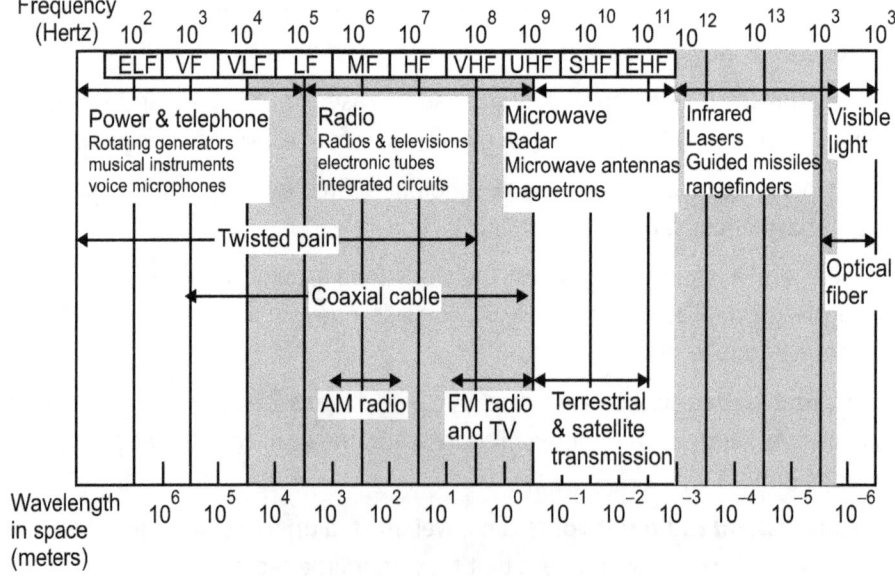

Fig. 4.13 : The Electromagnetic Spectrum

- The parts of the electromagnetic spectrum which can be used for transmitting information using amplitude, frequency or phase modulation are shown using a darker shading and include radio, microwave, infrared and visible light.

4.4 RADIO TRANSMISSION

- Radio waves are widely used for both indoor and outdoor communication because they are easy to generate, can travel over long distances, and can penetrate buildings easily.
- Because they travel in all directions from the transmitter (i.e. they are omni directional), the transmitter and receiver do not need to be carefully aligned.
- The properties of radio waves are dependent on frequency.
- At low frequencies, they pass through obstacles well, but the power falls off sharply as the distance from the transmitter increases.
- At high frequencies, radio waves tend to travel in straight lines and bounce off obstacles.
- They are also absorbed by rain.
- At all frequencies, they are subject to electromagnetic interference from electrical equipment such as electric motors.
- The ability to travel over large distances means that radio transmissions can also interfere with each other, which is one of the main reasons why the use of radio transmitters is tightly controlled by governments.
- In the very low to medium frequency bands, radio waves follow the ground, as illustrated below, and can be detected at distances of about 1000 kilometers. (Also called as Ground Wave Propagation)
- Radio waves at these frequencies can easily pass through buildings and are subsequently widely used by terrestrial radio stations.
- The relatively low bandwidth, however, means that they are not suitable for data communication.

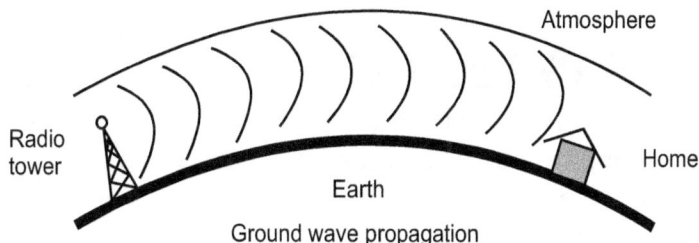

Fig. 4.14 : Radio Transmission using Ground Wave Propagation

- RF is part of electromagnetic spectrum that ranges from 3 Hz - 300 GHz.
- Radio wave is radiated by an antenna and produced by alternating currents fed to the antenna.
- RF is used in many standard as well as proprietary wireless communication systems.

- **RF has been used since long time for radio and TV broadcasting, wireless local loop, mobile communication, and amateur radio.**

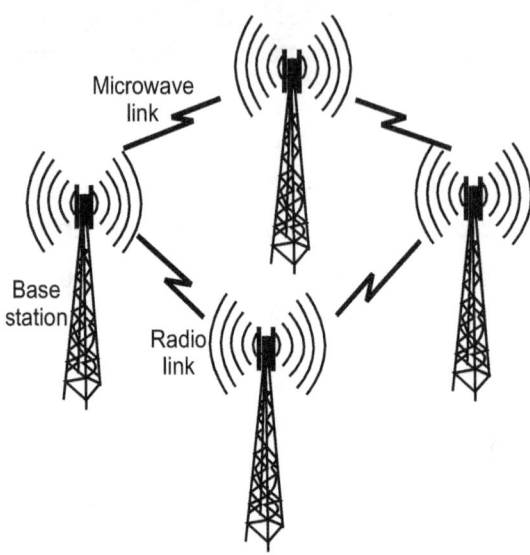

Fig. 4.15 : Radio waves radiated by a Base Station's antenna

- High (HF) and very high (VHF) frequency radio waves that reach the ionosphere, which is a layer of charged particles approximately 100-500 km above the earth's surface, are refracted by it and sent back to earth.

- These bands are used by amateur radio operators to talk over long distances, and are also used for military radio communication.

- **Radio waves** have virtually no distance limitations. However the radio waves are government regulated, expensive, and can be tapped into. This can be used across continents.

4.5 MICROWAVE TRANSMISSION

- At frequencies of 1 GHz and above, electromagnetic waves travel in straight lines and can be narrowly focused. Microwave is the upper part of RF spectrum. Because of the availability of larger bandwidth in microwave spectrum, microwave is used in many applications such as wireless PAN, wireless LAN, fixed broadband wireless access (wireless MAN), satellite communications, radar, and as backhaul in cellular networks.

- A parabolic dish antenna can be used to focus the transmitted power into a narrow beam to give a high signal to noise ratio, and before the advent of optical fiber, some long distance telephone transmission systems were heavily dependent on the use of a series of microwave towers.

Fig. 4.16 : Typical example of Microwave Link using Dish Antenna and Satellite

- Because microwaves travel in a straight line, the curvature of the earth limits the maximum distance over which microwave towers can transmit, so repeaters are needed to compensate for this limitation. As a general rule, the higher the towers are, the further apart they can be.
- At these higher frequencies, the transmitted waves do not easily pass through buildings.
- In addition, however well focused the transmitter may be, some waves may be refracted by low-lying atmospheric layers, and will take longer to arrive at their destination than direct waves.
- The delayed waves may therefore arrive out of phase with the direct waves and cancel out the signal. This effect is known as multipath fading.
- Rain can also be a problem, as frequencies around 8 GHz are absorbed by water.
- At higher frequencies, more expensive electronics are required, and transmissions can be subject to interference from radar installations and microwave ovens.
- **Microwave does, however, have several advantages over fiber.**
- Obstacles such as roads, railways and rivers may make laying cables difficult whereas these problems do not exist for microwave, and rights of way are not an issue.

- Erecting simple towers or mounting antenna on top of tall buildings is usually far cheaper than laying several kilometers of cable.
- Microwave also removes the need for reliance on telephone companies.
- In addition, governments worldwide have set aside the frequency band from 2.400 GHz to 2.484 GHz for unlicensed transmissions, so use of these frequencies does not require a license, and is therefore popular for various forms of short range wireless networking.
- **Microwaves** have a medium distance limitation and require line of sight. This is good between buildings or between satellites and satellite dishes. Weather and solar conditions may affect transmission.
- Microwaves are used for long distance communication like cellular phones, garage door openers, and much more.
- Microwave transmission is line of sight transmission. The transmitting station must be in visible contact with the receiving station.
- This sets a limit on the distance between stations depending on the local geography. Typically the line of sight due to the Earth's curvature is only 50 km to the horizon ! Repeater stations must be placed so the data signal can hop, skip and jump across the country.

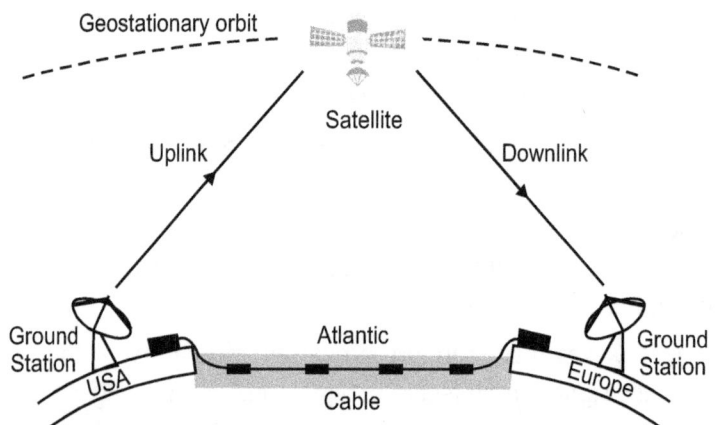

Fig. 4.17 : Other example of Microwave Transmission

- Microwaves operate at high operating frequencies of 3 to 10 GHz. This allows them to carry large quantities of data due to the large bandwidth.

4.5.1 Terrestrial Microwave Transmission

- Communication is accomplished through line of sight parabolic dish antenna located on elevated sites.

- Long distance communication is possible by using a series of relay stations.
- The distance between the stations is dependent on the height above the ground.
- Used for voice, television transmission, private communications and telephone networks e.g. emergency services, utilities etc.
- Utilizes a wide frequency band, 2 to 40 GHz but is susceptible to attenuation and interference.
- Attenuation can rise markedly in poor atmospheric conditions e.g. rain, but adversely affects the higher end of the frequency band, which is only used for short distance transmission.
- Natural noise severely affects transmission frequencies below 2GHz.
- Quick to install and overcomes the problems of laying cables in congested locations or over difficult terrain.

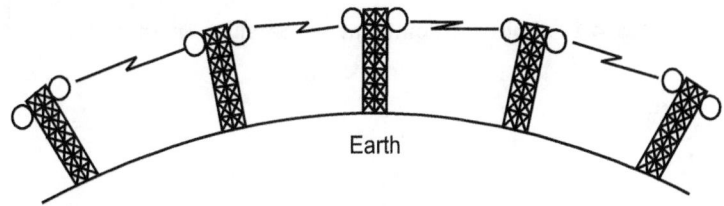

Fig. 4.18 : Typical Example of Terrestrial and Satellite Microwave Links

4.5.2 Satellite Microwave Transmission

- Overcomes the line of sight problems of terrestrial microwave and can be used for point-to-point or broadcast transmission.
- Uses an uplink and downlink frequency, a common frequency set is referred to as the 4/6 range which uses a downlink frequency of 4 GHz and an uplink frequency of 6 GHz.
- Typical uses of satellite microwave - television distribution, long distance telephone transmission, private business networks for global organizations.
- Suffers the same attenuation problems as terrestrial microwave.
- Microwave transmitters and receivers, especially satellite systems, are commonly used to transmit network signals over great distances.
- A microwave transmitter uses the atmosphere or outer space as the transmission medium to send the signal to a microwave receiver.
- The microwave receiver then either relays the signal to another microwave transmitter or translates the signal to some other form, such as digital impulses, and relays it on another suitable medium to its destination.

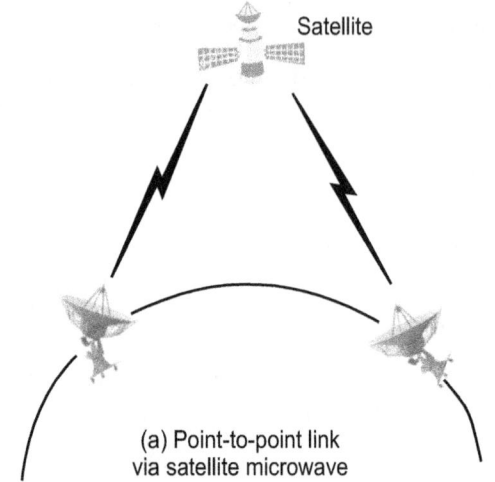

Fig. 4.19 : Point-to-Point Link via Satellite Microwave

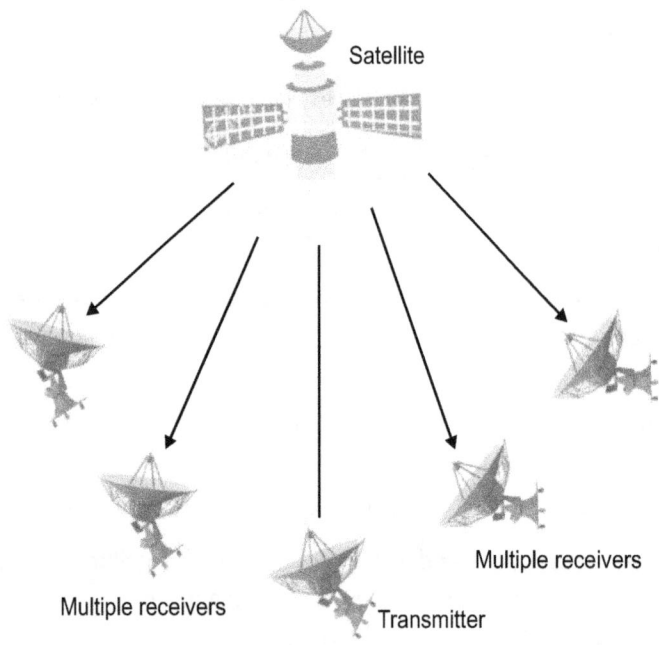

Fig. 4.20 : Broadcast Link via Satellite Microwave

Fig. 4.21 shows a satellite microwave link.

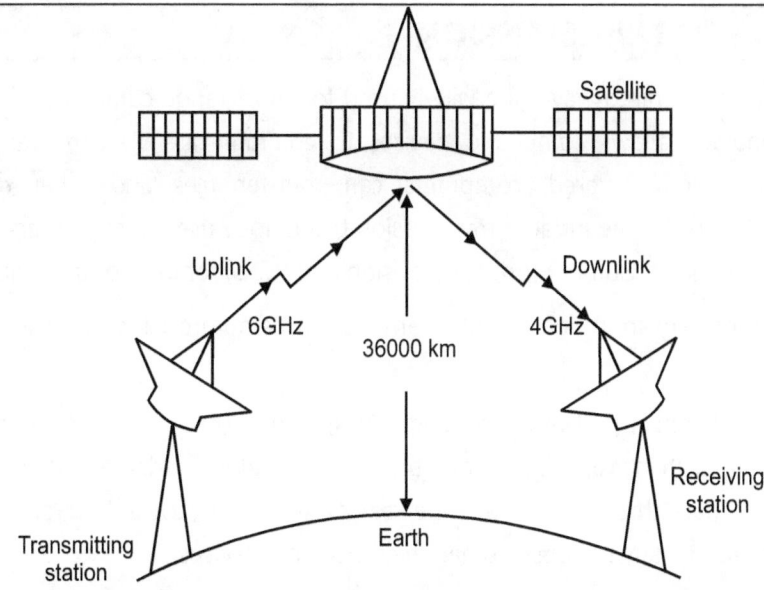

Fig. 4.21 : Satellite Microwave Link for Worldwide Communication

- Originally, this technology was used almost exclusively for satellite and long-range communication.
- Recently, however, there have been developments in cellular technology that allow you complete wireless access to networks, intranets, and the Internet.
- IEEE 802.11 defines a MAC and physical access control for wireless connection to networks.
- Used for TV distribution, long-distance telephone, and business networks.

Advantages :

- They require no right of way acquisition between towers.
- They can carry high quantities of information due to their high operating frequencies.
- Low cost land purchase : each tower occupies small area.
- High frequency/short wavelength signals require small antenna.

Disadvantages :

- Attenuation by solid objects : birds, rain, snow and fog.
- Reflected from flat surfaces like water and metal.
- Diffracted (split) around solid objects.
- Refracted by atmosphere, thus causing beam to be projected away from receiver.

4.6 INFRARED TRANSMISSION

- Unguided infrared waves are widely used for short-range communication. **Infrared** technology allows computing devices to communicate via short-range wireless signals. With infrared, computers can transfer files and other digital data bidirectionally. The infrared transmission technology used in computers is similar to that used in consumer product (television and VCRs) remote control units.

- Used for very short line of sight transmission, remote car locking systems, wireless security alarms.

- **Infrared** light is part of electromagnetic spectrum that is shorter than radio waves but longer than visible light. Computer infrared network adapters both transmit and receive data through ports on the rear or side of a device. Infrared adapters are installed in many laptops and handheld personal devices.

- Its frequency range is between 300 GHz and 400 THz, that correspond to wavelength from 1 mm to 750 nm.

- Infrared has long been used in night vision equipment and TV remote control.

- Infrared is also one of the physical media in the original wireless LAN standard, that is IEEE 802.11. Infrared networks were designed to support direct two-computer connections only, created temporarily as the need arises. However, extensions to infrared technology also support more than two computers and semi-permanent networks.

- Infrared use in communication and networking was defined by the IrDA (Infrared Data Association).

- **Using IrDA specifications, infrared can be used in a wide range of applications, e.g. file transfer, synchronization, dial-up networking, and payment.**

- However, IrDA is limited in range (up to about 1 meter). It also requires the communicating devices to be in LOS (Line of Sight) and within its 30-degree beam-cone. Infrared technology used in local networks exists in three different forms :

    - IrDA-SIR (slow speed) infrared supporting data rates up to 115 kbps.
    - IrDA-MIR (medium speed) infrared supporting data rates up to 1.15 Mbps.
    - IrDA-FIR (fast speed) infrared supporting data rates up to 4 Mbps.

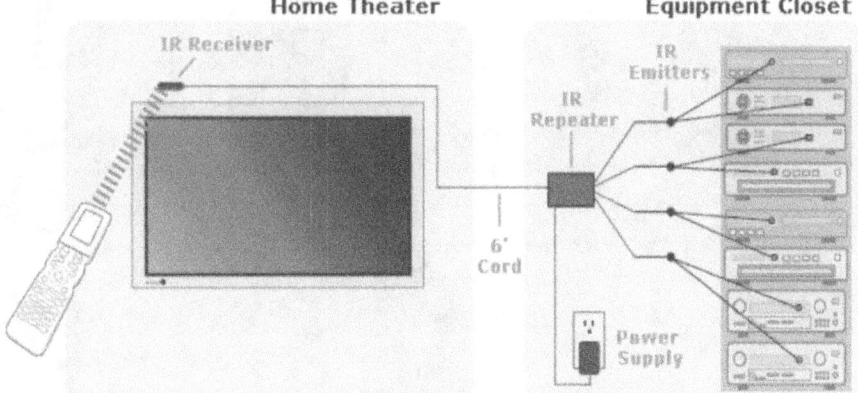

Fig. 4.22 : TV Remote Control Uses Infrared

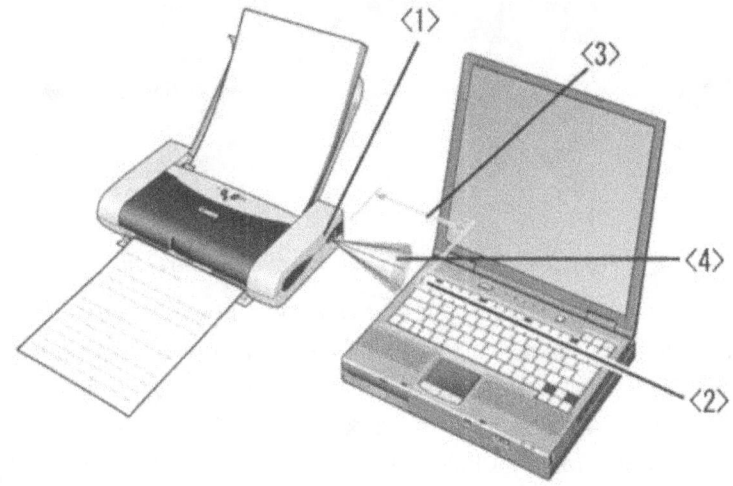

Fig. 4.23 : Computer Communication uses Infrared

- Infrared transmitters are (relatively) directional, cheap, and easy to manufacture. Infrared data and communication is a mode of communication that now plays an important role in wireless data communication. It suits the use of laptop computers, wireless data communication and other digital equipment such as personal assistants, cameras, mobile telephones and pagers.

- The major drawback is that infrared waves will not pass through solid objects. The communication between the devices requires that each have a transceiver (a combination of a transmitter and a receiver) in order to communicate. This capability is provided by microchip technology. However, devices may also require further, specialized software allowing communication to be synchronized.

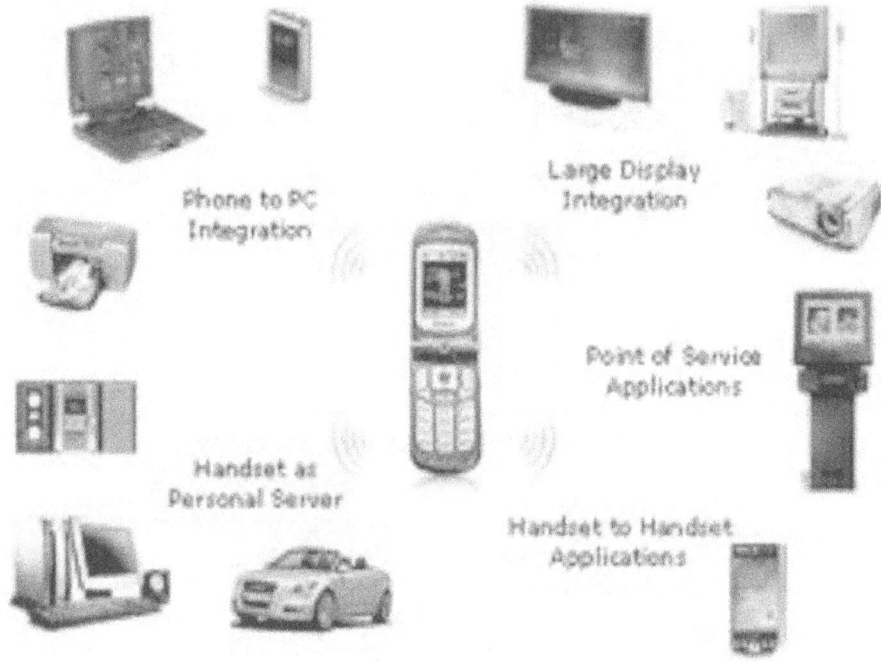

Fig. 4.24 : Devices Communicate using Infrared

- On the plus side, an infrared system in one room of a building will not interfere with similar systems in nearby rooms, and the possibility of eavesdropping is far lower than with radio-based systems. IR can be used over longer interconnections and has applicability to local area networks (LANs). However, the maximum effective distance is approximately 1 mile, with a maximum bandwidth of 16 Mbps.

- Infrared is therefore a realistic alternative for indoor wireless LANs, and the computers and offices within a building can be equipped with infrared transmitters and receivers which can be designed to be either directional or *diffuse*.

- In the latter case, signals bounce off walls and other objects to reach the receiver.

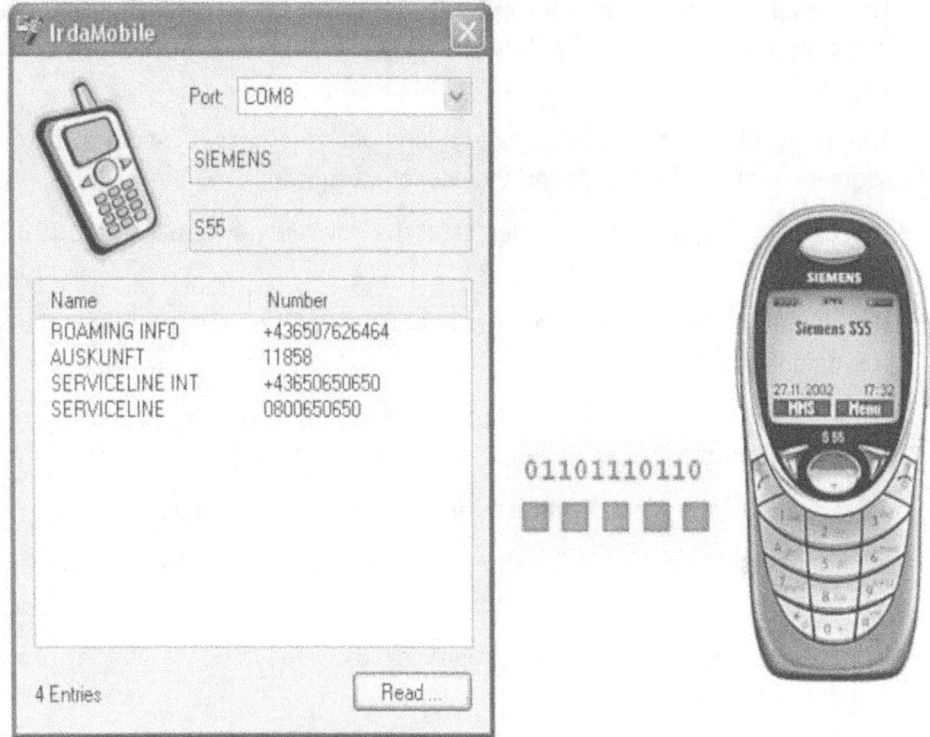

Fig. 4.25 : Mobile Handsets Communicate using Infrared

- As you can see from the two examples infrared communications work by sending and receiving pulses of infrared light.
- These pulses consist of periods of light and darkness.
- In the case of a TV or stereo, these pulses are nothing more than recognized patterns.
- However, in the case of computing devices, the pulses are binary code.
- When the infrared emitter is on, it is essentially sending a binary one.
- Likewise, when the infrared emitter is dark, it is considered to be sending a binary zero.
- This is where the need for infrared-based protocols comes in.
- The protocol regulates the timing of the infrared signal.
- It makes sure that the receiving device is checking the on/off status of the emitter at the same frequency the emitter intends.

- For example, if the emitter sent pulses at 4-millisecond intervals, but the receiver was expecting 2-millisecond pulses, then a single pulse of light could be mistaken for two pulses.
- The protocols must also negotiate things such as packet length (where one segment of binary code ends and the next one begins).
- For example, suppose the sender sent the following two packets : 10101100 00110010.
- Without proper timing, the receiver might pick up part of both packets and think it was a single packet.
- For example, if the receiver picked up the last four bits of the first packet and the first four bits of the second packet, it would receive the code as 11000011.
- As you can see, this is much different from the intended message.
- Infrared transmitters are similar to microwave systems : they use the atmosphere and outer space as transmission media.
- However, because they transmit light waves rather than radio waves, they require a line-of-sight transmission path.
- Infrared and laser transmissions are useful for signaling across short distances where it is impractical to lay cable for instance, when networks are at sites a few miles apart.
- Because infrared signals are in the light spectrum, rain, fog, and other environmental factors can cause transmission problems.
- Infrared communication is now common as a means of wireless communication between devices. It will not penetrate buildings and therefore is secure.
- Infrared communication is more secure than other options, such as radio, but it cannot be used outside due to interference by the Sun.

4.6.1 Applications of Infrared

As mentioned above, the short distance of interconnection drives the main application of this technology between appliances. Thus, according to the IrDA, at present, the main benefits and applications are :

- Sending a document from your notebook computer to a printer.
- Co-ordinating schedules and telephone books between desktop and hand-held (notebook) computers.

- Sending faxes from a hand-held computer, via a public telephone, to a distant fax machine.
- Beaming images from digital cameras to a desktop computer.
- Exchanging messages, business cards, and other information between hand-held personal computers.

For some of these functions, an interconnection between the hand-held or laptop computer and the desktop PC/printer in the form of an IR port, is required. Alternatively an IR adapter can be used.

4.6.2 The Future of Infrared Technology

- Infrared technology claims to be as secure as cable applications.
- For example, the access to LANs requires the user to be an authorized user of the network.
- Also, it claims to be more reliable than wired technology as it obviates wear and tear on the hardware used.
- In the future, it is forecast that this technology will be implemented in copiers, fax machines, overhead projectors, bank ATMs, credit cards, game consoles and headsets.
- All of these have local applications and it is really here where this technology is best suited, owing to the inherent difficulties in its technological process for interconnecting over distances.

EXERCISES

1. Classify the different transmission media.
2. Write notes on :
   (a) UTP cable
   (b) STP cable
   (c) Coaxial cable
3. What are the Cat 3, Cat 4, Cat 5, Cat 5e cables ?
4. Explain Cat 6 and Cat 7 wires in detail.
5. What is the difference between thin Ethernet cable and thick Ethernet cable ?

6. Draw and explain the construction of fiber cable.
7. Explain the typical fiber optic communication system.
8. Classify the fiber optic cable depending upon material and principle of operation.
9. Explain the advantages and disadvantages of fiber optic cable.
10. Compare Coaxial cable Vs. Fiber optic cable.
11. Draw and explain typical electromagnetic spectrum.
12. What is radio transmission ?
13. Explain the concept and types of microwave communication.
14. Write short notes on :
    (a) Infrared transmission.
    (b) Terrestrial and satellite microwave transmission.

Chapter 5
NETWORK HARDWARE COMPONENTS

OBJECTIVES

After reading this chapter you will understand :

- Concept of trans receivers and media converters
- Connecting devices like Passive Hub, Hub or Repeater, Bridge, Layer-2 Device, Router, Brouter and Layer-3 Switch.
- NIC and PC cards
- 802-X to 802-Y Bridges Variants, Advantages, Disadvantages of Bridges.
- Routers, Types of Routers, Routing Schemes, Gateway Device Uses.
- Comparison between Hub and Switch, Bridging Vs. Routing, Bridge Vs. Layer-2 Switch, Layer-2 Switch Vs. Layer-3 Switch, Router Vs. Switch etc.

5.1 TRANSRECEIVERS

A transceiver is a device comprising both a transmitter and a receiver which are combined and share common circuitry or a single housing. When no circuitry is common between transmit and receive functions, the device is a transmitter-receiver. Technically, transceivers must combine a significant amount of the transmitter and receiver handling circuitry. Similar devices include transponders, transverters, and repeaters.

A modern HF transceiver withspectrum analyzer and DSPcapabilities In radio terminology, a transceiver means a unit which contains both a receiver and a transmitter. From the beginning days of radio the receiver and transmitter were separate units and remained so until around 1920. Amateur radio or "ham" radio operators can build their own equipment and it is now easier to design and build a simple unit containing both of the functions: transmitting and receiving. Almost all modern amateur radio equipment is now a transceiver but there is an active market for pure radio receivers, mainly for shortwave listening (SWL) operators. An example of a transceiver would be a walkie-talkie, or a CB radio.

RF Transceiver

The RF Transceiver uses RF modules for high speed data transmission. The micro electronic circuits in the digital-RF architecture work at speeds up to 100 GHz. The objective in the design was to bring digital domain closer to the antenna, both at the receive and transmit ends using software defined radio (SDR).

The software-programmable digital processors used in the circuits permit conversion between digital baseband signals and analog RF.

Telephony

On a wired telephone, the handset contains the transmitter and receiver for the audio and in the 20th century was usually wired to the base unit by tinsel wire. The whole unit is colloquially referred to as a "receiver." On a mobile telephone or other radiotelephone, the entire unit is a transceiver, for both audio and radio.

A cordless telephone uses an audio and radio transceiver for the handset, and a radio transceiver for the base station. If a speakerphone is included in a wired telephone base or in a cordless base station, the base also becomes an audio transceiver in addition to the handset.

A modem is similar to a transceiver, in that it sends and receives a signal, but a modem uses modulation and demodulation. It modulates a signal being transmitted and demodulates a signal being received.

5.2 MEDIA CONVERTERS

Media converters are flexible and cost-effective devices for implementing and optimizing fiber links in all types of networks. The most common type of media converter is a device that functions as a transceiver; converting the electrical signal used in copper Unshielded Twisted Pair (UTP) network cabling into light waves used in fiber optic cabling. Fiber optic connectivity is necessary when the distance between two network devices exceeds the transmission distance of copper cabling. Copper-to-fiber conversion using media converters enables two network devices with copper ports to be connected over extended distances via fiber optic cabling.

Media converters also provide fiber-to-fiber conversion from multi-mode fiber to singlemode fiber, and convert a dual fiber link to single fiber using Bi-directional (BIDI) data flow. Media converters can also convert between wavelengths for Wavelength Division Multiplexing (WDM) applications.

Media converters are typically protocol specific and are available to support a wide variety of network types and data rates. They are available as physical layer or Layer 2 switching devices, and media converters with Layer 2 switching capability provide rate-switching and other advanced features.

5.2.1 The Advantages of Media Conversion Technology

Network complexity, demanding applications, and the growing number of devices on the network are driving network speeds and bandwidth requirements higher and forcing longer distance requirements within the Local Area Network (LAN). Media converters present solutions to these problems, by allowing the use of fiber when it is needed, and integrating new equipment into existing cabling infrastructure. Media converters provide seamless integration of copper and fiber, and different fiber types in Enterprise LAN networks. They support a wide variety of protocols, data rates and media types to create a more reliable and cost-effective network.

Demands on the Network are Increasing:

- LANs and WANs are converging, and networks are growing in physical area
- Budget constraints are pushing preservation of capital investment in legacy switches and routers
- New network services are driving up bandwidth demand

Solutions Provided by Media Converters:

- Increase network distances by converting UTP to fiber and extending fiber links
- Maintain investments in existing equipment
- Increase the capacity of existing fiber with WDM wavelengths (when used with multiplexers)

New Applications for Media Converters:

- Remotely managed converter and multi-port switch configurations
- Convert WDM wavelengths for bandwidth capacity enhancement
- Enable Fiber-to-the-Desktop

Media converters do more than convert copper-to-fiber and convert between different fiber types. Media converters for Ethernet networks can support integrated switch technology, and provide the ability to perform 10/100 and 10/100/1000 rate switching. Additionally, media converters can support advanced bridge features – including VLAN, Quality of Service (QoS) prioritization, Port Access Control and Bandwidth Control – that facilitate the deployment of new data, voice and video to end users. Media converters can provide all these sophisticated switch capabilities in a small, cost-effective device.

Media converters save capital equipment expenditures (CAPEX) by enabling interconnection between existing switches, servers, routers and hubs; preserving the investment in legacy equipment. They also reduce CAPEX by avoiding the need to install new fiber links by enabling WDM technology through wavelength conversion.

Media converters also reduce network operating costs (OPEX) by helping to troubleshoot and remotely configure network equipment that is at distant locations, saving time and money when there is not a network administrator at the distant location.

5.2.2 Types of Media Converters

There are a wide variety of copper-to-fiber and fiber-to-fiber media converters available that support different network protocols, data rates, cabling and connector types.

Network Protocols Supported:

- 10, 100, 10/100, Gigabit, 10/100/1000 and 10 Gigabit Ethernet
- Serial RS-232, RS-422, RS-485, RS-530 and X.21
- T1/E1 and T3/E3 TDM Protocols
- OC-3/STM1 and OC-12/STM4 SONET/SDH Protocols

Fiber Cable and Connector Types Supported:

- Multimode, single-mode, dual fiber and single-fiber
- SC, ST, LC, MT-RJ and FC connectors
- SFP, SFP+ and XFP transceivers

Copper Cable Types Supported:

- Coax
- UTP Category 4, 5 and 6

Unmanaged vs. Managed

An unmanaged media converter simply allows devices to communicate, and does not provide the same level of monitoring, fault detection and configuration as equivalent managed media converters. Connect the devices to the unmanaged media converter and they usually communicate automatically. Unmanaged media converters are simple to use and install. For most unmanaged converters, minimal configuration is required. A managed media converter is typically more costly than an unmanaged media converter; however, a managed converter provides additional network monitoring, fault detection and remote configuration functionality not available with an unmanaged media converter.

Ethernet Copper-to-Fiber Media Converters

Supporting the IEEE 802.3 standard, Ethernet copper-to-fiber media converters provide connectivity for Ethernet, Fast Ethernet, Gigabit and 10 Gigabit Ethernet devices. Some converters support 10/100 or 10/100/1000 rate switching, enabling the integration of equipment of different data rates and interface types into one seamless network.

Point-to-Point Applications

A pair of media converters can be used in point-to-point connections that connect two UTP Ethernet switches (or routers, servers, hubs, etc.) via fiber, or to connect UTP devices to workstations and file servers.

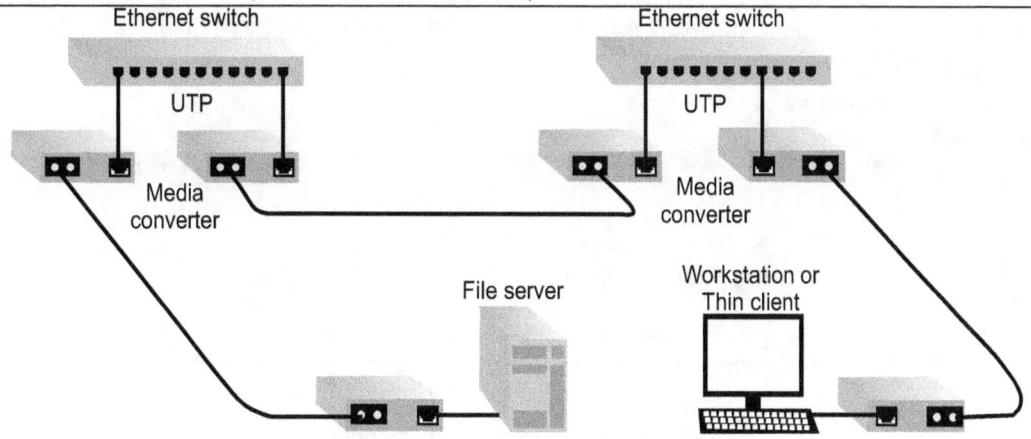

Fig. 5.1 : Point to Point Application

Campus Fiber Application

In this application example, 10/100 media converters are installed in a Redundant Power chassis for high-density fiber distribution from UTP switch equipment (A) at the network core. A UTP workgroup switch (B) is connected via fiber to the network core with a standalone 10/100 media converter. Another 10/100 converter enables fiber connectivity to a PC UTP port in a fiber-to-desktop application (C). An Ethernet switch (D) is connected directly via fiber to the media converter module at the network core.

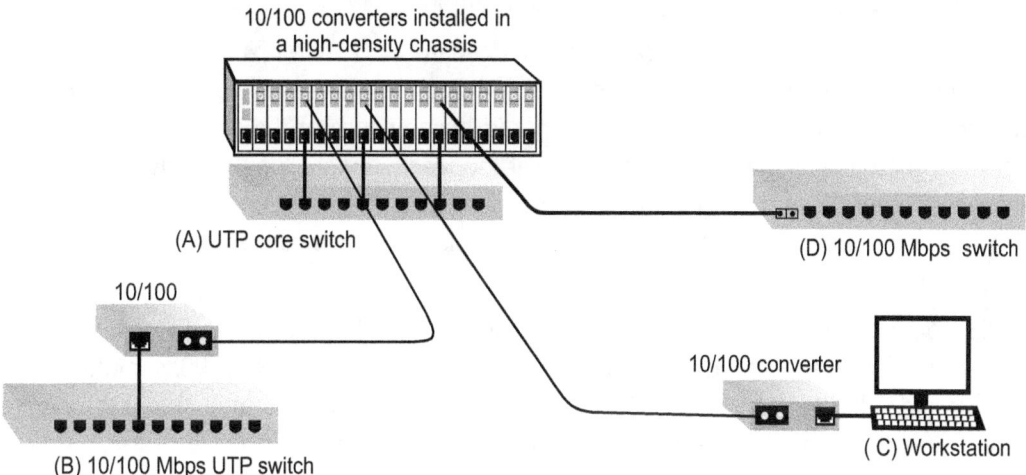

Fig. 5.2 : Campus Fibre Application

Redundant Fiber/Copper Application

Redundant Fast Ethernet media converters provide fiber or copper link redundancy. In the event that one cable link is broken, the redundant link is enabled to ensure 100% uptime. Redundant converter modules can provide link fault detection and switch over in 100 microseconds or less to provide rapid response time required for mission-critical network applications. Redundant links can run in parallel paths or geographically diverse paths (as shown in the fiber example below).

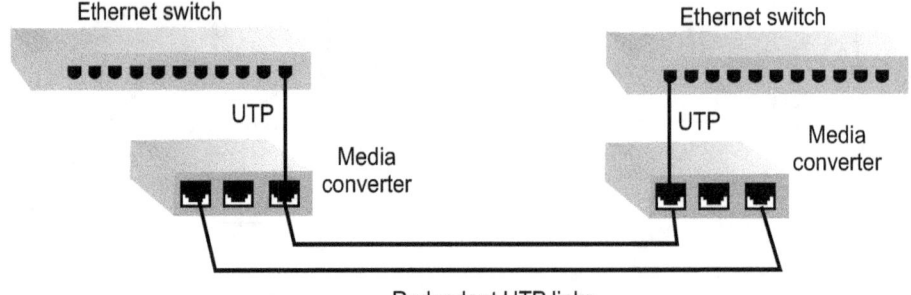

Fig. 5.3 : Redundant Fibre/Copper Application

TDM Copper-to-Fiber Media Converters :

T1/E1 and T3/E3 :

T1/E1 and T3/E3 copper-to-fiber converters provide a reliable and cost-effective method to extend traditional TDM (Time Division Multiplexing) telecom protocols copper connections using fiber optic cabling. T3/E3 and T1/E1 converters operate in pairs extending distances of TDM circuits over fiber, improving noise immunity, quality of service, intrusion protection and network security. This application is often useful within a building or as a connection between buildings in the building complex or a campus.

T1/E1 copper-to-fiber converters can support standard T1 (1.544Mbps), E1 (2.048Mbps) and can be compatible with AMI, B8ZS and HDB3 line codes. These converters often provide diagnostic features to aid in the installation and maintenance of the T1 or E1 connections. Some of the diagnostic features include local loopback, remote loopback and test-modes that insert data or alarm notification patterns such as all 1's insertion (AIS). These features enable the testing and troubleshooting of individual segments as well as the entire T1/E1 connection.

T3/E3 copper-to-fiber converters provide standard T3 (44.736Mbps) or E3 (34.368Mbps) coax-to-fiber conversion and can be used to connect to devices such as PBXs, multiplexers, routers and video servers via fiber. T3/E3 converters can be framing independent to operate with framed or unframed, channelized or fractional unchannelized data streams, and support B3ZS line coding for T3 (DS3) and HDB3 for E3.

T3/E3 Application :

T3/E3 media converters also provide a cost-effective solution for extending telecom demarcation points. In this example, a pair of T3/E3 converters is used to extend the demarcation between buildings via fiber.

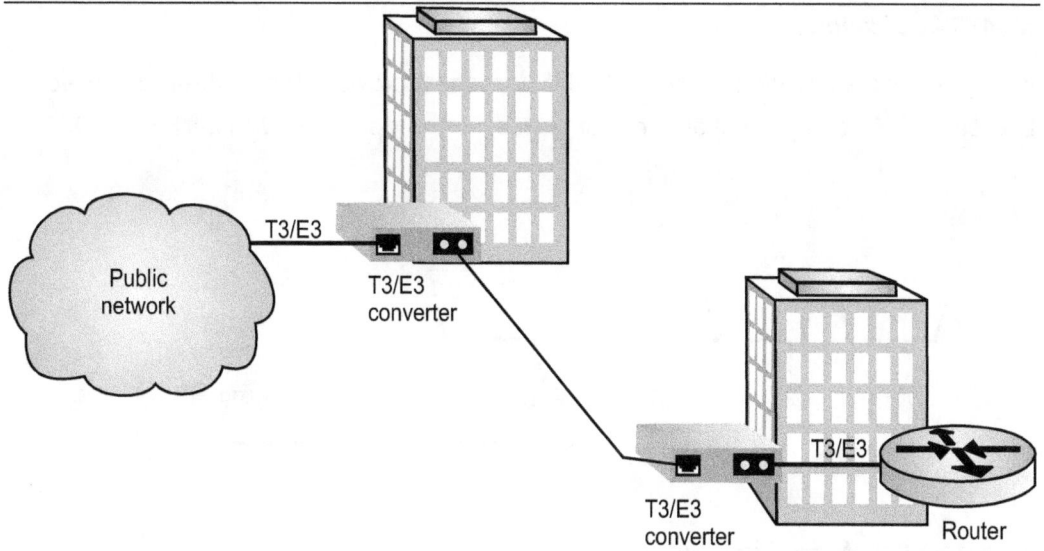

Fig. 5.6 : T3/E3 Application

Serial-to-Fiber Media Converters :
Serial-to-fiber converters provide fiber extension for serial protocol copper connections. They can automatically detect the signal baud rate of the connected Full-Duplex serial device, and support point-to-point and multi-point configurations.

RS-232 Application :
RS-232 fiber converters can operate as asynchronous devices, support speeds up to 921,600 baud, and support a wide variety of hardware flow control signals to enable seamless connectivity with most serial devices. In this example, a pair of RS-232 converters provides the serial connection between a PC and Terminal Server allowing access to multiple data devices via fiber.

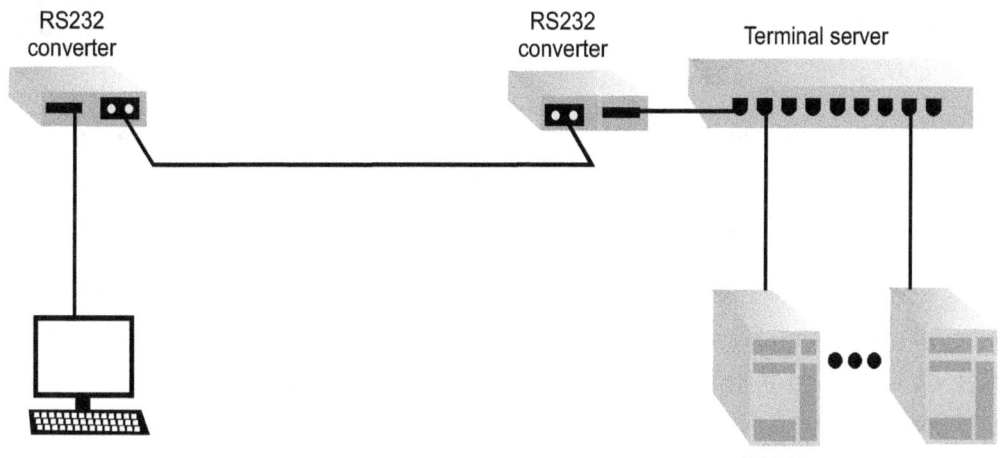

Fig. 5.7

RS-485 Application :

In this example application a pair of RS-485 converters provides the multi-drop connection between the Host equipment and the connected multi-drop devices via fiber.

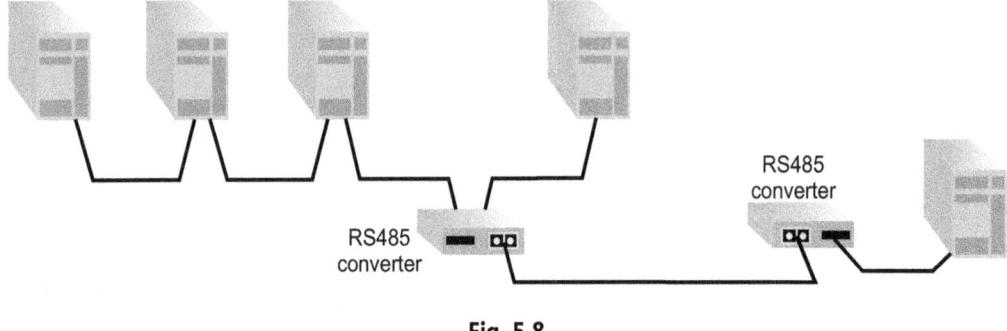

Fig. 5.8

Fiber-to-Fiber Media Converters :

Fiber-to-fiber media converters can provide connectivity between multimode (MM) and single-mode (SM) fiber, between different "power" fiber sources and between dual fiber and single-fiber. In addition, they support conversion from one wavelength to another. Fiberto-fiber media converters are normally protocol independent and available for Ethernet, and TDM applications.

Multimode to Single-mode Fiber Conversion :

Enterprise networks often require conversion from MM to SM fiber, which supports longer distances than MM fiber. Mode conversion is typically required when:

1) lower cost legacy equipment uses MM ports, and connectivity is required to SM equipment,

2) a building has MM equipment, while the connection to the service provider is SM, 3) MM equipment is in a campus building and SM fiber is used between buildings.

Multimode to Single-mode Fiber Application :

A fiber-to-fiber media converter can extend a MM network across SM fiber with distances up to 140km. In this application, two Gigabit Ethernet switches equipped with MM fiber ports are connected utilizing a pair of Gigabit fiber-to-fiber converters, which convert the MM fiber to SM and enable the long distance connection between the switches.

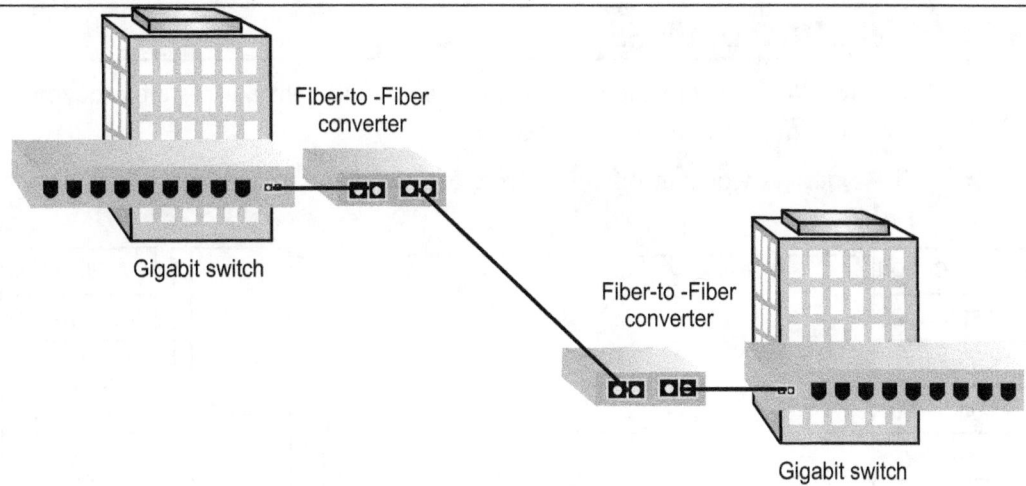

Fig. 5.9

Dual Fiber to Single-Fiber Conversion :
Enterprise networks may also require conversion between dual and single-fiber, depending on the type of equipment and the fiber installed in the facility. Single-fiber is single-mode and operates with bi-directional wavelengths, often referred to as BIDI. Typically BIDI single-fiber uses 1310nm and 1550nm wavelengths over the same fiber strand in opposite directions. The development of bi-directional wavelengths over the same fiber strand was the precursor to Wavelength Division Multiplexing.

Dual Fiber to Single-Fiber Conversion Application :
In this application, two dual fiber switches are connected via single-fiber. Since BIDI single fiber uses two separate wavelengths over the same fiber strand, the transmit (Tx) at one end of the fiber link matches the receive (Rx) from the other end, and vice versa.

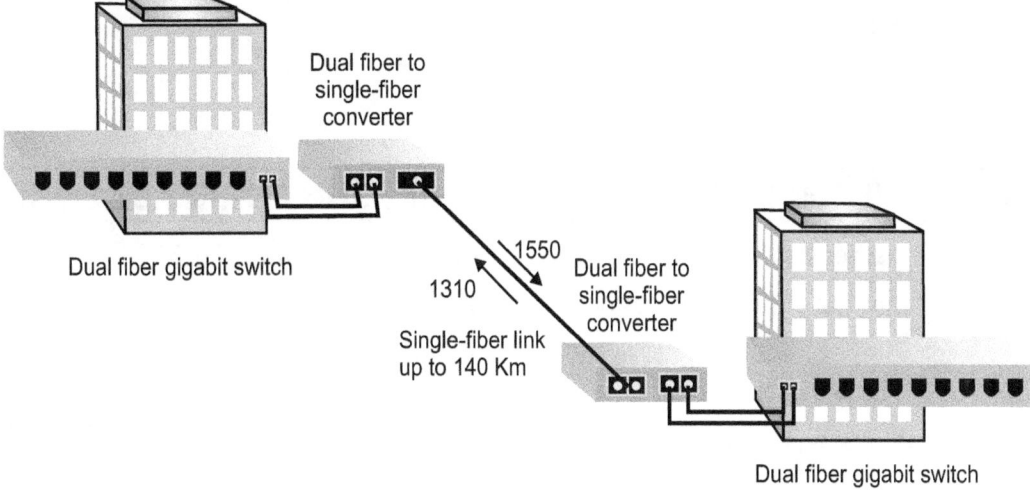

Fig. 5.10

5.3 CONNECTING DEVICES

- In LAN, MAN, WAN or Internet communication, different devices are required to connect different systems to each other.
- These devices works at different layers of ISO-OSI reference model as shown in Fig. 5.1.

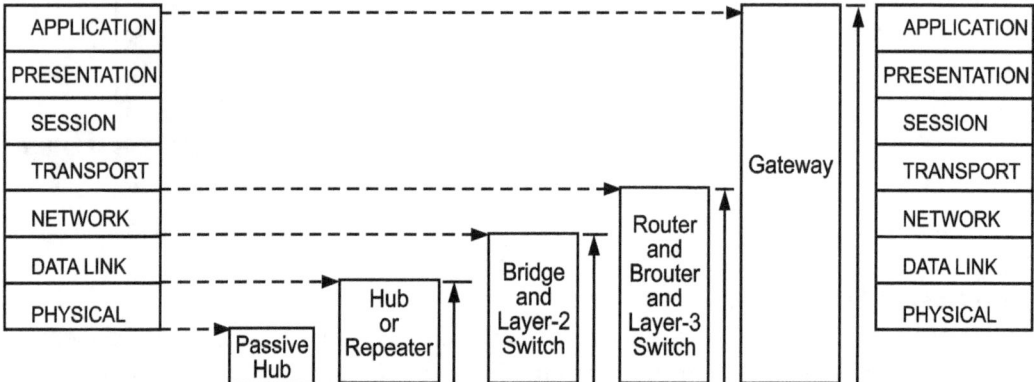

Fig. 5.11 : Connecting Devices as Part of Different Layers

- Passive hub (or connector) works below physical layer of ISO-OSI reference model.
- Hub or repeater works at physical layer of ISO-OSI reference model.
- Bridging device (Bridge) and other device like Layer-2 switch works upto datalink layer of ISO-OSI reference model.
- Router, Brouter (Bridge + Router) and Layer-3 switch devices work upto network layer of ISO-OSI reference model.
- Gateway works upto application layer of the ISO-OSI reference model.

5.4 PASSIVE HUBS (OR CONNECTOR) (BELOW PHYSICAL LAYER)

- Passive hub is nothing but simple connector unit as shown in Fig. 5.12.
- This type of passive hub is basically a part of media.
- This passive hub is just like a wire connector and acts below physical layer of the ISO-OSI reference model.
- All the signals coming from station 1 to station 16, collides at collision point as shown in Fig. 5.12.

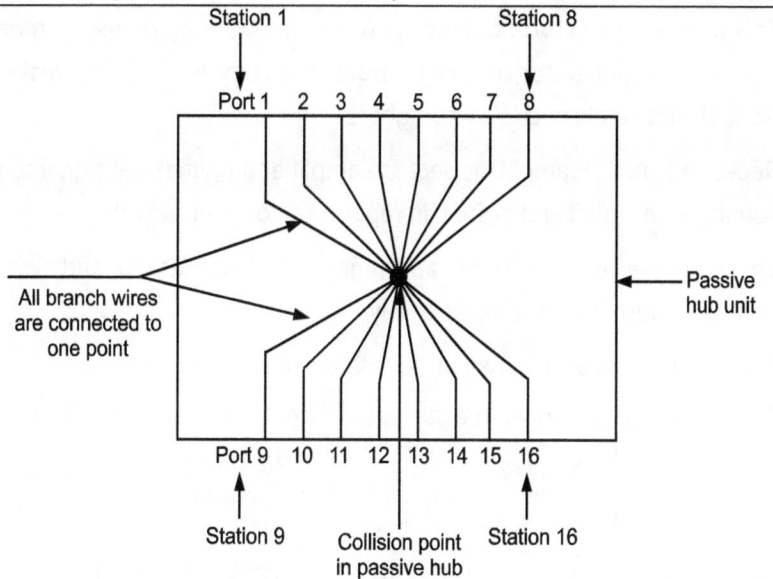

Fig. 5.12 : Typical Passive Hub Unit Internals

5.5 REPEATERS AND ACTIVE HUB

- It works at physical layer of the ISO-OSI reference model.
- We have seen 10Base5 Ethernet length restriction upto 500 meters. To extend the length, we divide the cable into segments and install repeater section between two segments.
- Thus, repeater connects two segments of LAN, not two different LANs.

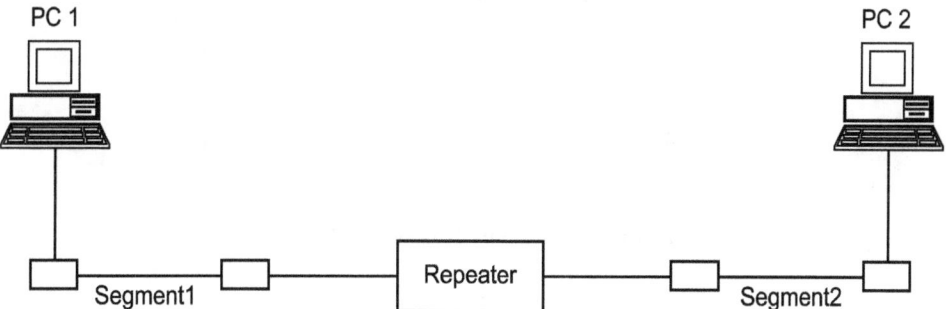

Fig. 5.13 : Repeater connects two segments of LAN

- For long distance data communication, signal becomes weak or corrupted.

- This weakened or corrupted data is regenerated bit by bit using repeater. Hence, repeater is regenerator or it regenerates the copy of data i.e. weakened '0' → to right '0' and weakened '1' → to right '1'.

- Repeater is not an amplifier, because amplifier amplifies the signal as well as noise coming with signal and noise can replace the original signal.

- Thus, repeater is regenerator and regenerates the data '0' and '1' for weakened and corrupted '0' and '1' respectively.

- Thus, repeater is also known as hub device in networking.

- The repeater regenerates the corrupted signal as shown in Fig. 5.14.

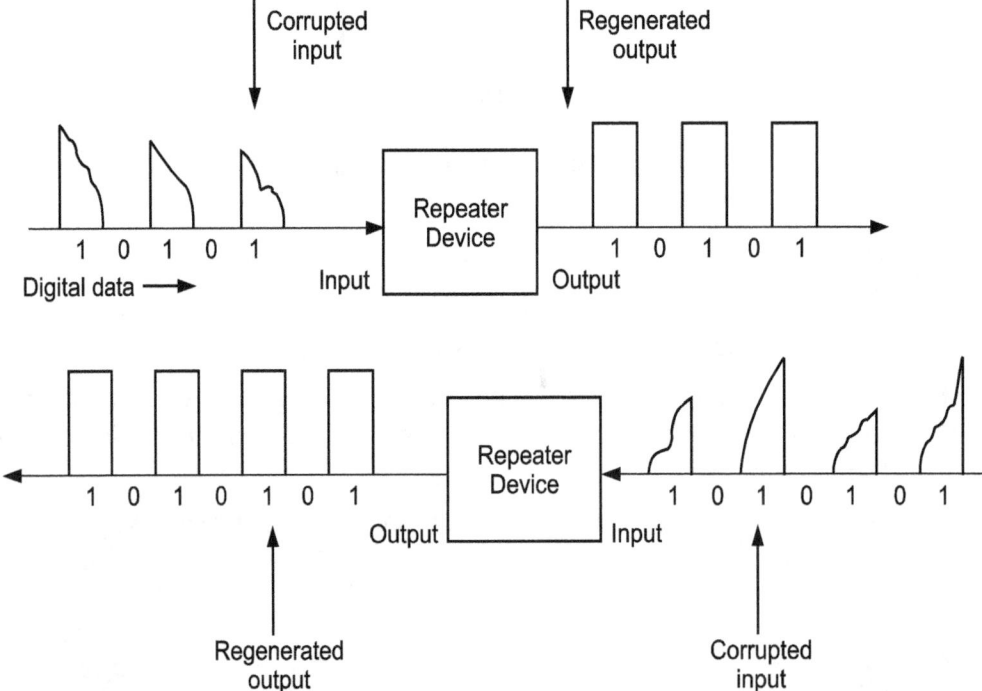

Fig. 5.14 : Function of Repeater Device

- Active hub is basically a multiport repeater as shown in Fig. 5.15.

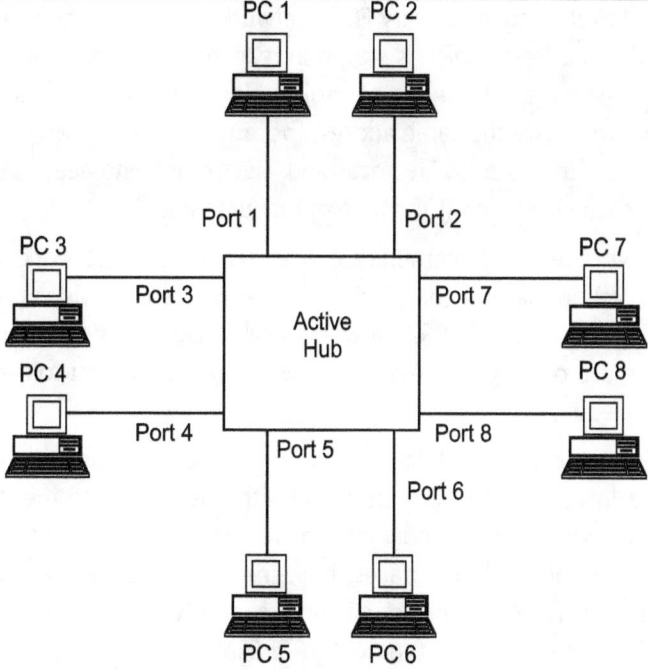

Fig. 5.15 : Active Hub is basically a Multiport Repeater

5.6 NIC AND PC CARD

5.6.1 NIC

A network interface controller (NIC, also known as a network interface card, network adapter, LAN adapter, and by similar terms) is a computer hardware component that connects a computer to a computer network. Early network interface controllers were commonly implemented on expansion cards that plugged into a computer bus; the low cost and ubiquity of the Ethernet standard means that most newer computers have a network interface built into the motherboard.

Purpose

The network controller implements the electronic circuitry required to communicate using a specific physical layer and data link layer standard such as Ethernet, Wi-Fi or Token Ring. This provides a base for a full network protocol stack, allowing communication among small groups of computers on the same LAN and large-scale network communications through routable protocols, such as IP.

Madge 4/16 Mbit/s TokenRing ISA-16 NIC

Although other network technologies exist (e.g. token ring), Ethernet has achieved near-ubiquity since the mid-1990s. Every network controller for an IEEE 802 network such as

Ethernet, Wi-Fi, or Token Ring, and every FDDI network controller, has a unique 48-bit serial number called a MAC address, which is stored in read-only memory. Every computer on an Ethernet network must have at least one controller. Normally it is safe to assume that no two network controllers will share the same address, because controller vendors purchase blocks of addresses from the Institute of Electrical and Electronics Engineers (IEEE) and assign a unique address to each controller at the time of manufacture.

The NIC allows computers to communicate over a computer network. It is both an OSI layer 1 (physical layer) and layer 2 (data link layer) device, as it provides physical access to a networking medium and, for IEEE 802 networks and FDDI, provides a low-level addressing system through the use of MAC addresses. It allows users to connect to each other either by using cables or wirelessly.

Whereas network controllers used to operate on expansion cards that plugged into a computer bus, the low cost and ubiquity of the Ethernet standard means that most new computers have a network interface built into the motherboard. Newer server motherboards may even have dual network interfaces built-in. The Ethernet capabilities are either integrated into the motherboard chipset or implemented via a low-cost dedicated Ethernet chip, connected through the PCI (or the newer PCI Express) bus. A separate network card is not required unless additional interfaces are needed or some other type of network is used.

The NIC may use one or more of two techniques to indicate the availability of packets to transfer: Polling is where the CPU examines the status of the peripheral under program control; Interrupt-driven I/O is where the peripheral alerts the CPU that it is ready to transfer data; and may use one or more of two techniques to transfer packet data: Programmed input/output is where the CPU moves the data to or from the designated peripheral to memory; Direct memory access is where an intelligent peripheral assumes control of the system bus to access memory directly. This removes load from the CPU but requires more logic on the card. In addition, a packet buffer on the NIC may not be required and latency can be reduced.

An Ethernet network controller typically has an 8P8C socket where the network cable is connected. Older NICs also supplied BNC, or AUI connections. A few LEDs inform the user of whether the network is active, and whether or not data transmission occurs. Ethernet network controllers typically support 10 Mbit/s Ethernet, 100 Mbit/s Ethernet, and 1000 Mbit/s Ethernet varieties. Such controllers are designated10/100/1000 - this means they can support a notional maximum transfer rate of 10, 100 or 1000 Megabits per second.

5.6.2 PC Card

PC Card is a form factor peripheral interface designed for laptop computers. Originally introduced as PCMCIA Card, the PC Card standard as well as its successors like CardBus were defined and developed by the Personal Computer Memory Card International

Association (PCMCIA). It was originally designed as a standard for memory-expansion cards for computer storage. The existence of a usable general standard for notebook peripherals led to many kinds of devices being made available based on its form factor, including network cards, modems, and hard disks.

PC Card types :

All PC Card devices use a similar sized package which is 85.6 mm long and 54.0 mm wide, the same size as a credit card.[6] The form factor is also used by the Common Interfaceform of conditional-access modules for DVB broadcasts, and by Panasonic for their professional "P2" video acquisition memory cards. The original standard was defined for both 5 volt and 3.3 volt cards, with 3.3 V cards having a key on the side to prevent them from being inserted fully into a 5 V-only slot. Some cards and some slots operate at both voltages as needed. The original standard was built around an 'enhanced' 16-bit ISA bus platform. A newer version of the PCMCIA standard is CardBus (see below), a 32-bit version of the original standard. In addition to supporting a wider bus of 32 bits (instead of the original 16), CardBus also supports bus masteringand operation speeds up to 33 MHz.

(1) Type I :

Cards designed to the original specification (PCMCIA 1.0) are type I and feature a 16-bit interface. They are 3.3 mm thick and feature a dual row of 34 holes (68 in total) along a short edge as a connecting interface. Type-I PC Card devices are typically used for memory devices such as RAM, flash memory, OTP (One-Time Programmable), and SRAMcards.

(2) Type II :

Type-II and above PC Card devices use two rows of 34 sockets, and feature a 16- or 32-bit interface. They are 5.0 mm thick. Type-II cards introduced I/O support, allowing devices to attach an array of peripherals or to provide connectors/slots to interfaces for which the host computer had no built-in support. For example, many modem, network, and TV cards use this form factor. Due to their thinness, most Type II interface cards feature miniature interface connectors on the card connecting to a dongle, a short cable that adapts from the card's miniature connector to an external full-size connector. Some cards instead have a lump on the end with the connectors. This is more robust and convenient than a separate adapter but can block the other slot where slots are present in a pair. Some Type II cards, most notably network interface and modem cards, have a retractable jack, which can be pushed into the card and will pop out when needed, allowing insertion of a cable from above. When use of the card is no longer needed, the jack can be pushed back into the card and locked in place, protecting it from damage. Most network cards have their jack on one side, while most modems have their jack on the other side, allowing the use of both at the same time as they do not interfere with each other. Wireless Type II cards often had a plastic shroud that jutted out from the end of the card to house the antenna.

(3) Type III :

Type-III PC Card devices are 16-bit or 32-bit. These cards are 10.5 mm thick, allowing them to accommodate devices with components that would not fit type I or type II height. Examples are hard disk drive cards,[6] and interface cards with full-size connectors that do not require dongles (as is commonly required with type II interface cards).

(4) Type IV

Type-IV cards, introduced by Toshiba, have not been officially standardized or sanctioned by the PCMCIA. These cards are 16 mm thick.

5.7 BRIDGE DEVICE

1. Bridge device works upto Layer-2 of the ISO-OSI reference model.
2. Bridge device works upto Layer-2 means it works in both physical and data link layer of ISO-OSI reference model.
3. A **network bridge** connects multiple network segments at the data link layer (Layer-2) of the OSI model, and the term **Layer-2 switch** is very often used interchangeably with bridge.
4. Bridges are similar to repeaters or network hubs, devices that connect network segments at the physical layer; however, with bridging, traffic from one network is managed rather than simply rebroadcast to adjacent network segments.
5. In Ethernet networks, the term "bridge" formally means a device that behaves according to the IEEE 802.1D standard—the popular term "switch" originated in marketing literature.
6. Bridges tend to be more complex than hubs or repeaters. Bridges can analyze incoming data packets to determine if the bridge is able to send the given packet to another segment of the network.
7. Since bridging takes place at the data link layer of the OSI model, a bridge processes the information from each frame of data it receives.
8. In an Ethernet frame, this provides the MAC address of the frame's source and destination.
9. Bridges use two methods to resolve the network segment that a MAC address belongs to **Transparent bridging and Source route bridging.**
10. **Transparent bridging :**
    - This method uses a forwarding database to send frames across network segments.

- The forwarding database is initially empty and entries in the database are built as the bridge receives frames.
- If an address entry is not found in the forwarding database, the frame is rebroadcast to all ports of the bridge, forwarding the frame to all segments except the source address.
- By means of these broadcast frames, the destination network will respond and a route will be created.
- Along with recording the network segment to which a particular frame is to be sent, bridges may also record a bandwidth metric to avoid looping when multiple paths are available.
- Devices that have this transparent bridging functionality are also known as *adaptive bridges*. **They are primarily found in Ethernet networks.**
- Transparent bridge must meet three criteria :
  (a) Frames must be forwarded from one system to another.
  (b) Forwarding table is automatically updated/made by learning frame movements in the LAN.
  (c) Loops in the system must be prevented.

11. **Source Route Bridging :**
    - With source route bridging, two frame types are used in order to find the route to the destination network segment.
    - Single-Route (SR) frames make up most of the network traffic and have set destinations, while All-Route (AR) frames are used to find routes.
    - Bridges send AR frames by broadcasting on all network branches; each step of the followed route is registered by the bridge performing it.
    - Each frame has a maximum hop count, which is determined to be greater than the diameter of the network graph, and is decremented by each bridge.
    - Frames are dropped when this hop count reaches zero, to avoid indefinite looping of AR frames.
    - The first AR frame which reaches its destination is considered to have followed the best route, and the route can be used for subsequent SR frames; the other AR frames are discarded.
    - This method of locating a destination network can allow for indirect load balancing among multiple bridges connecting two networks.
    - The more a bridge is loaded, the less likely it is to take part in the route finding process for a new destination as it will be slow to forward packets.

- A new AR packet will find a different route over a less busy path if one exists.
- This method is very different from transparent bridge usage, where redundant bridges will be inactivated; however, more overhead is introduced to find routes, and space is wasted to store them in frames.
- A switch with a faster backplane can be just as good for performance, if not for fault tolerance. **They are primarily found in Token Ring networks.**

5.7.1 802.x to 802.y Bridges and Variants

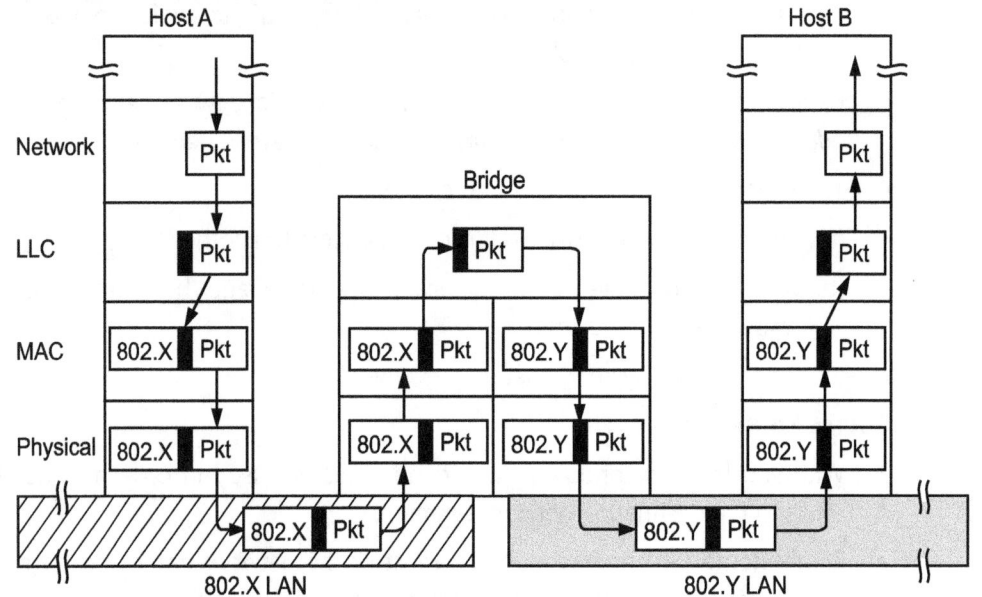

Fig. 5.16 : 802.X to 802.Y Bridge

- At Host 'A' network layer packet is indicated as packet. This comes to LLC layer and LLC header is added.
- At MAC Layer 802.X header is added to packet coming from LLC layer.
- At bridge end, 802.X header is removed and 802.Y header is added.
- Hence, at Host 'B', it understands only 802.Y header packet. Hence bridge converts 802.X to 802.Y header frame and communication of data is possible.

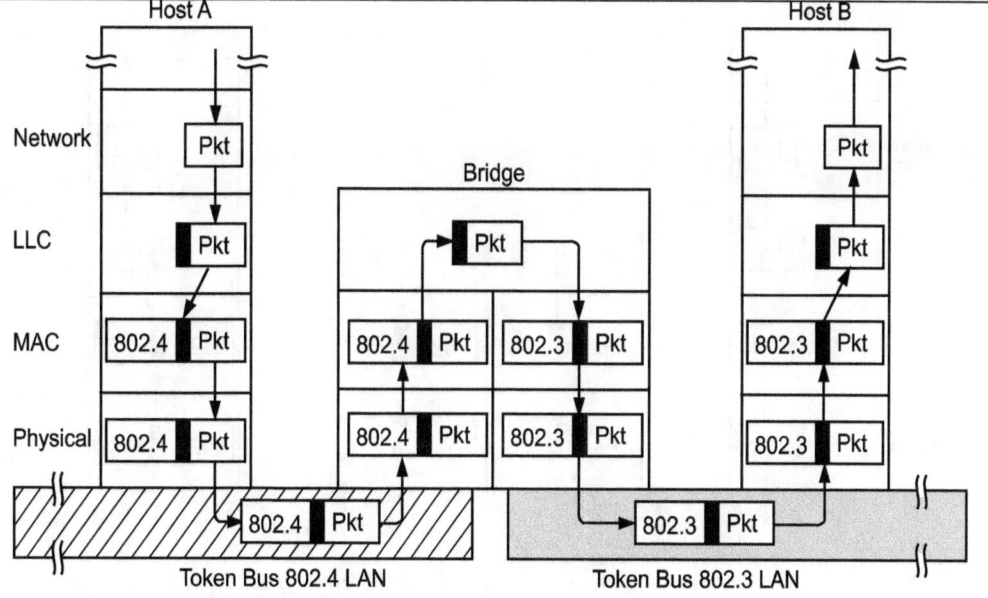

Fig. 5.17 : 802.4 to 802.3 Bridge

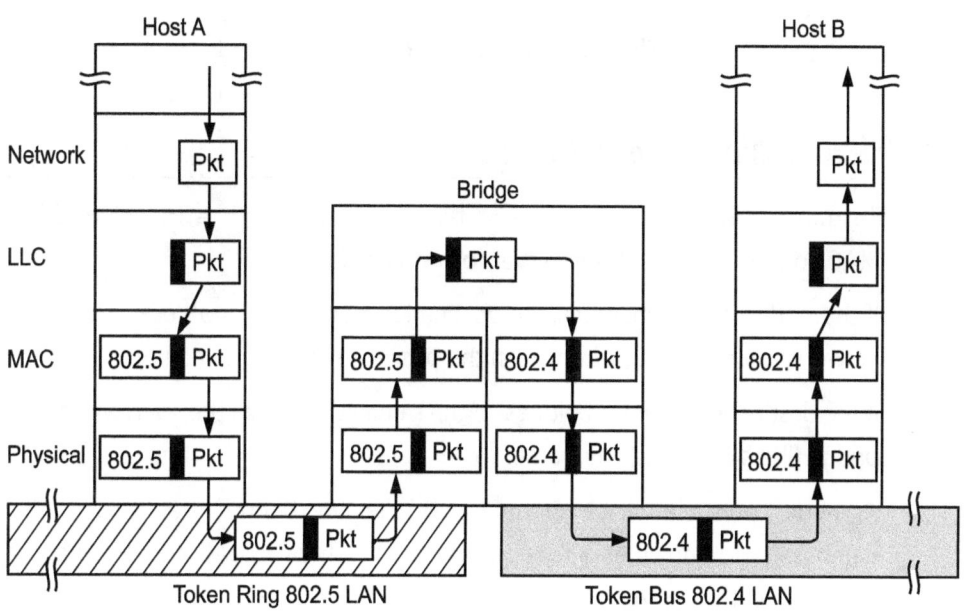

Fig. 5.18 : 802.5 to 802.4 Bridge

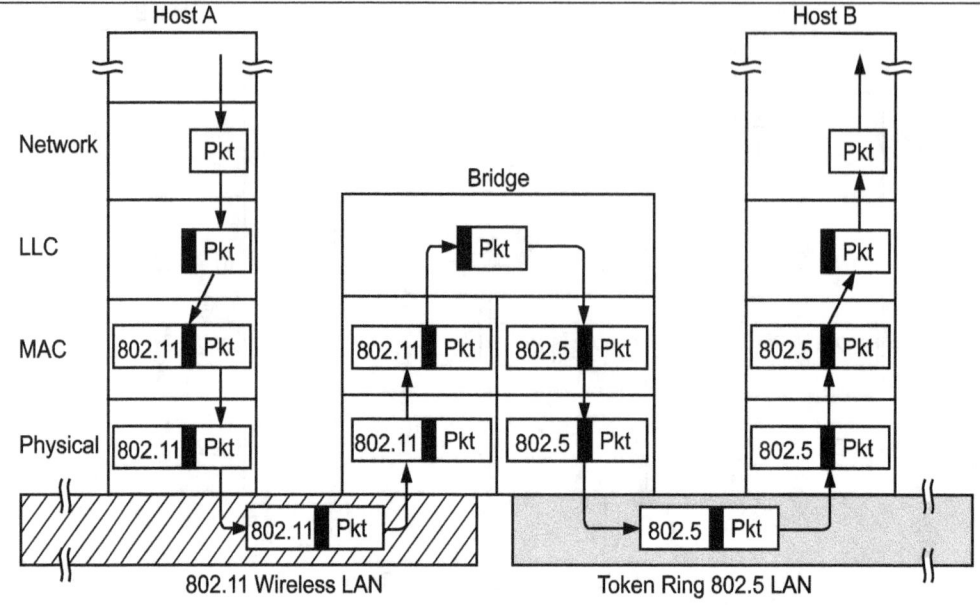

Fig. 5.19 : 802.11 to 802.5 Bridge

5.7.2 Filtering Database in Bridge

1. To translate between two segment types, a bridge reads a frame's destination MAC address and decides to either forward or filter.

2. If the bridge determines that the destination node is on another segment on the network, it forwards it (retransmits) the packet to that segment.

3. If the destination address belongs to the same segment as the source address, the bridge filters (discards) the frame.

4. As nodes transmit data through the bridge, the bridge establishes a filtering database (also known as a forwarding table) of known MAC addresses and their locations on the network.

5. The bridge uses its filtering database to determine whether a packet should be forwarded or filtered. Bridge maintains the table which maps MAC addresses to the specific port.

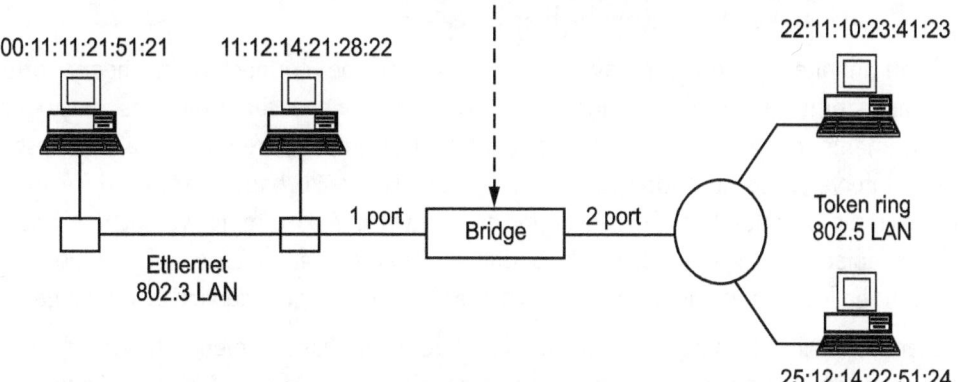

Fig. 5.20 : Bridge Table (MAC Address and Port Number)

5.7.3 Advantages of Network Bridges

- Self-configuring.
- Primitive bridges are often inexpensive.
- Isolate collision domain.
- Reduce the size of collision domain by microsegmentation in non-switched networks.
- Transparent to protocols above the MAC layer.
- Allows the introduction of management/performance information and access control.
- LANs interconnected are separate, and physical constraints such as number of stations, repeaters and segment length don't apply.
- Helps minimize bandwidth usage.
- Used to interconnect two LANs.

5.7.4 Disadvantages of Network Bridges9

- Does not limit the scope of broadcasts.
- Does not scale to extremely large networks.

- Buffering introduces store and forward delays; on average, traffic destined for bridge will be related to the number of stations on the rest of the LAN.
- Bridging of different MAC protocols introduces errors.
- Because bridges do more than repeaters by viewing MAC addresses, the extra processing makes them slower than repeaters.
- Bridges are more expensive than repeaters.

Although infinite bridges (or Layer-2 switches) can be connected in theory, often a broadcast storm will result as more and more collisions occur. Collisions delay service advertisements, causes the hosts to back off and attempt to retransmit after a pseudo-random interval. Because bridges simply repeat any Layer-2 broadcast traffic, this can result in undesirable broadcast traffic consuming the network. An example would be a bridge in between adjacent office buildings. It is unlikely that the advantages of bridging would outweigh the loss of network bandwidth associated with all of the service advertisements.

Another major disadvantage is that any standards-compliant implementation of bridging cannot have any closed loops in a network. This limits both performance and reliability.

5.8 LAYER-2 SWITCHING

- **LAN switching** is a form of packet switching used in local area networks. Switching technologies are crucial to network design, as they allow traffic to be sent only where it is needed in most cases, using fast, hardware-based methods.
- Layer-2 switching is hardware based, which means it uses the Media Access Control address (MAC address) from the host's Network Interface Cards (NICs) to decide where to forward frames.
- Switches use Application-Specific Integrated Circuits (ASICs) to build and maintain filter tables (also known as MAC address tables). One way to think of a layer-2 switch is as a multiport bridge.
- Layer-2 switches effectively provide the same functionality. They are similar to multiport bridges in that they learn and forward frames on each port. The major difference is the involvement of hardware that ensures that multiple switching paths inside the switch can be activated at the same time.
- Layer-2 switching provides the following :
  - Hardware-based bridging (MAC)
  - Wire speed
  - High speed
  - Low latency
  - Low cost

- Layer-2 switching is highly efficient because there is no modification to the data packet, only to the frame encapsulation of the packet, and only when the data packet is passing through dissimilar media (such as from Ethernet to FDDI).
- Layer-2 switching is used for workgroup connectivity and network segmentation (breaking up collision domains).
- This allows a flatter network design with more network segments than traditional 10BaseT shared networks.
- Layer-2 switching has helped develop new components in the network infrastructure :
  - **Server farms :** Servers are no longer distributed to physical locations because virtual LANs can be created to create broadcast domains in a switched internetwork. This means that all servers can be placed in a central location, yet a certain server can still be part of a workgroup in a remote branch, for example.
  - **Intranets :** Allows organization-wide client/server communications based on a web technology.
- These new technologies allow more data to flow off from local subnets and onto a routed network, where a router's performance can become the bottleneck.
- There are three distinct functions of layer-2 switching :
  - Address learning
  - Forward/filter decisions
  - Loop avoidance
- **Address learning :**
  Layer-2 switches and bridges remember the source hardware address of each frame received on an interface, and they enter this information into a MAC database called a forward/filter table.
- **Forward/filter decisions :**
  When a frame is received on an interface, the switch looks at the destination hardware address and finds the exit interface in the MAC database. The frame is only forwarded out to the specified destination port.
- **Loop avoidance :**
  If multiple connections between switches are created for redundancy purposes, network loops can occur. Spanning Tree Protocol (STP) is used to stop network loops while still permitting redundancy.
- While layer-2 switch remains more of a marketing term than a technical term, the products that were introduced as "switches" tended to use microsegmentation and full duplex to prevent collisions among devices connected to Ethernets.

- **Microsegmentation** in computer networking is a term used to describe the segmentation of a collision domain into as many segments as there are circuits minus one.

  Segments = Circuits − 1

- This microsegmentation performed by the switch cuts the collision domain down so that only two nodes coexist within each collision domain. This way, collisions are decreased and only the two NICs which are directly connected via a point-to-point link are contending for the medium.

- By using an internal forwarding plane much faster than any interface, they give the impression of simultaneous paths among multiple devices.

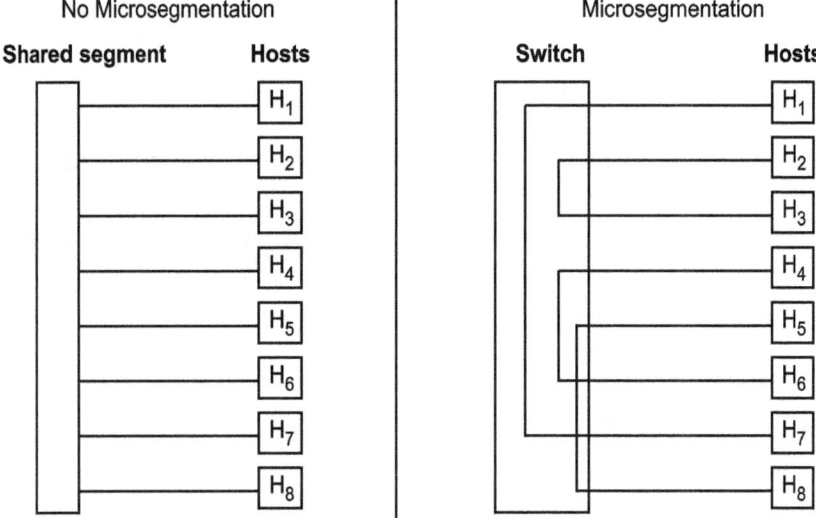

Fig. 5.21 : Microsegmentation and No Microsegmentation

- Once a bridge learns the topology through a spanning tree protocol, it forwards data link layer frames using a layer-2 forwarding method.

- There are four forwarding methods a bridge can use, of which the second to fourth methods are performance-increasing methods when used on "switch" products with the same input and output port speeds.

  - **Store and forward :** The switch buffers and typically performs a checksum on each frame before forwarding it on.

  - **Cut through :** The switch reads only up to the frame's hardware address before starting to forward it. There is no error checking with this method.

  - **Fragment free :** A method that attempts to retain the benefits of both "store and forward" and "cut through". Fragment free checks the first 64 bytes of the frame, where addressing information is stored. According to Ethernet specifications, collisions should be detected during the first 64 bytes of the frame, so frames that are in error because of a collision will not be forwarded. This way the frame will always reach its intended destination. Error checking of the actual data in the packet is left for the end device in Layer-3 or Layer-4 (OSI), typically a router.

- **Adaptive switching :** A method of automatically switching between the other three modes.

- Cut-through switches have to fall back to store and forward if the outgoing port is busy at the time when the packet arrives.
- While there are specialized applications, such as storage area networks, where the input and output interfaces are at same speed, this is rarely the case in general LAN applications.
- In LANs, a switch used for end user access typically concentrates lower speed (e.g., 10/100 Mbps) into a higher speed (at least 1 Gbps).
- Alternatively, a switch that provides access to server ports usually connects to them at a much higher speed than is used by end user devices.
- An Ethernet switch is used to interconnect a number of Ethernet local area networks (LANs) to form a large Ethernet network. Different ports of the switch are connected to different LAN segments. The purpose of the switch is to forward the packets only to the desired destination segment of the network whenever possible, minimizing traffic on the network.

Limitations of Layer-2 Switch :

- Layer-2 switches have the same limitations as bridge networks. Remember that bridges are good if a network is designed by the 80/20 rule: users spend 80 percent of their time on their local segment.
- Bridged networks break up collision domains, but the network remains one large broadcast domain.
- Similarly, layer-2 switches (bridges) cannot break up broadcast domains, which can cause performance issues and limits the size of your network.
- Broadcast and multicasts, along with the slow convergence of spanning tree, can cause major problems as the network grows.
- Because of these problems, layer-2 switches cannot completely replace routers in the internetwork.

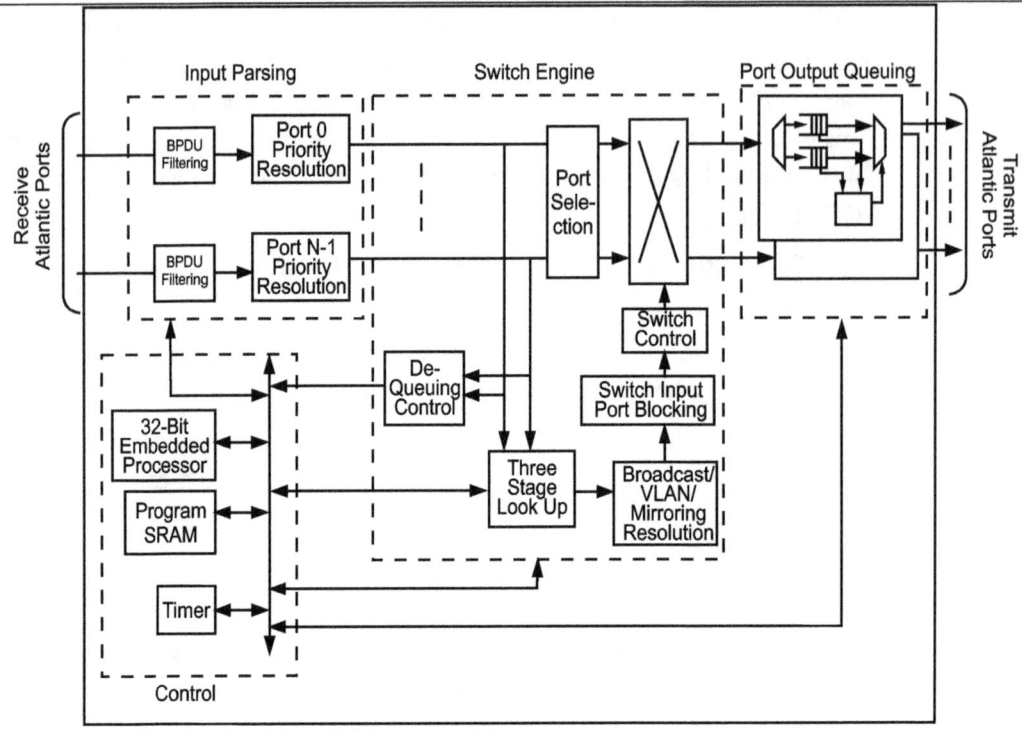

Fig. 5.22 : Ethernet Layer-2 Switch Block Diagram

5.9 ROUTER

- Technically, a router is a networking device whose software and hardware are usually tailored to the tasks of routing and forwarding information.
- Router works upto layer-3 of ISO-OSI reference model means Physical + Data link + Network layer.
- Router routes the packets based on their logical addresses like host to host IP addressing.
- Router connects LANs to WANs and decision is taken by routing table maintained by it.
- Routers connect two or more logical subnets, which do not necessarily map one-to-one to the physical interfaces of the router.
- The term "layer-3 switching" is often used interchangeably with routing, but switch is a general term without a rigorous technical definition.
- In marketing usage, a switch is generally optimized for Ethernet LAN interfaces and may not have other physical interface types.

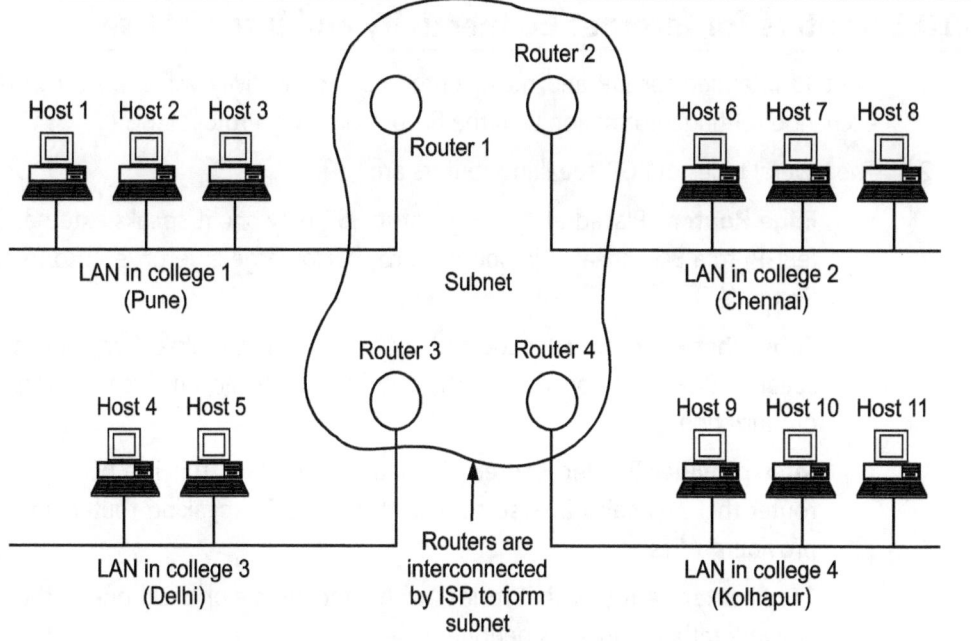

Fig. 5.23 : Typical Subnet (Host is not part of subnet)

- In comparison, the network hub (predecessor of the "switch" or "switching hub") does not do any routing, instead every packet it receives on one network line gets forwarded to all the other network lines.
- Routers operate in two different planes :
  - **Control plane**, in which the router learns the outgoing interface that is most appropriate for forwarding specific packets to specific destinations.
  - **Forwarding plane**, which is responsible for the actual process of sending a packet received on a logical interface to an outbound logical interface.

5.10 TYPES OF ROUTERS

Routers may provide connectivity inside enterprises, between enterprises and the Internet, and inside Internet Service Providers (ISPs). The smallest routers provide connectivity for small offices and home offices.
- Routers for Internet connectivity and internal use
- Small Office Home Office (SOHO) connectivity
- Enterprise routers
- Access routers
- Distribution routers
- Core routers.

5.10.1 Routers for Internet Connectivity and Internal Use

1. Routers intended for ISP and major enterprise connectivity will almost invariably exchange routing information with the Border Gateway Protocol (BGP).

2. The several types of BGP-speaking routers are :

    - **Edge Router :** Placed at the edge of an ISP network, it speaks external BGP (eBGP) to a BGP speaker in another provider or large enterprise Autonomous System(AS).

    - **Subscriber Edge Router :** Located at the edge of the subscriber's network, it speaks eBGP to its provider's AS(s). It belongs to an end user (enterprise) organization.

    - **Inter-provider Border Router :** Interconnecting ISPs, this is a BGP speaking router that maintains BGP sessions with other BGP speaking routers in other providers' ASes.

    - **Core router :** A router that resides within the middle or backbone of the LAN network rather than at its periphery.

3. **Within an ISP :** It is internal element of Autonomous System (AS), such a router speaks internal BGP (iBGP) to that provider's edge routers, other intra-provider core routers, or the provider's inter-provider border routers.

4. **Internet backbone :** The Internet does not have a clearly identifiable backbone, as did its predecessors. Nevertheless, it is the major ISP router acting as a core element. These ISPs operate all four types of the BGP-speaking routers described here. In ISP usage, a "core" router is internal to an ISP, and used to interconnect its edge and border routers. Core routers may also have specialized functions in virtual private networks based on a combination of BGP and Multi-Protocol Label Switching (MPLS). Routers are also used for port forwarding for private servers.

5.10.2 Small Office Home Office (SOHO) Connectivity

1. Residential gateways (often called routers) are frequently used in homes to connect to a broadband service, such as IP over cable or DSL.
2. Such a router may also include an internal DSL modem.
3. Residential gateways and SOHO routers typically provide network address translation and port address translation in addition to routing.
4. Instead of directly presenting the IP addresses of local computers to the remote network, such a residential gateway makes multiple local computers appear to be a single computer.
5. SOHO routers may also support Virtual Private Network tunnel functionality to provide connectivity to an enterprise network..

5.10.3 Enterprise Routers

1. All sizes of routers may be found inside enterprises.
2. The most powerful routers tend to be found in ISPs, academic and research facilities.
3. Large businesses may also need powerful routers.
4. A three-layer model is in common use, not all of which need be present in smaller networks.

5.10.4 Access Routers

Access routers, including SOHO, are located at customer sites such as branch offices that do not need hierarchical routing of their own. Typically, they are optimized for low cost.

5.10.5 Distribution Routers

1. Distribution routers aggregate traffic from multiple access routers, either at the same site, or to collect the data streams from multiple sites to a major enterprise location. Distribution routers often are responsible for enforcing quality of service across a WAN, so they may have considerable memory, multiple WAN interfaces, and substantial processing intelligence.
2. They may also provide connectivity to groups of servers or to external networks. In the latter application, the router's functionality must be carefully considered as part of the overall security architecture. Separate from the router may be a Firewalled or VPN concentrator, or the router may include these and other security functions.
3. When an enterprise is primarily on one campus, there may not be a distinct distribution tier, other than perhaps off-campus access. In such cases, the access routers, connected to LANs, interconnect via core routers.

5.10.6 Core Routers

1. In enterprises, a core router may provide a "collapsed backbone" interconnecting the distribution tier routers from multiple buildings of a campus, or large enterprise locations. They tend to be optimized for high bandwidth.
2. When an enterprise is widely distributed with no central location(s), the function of core routing may be subsumed by the WAN service to which the enterprise subscribes, and the distribution routers become the highest tier.

5.10.7 Routing Concept

1. **Routing** is the process of selecting paths in a network along which to send network traffic. Routing is performed for many kinds of networks, including the telephone network, electronic data networks (such as the Internet), and transportation networks. This article is concerned primarily with routing in electronic data networks using packet switching technology.

2. In packet switching networks, routing directs packet forwarding, the transit of logically addressed packets from their source towards their ultimate destination through intermediate nodes; typically hardware devices called routers, bridges, gateways, firewalls, or switches.

3. General-purpose computers with multiple network cards can also forward packets and perform routing, though they are not specialized hardware and may suffer from limited performance.

4. The routing process usually directs forwarding on the basis of routing tables which maintain a record of the routes to various network destinations.

5. Thus, constructing routing tables, which are held in the router's memory, is very important for efficient routing. Most routing algorithms use only one network path at a time, but multipath routing techniques enable the use of multiple alternative paths.

6. Routing schemes differ in their delivery semantics :
   - Unicast delivers a message to a single specified node;
   - Broadcast delivers a message to all nodes in the network;
   - Multicast delivers a message to a group of nodes that have expressed interest in receiving the message;
   - Anycast delivers a message to any one out of a group of nodes, typically the one nearest to the source.

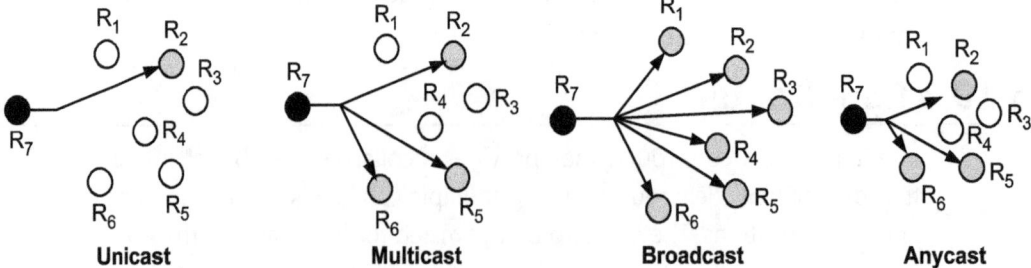

Fig. 5.24 : Different Routing Schemes

5.11 GATEWAY

1. Gateways work upto application layer of ISO-OSI reference model.
2. Different network architecture systems like TCP/IP, Novell netware, Microsoft, Macintosh AppleTalk etc. can communicate with the use of Application Gateway.
3. Application gateways, occasionally referred to as application proxies, are applications located between the end user and the Internet.
4. Application gateways are used in unified communication. Also known as *application proxy* or *application-level proxy*, an application gateway is an application program that runs on a firewall system between two networks.
5. When a client program establishes a connection to a destination service, it connects to an application gateway, or *proxy*.
6. The client then negotiates with the proxy server in order to communicate with the destination service.
7. In effect, the proxy establishes the connection with the destination behind the firewall and acts on behalf of the client, hiding and protecting individual computers on the network behind the firewall.
8. This creates two connections : One between the client and the proxy server and one between the proxy server and the destination.
9. Once connected, the proxy makes all packet-forwarding decisions. Since all communication is conducted through the proxy server, computers behind the firewall are protected.

5.11.1 Functioning Mechanism

1. The end user directly contacts the application gateway.
2. The application gateway performs the requested function on behalf of the user.
3. The application gateway also acts as a firewall by intercepting any IP packets from the Internet.
4. The application gateway can enforce the security policy since the end user never talks directly to a system on the Internet.

5.11.2 Pros and Cons

- **Security** - The application gateway runs on a secured host. Since the proxy stands between the user and the target system, they are not transparent to the users. Users will need to install custom applications to contact application gateways. No user accounts are saved on this host.
- **Simplicity** - The only function of the host running the application gateway is to proxy requests from end users.

5.11.3 Application Gateway Products

- Microsoft
- Cisco
- Nortel

5.12 LAYER-1 HUBS VERSUS SWITCH

1. A network hub, or repeater, is a fairly unsophisticated network device.
2. Hubs do not manage any of the traffic that comes through them.
3. Any packet entering a port is broadcast out or "repeated" on every other port, except for the port of entry.
4. Since every packet is repeated on every other port, packet collisions result, which slows down the network.
5. There are specialized applications where a hub can be useful, such as copying traffic to multiple network sensors.
6. High end switches have a feature which does the same thing called port mirroring. There is no longer any significant price difference between a hub and a low-end switch.

	Hub	Switch
Definition :	An electronic device that connects many computers together to form a single computer network	A way of routing electricity and data flow patterns through circuits based on binary decisions.
Technical Specifications :	Hubs classify as Layer-1 devices in the OSI model	Network switches operate at layer-two (Data Link Layer) of the OSI model.
Cost :	Cheaper than switches	Costlier than hubs
Manufacturers :	Sun Systems, Oracle and Cisco	Sun Systems, Oracle, Belkin, Linksys, and Net Gear, Huawei.
Function :	To connect a network of personal computers together, they can be joined through a central hub	Network switches inspect data packets as they are received, determining the source and destination device of that packet, and forwarding it appropriately.

5.13 BRIDGING VERSUS ROUTING

1. Bridging and routing are both ways of performing data control, but work through different methods.
2. Bridging takes place at OSI Model Layer-2 (data-link layer) while routing takes place at the OSI Model Layer-3 (network layer).
3. This difference means that a bridge directs frames according to hardware assigned MAC addresses while a router makes its decisions according to arbitrarily assigned IP addresses.
4. As a result of this, bridges are not concerned with and are unable to distinguish networks while routers can.
5. When designing a network, one can choose to put multiple segments into one bridged network or to divide it into different networks interconnected by routers.
6. If a host is physically moved from one network area to another in a routed network, it has to get a new IP address; if this system is moved within a bridged network, it does not have to reconfigure anything.
7. These days bridges are replaced with switches.

5.14 BRIDGE VERSUS LAYER-2 SWITCH

1. Bridge frame handling is controlled in the bridge's software. Conversely, layer-2 switch performs address recognition and frame forwarding with hardware. Similarly, a router and a layer-3 switch differ only by whether they forward in software, or hardware.
2. A bridge can typically analyze/forward only one packet at a time, while a layer-2 switch has multiple parallel data paths and can handle multiple frames simultaneously.
3. A bridge uses store-and-forward (it buffers the incoming frame, and then performs a CRC to ensure data integrity before forwarding the frame), while a layer-2 switch can be configured to either use store-and-forward, or to use cut-through (sending the frame as soon as the destination MAC address is realized, without checking the data for correctness).
4. Because a layer-2 switch can incorporate the functions of a bridge, the bridge has suffered commercially. New installations typically include layer-2 switches with bridge functionality, rather than bridges. This has led to the general mixing of the two terms.

5.15 LAYER-2 VERSUS LAYER-3 SWITCH

1. Essentially, a layer-2 switch is a multiport bridge.
2. A layer-2 switch will learn about MAC addresses connected to each port and passes frames marked for those ports.

3. It also knows that if a frame is sent out a port but is looking for the MAC address of the port it is connected and thereafter it drops that frame.
4. Whereas a single CPU bridge runs in serial, todays hardware based switches run in parallel, translating to extremly fast switching.
5. Layer-3 switching is a hybrid, as one can imagine a combination of a router and a switch.
6. There are different types of layer-3 switching, route caching and topology-based switching.
7. In route caching the switch requires both a Route Processor (RP) and a Switch Engine (SE).
8. The RP must listen to the first packet to determine the destination.
9. At that point the Switch Engine makes a shortcut entry in the caching table for the rest of the packets to follow.
10. Due to advancement in processing power and drastic reductions in the cost of memory, today's higher end layer-3 switches implement a topology-based switching which builds a lookup table and populates it with the entire network's topology.
11. The database is held in hardware and is referenced there to maintain high throughput. It utilizes the longest address match as the layer-3 destination.

5.16 ROUTER VERSUS SWTICH

Definition	Router	Switch
Cost :	More expensive than hubs or switches.	Costlier than hubs.
Manufacturers :	Cisco, Juniper Networks, Belkin, Extreme Networks, Huawei, Netgear.	Sun Systems, Oracle, Belkin, Linksys, and Net Gear, Huawei.
Function :	Routers connect two or more logical subnets, which do not necessarily map 1-1 to the physical interfaces of the router.	Network switches inspect data packets as they are received, determining the source and destination device of that packet, and forwarding it appropriately.
Definition :	A router is a computer tailored to the tasks of routing and forwarding information. Routers generally contain a specialized operating system, RAM, NVRAM, flash memory, and one or more processors, as well as two or more network interfaces.	A way of routing electricity and data flow patterns through circuits based on binary decisions.
Technical Specifications :	Router works at layer-3 of ISO-OSI reference model.	Network switches operate at layer-two (Data Link Layer) of the OSI model.

DATA COMMUNICATION (S.E. SEM. III SU – COMPUTER)　　　NETWORK HARDWARE COMPONENTS

1. Routers and switches are both computer networking devices. They allow one or more computers to be connected to other computers, network devices, or to other networks.

2. However, the functions of a hub, switch and router are quite different, even if at times they are integrated into a single device.

3. Routers connect two or more logical subnets, which do not necessarily map one-to-one to the physical interfaces of the router.

4. The term layer-3 switch is often used interchangeably with router, but switch is really a general term without a rigorous technical definition.

5. In marketing usage, it is generally optimized for Ethernet LAN interfaces and may not have other physical interface types.

EXERCISES

1. What are the different connecting devices used in computer data communication ?
2. Write short notes on following :
   (a) Passive hub
   (b) Hub or repeater
   (c) Bridge
   (d) Layer-2 switch
   (e) Router
   (f) Brouter
   (g) Layer-3 switch
3. Explain and correlate connecting devices with ISO-OSI reference model.
4. Explain 802.X to 802.Y bridge communication.
5. Explain the concept of filtering database in bridge.
6. What are different advantages of network bridges ?
7. What are different disadvantages of network bridges ?
8. What is Layer-2 switching ?
9. What is microsegmentation in switch ?
10. What are the limitations of Layer-2 switches ?
11. What is a router ? What are the different types of router ?
12. What is routing ? What are different routing schemes ?

13. What is "Gateway" connecting device ?
14. Compare Layer-1 hubs Vs. Switch device.
15. Compare Bridge Vs. Router.
16. Compare Bridge Vs. Layer-2 switch.
17. Compare Layer-2 switch Vs. Layer-3 switch.
18. Compare Router Vs. Switch.
19. Write short notes on the following :
    (a) Bus backbone networks
    (b) Star backbone networks
    (c) Virtual LANs
20. What are prerequisites of VLAN ?
21. What are different uses of VLAN ?
22. What technologies are able to implement VLANs ?
23. Explain IEEE 802.1Q VLAN standard tag used in Ethernet.
24. Explain the "VLAN Memberships" in detail.
25. What are the different advantages of VLANs ?
26. Explain the STS levels and related supporting data rate.
27. Write short notes on the following :
    (a) SONET devices in detail
    (b) Connections in SONET
    (c) SONET layers in detail
    (d) Device layer relationship in SONET
    (e) SONET frames
    (f) Frame, byte and bit transmission in SONET
    (g) STS-1 frame format in detail
    (h) SOH of STS-1 frame
    (i) LOH of STS-1 frame
    (j) SPE (Synchronous Payload Envelope)
    (k) Encapsulation Process in SONET.
28. Explain advantages of SONET.
29. Explain the benefits of SONET.

UNIT IV

Chapter 6

ERROR CONTROL AND DATA LINK LAYER

OBJECTIVES

After reading this chapter you will understand :
- Functions of Data Link Layer.
- How Linear Block Codes and Cyclic Block Codes are used for Error Control.
- What is Framing ?
- How Flow Control is done in DLL.
- HDLC and PPP Protocols.

6.1 INTRODUCTION

- Physical layer takes care of transmitting information over a communication channel.
- Information transmitted may be affected by noise or distortion caused in the channel.
- Hence, the transmission over communication channel is not reliable.
- The data transfer is also affected by delay and has finite rate of transmission. This reduces the efficiency of transmission.
- Data link layer is designed to take care of these problems i.e. data link layer improves reliability and efficiency of channel.
- We can also say that the services provided by physical layer are not reliable.
- Hence, we require some layer above physical layer which can take care of these problems. The layer above physical layer is Data Link Layer (DLL).

Following are some of the functions of a data link layer.

- **Error control :** Physical layer is error prone. The errors introduced in the channel need to be corrected.
- **Flow control :** There might be mismatch in the transmission rate of sender and the rate at which receiver receives. This mismatch must be taken care of.
- **Addressing :** In the network where there are multiple terminals, whom to send the data has to be specified.

- **Frame synchronization :** In physical layer, information is in the form of bits. These bits are grouped in blocks of frames at data link layer. In order to identify beginning and end of frames, some identification mark is put before and/or after each frame.

- **Link management :** In order to manage co-ordination and co-operation among terminals in the network, initiation, maintenance and termination of link is required to be done properly. These procedures are handled by data link layer. The control signals required for this purpose use the same channels on which data is exchanged. Hence, identification of control and data information is another task of data link layer.

- **Services provided to network layer :** Data link layer provides services to the layer above it viz. network layer. The basic service is transferring packets from network layer on source machine to network layer on destination machine as shown in Fig. 6.1.

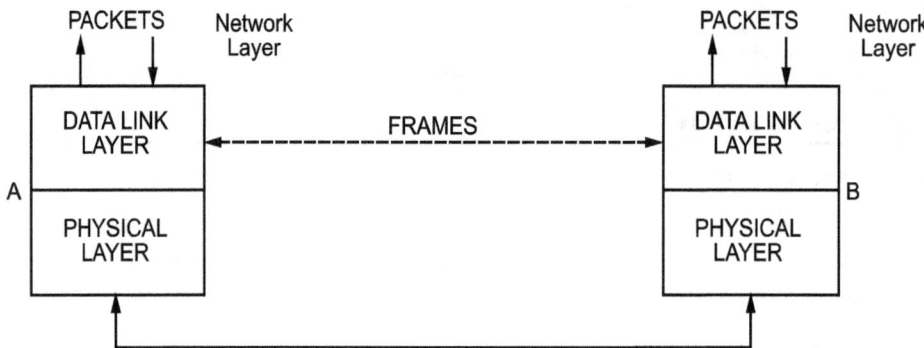

Fig. 6.1 : Service provided to Network Layer

The service model describes the service provided by a protocol.

There are two categories of service models :
- Connection-oriented service.
- Connectionless service.

In connection-oriented service, connection is established between the peer entities first and then data transfer begins. There will be connection setup, data transfer and connection release procedure required to be carried out. Connectionless services do not require a connection setup procedure. Information blocks are transmitted using address information in each Protocol Data Unit (PDU). Acknowledged connectionless services provide acknowledgement for each PDU so that data transfer is reliable.

Unacknowledged connectionless services do not provide acknowledgement for each PDU. This is also called best effort service. In such case, network layer has to provide reliable service i.e. acknowledged service.

The service model specifies the Quality of Service (QoS). It includes expected performance level in transfer of information. Examples of some QoS parameters are :

- Probability of error.
- Probability of loss.
- Transfer delay.

6.2 TYPES OF ERRORS

Whenever bits flow from one point to another, they are subjected to unpredictable changes, because of interference. This interference can change the shape of signals. In a single bit error a0 is changed to a1 or a1 to a0. In a burst error, multiple bits are changed. For example, 1/100s burst of impulse noise on a transmission with a data rate of 1200 bps might change all or some of the 12 bits of information.

(1) Single Bit Error :

It means that only 1 bit of a given data unit (as a byte, character or packet) is changed from 1 to 0 or 0 to 1.

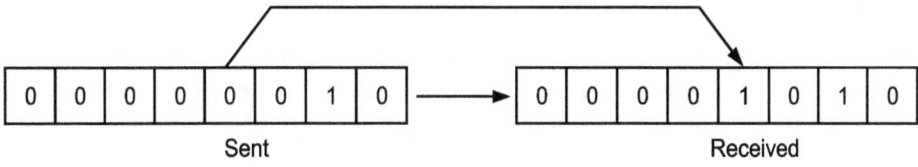

Fig. 6.2

Fig. 6.2 shows the effect of single bit error on a data unit. To understand the impact of change, imagine that each group of 8 bits is an ASCII character with a0 bit added to the left. In Fig. 6.2, 00000010 (ASCII/STX) was sent, meaning start of text but 00001010 (ASCII LF) was received, meaning line feed.

Single bit errors are the least likely type of errors in serial data transmission. To understand imagine data sent at 1 Mbps. This means that each bit lasts only 1/1,000,000s or 1 µs. For single bit error to occur, the noise must have a duration of only 1 µs, which is very rare. Noise normally lasts much longer than this.

(2) Burst Error :

The term means that 2 or more bits in the data unit have changed from 1 to 0 or from 0 to 1.

In this case 0100010001000011 was sent, but 0101110101100011 was received. A burst error does not necessarily mean that the errors occur in consecutive bits. The length of the burst is measured from the first corrupted bit to the last corrupted bit. Some bits in between may not have been corrupted.

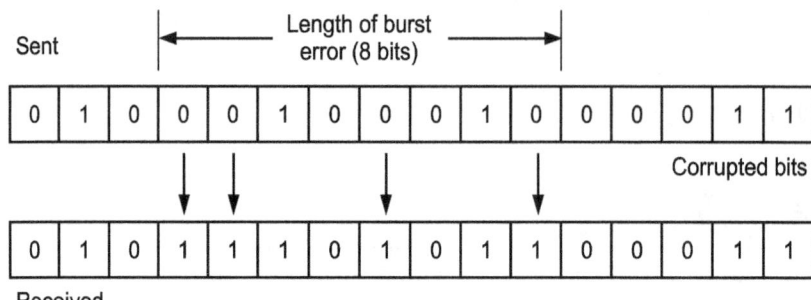

Fig. 6.3

A burst error is more likely to occur than a single bit error. The duration of noise is normally longer than the duration of 1 bit, this means when noise affects data, it affects a set of bits. The number of bits affected depends on the data rate and duration of noise. For example, if we are sending data at 1 kbps, a noise of 1/100s can affect 10 bits, if we are sending data at 1 Mbps, the same noise can affect 10,000 bits.

Redundancy :

The main concept in detecting errors is redundancy. To detect errors we need to send some extra bits with our data. These redundant bits are added by sender and removed by the receiver. Their presence allows the receiver to detect corrupted bits.

Detection Versus Correction :

The correction of error is more difficult than detection. In error detection, we are looking only to see if any error has occurred. The answer is a simple yes or no. We are not even interested in the number of errors. A single bit error is the same for us as a burst error.

In error correction, we need to know the exact number of bits that are corrupted and more importantly, their location in the message. The number of errors and the size of the message are important factors. If we need to correct one single error in an 8-bit data unit. We need to consider eight possible error locations. If we need to correct two errors in data unit of the same size, we need to consider 28 possibilities. You can imagine the receiver's difficulty in finding 10 errors in data unit of 1000 bits.

Forward Error Correction Versus Retransmission :

There are two main methods of error correction. Forward error correction is the process in which the receiver tries to guess the message by using redundant bits. This is possible, as we see later, if the number of errors is small.

Correction by retransmission is a technique in which the receiver detects the occurrence of an error and asks the sender to resend the message. Resending is repeated until a message arrives that the receiver believes in error-free.

Coding :

Redundancy is achieved through various coding schemes. The sender adds redundant bits through a process that creates a relationship between the redundant bits and the actual data bits. The receiver checks the relationship between the two sets of bits to detect the errors. The ratio of redundant bits to the data bits and the robustness of the process are important factors in any coding scheme.

We can divide coding schemes into two broad categories :

- Block coding.
- Convolution coding.

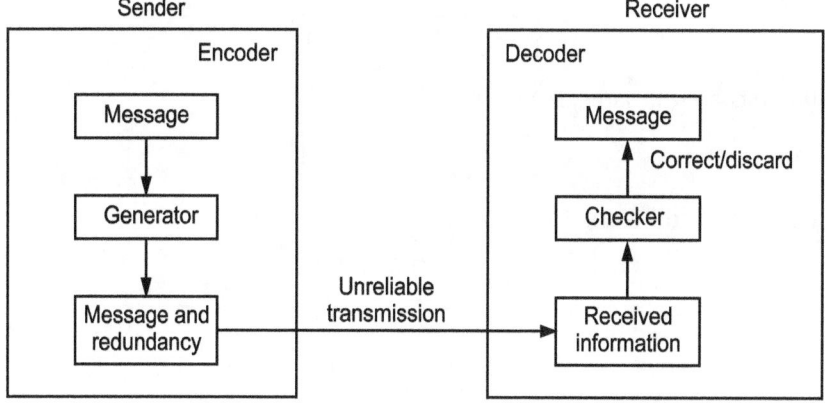

Fig. 6.4 : The Structure of Encoder and Decoder

Modular Arithmetic :

In modular arithmetic we use only limited range of integers. We define an upper limit, called modulus N. We use only the integers 0 to N – 1, inclusive. This is modulo-N arithmetic.

For example, if the modulus is 12, we use only the integers 0 to 11, inclusive. An example of modulo arithmetic is our clock system. It is based on modulo 12 arithmetic, substituting the number 12 for 0.

In a modulo-N system, if a number is greater than N, it is divided by N and the remainder is the result. If it is negative, as many Ns as needed are added to make it positive. Consider our clock system again, if we start job at 11 a.m. and the job takes 5 hrs., we can say that the job is to be finished at 16.00 if we are in the military, or we can say that it will be finished at 4 p.m. (the remainder of 16/12 is 4).

Addition and subtraction in modulo arithmetic are simple. There is no carry when you add two digits in a column. There is no carry when you subtract one digit from another in column.

Modulo-2 Arithmetic :

In this arithmetic, the modulus N is 2. We can use only 0 and 1. Operations in this arithmetic are very simple. The following shows how we can add or subtract 2 bits.

Adding : $0 + 0 = 0$ $0 + 1 = 1$ $1 + 0 = 1$ $1 + 1 = 0$

Subtracting : $0 - 0 = 0$ $0 - 1 = 1$ $1 - 0 = 1$ $1 - 1 = 0$

Notice particularly that addition and subtraction give the same results. In this arithmetic we use the XOR operation for both addition and subtraction. The result of an XOR operation is 0 if two bits are same, the result is 1 if two bits are different. Fig. 6.4 shows the operation :

XORing of two single bits or two words.

$$\boxed{0 + 0 = 0 \quad 1 + 1 = 0}$$

1. Two bits are the same, the result is 0.

$$\boxed{0 + 1 = 1 \quad 1 + 0 = 1}$$

2. Two bits are different, the result is 1.

$$\boxed{\begin{array}{r} 1\ 0\ 1\ 1\ 0 \\ +\ 1\ 1\ 1\ 0\ 0 \\ \hline 0\ 1\ 0\ 1\ 0 \end{array}}$$

3. Result of XORing two patterns.

Other Modulo Arithmetic :

We use modulo-N arithmetic through the book. The principle is the same. We use numbers between 0 and N − 1. If the modulus is not 2, addition and subtraction are distinct. If we get a negative result, we add enough multiples of N to make it positive.

6.3 BLOCK CODING

- A digital communication system must have higher data rate, minimum signal power, reliable transmission and minimum bandwidth requirement.
- The channel over which the transmission takes place is usually noisy and it will have limited bandwidth.
- If we have to keep the signal power minimum the signal to noise ratio will be lower. This will lead to increase in error probability (p_e), as it depends on E_b/N_0 ratio. Hence, reliability of the system suffers.

- Hence, in order to improve reliability for given E_b/N_0 ratio, we can use error control coding techniques.
- Error control coding techniques can correct errors, so that messages which are likely to go wrong in a noisy channel can be retrieved correctly at the receiver end.
- This is also known as Forward Error Correction (FEC).
- For a fixed value of error probability, it is also possible to reduce E_b/N_0 ratio (signal power) using error control coding.
- Since this technique tries to overcome channel noise, it is also called **channel coding**.
- The error correcting codes are generated by adding redundancy to original message before transmitting it on a noisy channel. The channel encoder block in the transmitter does this as shown in Fig. 6.5.

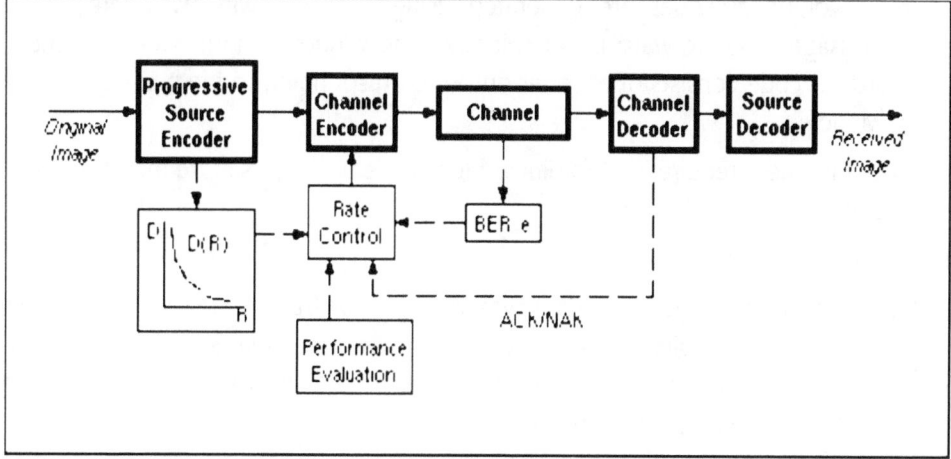

Fig. 6.5 : Channel Coding in Communication System

- At the receiver we can recover the original message if the errors are within the limit as per the design of code. The channel decoder block does this recovery.
- A good error control coding technique should have
    (i) Better error correcting capability.
    (ii) Faster and efficient method of coding and decoding.
    (iii) Maximum transfer of information in bit/sec. (or less overheads).
- If we try to increase error correcting capability, information rate will reduce and coding and decoding will also be slower. Complexity of design increases in order to achieve better coding technique. The addition of redundancy also increases the

- bandwidth requirement. Thus, reliability is at the cost of bandwidth and system complexity.
- Reliability can be increased by designing error detecting systems. In these systems, we add redundancy at the transmitter end in the message. The code is then transmitted. At the receiver end we will detect whether the code received is correct or not. If not, we request the transmitter to retransmit the code. The overheads required in this case are lower than that of FEC. This technique is called Automatic Repeat Request (ARQ).
- There are number of error correcting codes. They are classified as :
    (i) Block codes.
    (ii) Convolutional codes.
- In block codes a block of k-bit message is encoded into n bits by adding n–k redundant bits.
- Convolutional codes are generated using a sliding window where, incoming message slides forward in the window. The window length is usually small and output code consists of encoder output corresponding to the message bits in the window.
- The memory requirement for linear block code encoder is more than convolutional code.

Basic Definitions

In digital communication, we use binary symbols (I/O) for transmission of message hence, we will be using the word bits instead of symbols in our discussion. But correct and general word should be symbols as a message may generate more than two types of symbols. Let us first discuss some frequently used terms with coding.

1. **Word :** It is a sequence of symbols.

    e.g. Suppose we have a message consisting of 1010, then it is called a **message word.** Similarly, there will be code corresponding to this message called as **codeword.**

2. **Code :** It is a set of vectors called as codewords or code vectors.
3. **Parity bits :** The bits which are added to the message bits are called parity bits.
4. **Systematic code :** Code in which codewords consists of message bits and parity bits separately is called systematic code.
5. **Block codes :** These are fixed length codewords generated from a block of message words.

6. **Block code specification :** The block code is specified in terms of number of code bits and number of message bits. If there are k bits in the message word and n bits are generated to form codeword, the block code is called (n, k) block code.

7. **Code rate :** For an (n, k) block code the code rate is defined as the ratio of message bits and code bits (k/n). Code rate is always less than one.

8. **Parity check codes :** These are simplest possible block codes. These codes are generated by adding one bit to the message bits. They can be even parity check codes or odd parity check codes. Even parity check codes add 1 to message if number of 1's in message are odd and 0 if number of 1's in message are even.

   e.g.

Message	Code ↓	Parity bit
100101	1001011	
110101	1101010	

   Similarly,

   Odd parity check codes

Message	Code	Parity bit
010011	0100110	
010001	0100011	

   If single error occurs in these codewords, it can be detected at the receiver end.

9. **Weight of a codeword :** *The number of non-zero symbols in a codeword is called weight of the codeword.*

   e.g.

Codeword	Weight
10101	3
11110	4

10. **Hamming distance :** *It is a number of symbols in which two codewords differ.*

    e.g.
    $$c_1 = 10101$$
    $$c_2 = 11010$$

    Hamming distance between c_1 and c_2 is 4, denoted as $d(c_1, c_2) = 4$.

11. Minimum hamming distance between any two codewords of a code is called minimum hamming distance of that code. It is denoted as d_{min}.

12. **A linear code :** *It is a code which has following properties.*
    (i) The sum of any two codewords in the code will yield another codeword of that code.
    (ii) There is always all-zero codeword.
    (iii) The minimum hamming distance between any two codewords is equal to minimum weight of any non-zero codeword.

Example 6.1 :
Consider the following code.
$$C = \{000, 111\}$$

Solution :

It consists of the two codewords.

Weight of 000 is 0

Weight of 111 is 3.

Hamming distance between two codewords = 3.

Minimum hamming distance of the code = 3.

It is a linear code since addition of the two codewords yield one of the codewords 111.

Example 6.2 :
Consider a code.
$$C = \{000, 010, 001, 111\}$$

Codeword	Weight
000	0
010	1
001	1
111	3

Solution :

Minimum hamming distance = 1

It is not a linear code as addition of 001 and 010 does not yield valid codeword i.e. 011 is not a valid codeword of this code.

13. **Minimum hamming distance (d_{min}) :** Minimum Hamming distance of a linear code is equal to minimum weight of the non-zero codewords in that code.

    Consider a code C = {000, 010, 101, 111}

Codeword	Weight
000	0
010	1
101	2
111	3

Since, minimum weight of non-zero code is 1.

Minimum hamming distance $d_{min} = 1$.

6.4 LINEAR BLOCK CODES

Consider an (n, k) block code in which there are k message bits (or symbols) and n code bits (or symbols).

Let the code bits be,

$$C = (c_1, c_2, c_3, ... c_n) \quad ...(6.1)$$

Let the message bits be,

$$d = (d_1, d_2, d_3, ... d_k) \quad ...(6.2)$$

For general case, n bits of code C are generated by linear combinations of k message bits. This is called non-systematic code.

For a special case,

If $c_1 = d_1 \quad c_2 = d_2 \ ... \ c_k = d_k$

and c_{k+1} to c_n are generated from linear combinations of $d_1, d_2, ... d_k$ then the code is called systematic code. First k bits are message bits and (n − k) parity bits added to the message.

As we have seen in earlier section, any code C is a subspace of $GF(q^n)$ and any set of basic vectors S can be used to generate code space C = <S> by linear combinations of basis vectors. Hence, m can put all basic vectors in a matrix which is called generator matrix (G). This matrix is used to generate the codewords of C. If we have to generate the codewords of length n from k message bits we will need the generator matrix of the order k × n. Hence, we should have k basic vectors in the generator matrix. The code is generated by,

$$C = d \times G \quad ...(6.3)$$

Now, if we have to generate systematic code we should have relationship between c and d as below :

$$c_1 = d_1$$

$$c_2 = d_2$$
$$c_3 = d_3$$
$$\vdots$$
$$c_k = d_k$$
$$c_{k+1} = p_{11} \cdot d_1 \oplus p_{21} \cdot d_2 \oplus \ldots \oplus p_{k1} \cdot d_k$$
$$c_{k+2} = p_{12} \cdot d_1 \oplus p_{22} \cdot d_2 \oplus \ldots \oplus p_{k2} \cdot d_k$$
$$\vdots$$
$$c_n = p_{1n-k} \cdot d_1 \oplus p_{2n-k} \cdot d_2 \oplus \ldots \oplus p_{kn-k} \cdot d_k \quad \ldots (6.4)$$

Hence the generator matrix will be,

$$G = \begin{bmatrix} 1 & 0 & 0 & \ldots & 0 & p_{11} & p_{12} & p_{1n-k} \\ 0 & 1 & 0 & \ldots & 0 & p_{21} & p_{22} & p_{2n-k} \\ \vdots & \vdots & \vdots & & \vdots & & & \\ \vdots & \vdots & \vdots & & \vdots & & & \\ 0 & 0 & 0 & \ldots & 1 & p_{k1} & p_{k2} & p_{kn-k} \end{bmatrix} \quad \ldots (6.5)$$

Thus, generator matrix G consists of two parts Identity matrix I_k and Parity matrix P.

Order of I_k is $k \times k$.

Order of P is $k \times n - k$.

i.e.
$$G = [I_k \ P] \quad \ldots (6.6)$$

The generator matrix provides a concise and efficient way of representing linear block code i.e. a code can be written as,

$$C = dG \quad \ldots (6.7)$$

Thus, we need not store all codewords corresponding to all messages but we can generate them with the help of generator matrix which stores only few codewords.

Example 6.3 :

Generate all codewords of (7, 4) Linear Block Codes (LBC) for following generator matrix.

$$G = \begin{bmatrix} 1 & 0 & 0 & 0 & 1 & 1 & 0 \\ 0 & 1 & 0 & 0 & 0 & 1 & 1 \\ 0 & 0 & 1 & 0 & 1 & 1 & 1 \\ 0 & 0 & 0 & 1 & 1 & 0 & 1 \end{bmatrix} \quad \ldots (6.6)$$

$$\underbrace{\phantom{\begin{matrix}1 & 0 & 0 & 0\end{matrix}}}_{I_k} \quad \underbrace{\phantom{\begin{matrix}1 & 1 & 0\end{matrix}}}_{P}$$

Solution :

We know that,

$$C = dG$$

Here, n = 7, k = 4.

Hence, there will be $2^k = 2^4 = 16$.

To generate code we take each message word and multiply with G.

e.g. For message word d = [1 0 1 0]

$$C = [1\,0\,1\,0] \times \begin{bmatrix} 1 & 0 & 0 & 0 & 1 & 1 & 0 \\ 0 & 1 & 0 & 0 & 0 & 1 & 1 \\ 0 & 0 & 1 & 0 & 1 & 1 & 1 \\ 0 & 0 & 0 & 1 & 1 & 0 & 1 \end{bmatrix} \quad \ldots (6.9)$$

$[1 \cdot 1 \oplus 0 \cdot 0 \oplus 1 \cdot 0 \oplus 0 \cdot 0 = 1$
$1 \cdot 0 \oplus 0 \cdot 1 \oplus 1 \cdot 0 \oplus 0 \cdot 0 = 0$
$1 \cdot 0 \oplus 0 \cdot 0 \oplus 1 \cdot 1 \oplus 0 \cdot 0 = 1$
$1 \cdot 0 \oplus 0 \cdot 0 \oplus 1 \cdot 0 \oplus 0 \cdot 1 = 0$
$1 \cdot 1 \oplus 0 \cdot 1 \oplus 1 \cdot 1 \oplus 0 \cdot 0 = 0$
$1 \cdot 1 \oplus 0 \cdot 1 \oplus 1 \cdot 1 \oplus 1 \cdot 0 = 0$
$1 \cdot 0 \oplus 0 \cdot 1 \oplus 1 \cdot 1 \oplus 0 \cdot 1 = 1]$

$= [1\,0\,1\,0\,0\,0\,1]$

Similarly, we can generate code for all message words which are given below.

From given generator matrix we can write code bits in a code word as,

$$c_1 = d_1$$
$$c_2 = d_2$$
$$c_3 = d_3$$
$$c_4 = d_4$$

$$c_5 = d_1 \oplus d_3 \oplus d_4$$
$$c_6 = d_1 \oplus d_2 \oplus d_3$$
$$c_7 = d_2 \oplus d_3 + d_4 \qquad \ldots (6.10)$$

Hence, the generator circuit for above code is shown in Fig. 6.6.

Message word	Code word
0 0 0 0	0 0 0 0 0 0 0
0 0 0 1	0 0 0 1 1 0 1
0 0 1 0	0 0 1 0 1 1 1
0 0 1 1	0 0 1 1 0 1 0
0 1 0 0	0 1 0 0 0 1 1
0 1 0 1	0 1 0 1 1 1 0
0 1 1 0	0 1 1 0 1 0 0
0 1 1 1	0 1 1 1 0 0 1
1 0 0 0	1 0 0 0 1 1 0
1 0 0 1	1 0 0 1 0 1 1
1 0 1 0	1 0 1 0 0 0 1
1 0 1 1	1 0 1 1 1 0 0
1 1 0 0	1 1 0 0 1 0 1
1 1 0 1	1 1 0 1 0 0 0
1 1 1 0	1 1 1 0 0 1 0
1 1 1 1	1 1 1 1 1 1 1

Fig. 6.6

Parity Check Matrix

We have seen that generator matrix is used to generate codewords from message words. These codewords will be transmitted through a noisy channel. At the receiver end we have to validate these codewords i.e. they are to be checked whether they are correctly received or not. If not the codewords should be corrected with the help of redundant bits that we have added at the transmitter end. For this, consider a matrix H called parity check matrix which is given by,

$$H = [P_T \ I_{n-k}]_{n-k \times n} \quad \ldots (6.11)$$

i.e. H consists of two parts. Transpose of parity matrix whose order will be $n - k \times k$ and identity matrix whose order will be $(n - k) \times (n - k)$.

It can be verified for any codeword C.

$$CH^T = 0 \quad \ldots (6.12)$$

i.e. if we multiply any codeword with transpose of parity check matrix H result will be zero-vector.

Thus, the received codeword at the receiver is multiplied with H^T and we get zero vector if the codeword is correctly received. But if multiplication results into non-zero codeword, there will be error in the received codeword.

Substitute C = dG in equation (6.12),

$$d \, G \, H^T = 0$$

Thus, for equation (6.12) to hold true we should have,

$$G H^T = 0$$

Now consider,
$$G = [I_k \ P]$$

and
$$H = [P^T \ I_{n-k}]$$

$$G^T = \begin{bmatrix} I_k \\ P^T \end{bmatrix}$$

$$\therefore \quad H G^T = [P^T \ I_{n-k}] \begin{bmatrix} I_k \\ P^T \end{bmatrix}$$

$$= P^T \oplus P^T$$

$$= 0$$

$$\therefore \quad G H^T = 0$$

The process of coding and detection is shown in Fig. 6.7.

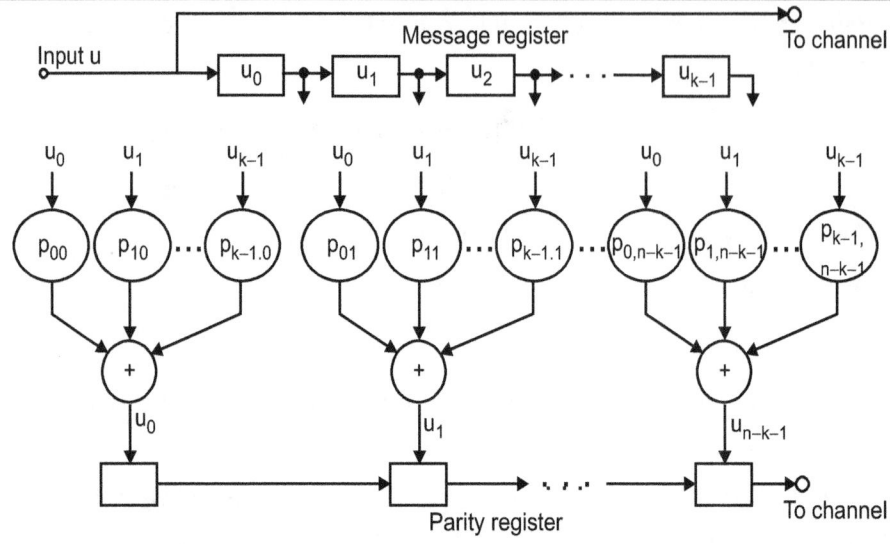

(i) Coding

```
                              Parity
         LSB                  (VRC)
    H  0 0 0 1 0 0 1 0
    e  1 0 1 0 0 1 1 0
    l  0 0 1 1 0 1 1 0
    P  0 0 0 0 1 1 1 1
    !  1 0 0 0 0 1 0 0
  LRC  0 0 0 0 1 0 0 1
```

(a) Correct LRC sent

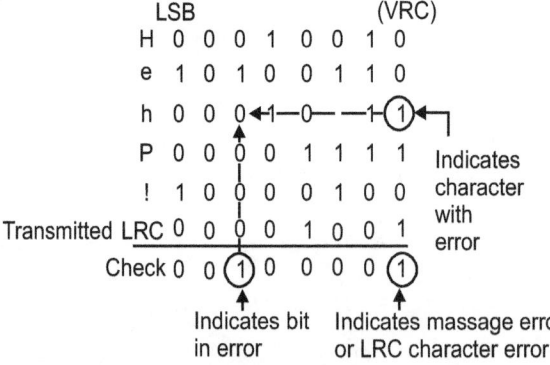

(b) Receive message with error

(ii) Detection

Fig. 6.7

Example 6.4 :

Consider a generator matrix given in example 6.3.

$$G = \begin{bmatrix} 1 & 0 & 0 & 0 & 1 & 1 & 0 \\ 0 & 1 & 0 & 0 & 0 & 1 & 1 \\ 0 & 0 & 1 & 0 & 1 & 1 & 1 \\ 0 & 0 & 0 & 1 & 1 & 0 & 1 \end{bmatrix}$$

Find parity check matrix and check whether following codewords are valid or not.

(i) 1000110   (ii) 0101011

Solution :

The given generator matrix is of the order 4 × 7.

Hence,   n = 7

               k = 4

The parity matrix in the generator is,

$$P = \begin{bmatrix} 1 & 1 & 0 \\ 0 & 1 & 1 \\ 1 & 1 & 1 \\ 1 & 0 & 1 \end{bmatrix}$$

Now parity check matrix is given by,

$$H = [P^T \; I_{n-k}]$$

$$= \begin{bmatrix} 1 & 0 & 1 & 1 & 1 & 0 & 0 \\ 1 & 1 & 1 & 0 & 0 & 1 & 0 \\ 0 & 1 & 1 & 1 & 0 & 0 & 1 \end{bmatrix}$$

$$\therefore \quad H^T = \begin{bmatrix} 1 & 1 & 0 \\ 0 & 1 & 1 \\ 1 & 1 & 1 \\ 1 & 0 & 1 \\ 1 & 0 & 0 \\ 0 & 1 & 0 \\ 0 & 0 & 1 \end{bmatrix}$$

To check whether given codewords are valid or not we find CH^T.

(i) Given: C = [1 0 0 0 1 1 0]

$$CH^T = [1\,0\,0\,0\,1\,1\,0] \begin{bmatrix} 1 & 1 & 0 \\ 0 & 1 & 1 \\ 1 & 1 & 1 \\ 1 & 0 & 1 \\ 1 & 0 & 0 \\ 0 & 1 & 0 \\ 0 & 0 & 1 \end{bmatrix}$$

∴ = [0 0 0]

Hence, given codeword is valid.

(ii) C = [0 1 0 1 0 1 1]

$$CH^T = [0\,1\,0\,1\,0\,1\,1] \begin{bmatrix} 1 & 1 & 0 \\ 0 & 1 & 1 \\ 1 & 1 & 1 \\ 1 & 0 & 1 \\ 1 & 0 & 0 \\ 0 & 1 & 0 \\ 0 & 0 & 1 \end{bmatrix}$$

∴ = [1 0 1]

Hence, given codeword is invalid.

Minimum Distance and H^T

- Hamming distance between two codewords is the number of positions in which their symbols differ.
- Hamming weight is number of non-zero elements in the codewords.
- The minimum distance d_{min} of a linear block code is the smallest distance between any pair of code vectors in the code.
- From the closure property of linear block codes the sum (or difference) of two codewords is another codeword.
- Minimum distance of a linear block code is the smallest hamming weight of the non-zero codeword in the code.

- Parity check matrix H and in turn generator matrix G are also related to minimum distance d_{min} of a code.
- Since $CH^T = 0$, the number of 1's in code vector C should be such that, corresponding rows of H^T add to zero i.e. corresponding columns of parity check matrix H must add to zero.

Consider the H^T discussed in earlier example.

$$H^T = \begin{bmatrix} 1 & 1 & 0 \\ 0 & 1 & 1 \\ 1 & 1 & 1 \\ 1 & 0 & 1 \\ 1 & 0 & 0 \\ 0 & 1 & 0 \\ 0 & 0 & 1 \end{bmatrix}$$

Now consider a valid code vector.

$$C = [1\ 0\ 0\ 0\ 1\ 1\ 0]$$

There are three non-zero elements at positions 1, 5 and 6 and the sum of 1st, 5th and 6th row of H^T is,

$$\begin{bmatrix} 1 \\ 1 \\ 0 \end{bmatrix} + \begin{bmatrix} 1 \\ 0 \\ 0 \end{bmatrix} + \begin{bmatrix} 0 \\ 1 \\ 0 \end{bmatrix} = \begin{bmatrix} 0 \\ 0 \\ 0 \end{bmatrix}$$

- The number of non-zero elements in the code is 3. If you check other codewords in the (7, 4) code discussed earlier, the minimum number of non-zero elements is 3 which is nothing but minimum weight of that code and it is also minimum hamming distance.
- Hence, the minimum distance of linear block code (d_{min}) is equal to minimum number of rows of H^T (or columns of H) whose sum is equal to zero vector.

Decoding of a Linear Block Code

Decoding is a process of detecting and correcting errors when messages in the form of codewords are transmitted on a noisy channel. The important question here is how many errors can we detect and correct. It will depend on the design of the code. The number of errors the code can correct or detect errors is called error correcting or detecting capability of that code.

A code contains certain number of codewords which are at some distance from each other which is specified in terms of hamming distance.

e.g. Consider the following code.

Message word	Code word
0	0 0 0
1	1 1 1

There are two codewords in the code whose hamming distance is 3.

When one of the codewords is transmitted the noise or distortion is likely to change some bits. e.g. when 0 0 0 is transmitted we might receive 0 0 1. As long as one codeword is not transformed into another codewords we can detect whether there was error in transmission or not. Thus, the number of errors that can be detected depends on minimum hamming distance of the code, as it is the minimum distance between any two codewords.

i.e. if a code has hamming distance d_{min} the number of errors that can be detected is,

$$\boxed{t_d \leq d_{min} - 1} \quad \ldots (6.13)$$

The number of errors that can be corrected also depends on minimum hamming distance. When a codeword is received with error we have to find which codeword was actually transmitted ? Obviously, the codeword nearest to the valid codewords will be the answer. But then the received codeword might be at same hamming distance from two or more valid codewords. Hence, it is not possible to correct the code with this criteria. Also, if more errors occur, the received codeword will go near to another valid codeword which was not transmitted.

e.g. If 0 0 0 is transmitted and 0 1 0 is received we can make decision in favour of 0 0 0 as 0 1 0 is nearer to 0 0 0 than 1 1 1. But if 0 0 0 is transmitted and 0 1 1 is received we will make decision in favour of 1 1 1 as 0 1 1 is nearer to 1 1 1 than 0 0 0 which is not correct. Hence, this code cannot correct two errors. For error correction capability any two codewords in the code should be separated such that the number of errors (t_c) should result into a received word which is closest to original codeword and away from all other codewords. The condition for this is,

$$\boxed{t_c \leq \frac{d_{min} - 1}{2}} \quad \ldots (6.14)$$

This can be well understood using pictorial view. We can consider the codewords to be placed in spheres separated from each other. The sphere are of radius t_c, where, t_c is number of errors that can be corrected. If t_c errors occur in code c_1/c_2, the new codeword will be within their spheres and remain nearer to the valid codeword. Hence, the minimum hamming distance has to be greater than $2t_c + 1$. If we consider the code C = {0 0 0, 1 1 1}, the codewords will be placed from other possible distortions as below on the vertices of a cube. If (0 0 0) is transmitted and (0 0 1) is received we find 0 0 1 is near to 0 0 0 than (1 1 1). Hence, we can make the correction in favour of (0 0 0). But if (0 0 0) is transmitted and (0 1 1) is received we find (0 1 1) is nearer to (1 1 1) than (0 0 0), hence we cannot correct the two errors here. Thus, this code has error correcting capability of 1 error. This can be verified from the formula also. The code has $d_{min} = 3$.

$$\therefore \quad t_c \leq \frac{d_{min} - 1}{2}$$

$$\leq \frac{3 - 1}{2}$$

$$\leq 1$$

Note that, if 0 1 1 is received when 0 0 0 was transmitted, decision will be made in favour of 1 1 1, even though it is incorrect. Here, we assume that probability of occurrence of 2 errors is far less than that of 1 error.

Example 6.5 :
Find the error correcting capability of code generated in example 6.5.
Solution :

Code word	Hamming weight
0 0 0 0 0 0 0	0
0 0 0 1 1 0 1	3
0 0 1 0 1 1 1	4
0 0 1 1 0 1 0	4
0 1 0 0 0 1 1	3
0 1 0 1 1 1 0	4
0 1 1 0 1 0 0	3
0 1 1 1 0 0 1	4
1 0 0 0 1 1 0	3
1 0 0 1 0 1 1	4
1 0 1 0 0 0 1	3
1 0 1 1 1 0 0	4
1 1 0 0 1 0 1	4
1 1 0 1 0 0 0	3
1 1 1 0 0 1 0	4
1 1 1 1 1 1 1	7

Since minimum weight of the non-zero codewords is 3.

$$d_{min} = 3$$

∴ Error correcting capability

$$t_c \leq \frac{d_{min} - 1}{2}$$

$$t_c \leq \frac{3 - 1}{2}$$

$$t_c \leq 1$$

If the code is such that there is ambiguity in deciding closest codeword, then it is called incomplete decoder. A complete decoder can decode every received word even if there are not more than t_c errors. They will make a good guess about the codeword.

There will be limit on maximum distance, on the code which will be,

$$d_{max} \leq n - k + 1 \qquad \ldots (6.15)$$

where, k is number of message bits.

n is number of code bits.

This is called Singleton Bound.

Syndrome Decoding

Minimum hamming distance d_{min} of a code decides error correcting capability of a code. Now, let us see how these errors can be corrected.

The generator matrix (G) is used at the transmitter to generate the code corresponding to message. The parity check matrix can be used to decode the received codeword.

- Let r be the received code vector.
- This code vector may or may not differ from transmitted code vector C.
- Let there be another vector e which will be called error vector defining the corresponding error pattern.
- Hence, $\qquad r = C \oplus e \qquad \ldots (6.16)$

If there is no error, e will be having all zero symbols. If there are some errors, then there will be that many number of 1's in the corresponding location.

i.e. $\qquad e_i = \begin{cases} 1 & \text{If an error has occurred in the } i^{th} \text{ location} \\ 0 & \text{Otherwise} \end{cases} \qquad \ldots (6.17)$

The received code vector is multiplied with H^T to get syndrome vector. As we see if received codeword is same as transmitted codeword, this multiplication will result into 0 as $CH^T = 0$.

Since the received code vector is $1 \times n$ and H^T is of the order $n \times n - k$.

The syndrome vector will have n – k bits.

Thus, $$S = rH^T \quad \text{...(6.18)}$$

If r = C, S will have all 0 vector.

If r ≠ C
$$\begin{aligned}S &= rH^T \\ &= (C \oplus e)H^T \\ &= C \cdot H^T \oplus e\,H^T \\ &= e\,H^T \quad \text{...(6.19)}\end{aligned}$$

Thus, the syndrome depends on error pattern e.

Another property of the syndrome is that all error patterns that differ by a codeword have the same syndrome. Let us look into this.

Let there be k message bits.

Hence, there will be 2^k codewords $C_1, C_2, C_3, \ldots C_{2^k}$.

Let there be some error pattern e which will also have 2^{k-1} distinct vectors $e_1, e_2, \ldots e_{2^k}$.

$$\therefore \quad e_i = e \oplus C_i \quad \text{...(6.20)}$$

Set of vectors $\{e_1, e_2, e_3, \ldots e_{2^k}\}$ is called coset of the code. There will be 2^{n-k} possible cosets of an (n, k) block code.

Now,
$$\begin{aligned}e_i \cdot H^T &= (e \oplus C_i)H^T \\ &= e\,H^T \oplus C_i\,H^T \\ &= e\,H^T = S \quad \text{...(6.21)}\end{aligned}$$

Thus, each coset of the code is characterised by unique syndrome.

The vector having minimum weight in the coset is called coset leader.

A standard array is constructed using these coset leaders.

In the first row all valid codewords are written starting with all-zero codewords.

In the second row we write vector e_2 which is not in first row as coset leader and then write the cosets $e_2 + c$ below each valid code vector. We continue this till all the cosets are listed.

e.g. $\quad C = \{0\,0\,0, 1\,1\,1\}$

Standard array:

Syndrome	Coset Leaders	n-tupes
0 0	0 0 0	1 1 1
1 1	1 0 0	0 1 1
1 0	0 1 0	1 0 1
0 1	0 0 1	1 1 0

← Code vectors

} Single errors

The decoding procedure for a linear block code will be as below.

1. Compute $S = r H^T$, where, r is received code.
2. Identify the error pattern i.e. coset leader corresponding to the syndrome. Let it be e.
3. Compute code vector.

$$C = r \oplus e$$

Example 6.6:

Decoding procedure for (7, 4) block code whose generator matrix is given in example 6.4.

$$G = \begin{bmatrix} 1 & 0 & 0 & 0 & 1 & 1 & 0 \\ 0 & 1 & 0 & 0 & 0 & 1 & 1 \\ 0 & 0 & 1 & 0 & 1 & 1 & 1 \\ 0 & 0 & 0 & 1 & 1 & 0 & 1 \end{bmatrix}$$

Also find the corrected codewords for following received words.

(i) 1 0 0 0 1 1 0   (ii) 0 1 0 1 0 1 1   (iii) 0 0 0 1 1 0 0

Solution:

Step I:

The given code has error correcting capability of 1. Hence, there will be $2^{n-k} = 2^3 = 8$ single error patterns.

Step II:

The parity check matrix is given by,

$$H = [P^T \; I_{n-k}]$$

$$= \begin{bmatrix} 1 & 0 & 1 & 1 & 1 & 0 & 0 \\ 1 & 1 & 1 & 0 & 0 & 1 & 0 \\ 0 & 1 & 1 & 1 & 0 & 0 & 1 \end{bmatrix}$$

$$H^T = \begin{bmatrix} 1 & 1 & 0 \\ 0 & 1 & 1 \\ 1 & 1 & 1 \\ 1 & 0 & 1 \\ 1 & 0 & 0 \\ 0 & 1 & 0 \\ 0 & 0 & 1 \end{bmatrix}$$

∴

Step III :

We find syndrome vectors corresponding to each error pattern using,

$$S = e H^T$$

e.g. for error pattern 0 0 0 0 0 0 1 the syndrome will be,

$$S = [0000001] \begin{bmatrix} 1 & 1 & 0 \\ 0 & 1 & 1 \\ 1 & 1 & 1 \\ 1 & 0 & 1 \\ 1 & 0 & 0 \\ 0 & 1 & 0 \\ 0 & 0 & 1 \end{bmatrix}$$

$$= [0\ 0\ 1]$$

Following table gives all syndrome with their error patterns.

Error pattern	Syndrome
0000000	000
1000000	110
0100000	011
0010000	111
0001000	101
0000100	100
0000010	010
0000001	001

Note : If you observe above syndrome they are nothing but matrix H^T itself.

Thus, if there is single error in i^{th} bit, the syndrome will be i^{th} row of H^T.

Step IV :

Once above table is ready we can now correct the errors in the received codewords.

(i)   r = [1 0 0 0 1 1 0]

∴   S = r H^T

    = [0 0 0]

Hence, there is no error.

∴   Corrected codeword

    C = r

(ii)   r = [0 1 0 1 0 1 1]

    S = r H^T = [1 0 1]

Corresponding error pattern from above table,

    e = 0 0 0 1 0 0 0 [Error in 4th bit]

∴   Corrected codeword

    C = r ⊕ e

     = [0 1 0 1 0 1 1] ⊕ [0 0 0 1 0 0 0]

     = [0 1 0 0 0 1 1]

(iii)   r = [0 0 0 1 1 0 0]

    S = r H^T = [0 0 1]

∴   Error pattern is,

    e = [0 0 0 0 0 0 1]

∴   Corrected codeword

    C = r ⊕ e

     = [0 0 0 1 1 0 0] + [0 0 0 0 0 0 1] = [0 0 0 1 1 0 1]

6.5 CYCLIC CODES

Cyclic codes are subclass of linear block codes. Generator matrix is used for generating linear block codes. Hence, for higher order codes we have to use large memory requirements and circuit becomes complex. Cyclic codes are linear block codes with an additional constraint. Cyclic codes are very easy to encode. Cyclic codes possess a well defined mathematical structure which makes them efficient in decoding.

Thus, cyclic codes are simple for implementation which is an important feature of cyclic code. A binary code is said to be cyclic if it satisfies following two fundamental properties.

- **Linearity** : The sum of any two codewords in a cyclic code is also a valid codeword.
- **Cyclic property** : A cyclic shift of bits in a codeword gives rise to another valid codeword.

As per the cyclic property if $(c_1, c_2, c_3, ... c_n)$ is a codeword, then,

$$(c_2, c_3, ... c_n, c_1)$$
$$(c_3, c_4, ... c_n, c_1, c_2)$$
$$\vdots$$
$$\vdots$$
$$(c_n, c_1, c_2, ... c_{n-2}, c_{n-1})$$

are all codewords in that code.

Example 6.7 :

C = {0 0 0 0, 0 1 0 1, 1 0 1 0, 1 1 1 1} is a cyclic code.

As this code satisfies both linearity property and cyclic property.

Example 6.8 :

C = {0 0 0, 0 1 0, 0 0 1, 1 0 0, 1 1 1} is not cyclic code. It satisfies cyclic property but does not satisfy linearity property.

Polynomials :

Cyclic code can be represented in polynomial form. e.g. given a codeword of code C,

$$c_1, c_2, c_3, ... c_n$$

We can write it as,

$$c(x) = c_1 x^{n-1} + c_2 x^{n-2} + c_3 x^{n-3} + ... + c_{n-1} x + c_n \quad ...(6.22)$$

In general, if $a_1, a_2, a_3, ... a_n$ are elements of GF(q) then a polynomial of these sequence of elements is expressed as,

$$p(x) = a_1 x^{n-1} + a_2 x^{n-2} + a_3 x^{n-3} + ... + a_{n-1} x + a_n \quad ...(6.23)$$

- If q = 2, coefficients $a_1, a_2, ...$ will be 1 or 0.
- a_1 is called leading coefficient.
- n – 1 is called degree of polynomial.

- If a_1 is unity, it is called monic polynomial.
- Let p[x] represent a set of polynomials in x with coefficients in GF(q). It is called a ring e.g. c[x] will be a set of polynomials of all valid codewords.

These polynomials satisfy first seven of eight properties that define a field.

e.g. addition or multiplication of two polynomials will result into coefficients in GF(q) only.

Consider 2 polynomials.

$$a(x) = x + 1$$
$$b(x) = x^3 + x + 1 \text{ defined over GF(2)}$$

Then,

$$a(x) + b(x) = (x \oplus 1) \oplus (x^3 \oplus x \oplus 1)$$
$$= x^3 \oplus [x \oplus x] \oplus [1 \oplus 1]$$
$$= x^3 \oplus [1 \oplus 1] x \oplus [1 \oplus 1]$$
$$= x^3 + 0x + 0$$
$$= x^3$$

$$a(x) \cdot b(x) = (x^3 \oplus x \oplus 1) \cdot (x \oplus 1)$$
$$= x^3 \cdot x \oplus x^3 \cdot 1 \oplus x \cdot x \oplus x \cdot 1 \oplus 1 \cdot x \oplus 1 \cdot 1$$
$$= x^4 \oplus x^3 \oplus x^2 \oplus x \oplus x \oplus 1$$
$$= x^4 \oplus x^3 \oplus x^2 \oplus (1 \oplus 1) x \oplus 1$$
$$= x^4 \oplus x^3 \oplus x^2 + x + 1$$
$$= x^4 + x^3 + x^2 + 1$$

(A) Division Algorithm for Polynomials :

Consider two polynomials a(x) and b(x).

If divide a(x) by b(x) [b(x) ≠ 0)]

we can write,

$$a(x) = q(x) b(x) + r(x) \qquad \ldots (6.24)$$

where, q(x) is quotient.

r(x) is remainder or residue whose degree will be less than b(x).

e.g. Let $a(x) = x^4 + x^2 + 1$
$b(x) = x + 1$

$x^3 + x^2 \quad \leftarrow q(x)$

$x + 1 \quad x^4 + x^2 + 1$

$$x^4 + x^3$$
$$\overline{x^3 + x^2 + 1}$$
$$x^3 + x^2$$
$$\overline{1} \leftarrow r(x)$$

Note that in GF(2), $1 - 1 = 0$ and $0 - 1 = -1 = 1$, $1 - 0 = 0$ and $0 - 0 = 0$ which is equivalent to modulo-2 addition. Hence, the subtraction is equivalent to modulo-2 addition.

$$\therefore \quad (x^4 + x^2 + 1) = (x^3 + x^2) \cdot (x + 1) + 1$$
$$\quad\quad\quad\quad \downarrow \quad\quad\quad\quad \downarrow \quad\quad \downarrow \quad\quad \downarrow$$
$$\quad\quad\quad\quad a(x) \quad\quad\quad q(x) \quad b(x) \quad r(x)$$

A polynomial $p(x)$ in $p[x]$ is said to be reducible if $p(x) = a(x) \cdot b(x)$, where $a(x)$ and $b(x)$ are elements of $p[x]$ and degree of $a(x)$ and $b(x)$ are smaller than degree of $p(x)$.

A monic polynomial is a polynomial whose leading coefficient is one. A monic polynomial which is irreducible and has a degree atleast one is called prime polynomial. Some examples of prime polynomials are x, $x + 1$, $x^2 + 1$, $x^2 + x + 1$, $x^3 + x^2 + 1$, $x^3 + x + 1$, etc.

(B) Representation of Cyclic codes using Polynomials :

We have seen that a codeword can be represented using polynomial as,

$$c(x) = c_1 x^{n-1} + c_2 x^{n-2} + c_3 x^{n-3} + \ldots + c_{n-1} x + c_n$$

e.g. if you are given a code word $C = (1\ 0\ 1\ 1\ 0)$, it will be written as,

$$C = (1 \quad 0 \quad 1 \quad 1 \quad 0)$$
$$\quad\quad \downarrow \quad \downarrow \quad \downarrow \quad \downarrow \quad \downarrow$$
$$c(x) = 1 \cdot x^4 + 0 \cdot x^3 + 1 \cdot x^2 + 1 \cdot x + 0 \cdot x$$
$$\therefore \quad\quad c(x) = x^4 + x^2 + x$$

We have seen that cyclic code satisfies cyclic property. We can verify that if $c(x)$ is a code polynomial corresponding to a codeword then the remainder after dividing $x^i\ c(x)$ by $x^n + 1$ also represents a valid codeword.

e.g. $\quad\quad x^i \cdot c(x) = c_1 x^n + c_2 x^{n-1} + c_3^{n-2} + \ldots + c_{n-1} x^2 + c_n x \quad\quad \ldots (6.25)$

Divide $x^i\ c(x)$ by $x^n + 1$ and find remainder.

$$\begin{array}{r} c_1 \\ x^n + 1 \overline{\smash{\big)} c_1 x^n + c_2 x^{n-1} + c_3 x^{n-2} + \ldots + c_{n-1} x^2 + c_n x} \\ c_1 x^n + c_1 \end{array}$$

Remainder $\Rightarrow c_2 x^{n-1} + c_3 x^{n-2} + \ldots + c_{n-1} x^2 + c_n x + c_1$

The remainder represents the codeword

$$C_1 = (c_2, c_3, \ldots c_{n-1}, c_n, c_1) \quad \ldots (6.26)$$

which is a cyclic shifted version of original code word C. Similarly, you can verify that remainder after divisor of $x^2 c(x)$ and $x^n + 1$ will give rise to another cyclic shifted codeword.

In general,

$$\text{Rem}\left[\frac{x^i \cdot c(x)}{x^n + 1}\right] = c_{i+1} x^{n-1} + c_{i+2} x^{n-2} + \ldots + c_n x^i + c_1 x^{i-1} + \ldots c_i \quad \ldots (6.27)$$

It is denoted as $c^i(x)$.

i.e. $\quad c^{(i)}(x) \quad = x^i c(x) \bmod (x^n + 1) \quad \ldots (6.28)$

[Mod is a remainder after division operation].

A Method for Generating Cyclic Code

Theorem:

Cyclic code polynomial c(x) can be generated using data polynomial d(x) of degree $k - 1$ and a generator polynomial g(x) of degree $n - k$ as,

$$c(x) = d(x) \cdot g(x) \quad \ldots (6.29)$$

where, g(x) is $(n - k)^{th}$ order factor of $x^n + 1$.

Proof:

Let d(x) represent data polynomial of k message bits $d_1, d_2, d_3, \ldots d_k$ as,

$$d(x) = d_1 x^{k-1} + d_2 x^{k-2} + d_3 x^{k-3} + \ldots + d_{k-1} x + d_k \quad \ldots (6.30)$$

Now, consider the polynomial.

$$c(x) = d(x) \cdot g(x)$$

$$\therefore \quad c(x) = d_1 x^{k-1} g(x) + d_2 x^{k-2} g(x) + \ldots + d_k g(x) \quad \ldots (6.31)$$

Since g(x) is $(n - k)^{th}$ order polynomial, c(x) will be of degree $n - 1$ or less. i.e. degree of c(x) will be atmost $n - 1$.

Now, we have to prove that this code is cyclic.

Let,

$$c(x) = c_1 x^{n-1} + c_2 x^{n-2} + \ldots + c_n$$

$$x \, c(x) = c_1 x^n + c_2 x^{n-1} + \ldots + c_n x$$

$$= (c_1 x^n + c_1) + (c_2 x^{n-1} + c_3 x^{n-2} + \ldots + c_n x + c_1) \quad \ldots (6.32)$$

Adding $c_1 \oplus c_2$,

$$= c_1(x^n + 1) + (c_2 x^{n-1} + c_3 x^{n-2} + \ldots + c_n x + c_1)$$

$$= c_1(x^n + 1) + c^{(1)}(x) \qquad \ldots (6.33)$$

But, $\qquad x \cdot c(x) = x \cdot d(x) \, g(x) \qquad \ldots (6.34)$

Thus, from equations (6.33) and (6.34), we get,

$$x \, c(x) \cdot g(x) = c_1 \cdot (x^n + 1) + c^{(1)}(x) \qquad \ldots (6.35)$$

But g(x) is a factor of $(x^n + 1)$ and if equation (6.35) has to hold good, $c^{(1)}(x)$ also has to be multiple of $(x^n + 1)$. But $c^{(1)}(x)$ is a cyclic shifted version of c(x). Hence, the code c(x) generated by multiplying d(x) and g(x) is cyclic.

Example 6.9 :

Find generator polynomial g(x) for a (7, 4) cyclic code and final codewords for following data words.

(i) 1 1 0 0

(ii) 1 0 1 0

(iii) 0 1 1 1

Solution :

Given : $\qquad$ n = 7

$\qquad\qquad$ k = 4

The generator polynomial should be of the degree n – k = 3.

The generator polynomial should be factor of $x^7 + 1$.

$$
\begin{aligned}
(x^7 + 1) &= (x + 1)(x^6 + x^5 + x^4 + x^3 + x^2 + x + 1) \\
&= (x + 1)(x^6 + x^5 + x^4 + x^3 + x^3 + x^3 + x^2 + x + 1) \\
&= (x + 1)(x^6 + x^4 + x^3 + x^5 + x^3 + x^2 + x^3 + x + 1) \\
&= (x + 1)[x^3(x^3 + x + 1) + x^2(x^3 + x + 1) + 1(x^3 + x + 1)] \\
&= (x + 1)(x^3 + x^2 + 1)(x^3 + x + 1)
\end{aligned}
$$

We have two polynomials of order 3, one of which can be selected as generator polynomial.

Let $\qquad\qquad g(x) = x^3 + x^2 + 1$

Now, a code is generated using,

$$c(x) = d(x) \, g(x)$$

(i) $\quad$ 1 1 0 0

$\qquad\qquad d(x) = x^3 + x^2$

$\therefore \qquad\qquad c(x) = (x^3 + x^2)(x^3 + x^2 + 1)$

$$= (x^6 + x^5 + x^3 + x^5 + x^4 + x^2)$$
$$= x^6 + x^4 + x^3 + x^2$$
$$= 1.x^6 + 0.x^5 + 1.x^4 + 1.x^3 + 1.x^2 + 0.x + 0.x$$

∴ $\quad C = [1\ 0\ 1\ 1\ 1\ 0\ 0]$

(ii) 1 0 1 0

$$d(x) = x^3 + x$$
$$c(x) = (x^3 + x)(x^3 + x^2 + 1)$$
$$= x^6 + x^5 + x^3 + x^4 + x^3 + x$$
$$= x^6 + x^5 + x^4 + x$$
$$= 1.x^6 + 1.x^5 + 1.x^4 + 0.x^3 + 0.x^2 + 1.x + 0$$

∴ $\quad C = [1\ 1\ 1\ 0\ 0\ 1\ 0]$

(iii) 0 0 1 1

$$d(x) = x + 1$$

∴ $\quad c(x) = (x+1)(x^3 + x^2 + 1)$
$$= x^4 + x^3 + x + x^3 + x^2 + 1$$
$$= x^4 + x^2 + x + 1$$
$$= 0.x^6 + 0.x^5 + 1.x^4 + 0.x^3 + 1.x^2 + 1.x + 1$$

∴ $\quad C = [0\ 0\ 1\ 0\ 1\ 1\ 1]$

It can be observed from above example that the code generated is non-systematic code as message bits and parity bits are not in separate blocks.

Example 6.10 :

Find generator polynomial for a (7, 3) cyclic code.

Solution :

Given :
$$n = 7$$
$$k = 3$$

∴ The order of generator polynomial will be,
$$n - k = 4$$

g(x) will factor of $x^7 + 1$.

$$x^7 + 1 = (x + 1)(x^6 + x^5 + x^4 + x^3 + x^2 + 1)$$
$$= (x + 1)(x^6 + x^5 + x^4 + x^3 + x^3 + x^3 + x^2 + 1)$$
$$= (x + 1)[x^3(x^3 + x + 1) + x^2(x^3 + x + 1) + 1(x^3 + x + 1)]$$

$$= (x+1)(x^3+x^2+1)(x^3+x+1)$$
$$= (x^4+x^3+x+x^3+x^2+1)(x^3+x+1)$$
$$= (x^4+x^2+x+1)(x^3+x+1)$$

∴ Generator polynomial of order 4 is,
$$g(x) = x^4+x^2+x+1$$

(A) Systematic Cyclic Code :

In order to encode message sequence into systematic form, it is necessary to have message bits and parity bits in separate block in the codeword.

Consider a message polynomial.
$$d(x) = d_1 x^{k-1} + d_2 x^{k-2} + \ldots + d_k \qquad \ldots (6.36)$$

Multiply above polynomial by x^{n-k}.

where,   n = Number of code bits

            k = Number of message bits

∴ $x^{n-k} d(x) = d_1 x^{n-1} + d_2 x^{n-2} + \ldots + d_k x^{n-k} \qquad \ldots (6.37)$

Dividing equation (6.37) by g(x), we get,

$$\frac{x^{n-k} d(x)}{g(x)} = q(x) + \frac{p(x)}{g(x)} \qquad \ldots (6.38)$$

or

$$x^{n-k} d(x) = q(x) \cdot g(x) + p(x) \qquad \ldots (6.39)$$

Adding p(x) on both sides of equation (6.39), we get,

$$x^{n-k} d(x) \quad + \quad p(x) \quad = \quad q(x) \cdot g(x) \qquad \ldots (6.40)$$
$$\downarrow \qquad\qquad\qquad \downarrow \qquad\qquad \downarrow$$
Message bits   Remainder   Code
shifted by n − k   (k − 1) bits

where, q(x) will be quotient after division whose order will be k − 1 or less, p(x) is remainder after division of the order n − k − 1. Since q(x) is of order k − 1 or less and g(x) of order n − k, q(x) · g(x) will be code polynomial. $x^{n-k} d(x)$ represents d(x) shifted by n − k digits or the left side and since p(x) is of the order k − 1, it represents parity bits.

Thus, procedure for generating systematic cyclic code is as below.

    (i)   Write d(x) for given message bits.

    (ii)   Find $x^{n-k} \cdot d(x)$.

(iii) Divide $x^{n-k} d(x)$ by $g(x)$ and find remainder $p(x)$.

(iv) Find $c(x) = x^{n-k} d(x) + p(x)$.

(v) Write codeword corresponding to $c(x)$.

Example 6.11 :

Construct a systematic (7, 4) cyclic code using generator polynomial $g(x) = x^3 + x^2 + 1$ for the messages.

(i) 1 0 1 0

(ii) 1 0 0 0

Solution :

Given : $g(x) = x^3 + x^2 + 1$

$n = 7, k = 4$

∴ $d(x) = x^3 + x$

∴ $x^{n-k} d(x) = x^3(x^3 + x)$

$= x^6 + x^4$

$$
\begin{array}{r}
x^3 + x^2 + 1 \overline{\smash{)}\, x^6 + x^4 } \\
\underline{x^6 + x^5 + x^3} \\
x^5 + x^4 + x^3 \\
\underline{x^5 + x^4 + x^2} \\
x^3 + x^2 \\
\underline{x^3 + x^2 + 1} \\
1 \leftarrow p(x)
\end{array}
$$

∴ $c(x) = x^{n-k} d(x) + p(x)$

$= x^3(x^3 + x) + 1$

$= x^6 + x^4 + 1$

∴ $c = [1 0 1 0 0 0 1]$

(ii) $d = [1 0 0 0]$

$d(x) = x^3$

$x^{n-k} d(x) = x^3 \cdot x^3$

$= x^6$

$$
\begin{array}{rl}
& x^3 + x^2 + x \\
x^3 + x^2 + 1 \overline{)} & x^6 \\
& x^6 + x^5 + x^3 \\
& \overline{} x^5 + x^3 \\
& x^5 + x^4 + x^2 \\
& \overline{} x^4 + x^3 + x^2 \\
& x^4 + x^3 + x \\
& \overline{} x^2 + x \leftarrow p(x)
\end{array}
$$

$\therefore$ $c(x) = x^{n-k} d(x) + p(x)$

$ = x^3 \cdot x^3 + x^2 + x$

$ = x^6 + x^2 + x$

$c = [1\ 0\ 0\ 0\ 1\ 1\ 0]$

(B) Parity Check Polynomial :

For linear block code we have seen that there is a generator matrix (G) and a parity check matrix (H) pair used at transmitter and receiver respectively.

A cyclic code can be specified by its generator polynomial $g(x)$. There can be another polynomial called parity check polynomial $h(x)$ such that,

$$[g(x) \cdot h(x)] \bmod [x^n + 1] = 0 \qquad \ldots (6.41)$$

or $\qquad g(x) \cdot h(x) = x^n + 1 \qquad \ldots (6.42)$

(Analogous to $GH^T = 0$)

The parity check polynomial is of the order k and is specified as,

$$h(x) = 1 + \left(\sum_{i=1}^{k-1} h_i x^i \right) + x^k \qquad \ldots (6.43)$$

- Equation (6.21) shows that just like $g(x)$, $h(x)$ is also a factor of $x^n + 1$.

e.g. for (7, 4) cyclic code, let $g(x) = x^3 + x + 1$.

$\therefore \qquad x^7 + 1 = (x + 1)(x^3 + x^2 + 1)(x^3 + x + 1)$

$ = (x^4 + x^2 + x + 1)(x^3 + x + 1)$

$\therefore \qquad h(x) = x^4 + x^2 + x + 1$

Decoding of Cyclic Code :

The decoding process of cyclic code is same for both systematic and non-systematic cyclic codes. Every valid codeword polynomial c(x) is a multiple of g(x). When this codeword is transmitted there may be some errors introduced, hence the received codeword polynomial r(x) may not be same as c(x). If received codeword is same as transmitted codeword then r(x) mod g(x) = 0. Otherwise it will be non-zero polynomial. Consider $\frac{r(x)}{g(x)}$. It can be written as,

$$\frac{r(x)}{g(x)} = q(x) + \frac{s(x)}{g(x)} \quad \ldots (6.44)$$

where, q(x) is quotient polynomial and s(x) is remainder polynomial also called as syndrome polynomial.

Degree of q(x) will be k – 1 and that of s(x) will be n – k – 1.

r(x) can be written in terms of c(x) as,

$$r(x) = c(x) \oplus e(x) \quad \ldots (6.45)$$

where, e(x) is an error polynomial decided by the bit error pattern in r(x).

$$\therefore \quad \frac{r(x)}{g(x)} = \frac{c(x) \oplus e(x)}{g(x)} \quad \ldots (6.46)$$

$$= \frac{c(x)}{g(x)} \oplus \frac{e(x)}{g(x)} \quad \ldots (6.47)$$

$$\therefore \quad \text{Remainder}\left[\frac{r(x)}{g(x)}\right] = \text{Rem}\left[\frac{c(x)}{g(x)}\right] + \text{Rem}\left[\frac{c(x)}{g(x)}\right] \quad \ldots (6.48)$$

But Remainder after division of c(x) and g(x) will be zero.

$$\therefore \quad \text{Rem}\left[\frac{r(x)}{g(x)}\right] = \text{Rem}\left[\frac{e(x)}{g(x)}\right] \quad \ldots (6.49)$$

Comparing equations (6.44) and (6.49), we can write,

$$s(x) = \text{Rem}\left[\frac{e(x)}{g(x)}\right] \quad \ldots (6.50)$$

Equation (6.50) shows that the syndrome polynomial of error polynomial e(x) is same as received word polynomial. Thus, the decoding process of a cyclic code will be as below.

If our aim is to only detect errors, then the received codeword polynomial is divided by g(x). If the remainder i.e. syndrome polynomial is zero, there will be no error and if it is non-zero then there will be error. If it is required to correct those errors, then the procedure will be,

- Prepare a table of error patterns and syndromes using relation (6.50).

- Find syndrome after diving received word polynomials r(x) and g(x).
- Select the error pattern corresponding to the syndrome.
- Add error pattern to the received codeword.

Example 6.12 :

Design (3, 1) cyclic repetition code and its decoding method. Find corrected codewords for

(i) 0 1 0

(ii) 1 1 0

Solution :

Given : $n = 3$

$k = 1$

The generator polynomial $g(x)$ order $= 3 - 1 = 2$.

Generator polynomial should be factor of $x^3 + 1$.

Now, $(x^3 + 1) = (x + 1)(x^2 + x + 1)$

∴ $g(x) = x^2 + x + 1$

Since, $k = 1$, there will be two message words 0 and 1.

(I) Coding :

(i) $d = [0]$

$d(x) = 0$

$x^{n-k} d(x) = x^2 \cdot 0 = 0$

∴ $p(x) = 0$

∴ $c(x) = x^{n-k} d(x) + p(x)$

$= 0 + 0$

$= 0$

∴ $c = [0\ 0\ 0]$

(ii) $d = [1]$

$d(x) = 1$

∴ $x^{n-k} d(x) = x^2 \cdot 1$

$= x^2$

To find p(x).

$$\begin{array}{r} 1 \\ x^2 + x + 1 \overline{\smash{)}\ x^2} \end{array}$$

$$x^2 + x + 1$$
$$x + 1 \leftarrow p(x)$$

$$\therefore \quad c(x) = x^{n-k} d(x) + p(x)$$
$$= x^2 + x + 1$$

$$\therefore \quad c = [1\ 1\ 1]$$

Hence, codewords are

Message	Code
0	0 0 0
1	1 1 1

(II) Decoding :

Since $d_{min} = 3$

Error correcting capability

$$t_c \leq \frac{d_{min} - 1}{2}$$

$$\leq \frac{3-1}{2}$$

$$\leq 1 \text{ error}$$

The error patterns will be,

1 0 0
0 1 0
0 0 1

Find $s(x) = e(x) \bmod g(x)$ for each error pattern.

(i) For e = 1 0 0

$$e(x) = x^2$$

$$\begin{array}{r} 1 \\ x^2 + x + 1 \overline{)\ x^2\ } \\ x^2 + x + 1 \\ \hline x + 1 \leftarrow s(x) \end{array}$$

$$\therefore \quad s = [1\ 1]$$

(ii) For e = 0 1 0

$$e(x) = x$$

$$\frac{x}{x^2 + x + 1} \frac{0}{\begin{array}{c} x \\ 0 \\ \hline x \leftarrow s(x) \end{array}}$$

∴ s = [1 0]

(iii) For e = 0 0 1

$$e(x) = 1$$

$$\frac{1}{x^2 + x + 1} \frac{0}{\begin{array}{c} 1 \\ 0 \\ \hline 1 \end{array}}$$

∴ s = [0 1]

Hence, syndrome and error vector table will be as below.

Syndrome	Error Vector
1 0 0	1 1
0 1 0	1 0
0 0 1	0 1

Now, let us decode given received words.

(i) r = 0 1 0

∴ $$r(x) = x$$

$$\frac{x}{x^2 + x + 1} \frac{0}{\begin{array}{c} x \\ 0 \\ \hline x \leftarrow s(x) \end{array}}$$

∴ s = [1 0]

This syndrome corresponds to e = [0 1 0].

∴ Corrected codeword c = r ⊕ e

= [0 1 0] ⊕ [0 1 0] = [0 0 0]

(ii) r = 1 1 0

$$\therefore \quad r(x) = x^2 + x$$

```
              1
x² + x + 1 ) x² + x
             x² + x + 1
             ─────────
                     1  ← s(x)
```

∴   s = [0 1]

This syndrome corresponds to e = [0 0 1]

∴   Corrected codeword c = r ⊕ e

$$= [1\ 1\ 0] \oplus [0\ 0\ 1]$$

$$= [1\ 1\ 1]$$

Error Detecting Codes :

Error detection system consists of encoding procedure similar to error correcting codes but at the receiver end the errors are detected by using pattern checking. The system has a provision of feedback which tells the transmitter to retransmit a message in error.

The number of errors that can be detected $t_d = d_{min} - 1$, where d_{min} is minimum hamming distance of the code.

The parity check code discussed earlier is an example of error detecting codes. In case of even parity code, there are even number of 1's in the code. If the receiver detects odd number of 1's the received codeword is incorrect. This system will fail if there are even number of errors. The effectiveness of an error detection code is measured by the probability that the system fails to detect an error. It depends on the properties of communication channel.

Following are some examples of error detecting codes.

- **Parity Check Code :** A parity bit is added to the message such that number of 1's in the code becomes even in case of even parity and odd in case of odd parity. Errors can be detected by wanting number of 1's at the receiver end.

- **Two-Dimensional Parity Code :** k information bits from m messages are arranged in m × k matrix form. Even parity of each row is calculated and stored in k+1th column and even parity of each of m columns is calculated and stored in m+1th row as shown in Fig. 6.8. If there are 3 or less errors anywhere in the matrix, error can be detected as atleast one row will fail the parity check. But some patterns with 4 errors cannot be detected as shown.

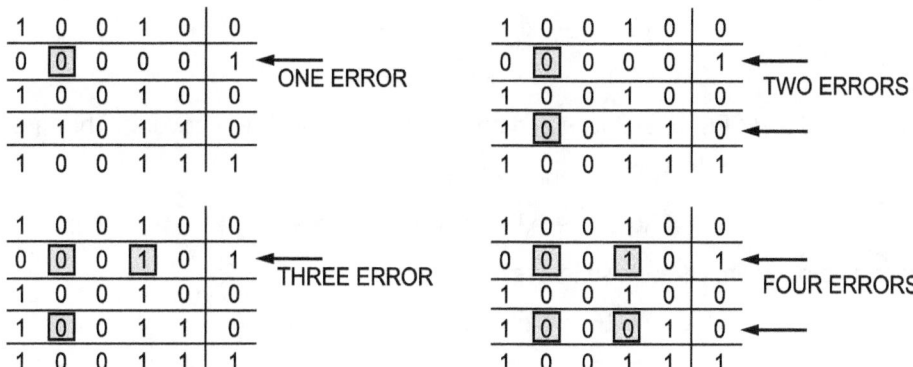

Fig. 6.8 : Two-dimensional parity code

- **Polynomial codes :**
- They are used both in error detection as well as error correction as discussed earlier.
- Polynomial codes are easy to implement using shift register.
- Cyclic Redundancy Check (CRC) codes are used to generate check bits for error detection.
- As seen earlier the message, codeword and error vectors are represented in terms of polynomials with binary coefficient.
- The codeword is generated using

$$c(x) = x^{n-k} d(x) + p(x)$$

where,

$$p(x) = \text{Rem}\left[\frac{x^{n-k} d(x)}{g(x)}\right]$$

- Detection involves finding syndrome

$$s(x) = \text{Rem}\left[\frac{r(x)}{g(x)}\right]$$

If remainder is zero, codeword is correctly received otherwise there will be error.

- Implementation of encoder and detector using shift register is already discussed.

Standardized Polynomial Codes :

Three polynomials listed below are used as standard polynomials in many applications.

They are

$$\text{CRC-12} - x^{12} + x^{11} + x^3 + x^2 + x + 1$$
$$\text{CRC-16} - x^{16} + x^{15} + x^2 + 1$$
$$\text{CRC-CCITT} - x^{16} + x^{12} + x^5 + 1$$

Recently, CRC-8 and CRC-10 are also recommended for use in ATM networks. They are

$$\text{CRC-8} - x^8 + x^2 + x + 1$$
$$\text{CRC-10} - x^{10} + x^9 + x^5 + x^4 + x + 1$$

Following two polynomials are also in use.

$$\text{CCITT-16} - x^{16} + x^{12} + x^5 + 1$$
$$\text{CCITT-32} - x^{32} + x^{26} + x^{23} + x^{22} + x^{16} + x^{12} + x^{11} + x^{10} + x^8 + x^7 + x^5 + x^4 + x^2 + x + 1$$

Error Detecting Capability of Polynomial Codes :

As seen earlier syndrome $s(x)$ is calculated by dividing $r(x)$ with $g(x)$. The error pattern $e(x)$ is given by

$$e(x) = r(x) \oplus d(x)$$

$\therefore \quad r(x) = d(x) \oplus e(x)$

$\therefore \quad s(x) = \text{Rem}\left[\dfrac{r(x)}{g(x)}\right]$

$$= \text{Rem}\left[\dfrac{d(x) + e(x)}{g(x)}\right]$$

$$= \text{Rem}\left[\dfrac{d(x)}{g(x)}\right] + \text{Rem}\left[\dfrac{e(x)}{g(x)}\right]$$

$$= \text{Rem}\left[\dfrac{e(x)}{g(x)}\right]$$

Thus, we can formulate $g(x)$ that will not divide the given error polynomials.

e.g.

- **To detect all single errors.**

$$e(x) = x^i \qquad 0 \leq i \leq n-1$$

If $g(x)$ has more than one term, it will not divide $e(x)$.

- **To detect all double errors.**

$$e(x) = x^i + x^j \qquad 0 \le i \le j \le n-1$$
$$= x^i (1 + x^{j-i})$$

As seen above, x^i is not divisible by $g(x)$. Hence, we should ensure that $1 + x^{j-i}$ is also not divisible by $g(x)$.

For this, $g(x)$ should be a primitive polynomial. Primitive polynomials have the property that, if degree of primitive polynomials is N then smallest value of m for which $1 + x^m$ is divisible by the polynomial is $2^N - 1$. Since $g(x)$ has degree n–k, it will detect all double errors if codeword has length less than or equal to $2^{n-k} - 1$.

The CRC-16 polynomial $x^{16} + x^{15} + x^2 + 1 = (x + 1)(x^{15} + x + 1)$ where, $x^{15} + x + 1$ is primitive. Hence, it can detect all double errors, if n <= $2^{15} - 1 = 32767$.

- **To detect all odd numbered errors :** If there are odd numbered errors, e(x) will have odd numbered terms. Such polynomial does not have x + 1 as a factor. Hence, by selecting (x + 1) as a factor, g(x) we can detect all odd numbered errors.

- **To detect all burst errors :** If a burst error of length L occurs starting from i^{th} bit position

$$e(x) = x^i b(x)$$

where, b(x) is of degree L–1 representing burst-error pattern. To detect this error, b(x) should not be divisible by g(x). For this, b(x) should have degree less than g(x) i.e. n–k. Thus, we can detect a burst error of length less than or equal to n–k. We can also detect a burst error of length n–k+1, if error pattern does not match g(x). Even we can detect some of the burst errors of length L > n–k+1.

All the CRC polynomials contain (x + 1) as a factor. Hence they can detect all odd numbered errors, all single and double errors and all burst errors of length ≤ n – k.

6.6 CHECKSUM

- It is an error detection method used in many protocols of internet.
- It is based on the concept of redundancy.
- As the name indicates it is a method in which error is "checked" by taking "sum" of the information in bits/digits.
- For example, if we want to transmit the digits (5, 2, 8, 7) we will transmit the sum of these digits along with them as additional (redundancy) information i.e. we will transmit (5, 2, 8, 7, 22). Now, when this information is received at the receiver end

we can "check" the sum of the first four digits. If it matches with 5th, the information is received correctly otherwise there will be error.

- We can have one more alternative which will make receiver's job simple. Transmit the negative of sum instead of sum so that if we add all received digits the sum will be 0.

- If you look at the information digits they will require only 4 bits for representation whereas the sum will require 5 bits and if negative sum is used we will require sign bit also. For this, we can use 1's complement arithmetic. Let us see how we can find the checksum using 1's complement arithmetic.

One's Complement Arithmetic :

In this method, a n bit number is represented in 1's complement form as below.

- If a number has more than n bits the extra leftmost bits are added to n right most bits.

- A negative number is represented by inverting all bits.

e.g. 1. In 4 bit representation number, 22 will be represented in 1's complement arithmetic as below.

NUMBER 22 is 10110

The 5th bit which is extra is added to leftmost bit as below.

```
  0110
+    1
  0111   which is 7.
```

Hence, 22 is represented as 0111 or 7.

2. In 4 bit representation, the number −10 will be represented as below.

Number 10 is 1010.

The negative number is represented by inverting the bits.

∴ −10 is represented as 0101 or 5.

Another way to find the complement is subtract the number from $2^n - 1$.

In above case, 4 bit representation $2^n - 1 = 15$. Hence, −10 will be represented as 15 − 10 = 5.

Example 6.13 :

Represent the following numbers using 1's complement arithmetics using 4 bits.

(i) 36, (ii) −6, (iii) 42, (iv) −20.

Solution :

(i) 36

Binary representation of 36 is

100100

More than 4 bits are added to leftmost bits

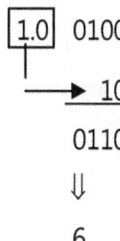

$$\boxed{1.0} \; 0100$$
$$\longrightarrow 10$$
$$0110$$
$$\Downarrow$$
$$6$$

(ii) −6

Binary representation of 6 is 0110.

Since negative number is represented by inverting bits.

$$0110$$
$$\downarrow$$
$$1001$$
$$\Downarrow$$
$$9$$

(iii) 42

Binary representation of 42 is 101010.

$$\boxed{10} \; 1010$$
$$\longrightarrow 10$$
$$1100$$
$$\Downarrow$$
$$12$$

(iv) −20

Binary representation of 20 is 10100.

More than 4 bits. Hence wrap.

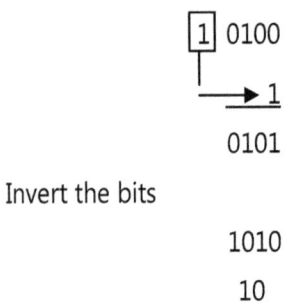

Invert the bits

1010

10

Now, let us find the checksum using one's complement arithmetic.

Let the transmitted digits be 5, 2, 8, 7.

The checksum will be (5 + 2 + 8 + 7) = −22.

−22 will be represented in one's complement arithmetic as below.

10110
↳ 1
0111

Inverting   1000
⇓
8

Hence, transmitted pattern will be,

(5, 2, 8, 7, 8).

If received pattern is same and if we add

5 + 2 + 8 + 7 + 8 = 30

Now, 30 in one's complement form is as below :

30 in binary 11110
wrap ↳ 1
Inverting 0000

If the final result is 0, it means there is no error in the transmitted digits/numbers.

Internet Checksum :

Internet uses 16 bit checksum. The information to be transmitted i.e. message has to be represented in terms of numbers so that it can be converted into 16 bit words. The steps to be followed for computing checksum at transmitter and receiver are as below :

I. Transmitter end :
1. Divide the message into 16 bit words.
2. Initialize checksum to 0.
3. Add words using one's complement arithmetic.
4. Complement the sum.

II. Receiver end :
1. Divide the received message (including checksum).
2. Add words using one's complement arithmetic.
3. Complement the sum.
4. If result is 0, no error. Otherwise there is error.

Let us take an example. Suppose we want to find the checksum for the word "communication". This word has to be expressed in ASCII format. The ASCII values of a-z are 97 to 122 in decimal, in hex they are 61 to 7A.

```
          ASCII value of c is   0x63
                        o is    0x6F
                        m is    0x6D
                        u is    0x75
                        n is    0x6E
                        t is    0x74
                        i is    0x69
                        a is    0x61
```

Now we add these alongwith checksum as below :

```
                                  4 2 3
                    c →         0 0 6 3
                   om →         6 F 6 D
                   mu →         6 D 7 5
                   ni →         6 E 6 9
                   ca →         6 3 6 1
                   ti →         7 4 6 9
                   on →         6 F 6 E
             checksum →         2 0 0 0 0
                 wrap           9 2 D 6
                                       2
                                9 2 D 8
           Complement           6 D 2 7
∴   Checksum is                 6 D 2 7
```

6.7 FRAMING

When the bits of information is received from physical layer, data link layer entity identifies beginning and end of block of information i.e. frames with the help of special pattern placed by the peer entity. The frames may be fixed length or variable length. The requirements of framing methods will vary accordingly. In case of fixed length frames, a frame consists of a single bit followed by a particular length sequence.

Variable length frames required additional information for frame identification.

For example :

- Special characters to identify beginning and end of frame.
- Starting and ending flags.
- Character counts.
- CRC Checking Methods (Checksum).

The first framing method uses ASCII characters DLE and STX at the start of each frame and DLE and ETX at the end of the frame. It is as shown in Fig. 6.9 (a), where DLE is Data Link Escape, STX is Start of Text and ETX is End of Text.

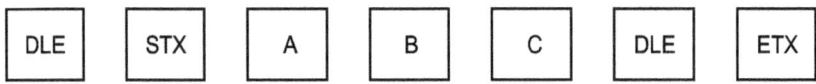

Fig. 6.9 (a) : Character Framing

But then this framing method has a problem. Consider the case where the data to be transmitted contains the character DLE STX in this case wrong identification of start of frame will be made. Similarly, if DLE ETX occur it will trigger end of frame. This problem can be solved by stuffing (adding) another DLE whenever DLE occurs in the data sequence. This technique is called **character stuffing**. The stuffed DLE can be destuffed (deleted) by receiving DLL entity. It is shown in Fig. 6.9 (b).

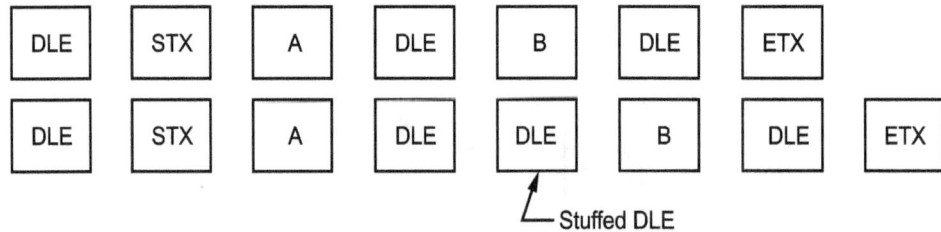

Fig. 6.9 (b) : Character Stuffing

This method is suitable only for data containing ASCII or printable characters and not for arbitrary sized characters. The second technique which is also called as bit stuffing allows arbitrary number of bits per character. At the beginning and end of each frame a special bit pattern 01111110 called as flag is used. Here also there is a possibility that the flag bits may occur in the data. The technique used to avoid this problem is bit stuffing. Whenever there are five 1's in data sequence, 0 is stuffed and at the receiving end it is destuffed. Bit stuffing is shown in Fig. 6.10.

ORIGINAL PATTERN : (Data)
1111111111101111110111110

AFTER BIT STUFFING :
11111[0] 11111[0] 110111110[0] 1011111[0]10

Fig. 6.10 : Bit Stuffing

Five 1's followed by 11 will indicate an error. If receiver looses synchronization all it has to do is scan for flag pattern. The character count method employs count of number of characters in the frame to be placed at the beginning of each frame. The receiver will look into character count and extract those many character from the frame and hence it knows the end of frame also. Problem will come when the count is changed due to error in transmission. The synchronization will be completely lost. Even if we use checksum, there will be no way of identifying the start of next frame. Hence this method is not used much. It is shown in Fig. 6.11.

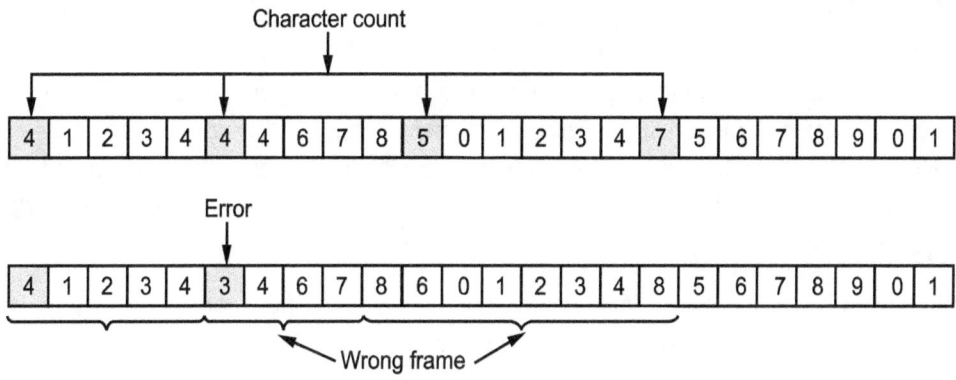

Fig. 6.11 : Character Count

In CRC based framing method, alongwith character count, CRC of count field is placed. Hence, the receiver examines four bytes at a time to see if CRC computed over first two bytes equals contents of next two bytes.

Many data link protocols use a combination of character count with other methods, for making it doubly sure that proper synchronization is achieved. For example, count of character is placed at the beginning of the frame and a flag is placed at the end of frame and may be checksum is also used. Count field is used to locate end of frame and only if appropriate flag is present at the end of frame and checksum is correct, the frame is accepted.

6.8 FLOW AND ERROR CONTROL

As pointed out earlier the two important functions of data link layer are flow control and error control.

Flow Control :

In a communication network the two communicating entities will have different speed of transmission and reception. There will be problem if sender is faster than receiver. The fast sender will swamp over the slow receiver. The "flow" of information between sender and receiver has to be "controlled". The technique used for this is called flow control technique. Also there will be time required to process incoming data at the receiver. This time required for processing is often more than the time for transmission. Incoming data must be checked and processed before they can be used. Hence, we require a buffer at the receiver to store the received data. This buffer is limited, therefore, before it becomes full the sender has to be informed to halt transmission temporarily. A set of procedures are required to be carried out to restrict the amount of data the sender can send before waiting for acknowledgement. This is called flow control.

Error Control :

When the data is transmitted it is going to be corrupted. We have seen how to tackle this problem by adding redundancy. Still the error is bound to occur. If such error occurs, the receiver can detect the errors and even correct them. What we can do is if error is detected by receiver, it can ask the sender to retransmit the data. This process is called Automatic Repeat Request (ARQ). Thus, error control is based on ARQ, which is retransmission of data.

Protocols :

The functions of data link layer viz. framing, error control and flow control are implemented in software. There are different protocols depending on the channel. For noiseless channel, there are two protocols :

    (i) Simplest,

    (ii) Stop-and-wait. For noisy channel, there are 3 protocols.

    (i)   Stop-and-wait ARQ

    (ii)   Go-back-N ARQ

    (iii) Selective repeat ARQ.

The protocols discussed here assume that the data flows only in one direction from sender to receiver. In practice, however, it is bidirectional. Hence, when the flow is bidirectional, we will be using piggybacking i.e. sending acknowledgement (positive/ negative) alongwith data if any to be sent to the other end.

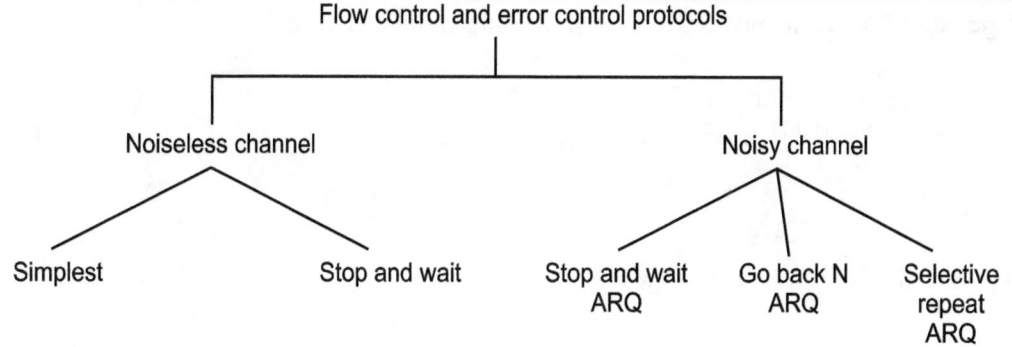

6.9 NOISELSS CHANNELS

If the channel is noiseless it will not corrupt the data or there will be no loss of information during transmission. There are two protocols for noiseless channel.

- Simplest protocol which does not require flow control.
- Stop-and-wait protocol which requires flow control.

Simplest Protocol :

Since the channel is noiseless, no error is introduced, hence it does not require error control. The receiver can receive all the data transmitted to by the sender at any speed. Hence, there will be no flow control.

Transmitter station A transmits a frame to receiver B whenever the network layer hands over the packet to data link layer in transmitter A. Fig. 6.12 shows the same.

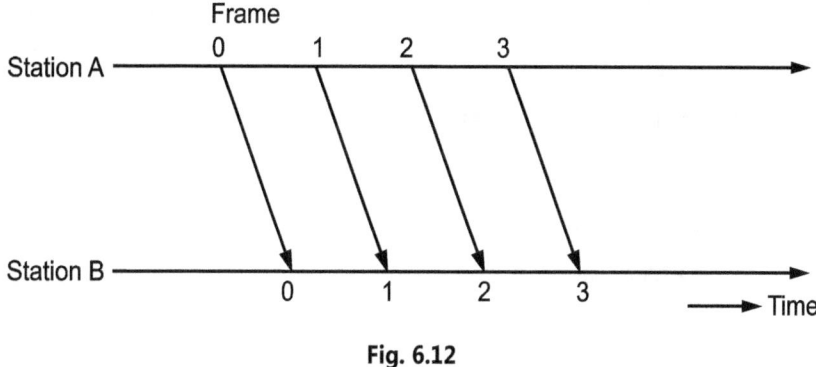

Fig. 6.12

The algorithms at transmitter and receiver will be as below :

Algorithm 6.1 : Transmitter site algorithm for Simplest Protocol

```
    start
1.  while(True)
2.  {
3.     wait_for_event( );
4.     if(Event(Request_to_send))
5.     {
6.         get_packet( )
7.         make_frame( );
8.         send_frame( );
9.     }
10. }
```

Explanation :

The algorithm runs continuously i.e. all the statements are repeated forever after the start. The transmitter DLL entity waits for the packet to be delivered by network layer, the wait_for_event( ) function does the same. If a packet comes it is accepted and DLL entity prepares frame by adding overheads (header tailer) to the packet. makeframe( ) function is used for this. The send_frame( ) function sends the frame and the DLL waits for a new packet.

Algorithm 6.2 : Receiver site algorithm for Simplest Protocol :

```
1.  while(true)
2.  {
3.     wait_for_event( )
4.        if(Event (frame_arrival))
5.        {
6.            accept_frame( );
7.            extract_packet( );
8.            deliver_packet( );
9.        }
10. }
```

Explanation :

The algorithm runs continuously. The receiver DLL entity waits for the frame to be received from physical layer, the wait_for_event( ) function does this. When the frame arrives it is accepted. This accept_frame( ) function does this. The extract_packet( ) function extracts the packet by processing and removing overheads added by transmitter DLL entity. The deliver_packet( ) function hands over the packet to network layer. Then the receiver DLL entity waits for the new event to occur.

Stop_and_wait protocol :

When there is a situation in which the sender is sending data faster than the receiver can process and accept it, there will be loss of frames. We must have a feedback mechanism in this case from receiver to sender to tell the sender when to send the next frame. In case of noiseless channel, there is no error control. Hence, we have to feedback the acknowledgement whenever the frame is received as shown in Fig. 6.13.

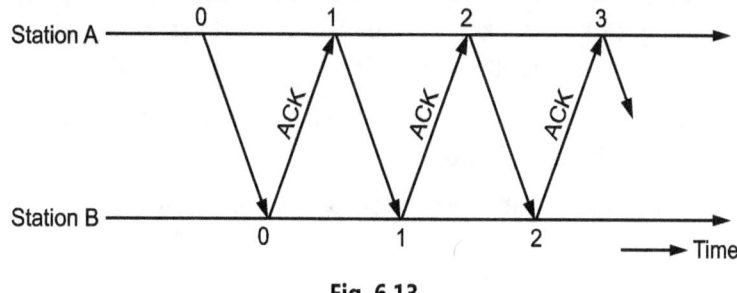

Fig. 6.13

The algorithms at transmitter and receiver will be as below :

Algorithm 6.3 : Transmitter site algorithm for stop_and_wait protocol

```
1.    ack=true
2.    while(true)
3.    {
4.          wait_for_event( );
5.          if(Event(Request_to_Send) && ack=true)
6.          {
7.                get_packet( );
8.                make_frame( );
9.                send_frame( );
10.               ack=false
11.   }
```

```
12.         wait_for_event( );
13.         if(event(ack_received))
14.         {
15.                 get_ack( );
16.                 ack=true;
17.         }
18. }
```

Explanation :
1. For first frame ack is set true.
2. Wait_for_event( ) waits for packet from network layer.
3. Whenever packet arrives and ack is true i.e. previous packet's acknowledgement is received get the packet, make frame and send it and wait for its acknowledgement by setting ack = false.
4. The second wait_for_event waits for acknowledgement whenever it arrives it is accepted and ack is made true.

Algorithm 6.4 : Receiver site algorithm for stop_and_wait protocol :

```
1.  while(true)
2.  {
3.         wait_for_event( );
4.         if(Event(frame_arrival))
5.         {
6.                 accept_frame( );
7.                 extract_packet( );
8.                 deliver_packet( );
9.                 send_ack( );
10.        }
11. }
```

Explanation :
1. The algorithm runs continuously.
2. Wait_for_event( ) waits for frame arrival from sender.

3. When frame arrives it is accepted, packet is extracted by processing the frame and the frame is delivered to network layer entity.
4. Acknowledgement is sent back.

6.10 NOISY CHANNELS

Noiseless channels are impossible practically. When the information is transmitted the channel is going to corrupt it and the receiver has to do error control. The three protocols that do error control are :

(i) Stop_and_wait ARQ.
(ii) Go back_N ARQ.
(iii) Selective Repeat (ARQ).

ARQ Protocols :

- Automatic repeat request is a combination of error detection and retransmission to ensure reliable data transmission.
- There are two basic types of ARQ protocols :
  (i) Simplex protocols.
  (ii) Sliding window protocols.
- Simplex protocols use stop-and-wait ARQ and sliding window protocols use Go-back-N ARQ and selective repeat ARQ.
- As shown in Fig. 6.14, the data link layer transmits information frames containing header and CRC alongwith payload. The receiving DLL entity checks for errors using CRC. Accordingly, a control frame is sent back to transmitting entity which includes acknowledgement (positive/negative). If Positive Acknowledgement (ACK) is received, next frame can be transmitted. In case of Negative Acknowledgement (NAK), retransmission of previous frame (s) is made.

Stop and Wait ARQ (Simplex Protocol) :

- In this technique, transmitter (A) transmits a frame to receiver (B) and waits for an acknowledgement from B.
- When acknowledgement from B is received, it transmits next frame.
- Now, consider a case where the frame is lost i.e. not received by B. B will not send an acknowledgement. A will wait and wait and wait ...... To avoid this, we can start a timer at A, corresponding to a frame. If the acknowledgement for a frame is not

received within the time timer is on, we can retransmit the frame, as shown in Fig. 6.15 (a).

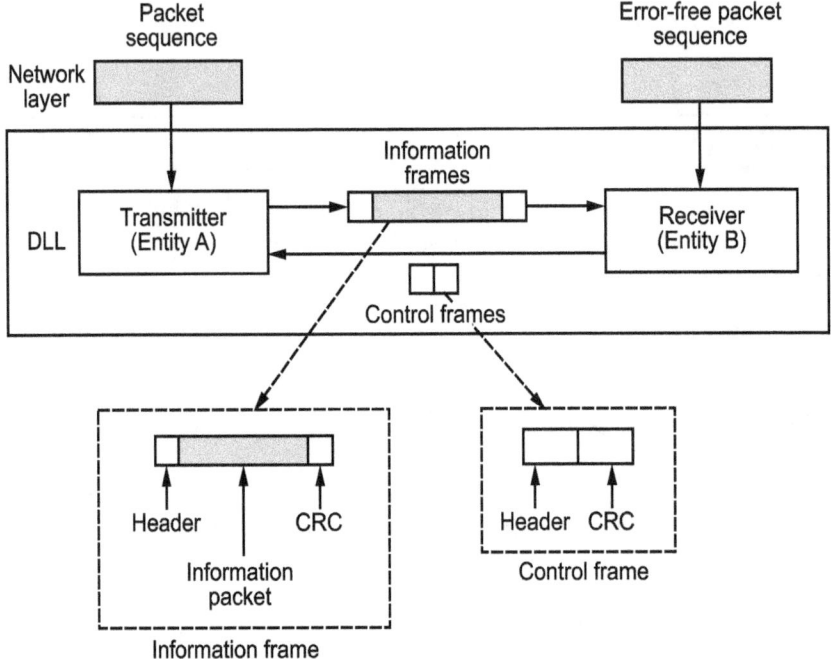

Fig. 6.14 : Frame Transmission in DLL

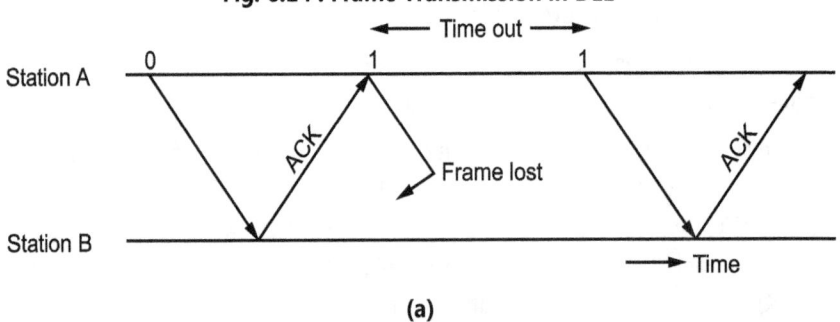

(a)

- Same thing can happen when frame is in error and B does not send acknowledgement. After A times out it will retransmit.
- There is another situation when some frame is transmitted but its acknowledgement is lost as shown in Fig. 6.15 (b).

The time out will send the same frame again which will result into accepting duplicate frame at B. For this, we have to bring in the concept of sequence number to frames. In case a duplicate frame is received due to loss of Ack, it can be discarded.

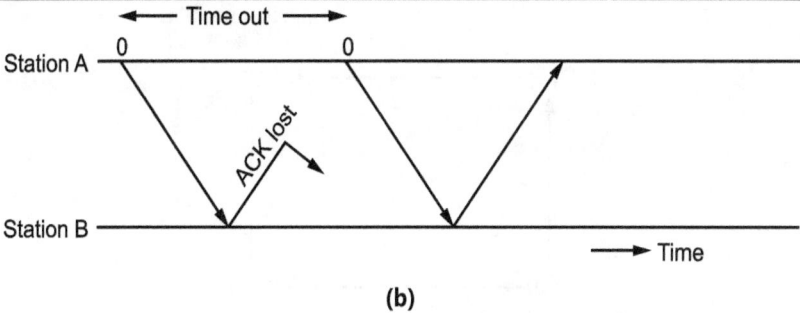

(b)

- A second ambiguity will arise due to delayed acknowledgement as shown in Fig. 6.15 (c).

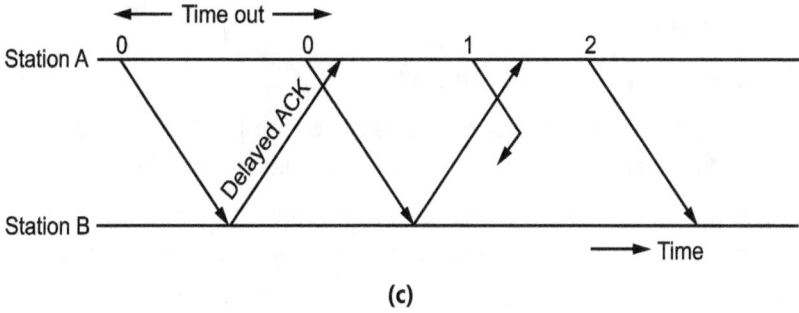

(c)

Fig. 6.15 : Stop_and_wait ARQ

As shown in figure, the acknowledgement received after frame 1 is transmitted would result into acknowledging frame 1 which is actually lost. We can give sequence number to acknowledgements so that transmitter knows the acknowledgement of which frame is received.

The acknowledgement number will be the number of next frame expected i.e. when frame 0 is received properly, we will be sending Acknowledgement number 1 as frame 1 is expected next.

Now, the next question is what should be the sequence numbers given to frame and acknowledgement. We cannot give large sequence numbers because they are going to occupy some space in frame header. Hence, sequence number should have minimum number of bits.

In stop_and_wait ARQ (simplex) protocol, one bit sequence number is sufficient. For this consider that frame 0 is transmitted and the receiver receives and sends acknowledgement number 1. Now, frame 1 is transmitted and sends acknowledgement for it since frame 0 is already received. We can use same number for next frame as shown in Fig. 6.16.

This ARQ technique is used in IBM's Binary Synchronous Communication (BISYNC) protocol and XMODEM, a file transfer protocol for modems.

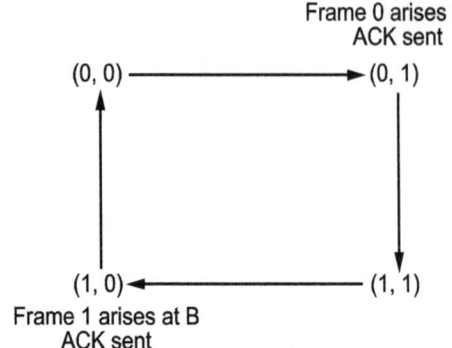

Fig. 6.16 : Sequence Number for stop_and_wait ARQ

Sliding Window Protocol

- The stop_and_wait ARQ is inefficient.
- We can also use full-duplex transmission to transmit and receive from both sides called piggybacking i.e. we send information alongwith acknowledgement.
- The protocols known as sliding window protocols are robust in nature and perform well, inspite of garbled frames, lost frames or premature timeouts.
- In all sliding window protocols, each frame transmitted from transmitter has sequence numbers. They are part of sending window whose size is W_S (Number of frames).
- Each frame received at the receiver is kept in a buffer called receiving window. Its size is W_R (Number of frames).
- There are two sliding window protocols :
  (i) Go_Back_N ARQ.
  (ii) Selective-Repeat ARQ.

Go-Back_N ARQ

- Unlike stop_and_wait ARQ, in this technique transmitter continues sending frames without waiting for acknowledgement.
- The transmitter keeps the frames which are transmitted in a buffer called sending window till its acknowledgement is received.
- Let the number of frames transmitter can keep in its buffer be W_S. It is called size of sender's window.
- The size of window is selected on the basis of delay-bandwidth product so that channel does not remain idle and efficiency is more.

- The transmitter keeps on transmitting the frames in window (buffer), till acknowledgement for the first frame in the window is received.

- When frames 0 to $W_S - 1$ are transmitted, the transmitter waits for acknowledgement of frame 0. When it is received the next frame is taken from network layer into the buffer i.e. window slides forward by one frame.

- If acknowledgement for an expected frame (i.e. first frame in the window) does not reach back and time-out occurs for the frame, all the frames in the buffer are transmitted again. Since there are $N = W_S$ frames waiting in the buffer, this technique is called Go_back_N ARQ.

- Thus, Go_back_N ARQ pipelines the processing of frames to keep the channel busy.

- Fig. 6.17 (a) shows Go_Back_N ARQ.

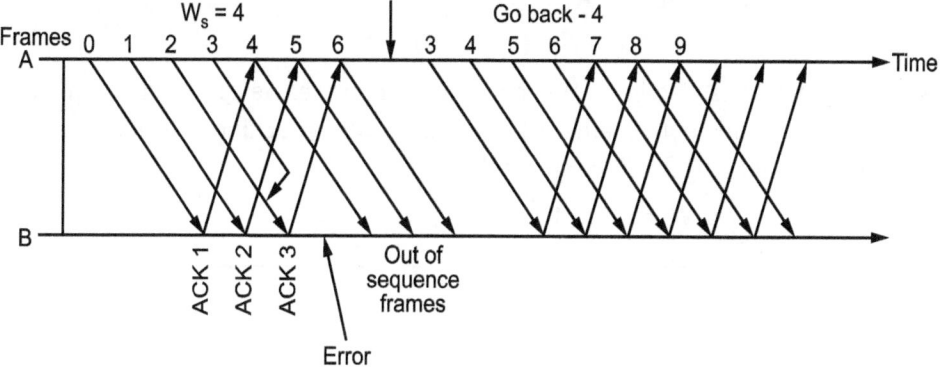

Fig. 6.17 (a)

- It can be seen that the receiver window size will be 1, since only one frame which is in order is accepted.

- Also, the expected frame number at the receiver end is always less than or equal to recently transmitted frame.

- What should be the maximum window size at the transmitter i.e. what should be value of W_S. It will depend on the number of bits used in sequence number field of the frame. So maximum window size at transmitter should be $W_S = 2^m$ i.e. if 3 bits are reserved for sequence number $W_S = 8$, but it will not ! For this consider following situation shown in Fig. 6.17 (b).

  i.e. if all the frames transmitted are acknowledged or their acknowledgement is lost. The transmitter will retransmit the frames in the buffer. The receiver will accept them as if they are new frames ! Hence, to avoid this problem, we reduce window size by 1 i.e. $W_S = 2^2 - 1 = 3$ i.e. make it Go_back_3. But the sequence number is maintained from 0 to 3. Now consider Fig. 6.18 (c), where the acknowledgements of all the received frames 0, 1, 2 are lost but the receiver is expecting frame 3. Hence, even if we transmit 0, 1, 2 again they will not be accepted as the expected sequence number does not match transmitted one. Hence, the window size should be $2^m - 1$ for Go_Back_N ARQ.

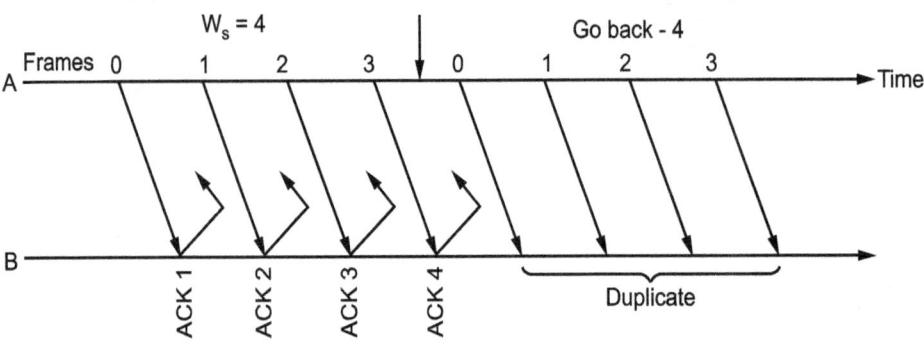

Fig. 6.17 (b)

- Go_Back_N can be implemented for both ends i.e. we can send information and acknowledgement together which is called **piggybacking**. This improves the use of bandwidth. Fig. 6.17 (c) shows the scheme.

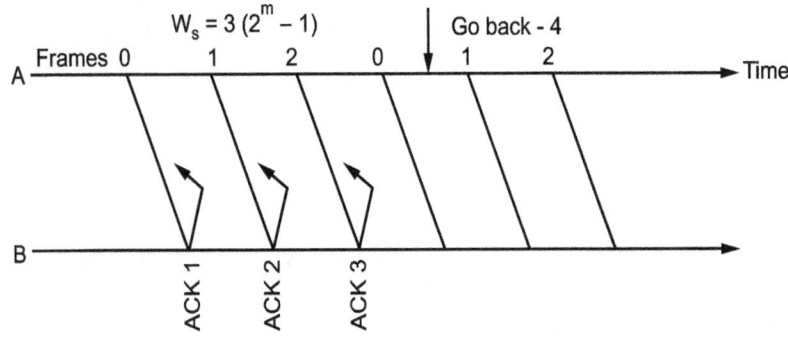

Fig. 6.17 (c)

Fig. 6.17 : Go_Back_N ARQ

Note that both transmitter and receiver need sending and receiving windows.
- Go_back_N ARQ is implemented in HDLC protocol and V-24 modem standard.

Selective Repeat ARQ :
- Go_Back_N ARQ is inefficient when channels have high error rates.
- Instead of transmitting all the frames in buffer, we can transmit only the frame in error.
- For this, we have to increase the window size of receiver so that it can accept frames which are error free but out of order (not in sequence).

- Normally, when an acknowledgement for first frame is received, the transmit window is advanced. Similarly, whenever acknowledgement for the first frame in receiver window is sent it advances.

- Whenever there is error or loss of frame and no acknowledgement is sent, the transmitter retransmits the frame whenever its timer expires. The receiver whenever accepts next frame which is out of sequence now sends negative acknowledgement NAK corresponding to the frame number it is expecting. Till the time the frame is received it keeps on accumulating frames received in the receiver window. Then, it sends the acknowledgement of recently accepted frame that was in error. It is shown in Fig. 6.18 (a).

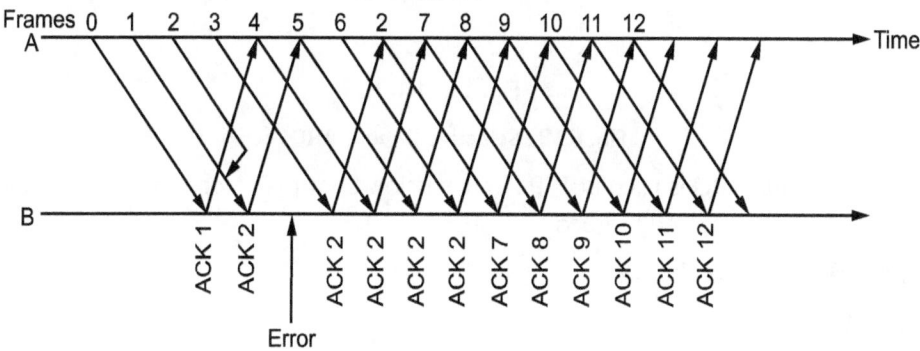

Fig. 6.18 (a)

To calculate the window size for given sequence numbering having m bits, consider the situation shown in Fig. 6.18 (b).

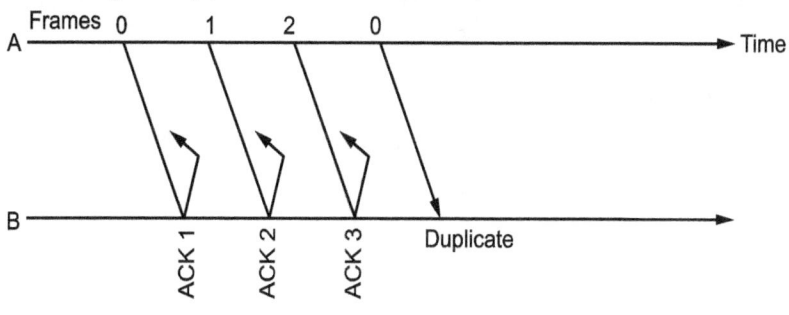

Fig. 6.18 (b)

Let us select window size for m = 2 as $W_S = 2^m - 1 = 3$. Let the frames 0, 1, 2 be in the buffer and are transmitted. They are received correctly but their acknowledgements are lost. Timer for frame 0 expires, hence is retransmitted. The receiver window is expecting frame 0 which it accepts as new frame but actually, it is duplicate !

Thus, the window size at transmitter and receiver are too large. Hence, we select $W_S = W_R = 2^m/2 = 2^{m-1}$. In above case, $W_S = W_R = 2^2/2 = 2$. Sequence numbers for frames will be 0, 1,

2, 3, as shown in Fig. 6.19 (c). The transmitter transmits frames 0, 1. But because of lost acknowledgements, timer for frame 0 expires. Hence, it retransmits frame 0. At the receiver we have expected frames {2, 3}. Hence, frame 0 is rejected as it is duplicate and not part of receiver window.

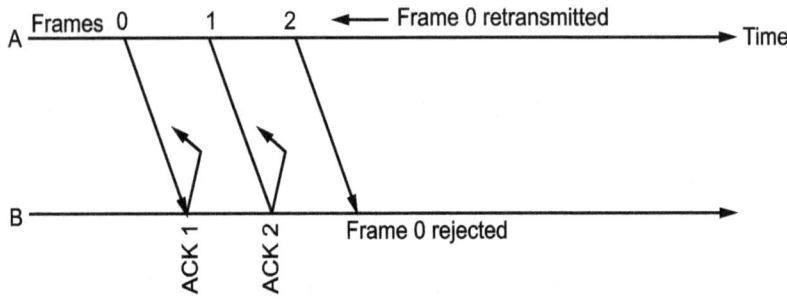

Fig. 6.18 (c)

Fig. 6.18 : Selective Repeat ARQ

The selective repeat ARQ is used in TCP (Transmission Control Protocol) and SSCOP (Service Specific Connection Oriented Protocol).

Performance of ARQ techniques

Stop_and_Wait ARQ

Let $T_F \rightarrow$ Frame time

$T_P \rightarrow$ Propagation Delay (One way)

∴ Total time taken to transmitting one frame

$$= T_F + 2T_P$$

(Neglecting acknowledgement time)

Efficiency or throughput is the ratio of time for one frame to the actual time taken to transmit the frame.

∴ $$\eta = \frac{T_F}{T_t} = \frac{T_F}{T_F + 2T_P}$$

Let R be the rate of transmission.

∴ Number of frame bits = $N_F = T_F \times R$

∴ $$\eta = \frac{\frac{N_F}{R}}{\frac{N_F}{R} + 2T_P}$$

If errors occur the frames are to be retransmitted. Let p be the error probability of frame. Let $\overline{N_r}$ be the average number of retransmissions required to transmit a frame successfully.

$$\therefore \overline{N_r} = \sum_{i=1}^{\infty} i \times p \text{ (i transmissions)}$$

$$= \sum_{i=1}^{\infty} i \times p_f^{i-1} (1 - p_f)$$

$$= \frac{1}{1 - p_f}$$

∴ Efficiency of stop_and_wait ARQ,

$$\eta = \frac{T_F}{(T_F + 2T_P) \times \overline{N_r}}$$

$$= \frac{T_F}{(T_F + 2T_P)} \times \frac{1}{1 - p_f}$$

$$= \frac{T_F}{T_F + 2T_P} \times (1 - p_f)$$

Sliding Window Protocol :

If there is no error, W_S frames are successfully transmitted in time $T_F + 2T_P$. Hence, the efficiency or throughput is given by,

$$\eta = \frac{W_S T_F}{T_F + 2T_P}$$

If rate of transmission is R,

$$\therefore T_F = \frac{N_F}{R}$$

$$\therefore \eta = \frac{W_S \times \frac{N_F}{R}}{\frac{N_F}{R} + 2T_P}$$

If there is an error in the frame Go_Back_N and Select Repeat ARQ will have different throughput.

(i) Go_Back_N ARQ :

The average number of retransmissions required will be,

$$\bar{N}_r = \sum_{i=1}^{\infty} f(i) P_f^{i-1} (1-p_f)$$

$$f(i) = 1 + (i-1)k$$

where, k is number of frames retransmitted when error occurs.

$$\bar{N}_r = (1-k) \sum_{i=1}^{\infty} p_f^{i-1} (1-p_f) + k \sum_{i=1}^{\infty} i P_f^{i-1} (1-p_f)$$

$$= 1 - k + \frac{k}{1-p_f}$$

Since,
$$k = W_S$$

$$\bar{N}_r = 1 - W_S + \frac{W_S}{(1-p_f)}$$

$$\therefore \quad \eta = \frac{W_S T_F}{\bar{N}_r (T_F + 2T_P)}$$

$$= \frac{W_S (1-p_f)}{\left(1 + \frac{2T_P}{T_F}\right)(1 - p_f + W_S p_f)}$$

(ii) Selective Repeat ARQ :

Since this case is similar to stop_and_wait ARQ, where we retransmit only one frame,

$$\bar{N}_r = \frac{1}{1-p_f}$$

$$\therefore \quad \text{Throughput } \eta = \frac{W_S T_F}{(T_F + 2T_P)} \times (1 - p_f)$$

Flow Control :

- When there is a mismatch in the speed of transmitting entity and receiving entity, data transfer will not be effective.
- Flow control is required in such case which is a function of data link layer.

- Example when there is a data transfer from high end server to a client flow control will be required.
- The ARQ techniques discussed earlier during error control can also be used for flow control viz. stop_and_wait ARQ and sliding window ARQ.

Stop and Wait Flow Control
- Stop_and_wait ARQ is simplest form of flow control.
- The transmitting entity transmits a frame and waits till the acknowledgement for the frame is received. After receiving acknowledgement it sends next frame i.e. receiver tells transmitter that Yes, I am ready to receive next frame. If acknowledgement is not received the frame is retransmitted. As seen earlier, this scheme is inefficient.

Sliding Window Flow Control :
- In situation where the link length is greater than frame length ($T_P >> T_F$) stop_and_wait ARQ proves to be inefficient, as line remains idle for long time.
- If multiple frames are allowed simultaneously on the link instead of one, efficiency can be improved.
- The two stations A and B allocate some buffer space for W_S frames.
- Each frame is given sequence number.
- A maintains list of sequence numbers it is allowed to send.
- B maintains list of sequence numbers it is prepared to receive.
- As shown in Fig. 6.19, the stations A and B transmit and receive information.

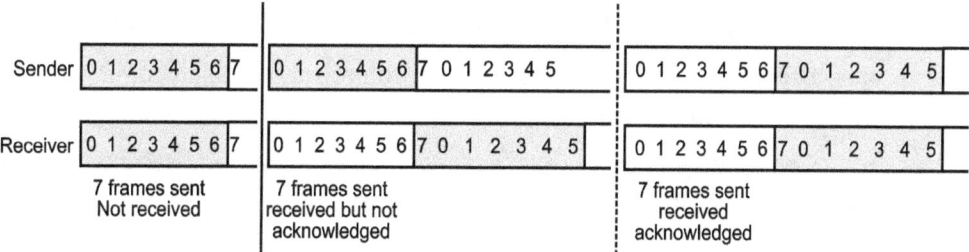

Fig. 6.19 : Sliding Window Flow Control

- The simplest procedure for flow control will be to tell sender to stop transmitting information.
- Whenever receiving station senses its buffer is getting full, it can send the stop signal to transmitting station.

- Note that receiving station is going to receive $2T_p \times R$ bits after it sends stop signal where T_p is propagation delay and R is transmitting rate.
- Sliding window protocols using ARQ techniques can also be used to provide flow control.
- The receiver's window size can be made equal to sender's window and whenever acknowledgement is received transmitter can accommodate next frame in buffer.
- Signals like Receive Ready (RR) and Receive Not Ready (RNR) can also be used.
- Receive Ready will indicate the expected frame to be received at the receiver.
- Receive Not Ready (RNR) will indicate buffer full and stop transmitting.
- A station can send both data and acknowledgement if it has both to send. It is called **piggybacking** which improves efficiency of transmission.
- A separate acknowledgement frame (RR or RNR) can be sent if station has only acknowledgement and no data to send.

6.11 HIGH LEVEL DATA LINK CONTROL (HDLC)

- It is the most widely used DLL protocol.
- It has a set of functions which provides communication service to network layer.
- HDLC supports variety of applications for which it has three types of stations, two link configurations and three data transfer modes.

Types of Stations :
- **Primary station :** It controls operation of link. It issues commands.
- **Secondary station :** Primary station controls it by issuing command frames transmitted by secondary station.
- **Combined station :** It has features of both primary and secondary stations i.e. it issues both commands and response.

Types of Configuration :
- **Unbalanced configuration :** It has one primary and one or more secondary stations. It supports both full duplex and half duplex configuration.
- **Balanced configuration :** It consists of two combined stations supporting half duplex and full duplex transmission.

These configurations are shown in Fig. 6.20 (a), (b) and (c).

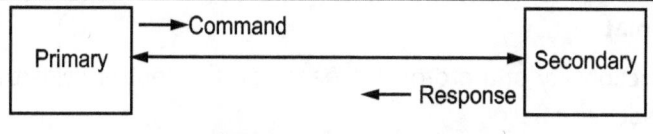

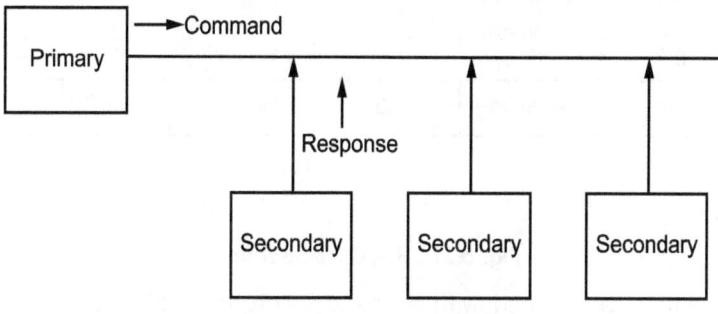

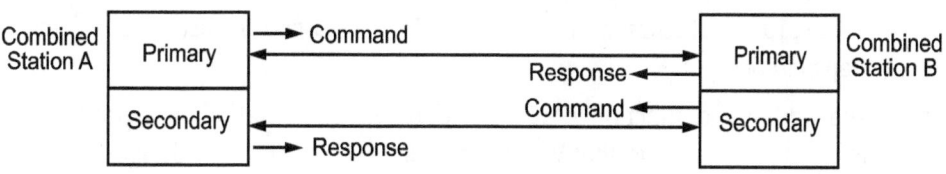

Fig. 6.20

- **Types of Data Transfer Modes :**

    - **Normal Response Mode (NRM) :** Used with unbalanced configuration. Primary can initiate data transfer to a secondary. Secondary can only transfer data in response to command from primary.

    - **Asynchronous Balanced Mode (ABM) :** Used with balanced configuration. Any one of the combined station can initiate transmission without the permission of other station.

    - **Asynchronous Response Mode (ARM) :** Used with unbalanced configuration secondary can initiate transmission without permission from primary. But primary has control of the link.

        NRM can be used on multidrop lines and point-to-point links. ABM is most widely used. ARM is rarely used.

HDLC Frame Format :

- The functionality of a protocol depends on the control fields that are defined in the header and trailer.
- The various data transfer modes are determined by the frame structure.
- Fig. 6.21 shows HDLC frame format.

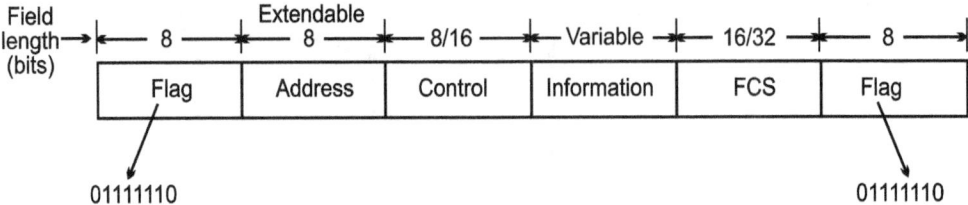

Fig. 6.21 : HDLC frame format

- Information is attached with an header consisting of flag, address and control fields and a trailer consisting of checksum and flag.
- Flag fields which are 8 bit long delimit the frame at both ends with a pattern 01111110 as discussed in Section 6.7. Bit stuffing is used to achieve data transparency.
- The addressing function of DLL is identifying the station that transmitted the frame and the station that will be receiving the frame. The address field specifies this. It is extendable over more than 8 bits in multiples. If this field is all 1's, the frame is broadcast to all secondaries.
- There are three types of control fields to identify three types of frames.
    - **Information frame (I-frame)** has 0 in the first bit of control field.
    - **Supervisory frame (S-frame)** has 10 in first two bits of control field.
    - **Unnumbered frame (U-frame)** has 11 in first two bits of control field.

    Error control and flow control functions of DLL are provided by I-frame and S-frame. The three frame fields are shown in Fig. 6.22.

    Information field consists of 3 bit sequence number N(S) and N(R) of sender and acknowledgement number of receiver respectively (piggybacked). All frames have a P/F bit. Its uses depend on situation. In command frames it is called P bit and is set to 1 whenever a response frame is expected (Polled) from peer entity. In response frames it is called F bit and is set to 1 to indicate that the frame is response to a command frame (Poll). The length of information frame can be variable.

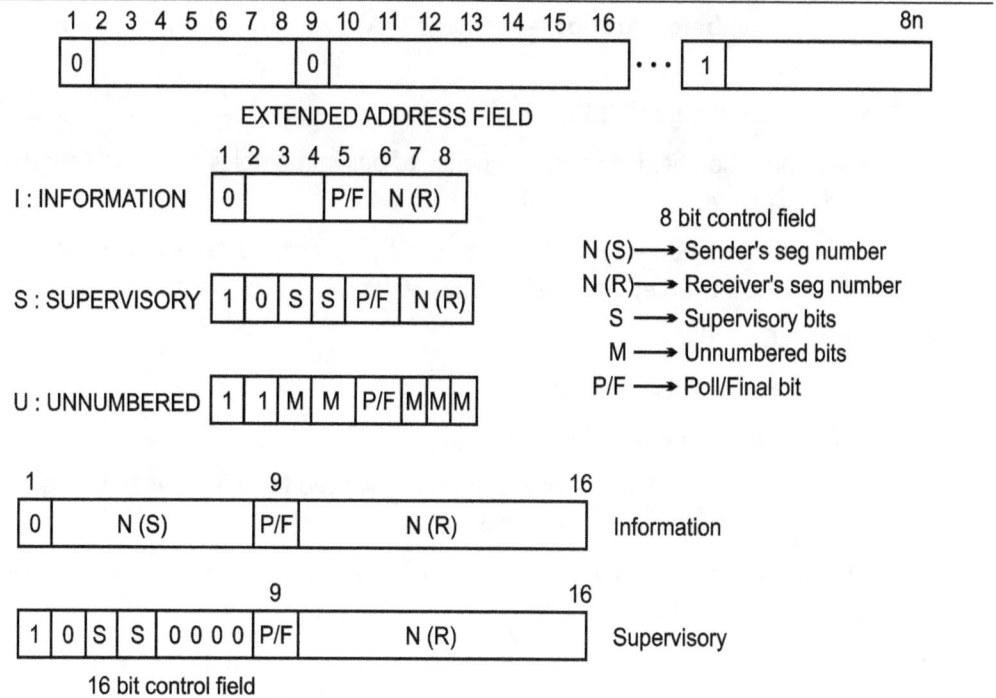

Fig. 6.22

There are four types of supervisory frames decided by S-field.

If SS = 00. It is receive ready (RR) which acknowledges received frames in absence of piggybacking.

If SS = 01. It is reject frame indicating negative acknowledgement and transmitter should go back and transmit frames N(R) onward.

SS = 10 means receive not ready (RNR). Buffer full condition.

SS = 11 indicates selective reject, where N(R) is frame to be retransmitted.

- Combination of I-frame and S-frame allows HDLC to implement ARQ techniques.
- The unnumbered frames implement number of control functions.

  The M bits decide the function.

  They are as below.

    - **Set Asynchronous Balanced Mode (SABM)** : To set up asynchronous balanced mode connection.
    - **Set Normal Response Mode (SNRM)** : To set up normal response mode.
    - **Disconnect (DISC)** : Indicates station wishes to disconnect connection.

- **Unnumbered Acknowledgement (UA)** : Acknowledges frames during call set up.
- **Frame Reject (FRMR)** : Reject unacceptable frame.
- The information field contains sequence of bits in multiples of octets. Length of F-field is variable.
- Frame Check Sequence (FCS) field consists of error detecting code calculated from frame bits except flag fields. It has 16 bit CRC CCITT code.

Operation of HDLC :

Let us now see how HDLC operates.

Connection Establishment and Release :

- Station A sends SAMB (Set Asynchronous Balanced Mode) frame indicating that it wants to establish a new connection.
- Station B sends unnumbered acknowledgement if it is ready to proceed. Otherwise it will REJECT the request by sending RNR frame.
- Whenever station wants to release connection it sends DISC frame and other station sends unnumbered acknowledgement. It is shown in Fig. 6.23.

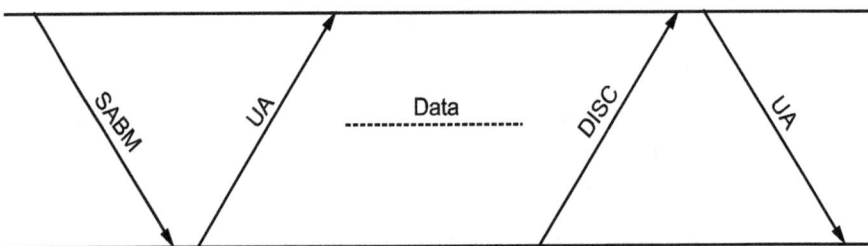

Fig. 6.23 : HDLC Connection Establishment and Release

Exchange of Frames using Normal Response Mode :

Assuming that connection is established between station A as primary and stations B and C as secondary, exchange of frames is shown in Fig. 6.24.

- Station A polls B with N(R) = 0. Station B responds by sending frames 0, 1, 2, 3, with F bits set in last frame.
- Station A sends rejection of frame 2 and polls station C, which responds with receive ready frame.
- Station A again sends request to transmit frame 2 to B with poll bit set. Station B responds by sending frames 2, 4, 5 with F bit set in last frame.
- Station A sends information frame piggybacking acknowledgement of 5.

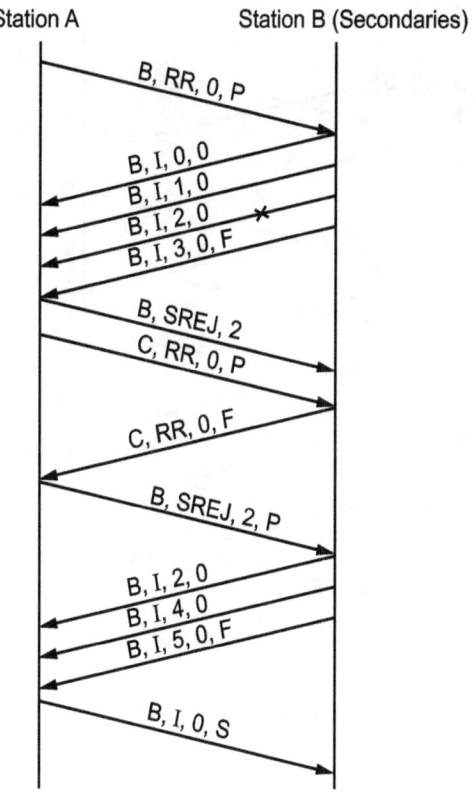

Fig. 6.24 : Exchange of Frames using NRM

Exchange of frames using Asynchronous Balanced Mode (Refer Fig. 6.25).

Address field consists of address of receiving station, if it is information frame and address of transmitting station, if it is command frame or a response frame. Whenever frame is in error a REJ frame is send indicating number of bad frame so that transmitting station resends all the frames starting from that frame (Go_back_N) as is seen in case frame 1 rejected by station B.

Information frame consists of N(S) and N(R), where N(S) is transmitted frame number and N(R) is expected frame number i.e. piggyback acknowledgement. In case station does not have information frame to send it sends RR frame with acknowledgement of previously received frame.

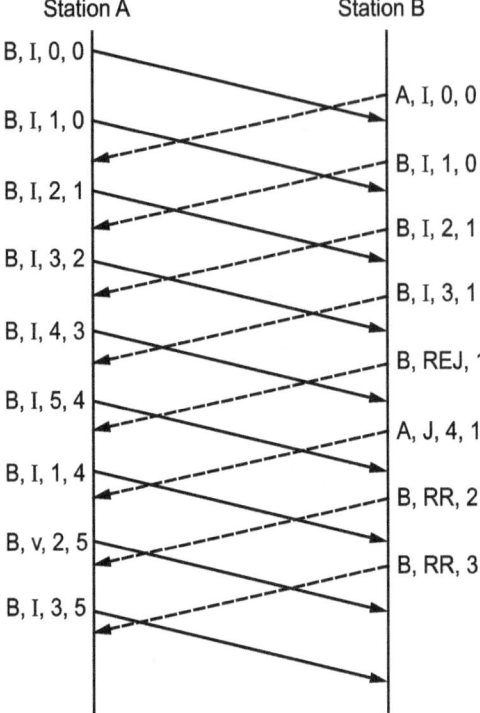

Fig. 6.25 : Exchange of Frames using ABM

6.12 POINT-TO-POINT PROTOCOL (PPP)

Introduction

The *Point-to-Point Protocol (PPP)* originally emerged as an encapsulation protocol for transporting IP traffic over point-to-point links. PPP also established a standard for the assignment and management of IP addresses, asynchronous (start/stop) and bit-oriented synchronous encapsulation, network protocol multiplexing, link configuration, link quality testing, error detection, and option negotiation for such capabilities as network layer address negotiation and data-compression negotiation. PPP supports these functions by providing an extensible Link Control Protocol (LCP) and a family of Network Control Protocols (NCPs) to negotiate optional configuration parameters and facilities. In addition to IP, PPP supports other protocols, including Novell's Internetwork Packet Exchange (IPX) and DECnet.

PPP Components :

PPP provides a method for transmitting datagrams over serial point-to-point links. PPP contains three main components :

- A method for encapsulating datagrams over serial links. PPP uses the High-Level Data Link Control (HDLC) protocol as a basis for encapsulating datagrams over point-to-point links.
- An extensible LCP to establish, configure, and test the data link connection.
- A family of NCPs for establishing and configuring different network layer protocols. PPP is designed to allow the simultaneous use of multiple network layer protocols.

General Operation :

To establish communications over a point-to-point link, the originating PPP first sends LCP frames to configure and (optionally) test the data link. After the link has been established and optional facilities have been negotiated as needed by the LCP, the originating PPP sends NCP frames to choose and configure one or more network layer protocols. When each of the chosen network layer protocols has been configured, packets from each network layer protocol can be sent over the link. The link will remain configured for communications until explicit LCP or NCP frames close the link, or until some external event occurs (for example, an inactivity timer expires or a user intervenes).

Physical Layer Requirements :

PPP is capable of operating across any DTE/DCE interface. Examples include EIA/TIA-232-C (formerly RS-232-C), EIA/TIA-422 (formerly RS-422), EIA/TIA-423 (formerly RS-423), and International Telecommunication Union Telecommunication Standardization Sector (ITU-T) (formerly CCITT) V.35. The only absolute requirement imposed by PPP is the provision of a duplex circuit, either dedicated or switched, that can operate in either an asynchronous or synchronous bit-serial mode, transparent to PPP link layer frames. PPP does not impose any restrictions regarding transmission rate other than those imposed by the particular DTE/DCE interface in use.

PPP Link Layer :

PPP uses the principles, terminology, and frame structure of the International Organization for Standardization (ISO) HDLC procedures (ISO 3309-1979), as modified by ISO 3309:1984/PDAD1 "Addendum 1: Start/Stop Transmission." ISO 3309-1979 specifies the HDLC frame structure for use in synchronous environments. ISO 3309 : 1984/PDAD1 specifies proposed modifications to ISO 3309-1979 to allow its use in asynchronous environments. The PPP control procedures use the definitions and control field encodings standardized in ISO 4335-1979 and ISO 4335-1979/Addendum 1-1979. The PPP frame format appears as shown in Fig. 6.26.

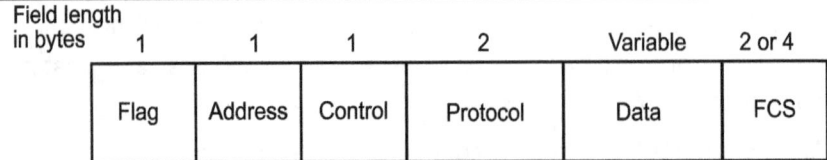

Fig. 6.26 : Six Fields make up the PPP Frame

The following descriptions summarize the PPP frame fields illustrated in Fig. 6.27.

- **Flag** : A single byte that indicates the beginning or end of a frame. The flag field consists of the binary sequence 01111110.

- **Address** : A single byte that contains the binary sequence 11111111, the standard broadcast address. PPP does not assign individual station addresses.

- **Control** : A single byte that contains the binary sequence 00000011, which calls for transmission of user data in an unsequenced frame. A connectionless link service similar to that of Logical Link Control (LLC) Type 1 is provided.

- **Protocol** : Two bytes that identify the protocol encapsulated in the information field of the frame. The most up-to-date values of the protocol field are specified in the most recent Assigned Numbers Request For Comments (RFC).

- **Data** : Zero or more bytes that contain the datagram for the protocol specified in the protocol field. The end of the information field is found by locating the closing flag sequence and allowing 2 bytes for the FCS field. The default maximum length of the information field is 1,500 bytes. By prior agreement, consenting PPP implementations can use other values for the maximum information field length.

- **Frame Check Sequence (FCS)** : Normally 16 bits (2 bytes). By prior agreement, consenting PPP implementations can use a 32-bit (4-byte) FCS for improved error detection.

The LCP can negotiate modifications to the standard PPP frame structure. Modified frames, however, always will be clearly distinguishable from standard frames.

PPP Link-Control Protocol :

The PPP LCP provides a method of establishing, configuring, maintaining, and terminating the point-to-point connection. LCP goes through four distinct phases.

First, link establishment and configuration negotiation occur. Before any network layer datagrams (for example, IP) can be exchanged, LCP first must open the connection and negotiate configuration parameters. This phase is complete when a configuration-acknowledgment frame has been both sent and received.

This is followed by link quality determination. LCP allows an optional link quality determination phase following the link-establishment and configuration-negotiation phase.

In this phase, the link is tested to determine whether the link quality is sufficient to bring up network layer protocols. This phase is optional. LCP can delay transmission of network layer protocol information until this phase is complete.

At this point, network layer protocol configuration negotiation occurs. After LCP has finished the link quality determination phase, network layer protocols can be configured separately by the appropriate NCP and can be brought up and taken down at any time. If LCP closes the link, it informs the network layer protocols so that they can take appropriate action.

Finally, link termination occurs. LCP can terminate the link at any time. This usually is done at the request of a user but can happen because of a physical event, such as the loss of carrier or the expiration of an idle-period timer.

Three classes of LCP frames exist. Link-establishment frames are used to establish and configure a link. Link-termination frames are used to terminate a link, and link-maintenance frames are used to manage and debug a link.

These frames are used to accomplish the work of each of the LCP phases.

SOLVED EXAMPLES

Example 6.14 :

Let $g(x) = x^3 + x + 1$.

Consider the information sequence 1001.

   (i) Find the codeword corresponding to the information sequence given.
   (ii) Suppose that the codeword has a transmission error in the first bit. What will be the syndrome generated at the receiver ?

Solution :

Given :
$$g(x) = x^3 + x + 1$$
$$d = [1\,0\,0\,1]$$
$$d(x) = x^3 + 1$$
$$\text{Here, } n - k = 3$$
$$k = 4$$
$$\therefore \quad n = 7$$

(i) Assuming systematic code generation.
$$c(x) = x^{n-k}\, d(x) + p(x)$$

where,

$$p(x) = \text{Rem}\left[\frac{x^{n-k} d(x)}{g(x)}\right]$$

$$\begin{array}{r} x^3 + x \\ x^3 + x + 1 \overline{)\, x^6 + x^3 } \\ x^6 + x^4 + x^3 \\ \hline x^4 \\ x^4 - x^2 + x \\ \hline x^2 + x \end{array}$$

$\therefore \quad p(x) = x^2 + 1$

$\therefore \quad c(x) = x^3 (x^3 + 1) + x^2 + 1$

$\qquad \qquad = x^6 + x^3 + x^2 + 1$

$\qquad \qquad = [1 0 0 1 1 0 1]$

(ii) If error is there in first bit,

$\qquad$ Error pattern $e = [1 0 0 0 0 0 0]$

$\therefore \qquad e(x) = x^6$

Now, syndrome

$$s(x) = \text{Rem}\left[\frac{r(x)}{g(x)}\right] = \text{Rem}\left[\frac{e(x)}{g(x)}\right]$$

$$\begin{array}{r} x^3 + x + 1 \\ x^3 + x + 1 \overline{)\, x^6 } \\ x^6 + x^4 + x^3 \\ \hline x^4 + x^3 \\ x^4 + x^2 + x \\ \hline x^3 + x^2 + x \\ x^2 + x + 1 \\ \hline x^2 + 1 \end{array}$$

$\therefore \qquad s = [1 0 1]$

Example 6.15 :

To provide more reliability than single parity bit can give, an error detecting coding scheme uses one parity bit for checking all the odd numbered bits and a second parity for all even numbered bit. What is the hamming distance of this code ?

Solution :

If 1 parity bit is provided for odd numbered bits and 1 parity for even numbered bits, two changes in odd or even numbered positions will generate a valid codeword. Hence, hamming distance = 2. e.g. Let message be 1010. Code will be 101000.

If two errors occur in 1st and 3rd position codeword will be 000000 which is valid codeword as it satisfies parity condition.

∴ The hamming distance between these codewords is 2.

Example 6.16 :

A bit stream 10011101 is transmitted using the standard CRC method. The generator polynomial is $x^3 + 1$. Show the actual bit string transmitted. Suppose the third bit from left is inverted during transmission. Show that this error is detected at the receiver's end.

Solution :

Given :

$d = [1 0 0 1 1 1 0 1]$

$g(x) = x^3 + 1$

∴ $d(x) = x^7 + x^4 + x^3 + x^2 + 1$

$x - k = 3 \quad k = 8$

∴ $x = 11$

(i) $x^{n-k} d(x) = x^3 (x^7 + x^4 + x^3 + x^2 + 1)$

$= x^{10} + x^7 + x^6 + x^5 + x^3$

$\begin{array}{r} x^7 + x^3 + x^2 \\ x^3 + 1 \overline{) x^{10} + x^7 + x^6 + x^5 + x^3} \\ \underline{x^{10} + x^7} \\ x^6 + x^4 + x^3 \\ \underline{x^6 + x^3} \\ x^5 \end{array}$

$$x^5 + x^2$$
$$x^2 = p(x)$$

∴ $c(x) = x^{n-k} d(x) + p(x)$

$= x^{30} + x^7 + x^6 + x^5 + x^3 + x^2$

$= [1 0 0 1 1 1 0 1 1 0 0]$

(ii) c = [1 0 0 1 1 1 0 1 1 0 0]

Third bit is inverted.

∴ r = [1 0 1 1 1 1 0 1 1 0 0]

$r(x) = x^{10} + x^8 + x^7 + x^6 + x^5 + x^3 + x^2$

$$\begin{array}{r} x^7 + x^5 + x^3 \\ x^3 + 1 \overline{) x^{10} + x^8 + x^7 + x^6 + x^5 + x^3 + x^2} \\ x^{10} + x^7 \\ \hline x^8 + x^6 + x^5 + x^3 + x^2 \\ x^8 + x^5 \\ \hline x^6 + x^3 + x^2 \\ x^6 + x^3 \\ \hline x^2 \end{array}$$

∴ $s(x) = x^2$

∴ s = [1 0 0]

Since syndrome in non-zero above error is detected.

Example 6.17 :

If you are given the following bit sequence of HDLC frame, identify various fields.

01111110	01111110	10100011	01100010
01110000	11000011	01010101	10101011
01111110	01111110		

Solution :

An HDLC frame has following format

8 bit	8 bit	8 bit	Variable	16 bit	8 bit
Flag	Address	Control	Information	FCS	Flag

There are two flag fields at the start and end.

Start Flag	01111110		
Flag	01111110		
Address	10100011		
Control	01100010		
Information	01110000	11000011	01010101
FCS	01010101	10101011	
Flag	01111110		
End Flag	01111110		

EXERCISES

1. Explain different types of errors that can occur in transmission of bits.
2. What are functions of data link layer ?
3. What is error control ? How it is achieved ?
4. Explain error correction and detection.
5. What are linear block codes ? Explain.
6. What are cyclic codes ? Explain.
7. What is hamming distance ? Explain with example.
8. What is generator matrix in LBC ? How it is created and used ?
9. What is generator polynomial in cyclic codes ?
10. How is systematic cyclic code generated ?
11. What is checksum ? Explain with example.
12. What is framing ? What are different types of framing ?
13. What is flow control in DLL ? Explain.

14. Explain :
    (i) Simplest Protocol, (ii) Stop_and_wait protocol.
15. What are ARQ protocols ? Explain.
16. What is stop_and_wait ARQ ?
17. What is Go_back_N ARQ ?
18. What is selective_repeat ARQ ?
19. Give frame format of HDLC protocol. Explain each field.
20. Give frame format of PPP protocol. Explain each field.

Chapter 7
MULTIACCESS CONTROL

OBJECTIVES

After reading this chapter you will understand :

- Multiple Access Communications
- Random Access : Aloha, Carrier Sense Multiple Access Protocols, CSMA/CD, Aloha and Collisions, Retransmission Back-off
- Controlled Access
- Collision free protocols, limited contention protocol
- Multiple Access Techniques

7.1 INTRODUCTION

There are two categories of networks based on the manner in which they provide interconnection.

• Switched Networks : They provide interconnection by means of transmission lines, multiplexers and switches. Addressing is hierarchical and routing is used.

• Broadcast Network : Information is broadcasted over a channel and is available to all users. Non-hierarchical addressing will identify correct user. Routing is not used.

Broadcast networks require what is called as medium access control protocol to co-ordinate the access of channels. A single medium is shared by number of users, hence these networks are called multiple access networks.

Multiple Access Communications :

When number of users share the same medium for transmission as shown in Fig. 7.1, all the stations sharing the medium can hear transmission from any given station.

If two or more stations try transmitting simultaneously their transmission will collide.

There are two schemes for allocating channels for transmission to a particular user.

• Static Channel Allocation :

It is static and collision free sharing of medium. If there are N users, the bandwidth of channel is divided into N subchannels and each user uses them separately. It is called Frequency Division Multiplexing (FDM).

FDM is efficient in case when all the channels have continuous traffic and inefficient when traffic is bursty. Another static channel allocation method is Time Division Multiplexing (TDM) where each user is allocated a fixed time slot for transmission.

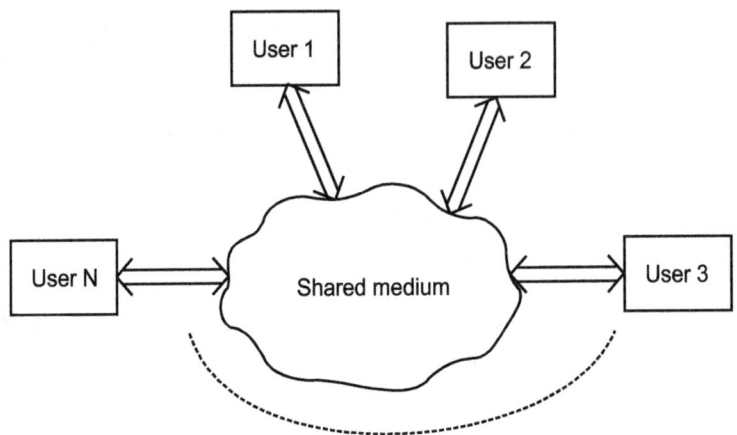

Fig. 7.1 (a) : Multiple Access Communication

- **Dynamic Channel Allocation :**

In situations where user traffic is bursty the channel is allocated on a per frame basis. This is called Medium Access Control Scheme.

There are two approaches of implementing this scheme :

- Scheduling
- Random Access

While allocating the channels dynamically, following assumptions are made :

- There are N independent stations which generate frames for transmission randomly. Once a frame is generated station is blocked i.e. it does nothing until frame is successfully transmitted.
- There is only one channel available.
- If two frames are transmitted simultaneously, it results into collision.
- Frame transmission can begin at any instant. Frames are transmitted in a fixed time slot.
- Stations can sense if channel is in use. If it is sensed busy no station will attempt to use it.

Stations cannot serve channel before use. Only after transmission they decide whether transmission was successful or not. There are number of protocols devised to handle the multiple access over a shared channel. These protocols can be classified as :

1. Random Access Protocols.

    e.g. Aloha, CSMA, CSMA/CD, CSMA/CA

2. Controlled Access Protocols

   e.g. Reservation, Polling, Token Passing.

3. Channelization Protocols

   e.g. FDMA, TDMA and CDMA.

7.2 RANDOM ACCESS

ALOHA

- It is a random access scheme for transmitting information for terminals sharing the same channel.
- It is simple in operation.
- Information is transmitted over the shared channel as soon as it becomes available.
- If there is collision because of more stations transmitting simultaneously, they will wait for random amount of time before transmitting the information again. It is called back-off.
- Fig. 7.1 (b) shows frame transmission using ALOHA.

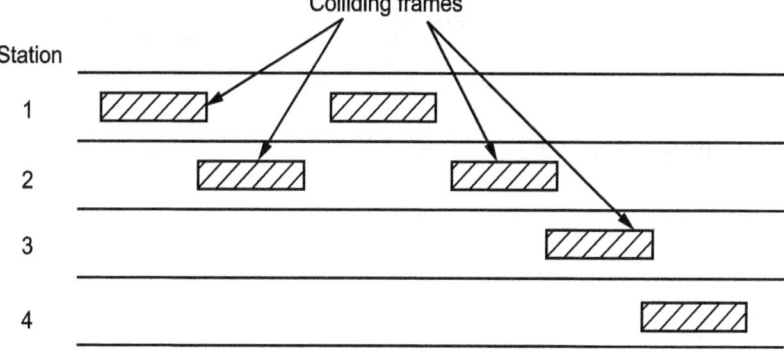

Fig. 7.1 (b) : ALOHA System

Efficiency of ALOHA :

Let L be the length of frame (bits) (constant).

R be rate of transmission.

$$\therefore \quad \text{Frame time} = X = \frac{L}{R}$$

Let some frame arrive at time t_0 and end at $t_0 + X$.

This frame will collide if there is transmission from other stations between $t_0 - X$ and $t_0 + X$ as shown in Fig. 7.1 (c).

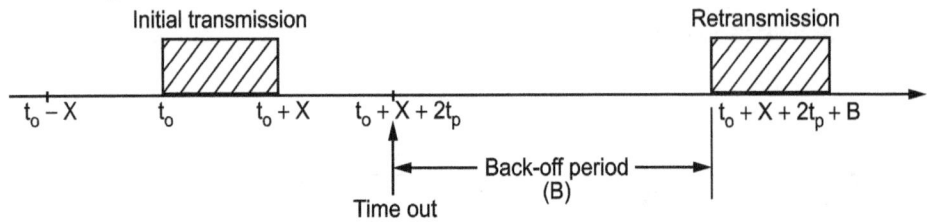

Fig. 7.1 (c) : ALOHA System

∴ Vulnerable time $= (t_0 + X) - (t_0 - X) = 2X$

Let G be the total arrival rate of the system in frames/X seconds. G is also throughput of the system. Let G be total arrival rate of the system in frames/X seconds. G is also called total load of the system. With the assumption that the back-off spreads retransmissions such that new and repeated frame transmission are equally likely to occur, the number of frames transmitted in a time interval has Poisson distribution with average number of arrivals of 2G arrivals/2X seconds. Hence, probability that k frames are generated during a given frame time are : $P[k \text{ transmissions in 2X seconds}] = \dfrac{(2G)^k}{k!} e^{-2G}$. Hence, throughput S is equal to total arrival rate G times probability of successful transmission.

∴ $S = P[\text{no collision}]$
$= P[\text{0 transmissions in 2X seconds}]$
$= G \dfrac{(2G)^0}{0!} e^{-2G} = Ge^{-2G}$

The plot of S versus G is shown in Fig. 7.1 (d).

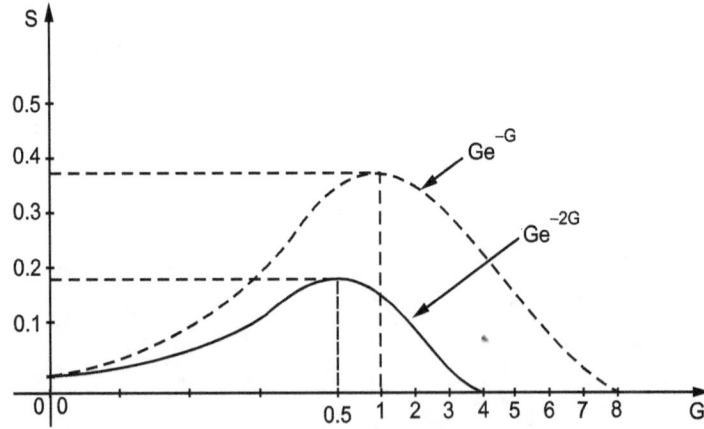

Fig. 7.1 (d) : Throughput CurveIt can be seen that the maximum value of $S = \dfrac{1}{2e}$ at $G = 0.5$.

That is system can achieve throughput of 18.4% only.

Slotted ALOHA :

Performance of ALOHA can be improved by putting a restriction on time of transmission i.e. stations will transmit only at a fixed time (Synchronize fashion). Thus, reducing the probability of collisions. All stations keep track of transmission time slots and are allowed to initiate transmission only at beginning of slot. Vulnerable time i.e. time of collision reduces to $t_o - X$ to X i.e. X second as shown in Fig. 7.2.

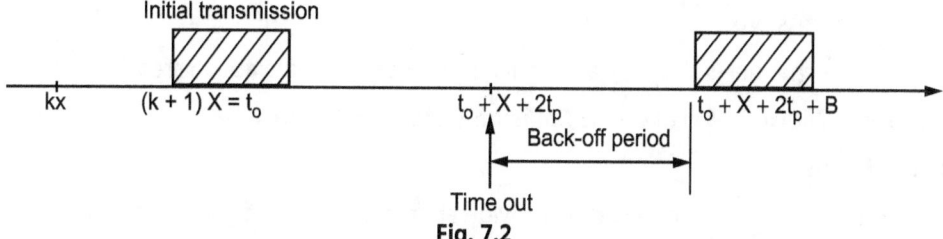

Fig. 7.2

There are G arrivals in X seconds, (G is total arrival rate)

∴
$$S = G \times P \text{ [no collision]}$$
$$= G \times P \text{ [0 transmission in X seconds]}$$
$$= G \times \frac{(G)^0}{0!} e^{-G}$$
$$= Ge^{-G}$$

Above equation is plotted in Fig. 7.1 (c). Slotted ALOHA has maximum throughput of $\frac{1}{e}$ = 36.8% at G = 1.

Carrier Sense Multiple Access Protocols :

Protocols in which stations listen for carriers and take suitable action are called Carrier Sense Protocols.

Following are some carrier sense protocols :

1. **1-Persistent CSMA :**
   - When a station has some data to send it listens to the channel.
   - If channel is busy it waits until it becomes free or idle continuously sensing the channel.
   - If channel is idle it transmits the frame.
   - It is called 1-persistent because whenever channel is idle the station transmits with probability 1.

2. **Non-Persistent CSMA :**
   - When station has some data to send, it listens to the channel and if channel is idle it sends data.
   - If channel is busy, it waits until it becomes free/idle.
   - But then it does not sense the channel continuously as in 1-persistent CSMA. It waits for random period and then again senses the channel.

3. **p-Persistent CSMA :**
   - It applies to slotted channels.
   - When a station is ready to transit data and channel is idle it transmits with probability p and decides not to transmit with probability q = 1 – p until next slot. If that slot is also idle it decides to transmit or defer with probability p and q. This process is repeated until either frame is transmitted or another station has started transmission.
   - If the channel is busy it waits until next slot and repeats above step.

Carrier Sense Multiple Access with Collision Detection (csma/cd)

A Shared Medium :

The Ethernet network may be used to provide shared access by a group of attached nodes to the physical medium which connects the nodes. These nodes are said to form a Collision Domain. All frames sent on the medium are physically received by all receivers, however the Medium Access Control (MAC) header contains a MAC destination address which ensure only the specified destination actually forwards the received frame (the other computers all discard the frames which are not addressed to them).

Consider a LAN with four computers each with a Network Interface Card (NIC) connected by a common Ethernet cable.

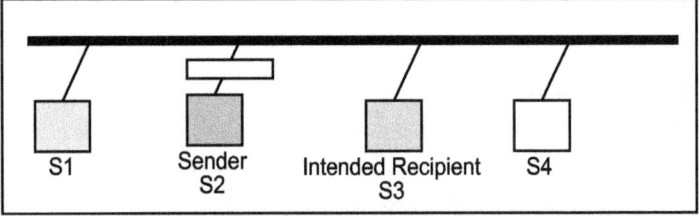

Fig. 7.3 (a)

One computer (S_2) uses a NIC to send a frame to the shared medium, which has a destination address corresponding to the source address of the NIC in the S_3 computer.

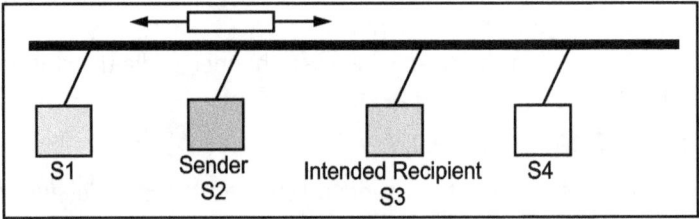

Fig. 7.3 (b)

The cable propagates the signal in both directions, so that the signal (eventually) reaches the NICs in all four of the computers. Termination resistors at the ends of the cable absorb the frame energy, preventing reflection of the signal back along the cable.

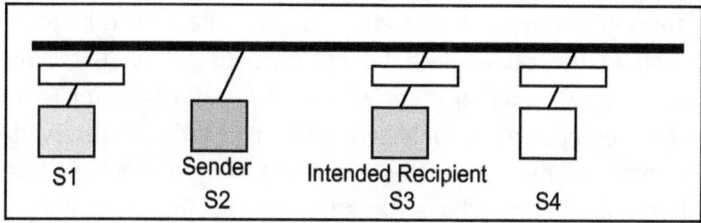

Fig. 7.3 (c)

All the NICs receive the frame and each examines it to check its length and checksum. The header destination MAC address is next examined, to see if the frame should be accepted, and forwarded to the network-layer software in the computer.

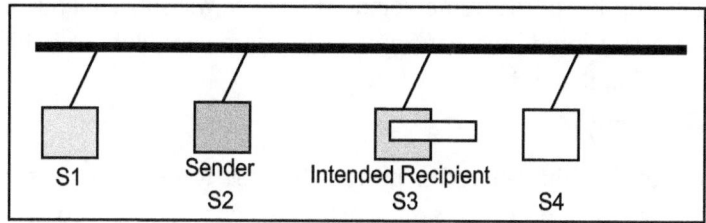

Fig. 7.3 (d)

Only the NIC in the computer S_3 recognises the frame destination address as valid, and therefore this NIC alone forwards the contents of the frame to the network layer. The NICs in the other computers discard the unwanted frame. The shared cable allows any NIC to send whenever it wishes, but if two NICs happen to transmit at the same time, a collision will occur, resulting in the data being corrupted.

ALOHA and Collisions :

To control which NICs are allowed to transmit at any given time, a protocol is required. As seen earlier, the simplest protocol is known as ALOHA (this is actually an Hawaiian word, meaning "hello"). ALOHA allows any NIC to transmit at any time, but states that each NIC must add a checksum/CRC at the end of its transmission to allow the receiver(s) to identify whether the frame was correctly received.

ALOHA is therefore a best effort service, and does not guarantee that the frame of data will actually reach the remote recipient without corruption. It therefore relies on ARQ protocols to retransmit any data which is corrupted. An ALOHA network only works well when the medium has a low utilization, since this leads to a low probability of the transmission colliding with that of another computer, and hence a reasonable chance that the data is not corrupted.

Carrier Sense Multiple Access (CSMA) :

Ethernet uses a refinement of ALOHA, known as Carrier Sense Multiple Access (CSMA), which improves performance when there is a higher medium utilization. When a NIC has data to transmit, the NIC **first** listens to the cable (using a transceiver) to see if a carrier (signal) is being transmitted by another node. This may be achieved by monitoring whether a current is flowing in the cable (each bit corresponds to 18-20 milliAmps (mA)). The individual bits are sent by encoding them with a 10 (or 100 MHz for Fast Ethernet) clock using Manchester encoding. Data is only sent when no carrier is observed (i.e. no current present) and the physical medium is therefore idle. Any NIC which does not need to transmit, listens to see if other NICs have started to transmit information to it.

However, this alone is unable to prevent two NICs transmitting at the same time. If two NICs *simultaneously* try transmit, then both could see an idle physical medium (i.e. neither will see the other's carrier signal), and both will conclude that no other NIC is currently using the medium. In this case, both will then decide to transmit and a *collision* will occur. The collision will result in the corruption of the frame being sent, which will subsequently be discarded by the receiver since a corrupted Ethernet frame will (with a very high probability) not have a valid 32-bit MAC CRC at the end.

Collision Detection (CD) :

A second element to the Ethernet access protocol is used to detect when a collision occurs. When there is data waiting to be sent, each transmitting NIC also monitors its own transmission. If it observes a collision (excess current above what it is generating,
i.e. > 24 mA for coaxial Ethernet), it stops transmission immediately and instead transmits a 32-bit jam sequence. The purpose of this sequence is to ensure that any other node which may currently be receiving this frame will receive the jam signal in place of the correct 32-bit MAC CRC, this causes the other receivers to discard the frame due to a CRC error.

To ensure that all NICs start to receive a frame before the transmitting NIC has finished sending it, Ethernet defines a minimum frame size (i.e. no frame may have less than 46 bytes of payload). The minimum frame size is related to the distance which the network spans, the type of media being used and the number of repeaters which the signal may have to pass through to reach the furthest part of the LAN. Together these define a value known as the *Ethernet Slot Time*, corresponding to 512 bit times at 10 Mbps.

When two or more transmitting NICs each detect a corruption of their own data (i.e. a collision), each responds in the same way by transmitting the jam sequence. The following sequence depicts a collision :

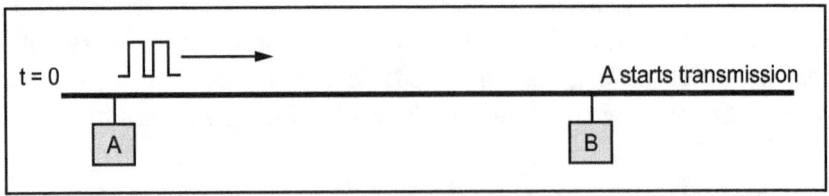

Fig. 7.4 (a)

At time t = 0, a frame is sent on the idle medium by NIC A.

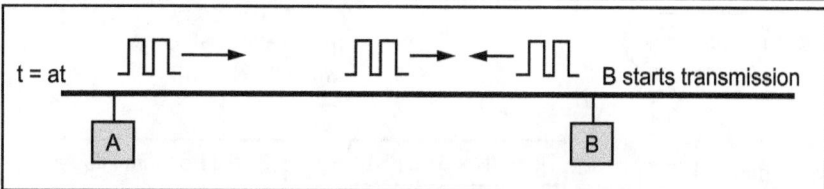

Fig. 7.4 (b)

A short time later, NIC B also transmits. (In this case, the medium, as observed by the NIC at B happens to be idle too.)

Fig. 7.4 (c)

After a period, equal to the propagation delay of the network, the NIC at B detects the other transmission from A, and is aware of a collision, but NIC A has not yet observed that NIC B was also transmitting. B continues to transmit, sending the Ethernet Jam sequence (32 bits).

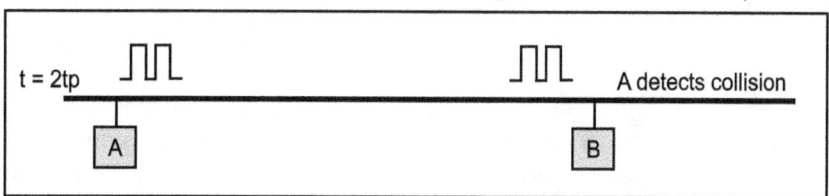

Fig. 7.4 (d)

After one complete round trip propagation time (twice the one way propagation delay), both NICs are aware of the collision. B will shortly cease transmission of the jam sequence, however A will continue to transmit a complete jam sequence. Finally the cable becomes idle.

Retransmission Back-Off :

An overview of the transmit procedure is shown below. The transmitter initializes the number of transmissions of the current frame (n) to zero, and starts listening to the cable (using the carrier sense logic (CS) - e.g. by observing the R_x signal at transceiver to see if any bits are being sent). If the cable is not idle, it waits (defers) until the cable is idle. It then waits for a small Inter-Frame Gap (IFG) (e.g. 7.6 microseconds) to allow to time for all receiving nodes to return to prepare themselves for the next transmission.

Transmission then starts with the preamble, followed by the frame data and finally the CRC-32. After this time, the transceiver Tx logic is turned-off and the transceiver returns to passively monitoring the cable for other transmissions.

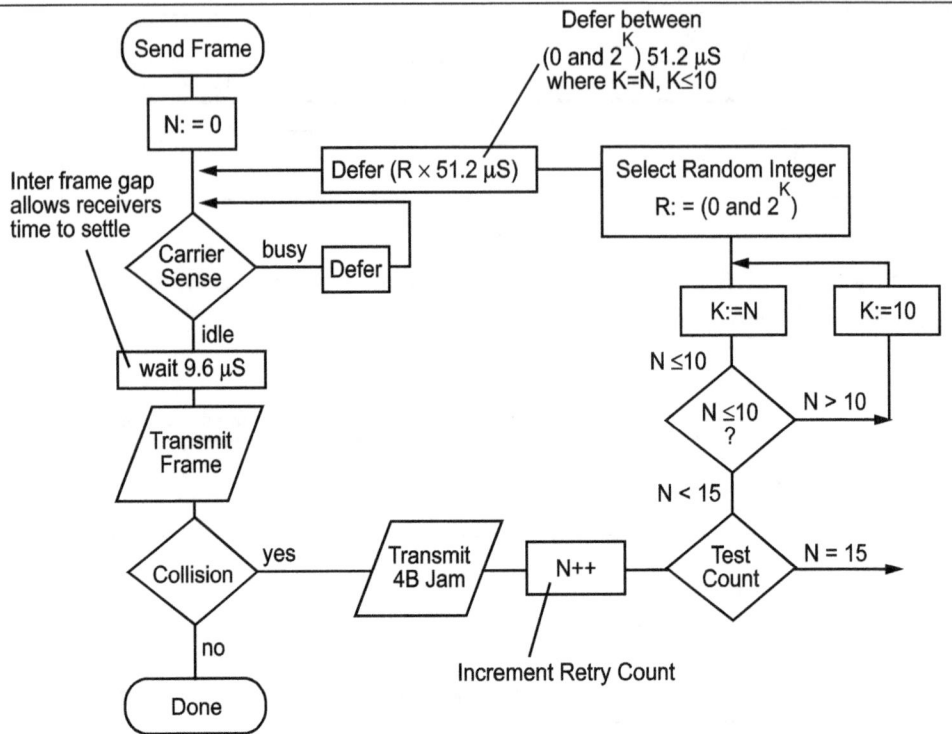

Fig. 7.5

During this process, a transmitter must also continuously monitor the collision detection logic (CD) in the transceiver to detect if a collision occurs. If it does, the transmitter aborts the transmission (stops sending bits) within a few bit periods, and starts the collision procedure, by sending a jam signal to the transceiver Tx logic. It then calculates a retransmission time.

If all NICs attempted to retransmit immediately following a collision, then this would certainly result in another collision. Therefore a procedure is required to ensure that there is only a low probability of simultaneous retransmission. The scheme adopted by Ethernet uses a random back-off period, where each node selects a random number, multiplies this by the slot time (minimum frame period, 51.2 µs) and waits for this random period before attempting retransmission. The small Inter-Frame Gap (IFG) (e.g., 7.6 µs) is also added.

On a busy network, a retransmission may still collide with another retransmission (or possibly new frames being sent for the first time by another NIC). The protocol therefore counts the number of retransmission attempts (using a variable N in Fig. 7.5) and attempts to retransmit the same frame up to 15 times.

For each retransmission, the transmitter constructs a set of numbers :

{0, 1, 2, 3, 4, 5, ... L} where L is ([2 to the power (K)]−1) and where K = N; K<= 10;

A random value R is picked from this set, and the transmitter waits (defers) for a period.

R × (slot time) i.e. R × 51.2 Micro Seconds

For example, after two collisions, N = 2, therefore K = 2, and the set is {0, 1, 2, 3} giving a one in four chance of collision. This corresponds to a wait selected from {0, 51.2, 102.4, 153.6} μs.

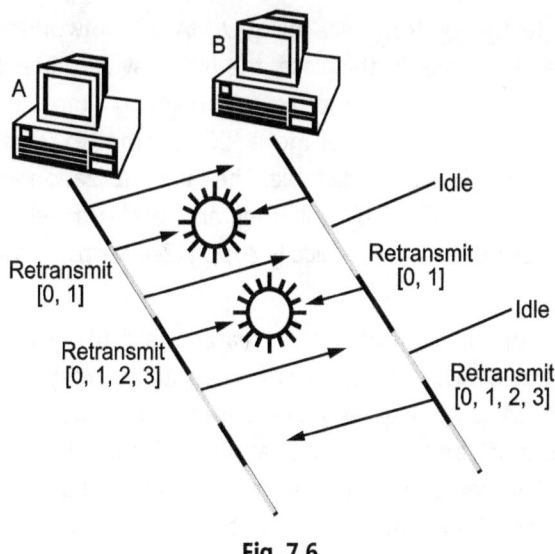

Fig. 7.6

After 3 collisions, N = 3, and the set is {0, 1, 2, 3, 4, 5, 6, 7}, that is a one in eight chance of collision. But after 4 collisions, N = 4, the set becomes {0, 1, 2, 3, 4, 5, 6, 7, 8, 9, 10, 11, 12, 13, 14, 15}, that is a one in 16 chance of collision.

The scaling is performed by multiplication and is known as exponential back-off. This is what lets CSMA/CD scale to large numbers of NICs - even when collisions may occur. The first ten times, the back-off waiting time for the transmitter suffering collision is scaled to a larger value. The algorithm includes a threshold of 1024. The reasoning is that the more attempts that are required, the more greater the number of NICs which are trying to send at the same time, and therefore longer the period which needs to be deferred. Since a set of numbers {0, 1, ..., 1023} is a large set of numbers, there is very little advantage from further increasing the set size.

Each transmitter also limits the maximum number of retransmissions of a single frame to 16 attempts (N=15). After this number of attempts, the transmitter gives up transmission and discards the frame, logging an error. In practice, a network that is not overloaded should never discard frames in this way.

Late Collisions :

In a proper functioning Ethernet network, a NIC may experience collision within the first slot time after it starts transmission. This is the reason why an Ethernet NIC monitors the CD signal during this time and use CSMA/CD. A faulty CD circuit, or misbehaving NIC or transceiver may lead to a late collision (i.e. after one slot time). Most Ethernet NICs therefore continue to monitor the CD signal during the entire transmission. If they observe a late collision, they will normally inform the sender of the error condition.

Performance of CSMA/CD :

It is simple to calculate the performance of a CSMA/CD network where only one node attempts to transmit at any time. In this case, the NIC may saturate the medium and near about 100% utilization of the link may be achieved, providing almost 10 Mbps of throughput on a 10 Mbps LAN. However, when two or more NICs attempt to transmit at the same time, the performance of Ethernet is less predictable. The fall in utilization and throughput occurs because some bandwidth is wasted by collisions and back-off delays. In practice, a busy shared 10 Mbps Ethernet network will typically supply 2-4 Mbps of throughput to the NICs connected to it.

As the level of utilization of the network increases, particularly if there are many NICs competing to share the bandwidth, an overload condition may occur. In this case, the throughput of Ethernet LANs reduces very considerably, and much of the capacity is wasted by the CSMA/CD algorithm, and very little is available for sending useful data. This is the reason why a shared Ethernet LAN should not connect more than 1024 computers. Many engineers use a threshold of 40% utilization to determine if a LAN is overloaded. A LAN with a higher utilization will observe a high collision rate, and likely a very variable transmission time (due to back off). Separating the LAN into two or more collision domains using bridges or switches would likely provide a significant benefit (assuming appropriate positioning of the bridges or switches).

Shared networks may also be constructed using Fast Ethernet, operating at 100 Mbps. Since Fast Ethernet always uses fibre or twisted pair, a hub or switch is always required.

Ethernet Capture :

A drawback of sharing a medium using CSMA/CD, is that the sharing is not necessarily fair. When each computer connected to the LAN has little data to send, the network exhibits almost equal access time for each NIC. However, if one NIC starts sending an excessive number of frames, it may dominate the LAN. Such conditions may occur, for instance, when one NIC in a LAN acts as a source of high quality packetized video. The effect is known as "Ethernet Capture".

Ethernet Capture by Node A :

Fig. 7.7 illustrates Ethernet Capture. Computer A dominates computer B. Originally both computers have data to transmit. A transmits first. A and B then both simultaneously try to transmit. B picks a larger retransmission interval than A and defers. A sends, then sends again. There is a short pause, and then both A and B attempt to resume transmission. A and B both back-off, however, since B was already in back-off (it failed to retransmit), it chooses from a larger range of back-off times (using the exponential back-off algorithm). A is therefore more likely to succeed, which it does in the example. A and B both attempt to send, however, since this fails in this case, B further increases its back-off and is now unable to fairly compete with A.

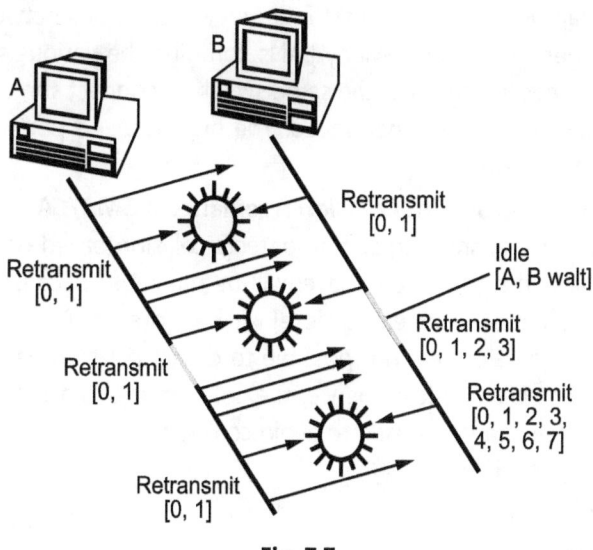

Fig. 7.7

Ethernet Capture may also arise when many sources compete with one source which has much more data to send. Under these situations some nodes may be "locked out" of using the medium for a period of time. The use of higher speed transmission (e.g. 100 Mbps) significantly reduces the probability of Capture, and the use of full duplex cabling eliminates the effect. Ethernet LANs may be implemented using a variety of media (not just the coaxial cable described above). The types of media segments supported by Ethernet are :

- 10 Base 5 Low loss coaxial cable (also known as "thick" Ethernet).
- 10 Base 2 Low cost coaxial cable (also known as "thin" Ethernet).
- 10 Base T Low cost twisted pair copper cable (also known as Unshielded Twisted Pair (UTP)).
- 10 Base F Fibre optic cable.

The network design rules for using these types of media are summarized below :

Segment type	Max Number of systems per cable segment	Max Distance of a cable segment
10 Base 5 (Thick Coax)	100	500 m
10 Base 2 (Thin Coax)	30	185 m
10 Base T (Twisted Pair)	2	100 m
10 Base F (Fibre Optic)	2	2000 m

Network Design Rules for Different types of Cable

There is also a version of Ethernet which operates using twisted pair cabling or fibre optic links at 100 Mbps and at 1 Gbps. 100 Mbps networks may operate full duplex (using a Fast Ethernet Switch) or half duplex (using a Fast Ethernet Hub). 1 Gbps networks usually operate between a pair of Ethernet Switches. Many LANs combine the various speeds of operation using dual-speed switches which allow the same switch to connect some ports to one speed of network, and other ports at another speed. The higher speed ports are usually used to connect switches to one another.

Carrier Sense Multiple Access with Collision Avoidance (CSMA/CA) :

In case of CSMA/CD, the transmitting station detects collision based on signal energy level. When there is no collision signal energy level will be minimum because only one station is transmitting. When there is collision energy level will be more.

In case of wireless transmission it is not possible to detect collision based on signal energy level. It is because there is more loss. Hence, the solution is avoid collision as it cannot be detected. There are three strategies used to avoid collisions :

1. Interframe Space (IFS)
2. Contention Window
3. Acknowledgements.

1. Interframe Space (IFS) :

When a station wants to transmit and finds the channel is idle it waits for a period of time called interframe space (IFS). After the IFS time for a station is over and it finds that the channel is idle it can send, but not immediately it still waits for contention time. IFS can be variable for each station.

2. Contention Window :

A station that is ready to send waits for a time equal to random number of slots, the algorithm used to generate the random number of slots is binary back-off.

3. Acknowledgement :

If there is collision even with implementation of above, we can have the mechanism of acknowledgement where the transmitting station waits for acknowledgement from receiving station for a particular time. If time out occurs it can retransmit. Fig. 7.8 depicts the three strategies.

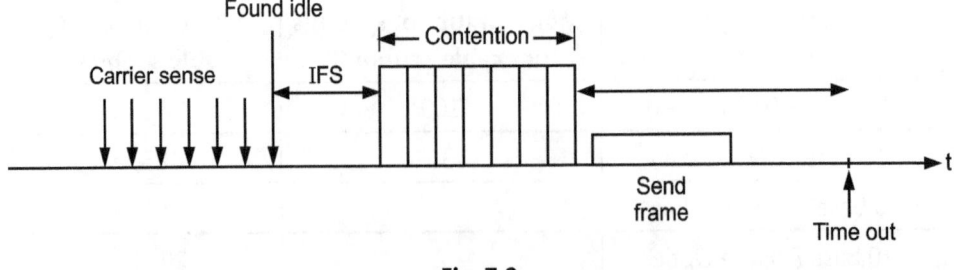

Fig. 7.8

The procedure is shown in flowchart below.

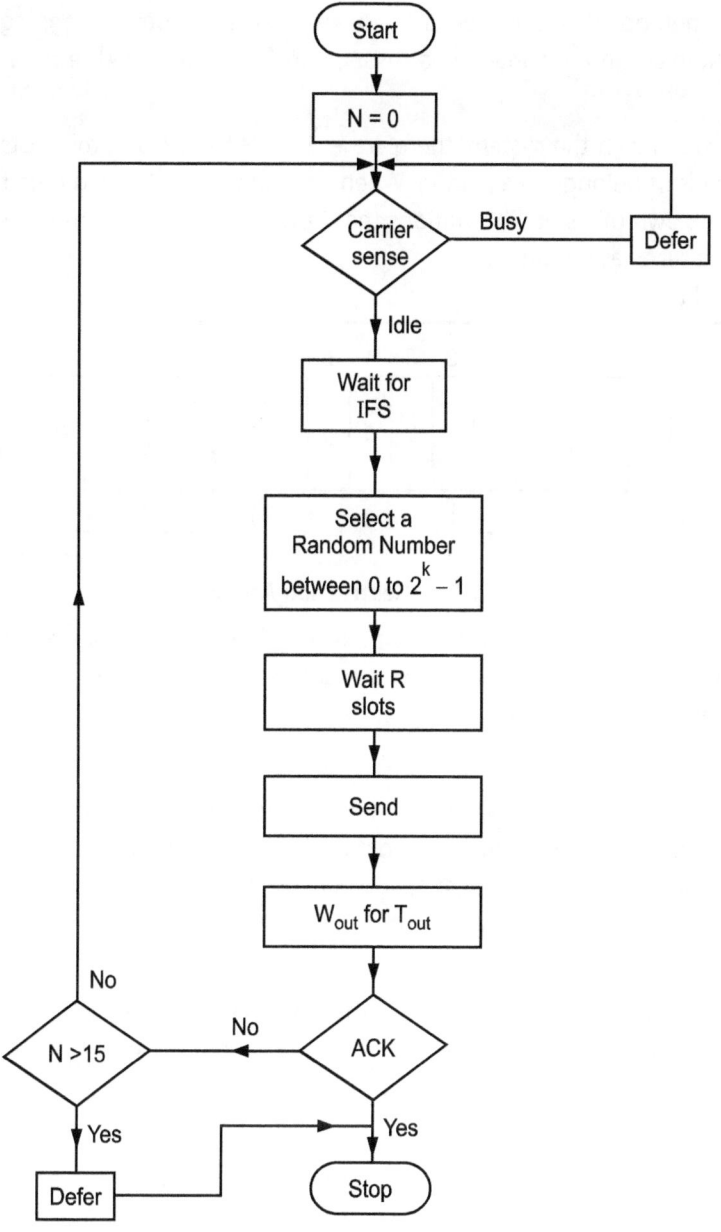

7.3 CONTROLLED ACCESS

In controlled access, the station consults one another to find which station has the right to send. We discuss three popular methods :

Reservation :

In reservation method, a station needs to make reservation before sending data. Time is divided into intervals. In each interval, a reservation frame preceds the data frames sent in that interval.

If there are N stations in the system, there are exactly N reservation minislots in reservation frame. Each minislot belongs to a station. When a station needs to send data frame, it makes reservation in its own minislot. The stations that have made reservations can send their data frames after the reservation frame.

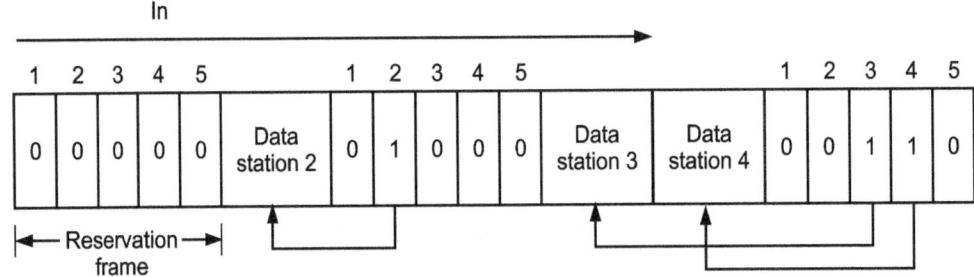

Fig. 7.9 : Reservation Access

In Fig. 7.9, it shows a situation with five stations and five minislot reservation frames. In the first interval, only stations 1, 3 and 4 have made reservations. In the second interval, only station 1 has made a reservation.

Polling :

Polling works with topologies in which one device is designated as a primary station and the other devices are secondary stations. All data exchanges must be made through primary device even when the ultimate destination is a secondary device. The primary device controls the link. The secondary devices follow its instructions. The primary device is always the initiator of session.

If the primary wants to receive data, it asks the secondaries. If they have anything to send, this is called poll function. If the primary wants to send data, it tells secondary to get ready to receive. This is called select function.

Poll :

The poll function is used for primary device to receive transmissions from the secondary devices. When the primary is ready for that, it must ask (poll) each device in turn if it has anything to send. When the first secondary is approached, it responds either with NAK frame if it has nothing to send or with data (in the form of data frame) if it does. If the response is negative (a NAK frame) then the primary polls the next secondary in the same manner until it finds one with data to send. When the response is positive (a data frame) the primary reads the frame and returns an acknowledgement (ACK frame) verifying its receipt.

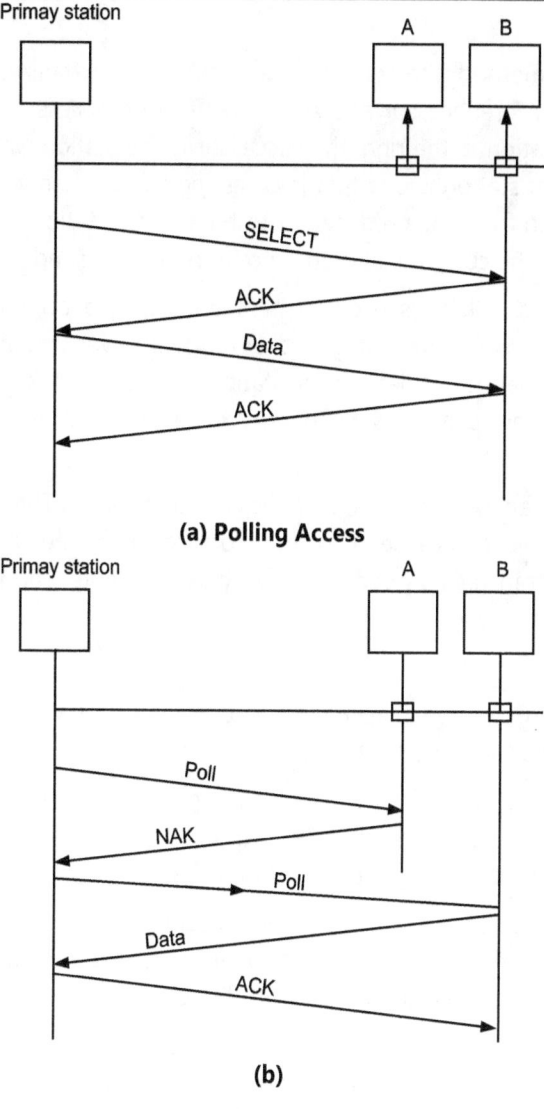

Fig. 7.10

Select :

The select function is used whenever the primary device has something to send. The primary device controls the link. If the primary is neither sending nor receiving data, it knows the link is available.

If it has something to send, the primary device sends it. But however, it does not know, whether the target device is prepared to receive. So the primary must alert the secondary to the upcoming transmission and wait for an acknowledgement of the secondary ready status. Before sending data the primary creates and transmits a select (SEL) frame, one field of which includes the address of intended secondary.

Token Passing :

In the token passing method, the stations in a network are organized in a logical ring. For each station, there is a predecessor and successor. The predecessor is the station which is logically before the station in the ring, the successor is the station which is after the station in the ring. The current station is one that is accessing to the channel now. The right to this access has been passed from the predecessor to the current station. The right will be passed to the successor when the current station has no more data to send.

A special packet called 'token' is used to pass the right to access from one station to another. The token keeps on circulating in the ring whichever station has the token it has right to access the channel. Whenever a station has data to send it waits for token. Whenever token is received it will send data. Whenever it has finished sending data, the token is passed to next station.

Token management is an important issue in this type of network. The network should ensure that the token is not lost because of some problem in the network. e.g. faulty station. Sometimes the data transfer may require priority assignments. The token can be used by stations as per their priority.

Logical Ring :

- This standard evolved from the needs of companies like General Motors implementing terminals for factory automation.
- 802.3 was not suitable for them as a station in ethernet has to wait for a long time to send a frame in worst case. 802.3 frames do not have priorities which makes important frames waiting for unimportant frames.
- A token bus system is a medium access control technique for bus/tree stations form a logical ring around which a token is passed. A station receiving the token may transmit data and then must pass the token on to next station in the ring.
- Though it is similar to token ring it does not implement the ring physically as it has drawback of getting entire network down in case one terminal is down.
- If there are n stations in the token bus network and T_p seconds are required to send a frame, it will take not more than nT_p seconds to get a turn for a station.
- A token bus network is shown in Fig. 7.11.
- The stations can be configured so that they can be part of the logical ring or may opt out of the ring.
- Initially highest number station gets the token. Then it passes the token to its neighbour (right or left).
- Token thus moves around the ring with token holder permitted to send the frame.
- If station has no data it must pass the token to next station.

- A 85 ohm broadband cable is used at physical layer.

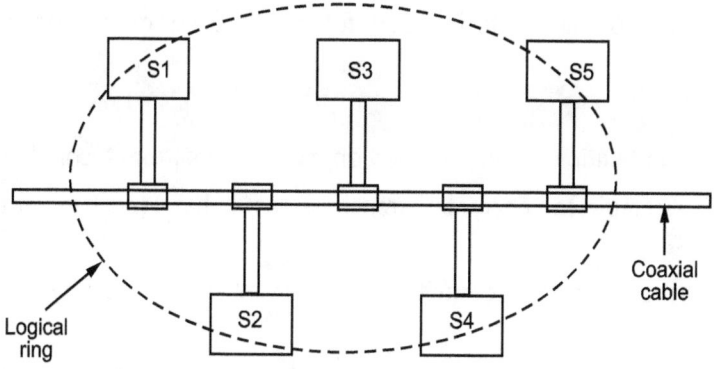

Fig. 7.11 : Token Bus

7.4 MULTIPLE ACCESS TECHNIQUES

A transponder channel aboard may be fully loaded by single transmission from an earth station in Satellite communications. This is referred to as **single access** mode of operation. It is also possible for for a transponder to be loaded by a number of carriers. These may originate from a number of earth stations geographically separate and each earth station may transmit one or more of the carriers. This mode of operation is termed **multiple access.** The most commonly used methods of multiple access are FDMA, TDMA and CDMA.

FDMA :

- Frequency Division Multiple Access (FDMA) is the most common analog system.
- It is a technique whereby spectrum is divided up into frequencies and then assigned to users.
- With FDMA, only one subscriber at any given time is assigned to a channel.
- The channel therefore is closed to other conversations until the initial call is finished, or until it is handed-off to a different channel.
- A "full-duplex" FDMA transmission requires two channels, one for transmitting and the other for receiving. FDMA has been used for first generation analog systems.

TDMA :

- Time Division Multiple Access (TDMA) improves spectrum capacity by splitting each frequency into time slots.
- TDMA allows each user to access the entire radio frequency channel for the short period of a call.
- Other users share this same frequency channel at different time slots.

- The base station continually switches from user to user on the channel.
- TDMA is the dominant technology for the second generation mobile cellular networks.

CDMA :
- Code Division Multiple Access is based on "spread" spectrum technology.
- Since it is suitable for encrypted transmissions, it has long been used for military purposes.
- CDMA increases spectrum capacity by allowing all users to occupy all channels at the same time.
- Transmissions are spread over the whole radio band, and each voice or data call are assigned a unique code to differentiate from the other calls carried over the same spectrum.
- CDMA allows for a **soft hand-off**, which means that terminals can communicate with several base stations at the same time.

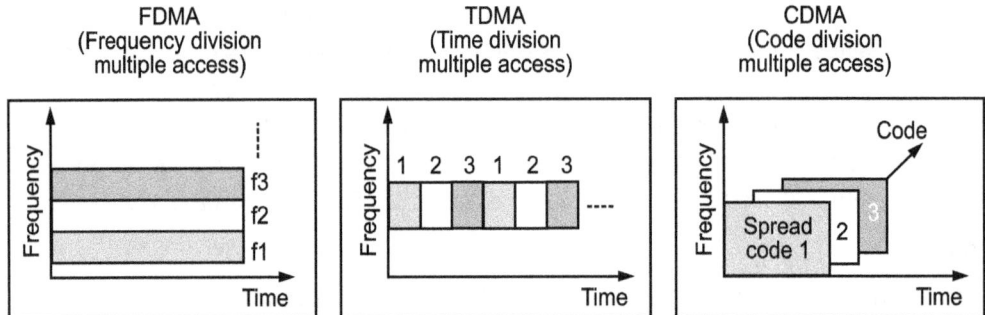

Fig. 7.12 : **FDMA-TDMA-CDMA graphical representation**

In addition to above multiple access techniques, we can have

(1) Fixed Assigned Multiple Access (FAMA) mode using either FDMA, TDMA, CDMA. In this mode, the format does not change even if traffic load changes.

(2) Demand Assigned Multiple Access (DAMA) mode using either FDMA, TDMA, CDMA. In this mode, the formats are changed depending on traffic demand. It is more efficient but costlier to implement and maintain.

Advantages of Digital Technology :

All multiple access techniques depend on the adoption of digital technology. Digital technology is now the standard for the public telephone system where all analog calls are converted to digital form for transmission over the backbone. Digital transmission has a number of advantages over analog transmission :

- It economizes on bandwidth.
- It allows easy integration with personal communication systems (PCS) devices.

- It maintains superior quality of voice transmission over long distances.
- It is difficult to decode.
- It can use lower average transmitter power.
- It enables smaller and less expensive individual receivers and transmitters.
- It offers voice privacy.

How FDMA Works ?

- TDMA is basically analog's FDMA with a time-sharing component built into the system.
- FDMA allocates a single channel to one user at a time (see Fig. 7.13).
- If the transmission path deteriorates, the controller switches the system to another channel.
- Although technically simple to implement, FDMA is wasteful of bandwidth : the channel is assigned to a single conversation whether or not somebody is speaking. Moreover, it cannot handle alternate forms of data, only voice transmissions.

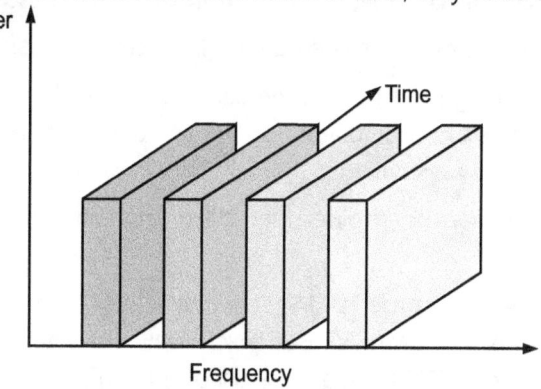

Fig. 7.13 : FDMA

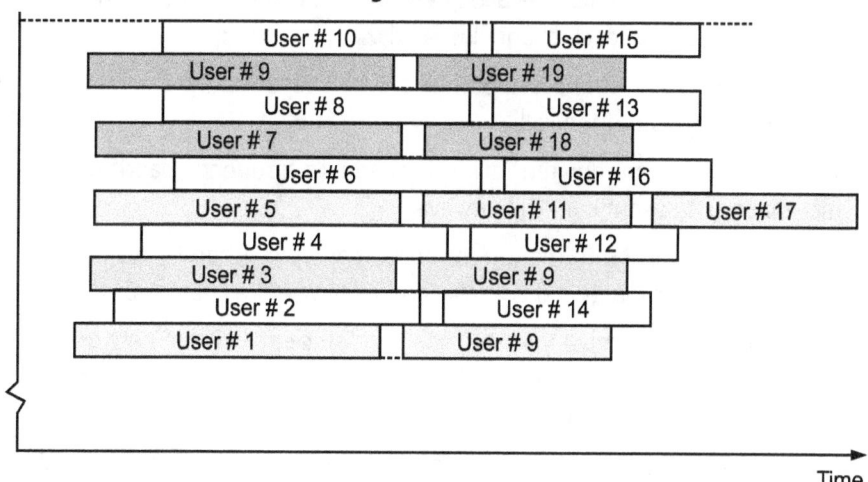

Fig. 7.14 : Schematic allocation of subscriber channels within an assigned frequency band (range)

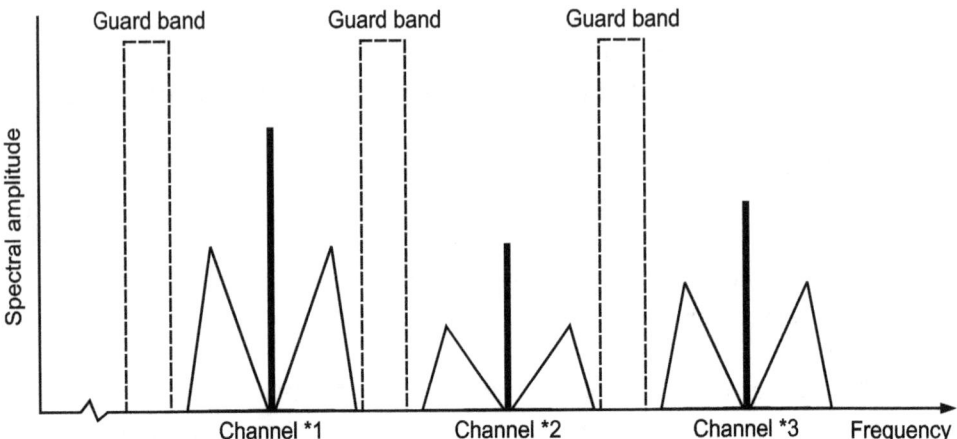

Fig. 10.15 : Schematic frequency spectrum of several subscriber channels

- Analog transmission is considered an "older" cellular phone technology.
- Analog technology was built in the early 1980's. Analog allows a cellular phone to transmit signals by sending voice, video, and data that are always changing, and so does the network systems.
- Analog is considered an older method of modulating voice or data information radio signals.
- Analog transmissions use FDMA technology. FDMA stands for "Frequency Division Multiple Access". FDMA is used exclusively for analog cellular systems, even though in theory FDMA can also be used with digital.
- Essentially, FDMA splits the allocated spectrum into many channels. In current analog cell systems, each channel is 30 kHz.
- When a FDMA cell phone establishes a call, it reserves the frequency channel for the entire duration of the call.
- The voice data is modulated into this channel's frequency band (using frequency modulation) and sent over the airwaves.
- At the receiver, the information is recovered using a band-pass filter. The phone then uses a common digital control channel to acquire channels.
- FDMA analog transmissions are the least efficient cellular networks since each analog channel can only be used one user at a time. Analog channels don't take full advantage of bandwidth.
- Not only are these FDMA channels larger than necessary given modern digital voice compression, but they are also wasted whenever there is silence during a cell phone conversation.

- Analog signals are especially susceptible to noise and the extra noise cannot get filtered out. Given the nature of the signal, analog cell phones must use higher power (between 1 and 3 watts) to get acceptable call quality.
- Given these analog features, it is easy to see why FDMA is being replaced by newer digital networks such as TDMA and CDMA.

Advantages of FDMA :
- If channel is not in use, it sits idle.
- Channel bandwidth is relatively narrow (30 kHz).
- Simple algorithmically, and from a hardware standpoint.
- Fairly efficient when the number of stations is small and the traffic is uniformly constant.
- Capacity increase can be obtained by reducing the information bit rate and using efficient digital code.
- No need for network timing.
- No restriction regarding the type of baseband or type of modulation.

Disadvantages of FDMA :
- The presence of guard bands.
- Requires right RF filtering to minimize adjacent channel interference.
- Maximum bit rate per channel is fixed.
- Small inhibiting flexibility in bit rate capability.
- Does not differ significantly from analog system.

How TDMA Works ?
- TDMA relies upon the fact that the audio signal has been digitized; that is, divided into a number of milliseconds-long packets.
- It allocates a single frequency channel for a short time and then moves to another channel.
- The digital samples from a single transmitter occupy different time slots in several ands at the same time as shown in Fig. 7.16.
- The access technique used in TDMA has three users sharing a 30 kHz carrier frequency.
- TDMA is also the access technique used in the European digital standard, GSM, and the Japanese digital standard, Personal Digital Cellular (PDC).
- The reason for choosing TDMA for all these standards was that it enables some vital features for system operation in an advanced cellular environment.

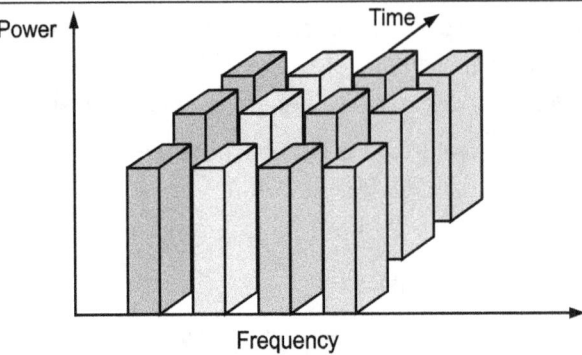

Fig. 7.16 : TDMA

- Today, TDMA is an available, well-proven technique in commercial operation in many systems.
- To illustrate the process, consider the following situation. Fig. 7.17 shows four different, simultaneous conversations occurring.

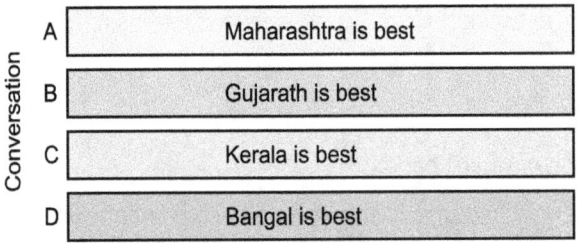

Fig. 7.17 : Four Conversations-Four Channels

- A single channel can carry all four conversations if each conversation is divided into relatively short fragments, is assigned a time slot, and is transmitted in synchronized timed bursts as shown in Fig. 7.18.
- After the conversation in time-slot four is transmitted, the process is repeated.

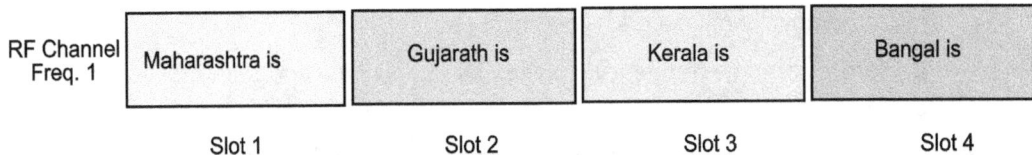

Fig. 7.18 : Four Conversations-One Channel

- Effectively, the implementations of TDMA immediately tripled the capacity of cellular frequencies by dividing a 30 kHz channel into three time slots, enabling three different users to occupy it at the same time.
- Currently, systems are in place that allow six times capacity. In the future, with the utilization of hierarchical cells, intelligent antennas, and adaptive channel allocation, the capacity should approach 40 times analog capacity.

Advanced TDMA :

- TDMA substantially improved upon the efficiency of analog cellular.
- However, like FDMA, it had the weakness that it wasted bandwidth : the time slot was allocated to a specific conversation whether or not anyone was speaking at that moment.
- Enhanced version of TDMA Extended Time Division Multiple Access (ETDMA) attempts to correct this problem. Instead of waiting to determine whether a subscriber is transmitting, ETDMA assigns subscribers dynamically.
- ETDMA sends data through those pauses which normal speech contains.
- When subscribers have something to transmit, they put one bit in the buffer queue.
- The system scans the buffer, notices that the user has something to transmit, and allocates bandwidth accordingly.
- If a subscriber has nothing to transmit, the queue simply goes to the next subscriber. So, instead of being arbitrarily assigned, time is allocated according to need.
- If partners in a phone conversation do not speak over one another, this technique can almost double the spectral efficiency of TDMA, making it almost 10 times as efficient as analog transmission.

Benefits of TDMA

- In addition to increasing the efficiency of transmission, TDMA offers a number of other advantages over standard cellular technologies.
- First and foremost, it can be easily adapted to the transmission of data as well as voice communication.
- TDMA offers the ability to carry data rates of 64 kbps to 120 Mbps (expandable in multiples of 64 kbps).
- This enables operators to offer personal communication-like services including fax, voice band data, and short message services (SMSs) as well as bandwidth-intensive applications such as multimedia and videoconferencing.
- Unlike spread-spectrum techniques which can suffer from interference among the users all of whom are on the same frequency band and transmitting at the same time, TDMA's technology, which separates users in time, ensures that they will not experience interference from other simultaneous transmissions.
- TDMA also provides the user with extended battery life and talk time since the mobile is only transmitting a portion of the time (from 1/3 to 1/10) of the time during conversations.
- TDMA installations offer substantial savings in base-station equipment, space and

maintenance, an important factor as cell sizes grow ever smaller.
- TDMA is the most cost-effective technology for upgrading a current analog system to digital.
- TDMA is the only technology that offers an efficient utilization of hierarchical cell structures (HCSs) offering pico, micro, and macrocells. HCSs allow coverage for the system to be tailored to support specific traffic and service needs.
- Because of its inherent compatibility with FDMA analog systems, TDMA allows service compatibility with the use of dual-mode handsets.

Advantages of TDMA :
- Flexible bit rate.
- No frequency guard band required.
- No need for precise narrowband filters.
- Easy for mobile or base stations to initiate and execute hands off.
- Extended battery life.
- TDMA installations offer savings in base station equipment, space and maintenance.
- The most cost-effective technology for upgrading a current analog system to digital.

Drawbacks of TDMA :
- One of the disadvantages of TDMA is that each user has a predefined time slot. However, users roaming from one cell to another are not allotted a time slot.
- Thus, if all the time slots in the next cell are already occupied, a call might well be disconnected. Likewise, if all the time slots in the cell in which a user happens to be in are already occupied, a user will not receive a dial tone.
- Another problem with TDMA is that it is subjected to multipath distortion. A signal coming from a tower to a handset might come from any one of several directions.
- It might have bounced off several different buildings before arriving (see *Fig. 7.19*) which can cause interference.
- One way of getting around this interference is to put a time limit on the system.
- The system will be designed to receive, treat, and process a signal within a certain time limit. After the time limit has expired, the system ignores signals.
- The sensitivity of the system depends on how far it processes the multipath frequencies. Even at thousandths of seconds, these multipath signals cause problems.

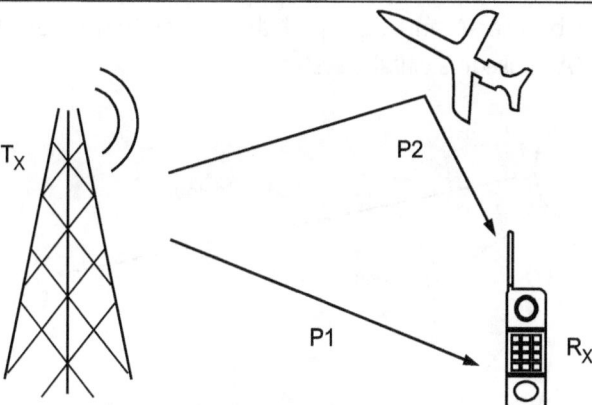

Fig. 7.19 : Multipath Interference

Disadvantages of TDMA in brief :

- Cross-link transmissions must occur one cross-link at a time.
- Time synchronization needed between all distributed users.
- Propagation delay corrections must be applied when cross-link signal path lengths vary in order to avoid signal collisions.
- The greater the number of spacecraft, the longer the duty interval for cross-link transmissions by a given spacecraft resulting in lowering the overall data throughput for the distribution.
- Changing the user distances of separation requires dynamic assessments of time slot allocations to compensate for variable signal delays.

How CDMA Works ?

- CDMA is a digital wireless technology.
- It is a general type of technology, implemented in many specific technologies.
- But the term "CDMA" is also commonly used to refer to one specific implementation : IS-95 - a mobile-phone technology that competes with technologies such as GSM. CDMA is a "spread spectrum" technology, which means that it spreads the information contained in a particular signal of interest over a much greater bandwidth than the original signal.
- *Code division multiple access,* CDMA, is a spread spectrum system in which two or more spread spectrum signals communicate simultaneously, each operating over the same frequency band.
- In a CDMA system, each user is given a unique sequence (pseudo-random code).
- This sequence identifies the user. For example, if user-A has sequence-a, and user-B has sequence-b, a receiver wanting to listen to user-A would use sequence-a to decode the wanted intelligence. It would then receive all the energy being

transmitted by user-A and disregard the power transmitted by user-B. Fig. 7.20 shows CDMA in use in a cellular system.

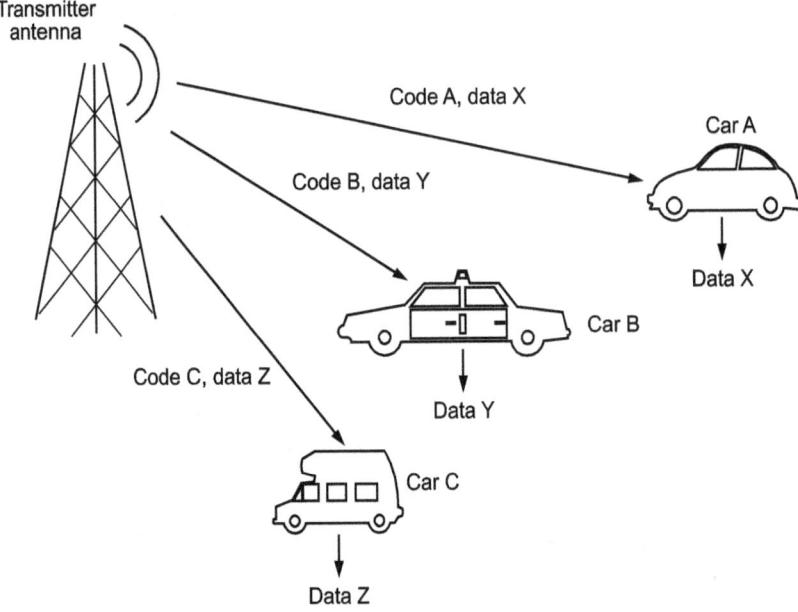

Fig. 7.20 : Spreading at Transmitter and De-spreading at Receivers

Some Benefits of CDMA :

- It has many advantages over TDMA.
- CDMA is less prone to deep multipath fading caused by transmissions arriving at the receiver that have followed different paths. i.e. one signal direct, and another reflecting off a large object.
- In fact, one approach in common use with CDMA systems, a rake receiver, takes advantage of multipath, normally a major source of interference and signal degradation in other systems. In a rake receiver, each receiver coherently combines the three strongest multipath signals to provide an enhanced signal with better voice quality.
- Rake receiver : A **rake receiver** is a radio receiver designed to counter the effects of multipath fading. It does this by using several "sub-receivers" each delayed slightly in order to tune in to the individual multipath components. Each component is decoded independently, but at a later stage combined in order to make the most use of the different transmission characteristics of each transmission path. This could very well result in higher SNR in a multipath environment than in a "clean" environment.
- CDMA can operate with much lower transmit powers leading to smaller handsets and smaller batteries and longer life. For example, some field trials in the different

countries claimed to demonstrate that the average transmits power of CDMA phones averaged 6 mW, or roughly 10% of analogue phones for similar coverage.
- CDMA can reduce interference between cells in cellular networks and improve 'hand-over' by summing and correlating transmissions from adjacent cells.
- CDMA systems have the ability to co-exist with conventional narrow-band transmissions.
- CDMA can simplify cell planning by removing the need to specify rigid frequency allocations to individual cells.
- CDMA is claimed to provide higher spectrum efficiency compared to TDMA, although real verification of these claims is still lacking.

Advantages of CDMA in brief :
- Multipath fading may be substantially reduced because of large signal bandwidth.
- No absolute limit on the number of users.
- Easy addition of more users.
- Impossible for hackers to decipher the code sent.
- Better signal quality.
- No sense of handoff when changing cells.

Disadvantages of CDMA in brief :
- As the number of users increases, the overall quality of service decreases.
- Self-jamming.
- Near- Far- problem arises.

However, it seems clear that for the near future at least, TDMA will remain the dominant technology in the wireless market.

Comparison of Multiple Access Techniques

	TDMA	FDMA	CDMA
1.	Users transmit inturn in their own unique time slots.	All users transmit at the same time but in unique frequency band.	Many users simultaneously transmit spread spectrum signals that occupy same frequency band.
2.	Guard times are kept between two users.	Guard bands are kept between two users.	Both guard band and guard times are kept.
3.	Power efficiency is high.	Power efficiency is low.	Power efficiency is highest.
4.	Time synchronization is required.	Synchronization is not necessary.	Synchronization is not required.
5.	Interference from adjacent users can degrade performance.	Interference from adjacent users can degrade performance.	Interference from adjacent users is negligible.
6.	Implementation is complex.	Implementation is simple.	Implementation is complex.

7.5 COLLISION FREE PROTOCOL

Since collision causes problem, we can use collision- free protocol.

They will provide constant overhead to achieve performance guarantee.

They are good when network load is high

(1) Static TDMA

WE can use static TDMA, but as we know there are problems with static TDMA. Problem of static TDMA: When a station has nothing to send, its time slot is idling and wastes resources

(2) Reservation-Bit-Map Protocol

In Bit-Map Protocol Stations are ordered and transmit a bit during their slot.At close of contention period, everyone knows who is transmitting. Transmitting done in station order.

This is how the Basic Bit-Map Protocol works.

- Assume N stations are numbered from 1 to N.
- There is a contention period of N slots (bits).
- Each station has one slot time during the contention period, numbered 1 to N.
- Station J sends a 1-bit reservation during Jth slot time if it wants to transmit a frame.
- Every station sees all the 1-bit reservation transmitted during the contention period, so each station knows which stations want to transmit.
- After the contention period, each station that asserted its desire to transmit sends its frame in the order of station number.

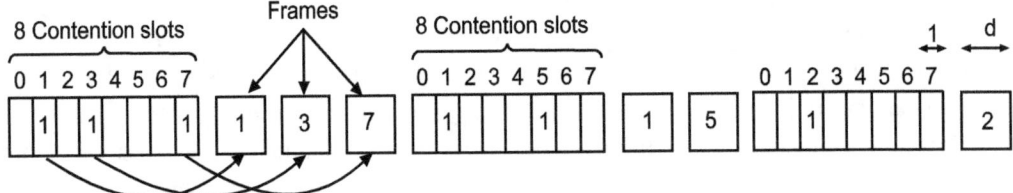

Fig. 7.21 : Bit-Map protocol

Issues with this scheme:

- Stations' access to the network is unfaire: the low numbered stations have implied priority over high numbered stations. That is, if station i and station j both want to transmit, and i < j, then station i gets the automatic bid.
- On the other hand, low numbered stations have to wait longer than high numbered stations for the reservation to complete. For example, the shortest time station 1 has to wait is N bits, the longest time station 1 has to wait is 2N - 1 bits; the shortest time station N has to wait is 0 when no one else in the network wants to transmit

and the reservation slot just arrived at station N, the longest time station N has to wait is N-1 bits.

- Efficiency: at low load, the protocol efficiency is low. For example, at the extreme case, one frame transfer per contention period, thus efficiency is d/(d+N) where d is the number of bits in frame, and N is the number of stations on the network. At high load, the protocol efficiency is high. At the extreme case, all stations have frames to transmit at all time, then the efficiency is Nd/(Nd + N) which is d/(d + 1). Typically, d >> N.

- The average waiting time is : $\frac{N_1 + N}{2}$ = N (d + 1/2) plus the waiting time inside the station queue.

(1) Polling/Binary Countdown :

One problem with Basic Bit-Map Protocol is that the overhead is 1 bit per frame per station. We can do better by using binary station addresses.

In networking, the physical link that carries data can be one of a number of different things: wire, cable or wireless, among others. The generic term for this is "media." Binary countdown is a media access protocol. It describes a method to get a turn putting data onto the media.

- A station wanting to use the channel now broadcasts its address as a binary bit string in serial fashion.
- As soon as a station sees that a high-order bit position that is 0 in its address has been overwritten by a 1, it gives up (meaning some high order station wants to transmit).
- The remaining stations keep sending their addresses on the network, until a winner merges.
- The wining station sends out the frame. The bidding process repeats.

For exapmle, if stations 0010, 0100, 1001, and 1010 are all trying to get the channel, in the first bit time the four stations transmit 0, 0, 1, and 1, respectively.

These are ORed together resulting in a 1. Stations 0010 and 0100 see the 1 and know that a higher-numbered station is competing for the channel, so they give up for the current round. Stations 1001 and 1010 continue. The next bit sent from both stations is 0, both continues.

The next bit is 1, so station 1001 gives up. The winner is 1010. This station transmits its frame. Then a new bidding process begins. The channel efficiency is now d/(d + ln N)

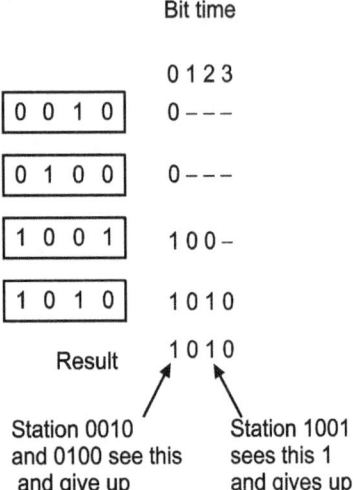

Fig. 7.22 : Binary countdown

Purpose :

Data is transported as an electric pulse. There may be many devices connected to the same wire and they can't all apply their signals onto the wire at the same time or those pulses will get intermingled. This is called collision. To avoid collision, a computer has to check that another computer is not using the wire before applying its data. If all check at the same time, they will see the media as available and all send data at the same time. Binary countdown is one method to stop this happening.

Function :

Data is transmitted in 0s and 1s -- known as binary transmission. If several nodes on a network start transmitting simultaneously, all transmit their network ID as a binary number. These numbers are compared starting at the most significant bit, which is the first number in the sequence, representing the highest value in the byte. All those containing a zero at this bit are knocked out, if there is still more than one node in contention, the next bit along is compared. Again, those with 1 stay in and those with 0 are out. This process continues along the bits of the network ID until there is only one node left and that gets control of the media.

Features :

The binary countdown method is also called bit dominance. Although, in this example, 1 always wins, the system could work equally nominating a 0 as the winner.

(2) Token passing :

The **Token-Passing Protocol** relies on a control signal called the token. A token is a 24-bit packet that circulates throughout the network from NIC to NIC in an orderly fashion. If a workstation wants to transmit a message, first it must seize the token. At that point, the workstation has complete control over the communications channel. The existence of only one token eliminates the possibility of signal collisions. This means that only one station can speak at a time.

Logical Ring Physical Star topology for Token-Passing Standard :

It is sure that any break in the ring at any point will interrupt communications for all machines. To solve this problem, IBM developed a modified ring topology, which they called the logical ring physical star. The central point of the physical star configuration is Token Ring hub called the multi-station access unit (MSAU, pronounced as masow).

Workstations and servers attached to the MSAU through special STP adapter cables. IBM converted stars into a logical ring by connecting all MSAU hubs together through special ring-in (RI) and ring-out (RO) ports.

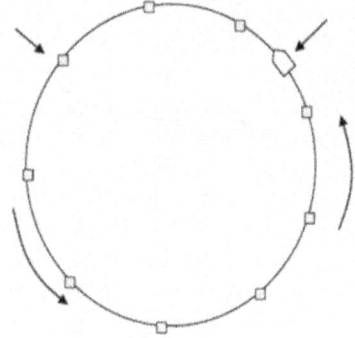

Fig. 7.23 : Token Ring

Advantages of Token Ring :

Here are Token ring's most useful advantages:
- It offers excellent throughput under high-load conditions.
- Token Ring facilitates LAN-to-LAN mainframe connections especially for interfacing with IBM's broader connectivity strategies.
- It has built-in troubleshooting mechanisms such as beaconing and auto-reconfiguration and may now be used with UTP cabling.
- It has the most reliable protocol (token-passing), the most trouble-free configuration (physical star) and the fastest connectivity scheme (r or 16 mb/s).

Disadvantages of Token Ring :

Few of the disadvantages of Token Ring are:
- Token Ring is very expensive. All topology components cost much more than other more popular standards.
- It is relatively proprietary. Token Ring's complexity is built into the hardware components. This means hat you need to choose a manufacturer and stick with it.
- Engineers must have considerable expertise to manage and troubleshoot token ring components.

7.6 LIMITED-CONTENTION PROTOCOL

At low traffic, contention is preferable due to its low delay. at high traffic collision-free protocol performs better. A contention-based protocol (CBP) is a communications protocol for operating wireless telecommunication equipment that allows many users to use the same radio channel without pre-coordination. The "listen before talk" operating procedure in IEEE 802.11 is the most well known contention-based protocol.

A protocol that allows multiple users to share the same spectrum by defining the events that must occur when two or more transmitters attempt to simultaneously access the same channel and establishing rules by which a transmitter provides reasonable opportunities for other transmitters to operate. Such a protocol may consist of procedures for initiating new transmissions, procedures for determining the state of the channel (available or unavailable), and procedures for managing retransmissions in the event of a busy channel.

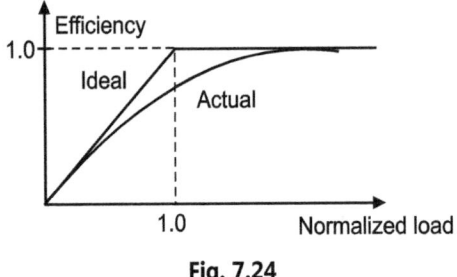

Fig. 7.24

The strategies are rated with two performance measures: delay at low load and channel efficiency at high load. Light load: contention (pure/slotted ALOHA) is preferable due to its low delay (collisions are rare). As the load increases, contention becomes increasingly less attractive. The channel efficiency becomes an important issue. Limited-Contention protocol: Use contention at low load and a collision-free technique at high load

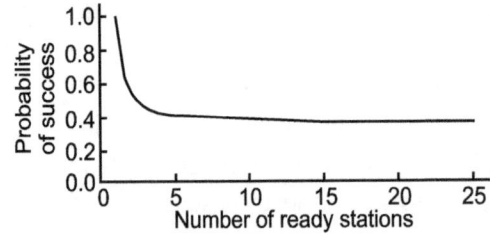

Fig. 7.25 :Acquisition probability for a symmetric contention channel.

Adaptive Treewalk Protocol :

The following is the method of adaptive tree protocol. Initially all the nodes are allowed to try to aquire the channel. If it is able to aquire the channel, it sends its frame. If there is collision then the nodes are divided into two equal groups and only one of these groups compete for slot 1. If one of its member aquires the channel then the next slot is reserved for the other group. On the other hand, if there is a collision then that group is again subdivided and the same process is followed. This can be better understood if the nodes are thought of as being organised in a binary tree as shown in the following figure. Many improvements could be made to the algorithm. For example, consider the case of nodes G and H being the only ones wanting to transmit. At slot 1 a collision will be detected and so 2 will be tried and it will be found to be idle. Hence it is pointless to probe 3 and one should directly go to 6,7.

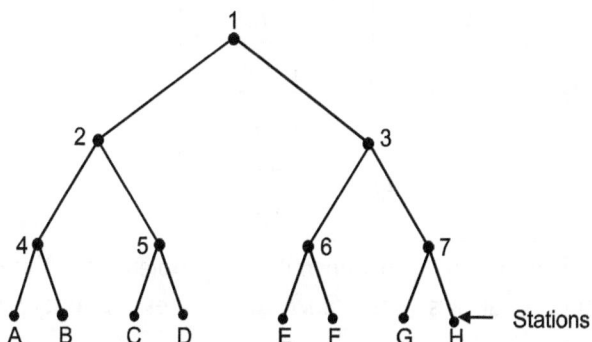

Fig. 7.26 : The tree for 8 stations

7.7 COLLISION FREE PROTOCOLS

Although collisions do not occur with CSMA/CD once a station has unambigously seized the channel, they can still occur during the contention period. These collisions adversely affect the efficiency of transmission. Hence some protocols have been developed which are contention free.

Bit-Map Method :

In this method, there N slots. If node 0 has a frame to send, it transmit a 1 bit during the first slot. No other node is allowed to transmit during this period. Next node 1 gets a chance to transmit 1 bit if it has something to send, regardless of what node 0 had transmitted. This is done for all the nodes. In general node j may declare the fact that it has a frsme to send by inserting a 1 into slot j. Hence after all nodes have passed, each node has complete knowledge of who wants to send a frame. Now they begin transmitting in numerical order. Since everyone knows who is transmitting and when, there could never be any collision.

The basic problem with this protocol is its inefficiency during low load. If a node has to transmit and no other node needs to do so, even then it has to wait for the bitmap to finish. Hence the bitmap will be repeated over and over again if very few nodes want to send wasting valuable bandwidth.

Binary Countdown :

In this protocol, a node which wants to signal that it has a frame to send does so by writing its address into the header as a binary number. The arbitration is such that as soon as a node sees that a higher bit position that is 0 in its address has been overwritten with a 1, it gives up. The final result is the address of the node which is allowed to send. After the node has transmitted the whole process is repeated all over again. Given below is an example situation.

Nodes	Addresses
A	0010
B	0101
C	1010
D	1001

	1010

Node C having higher priority gets to transmit. The problem with this protocol is that the nodes with higher address always wins. Hence this creates a priority which is highly unfair and hence undesirable.

7.7 LIMITED CONTENTION PROTOCOLS

Both the type of protocols described above - Contention based and Contention - free has their own problems. Under conditions of light load, contention is preferable due to its low delay.

As the load increases, contention becomes increasingly less attractive, because the overload associated with channel arbitration becomes greater. Just the reverse is true for contention - free protocols. At low load, they have high delay, but as the load increases, the channel efficiency improves rather than getting worse as it does for contention protocols.

Obviously it would be better if one could combine the best properties of the contention and contention - free protocols, that is, protocol which used contention at low loads to provide low delay, but used a cotention-free technique at high load to provide good channel efficiency. Such protocols do exist and are called Limited contention protocols.

It is obvious that the probablity of some station aquiring the channel could only be increased by decreasing the amount of competition. The limited contention protocols do exactly that. They first divide the stations up into (not necessarily disjoint) groups. Only the members of group 0 are permitted to compete for slot 0. The competition for aquiring the slot within a group is contention based.

If one of the members of that group succeeds, it aquires the channel and transmits a frame. If there is collision or no node of a particular group wants to send then the members of the next group compete for the next slot. The probablity of a particular node is set to a particular value (optimum).

Adaptive Tree Walk Protocol :

The following is the method of adaptive tree protocol. Initially all the nodes are allowed to try to aquire the channel. If it is able to aquire the channel, it sends its frame. If there is collision then the nodes are divided into two equal groups and only one of these groups compete for slot 1. If one of its member aquires the channel then the next slot is reserved for the other group. On the other hand, if there is a collision then that group is again subdivided and the same process is followed. This can be better understood if the nodes are thought of as being organised in a binary tree as shown in the following figure.

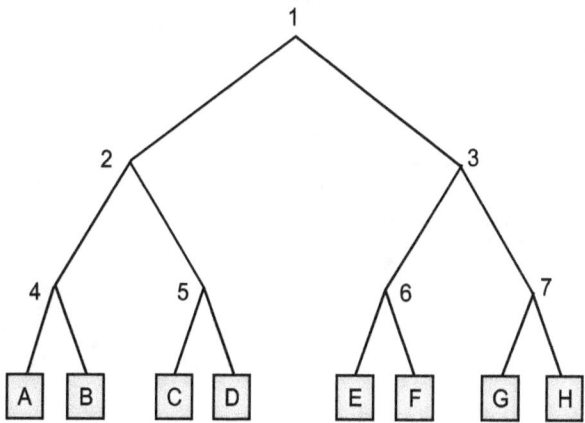

Fig. 7.27 : Adaptive Tree Walk Abstraction of Nodes in Binary Tree

Many improvements could be made to the algorithm. For example, consider the case of nodes G and H being the only ones wanting to transmit. At slot 1 a collision will be detected and so 2 will be tried and it will be found to be idle. Hence it is pointless to probe 3 and one should directly go to 6,7.

SOLVED EXAMPLES

Example 7.1 : Consider a 64 kbps geostationary satellite channel is used to send 512 byte data frames in one direction, with very short acknowledgement coming back the other way. What is maximum throughput for window size of 1, 7, 15 and 127 ? (Sliding window protocol is used).

Solution :

Given :

$$R = 64 \text{ kbps} = 64000 \text{ bits/sec}$$

$$\text{Frame size} = 512 \text{ byte} = 4096 \text{ bits}$$

$$\text{Frame time, } T_F = \frac{\text{Frame size}}{\text{Rate}} = \frac{4096}{64000} = 64 \times 10^{-3} \text{ sec} = 64 \text{ ms}$$

Round trip propagation delay.

$$2T_P = 540 \text{ ms}$$

Throughput is given by,

$$\eta = \frac{W_S T_F}{T_F + 2T_P}$$

(i) $W_S = 1$

$$\eta = \frac{1 \times 64}{64 + 540} = 0.1059$$

i.e. throughput is 10.59%

(ii)

$$\eta = \frac{7 \times 64}{64 + 540} = 0.7413$$

i.e. throughput is 74.13%

(iii) $W_S = 15$

Here, $W_S \geq \frac{2T_P}{T_F} + 1$

∴ $\eta = 1$

i.e. throughput is 100%.

(iv) $W_S = 127$

Here also,

$$W_S \geq \frac{2T_P}{T_F} + 1$$

∴ $\eta = 1$

i.e. throughput is 100%.

[i.e. when window size $W_S \geq \frac{2T_P}{T_F} + 1$, sender keeps on sending the frames and does not remain idle at any time].

Example 7.2 :

A 4 Mbps token ring has a token holding timer value of 10 m/sec. What is the longest frame that can be sent on this ring ?

Solution :

Given : $R = 4 \text{ Mbps} = 4 \times 10^6 \text{ bits/sec.}$

Token holding time = 10×10^{-3} sec.

∴ Number of bits that can be transmitted in 10 msec.

$$= 4 \times 10^6 \times 10 \times 10^{-3}$$
$$= 40000 \text{ bits}$$
$$= 5000 \text{ bytes}$$

Hence, longest frame is 5000 bytes including overheads. Data portion will be slightly less than this.

Example 7.3 :

Consider the use of 1000 bit frames on a 1 Mbps satellite channel. What is the maximum links utilization for

(i) Stop and Wait ARQ

(ii) Continuous ARQ with Windowsize 7.

(iii) Continuous ARQ with Windowsize 127.

(iv) Continuous ARQ with Windowsize 255.

Solution :

Given : Frame size = 1000 bits

Bit rate = 1×10^6 bits/sec.

∴ $T_F = \dfrac{1000}{1 \times 10^6} = 1 \times 10^{-3} = 1$ msec.

For satellite channel, T_P = 270 ms.

(i) Stop-and-Wait ARQ :

$$\text{Utilization} = U = \dfrac{1}{1 + 2\dfrac{T_P}{T_F}}$$

$$= \dfrac{1}{1 + 2 \times \dfrac{270}{1}}$$

$$= 0.0018 \text{ i.e. } 0.18\%$$

(ii) For Continuous ARQ (Sliding Window) :

$$\text{Utilization} = U = \dfrac{W_S}{1 + 2 \times \dfrac{T_P}{T_F}}$$

$W_S = 7$

∴ $U = 7 \times \dfrac{1}{541}$

$= 0.0129$

i.e. 1.29%

(iii) $W_S = 127$

$U = \dfrac{127}{541}$

$= 0.2343$

i.e. 23.43%

(iv) $W_S = 255$

$U = \dfrac{255}{541}$

$= 0.4713$ i.e. 47.13%

Example 7.4 :

A channel has a bit rate of 4 kbps and propagation delay 20 ms. For what range of frame size does stop-and-wait ARQ gives throughput $\geq 50\%$?

Solution :

Given :

$R = 4$ kbps

$\quad = 4 \times 10^3$ bits/sec

$T_P = ?$

$\eta \geq 50\%$

For stop-and-wait ARQ,

$$\eta = \dfrac{1}{1 + \dfrac{2T_P}{T_F}}$$

∴ $\dfrac{1}{1 + \dfrac{2T_P}{T_F}} \geq \dfrac{1}{2}$

∴ $\dfrac{1}{1 + \dfrac{2 \times 20}{T_F}} \geq \dfrac{1}{2}$

$\dfrac{T_F}{T_F + 40} \geq \dfrac{1}{2}$

$$2T_F \geq T_F + 40$$
$$T_F \geq 40$$
$$T_F \geq 40 \text{ ms}$$

∴ Frame size $= R \times T_F$

$$= \frac{4 \times 10^3}{10^3} \times 40 \times 10^{-3}$$

$$= 160 \text{ bits}$$

∴ Frame size ≥ 160 bits

≥ 20 bytes

Example 7.5 :

A group of N users share 56 kbps pure ALOHA channel. Each station outputs 1000 bit frame on an average of once every 100 sec., even if the previous has not yet been sent (buffered). What is maximum value of N ?

Solution :

For pure ALOHA,

Maximum throughput $= 0.184$

∴ Maximum usable channel bandwidth

$$R = 0.184 \times 56 \text{ kbps}$$
$$R = 10.3 \text{ kbps}$$

Rate of transmission of stations $= \dfrac{1000}{100} = 10$ bps

∴ Number of stations that can use the channel will be,

$$N = \frac{10.3 \times 10^3}{10} = 1030$$

Example 7.6 :

10,000 Airline reservation stations are competing for the use of a single slotted ALOHA channel. The average station makes 18 requests/hr. A slot is 125 μsec. What is approximate total channel load ?

Solution : Total channel load is number of transmissions per slot.

Given : One station makes 18 requests/hr.

i.e. 18/3000 requests/sec.

1/200 requests/sec.

∴ Number of requests made by 10000 stations in 1 sec

$$= 10000 \times \frac{1}{200} = 50$$

i.e. 50 requests in 1 sec.

Hence, number of requests per time slot of 125 μsec = $125 \times 10^{-6} \times 50$

i.e.　　　　Total load G = 0.006250

Example 7.7 :

A large population of ALOHA users manages to generate 50 requests/sec. including both originals and retransmissions. Time is slotted in units of 40 msec.

　(a)　What is the chance of success on first attempt ?

　(b)　What is the probability of exactly k collisions and then a success ?

　(c)　What is expected number of transmission attempts needed ?

Solution :

Given : Stations generate 50 requests/sec.

∴　Number of requests per time slot of 40 msec

$$= 40 \times 10^{-3} \times 50 = 2$$

∴　　　　G = 2

　(a)　For slotted ALOHA,

　　　Chance of success in first attempt will be

$$= e^{-G} \text{ (Poisson's Distribution)}$$
$$= e^{-2}$$
$$= 0.135$$

　(b)　The probability of exactly k collisions and a success

$$= (1 - e^{-G})^k \, e^{-G}$$
$$= 0.135 \times 0.865^{-k}$$

　(c)　The expected number of transmissions is,

　　　e^G = 7.4

Example 7.8 :

Calculate maximum throughput possible for ALOHA and pure ALOHA for a radio system with 9600 bps channel used for call setup request to base station. Let frame length be 200 bits.

Solution :

　(i) The maximum throughput for pure ALOHA = 0.184.

Given :

$$\text{Rate of transmission} = 9600 \text{ bps}$$
$$\text{Frame length} = 120 \text{ bits}$$

∴ Number of frames per sec.

$$= \frac{9600 \text{ bits/sec.}}{120 \text{ bits/frame}}$$
$$= 80 \text{ frames/sec}$$

∴ Throughput $= 80 \times 0.184 = 15$ frames/sec.

(ii) For slotted ALOHA

Maximum throughput $= 0.368$

∴ Throughput $= 0.368 \times 80$
$= 30$ frames/sec.

Example 7.9 :

Measurement of slotted ALOHA channel with infinite number of users. Show that 10% of slots are idle.

(a) What is channel load G ?
(b) What is throughput ?
(c) Is the channel under loaded or overloaded ?

Solution :

(i) **Given :** $N = \infty$

Idle slots $= 10\%$

∴ Probability of frame not generated $= 0.1$

Using Poisson's Law :

Probability that k transmissions are done in a slot is

$$= \frac{G^k \times e^{-G}}{k!}$$

∴ Probability that no frame generated

$$= \frac{G^0 \, e^{-G}}{k!}$$
$$= e^{-G}$$

∴ $0.1 = e^{-G}$

∴ $\ln 0.1 = -G$

∴
(ii)   Channel load, G = 2.3
Throughput s = Ge^{-G}
= $2.3 \, e^{-2.3}$
= 0.23

(iii) A channel is overloaded, if G > 1.
Since G = 2.3. It is overloaded.

Example 7.10 :

A CSMA/CD network running at 1 Gbps over 1 km cable with no repeators. The signal speed in the cable is 200000 km/sec. What is minimum frame size ?

Solution :

Given :
$$d = 1 \text{ km}$$
$$v = 2 \times 10^8 \text{ m/sec}$$

∴ Propagation time (T_P) = $\dfrac{d}{v} = \dfrac{1000}{2 \times 10^8} = 5 \times 10^{-6}$ sec

For CSMA/CSD the frame must not be transmitted in time $2T_P$.

∴ $2T_P = 10 \times 10^{-6} = 10$ μsec.

Rate of transmission = 1 Gbps

∴ 1×10^9 bits are transmitted in 1 sec.
∴   Number of bits transmitted in 10 μsec.
$$= 1 \times 10^9 \times 10 \times 10^{-6} = 10 \times 10^3$$
$$= 10000 \text{ bits}$$

∴   The frame size must be greater than 10000 bits which is minimum frame size.

Example 7.11 :

At a transmission rate of 5 Mbps and propagation speed of 200 m/μsec to how many metres of cable is the 1 bit delay in token ring interface is equivalent ?

Solution :

Bit rate R = 5 Mbps = 5×10^6

Bit duration = $\dfrac{1}{R} = 2 \times 10^{-7}$

Propagation speed = 200×10^6 m/s
= 2×10^8 m/s

Distance equivalent/bit   d = $v \times R = 2 \times 10^8 \times 2 \times 10^{-7}$ = 40 m

[i.e. if we add one more station it will introduce delay equivalent to 40 m cable].

Example 7.12 :

Draw sender and receiver windows for a system using Go-back N ARQ and selective repeat ARQ.

    (a) Frame 0 is sent; frame 0 is acknowledged.
    (b) Frame 1 and 2 are sent; frame 1 and 2 are acknowledged.
    (c) Frames 3, 4 and 5 are sent NAK 4 is received.
    (d) Frames 4, 5, 6, 7 are sent frames 4 through 7 are acknowledged.

Solution :
(i) Go-back N ARQ

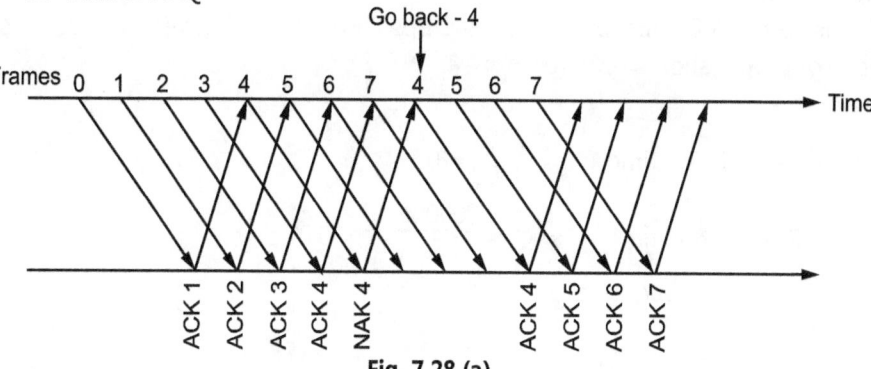

Fig. 7.28 (a)

(ii) Selective Repeat ARQ

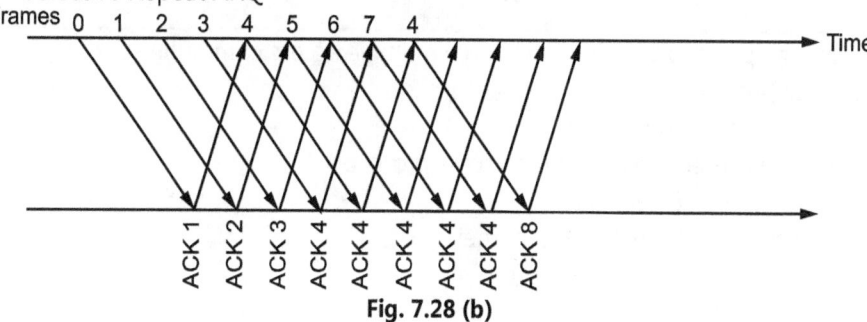

Fig. 7.28 (b)

Example 7.13 :
Computer A uses stop-and-wait ARQ protocol to send packets to computer B. Distance between A and B is 4000 km. How long does it take for computer A to send out a packet of size 1000 byte if throughput is 100000 kbps ? How much time the computer is idle ? (Assume propagation speed to be speed of light).

Solution : Given :
$$d = 4000 \text{ km}$$
$$N_F = 1000 \text{ byte} = 8000 \text{ bits}$$
$$v = 3 \times 10^8 \text{ m/s}$$
$$T_F = ?$$

∴ Propagation delay $T_P = \dfrac{4000 \times 10^3}{3 \times 10^8} = \dfrac{4}{3} \times 10^{-2}$

$s = 0.0133$ s Throughput for stop and wait ARQ is

(i) Here throughput means rate at which data is coming out of station A.
∴ Time token to transmit one packet is,
$$T_F = \dfrac{8000}{100000 \times 10^3} = 8 \times 10^{-6}$$

(ii) Idle time $= 2T_P - T_F$
$$= 0.01333 \times 2 - 8 \times 10^{-5} = 0.026658663$$

Example 7.14 :

Calculate the maximum link utilization efficiency for stop-and-wait flow control mechanism if the frame size is 2400 bits, bit rate is 4800 bps and distance between the devices is 2000 km. Speed of propagation be 2×10^8 m/s.

Solution :

$$\text{Frame transmission time } T_F = \frac{2400}{4800} = 0.5$$

$$\text{Propagation time } T_P = \frac{d}{v} = \frac{2000 \times 10^3}{2 \times 10^8} = 0.01 \text{ s}$$

Link utilization is throughput

$$\eta = \frac{T_F}{T_F + 2T_P} = \frac{0.5}{0.5 + 0.01 \times 2} = 96.15\%$$

EXERCISES

1. State the protocols devised to handle multiple access communication.
2. Explain pure aloha.
3. Explain slotted aloha.
4. What are carrier sense multiple access protocols ?
5. Explain CSMA/CD technique.
6. How collision is detected in Ethernet ?
7. What is retransmission Back-off ?
8. Explain CSMA/CA technique.
9. What is controlled access ? How it is achieved ?
10. What is logical ring ? Explain.
11. State and explain various multiple access techniques.
12. Compare FDMA, TDMA and CDMA.
13. What are advantages and disadvantages of FDMA ?
14. What are advantages and disadvantages of TDMA ?
15. What are advantages and disadvantages of CDMA ?
16. What is Ethernet ?
17. State various forms of Ethernet based on data rate.
18. Explain standard Ethernet and frame format of standard ethernet.
19. What is bridged ethernet ?
20. What is switched ethernet ?
21. Explain various physical layer implementations of 10 Mbps Ethernet.
22. What is Fast Ethernet ? Give its frame format.
23. What is Gigabit Ethernet ? Give its frame format.
24. Explain Ten Gigabit ethernet.

Chapter 8
IEEE STANDARDS FOR LANS AND MANS

OBJECTIVES

After reading this chapter, the student will understand :

- 802.3 standard and Ethernet.
- 802.4 standard and token bus
- 802.5 standard and token ring
- Comparison of 802.3, 802.4 and 802.5.

8.1 ETHERNET

Local Area Network (LAN) is a data communications network connecting terminals, computers and printers within a building or other geographically limited areas. These devices could be connected through wired cables or wireless links. Ethernet, Token Ring and Wireless LAN using IEEE 802.11 are examples of standard LAN technologies.

Ethernet is by far the most commonly used LAN technology. Token Ring technology is still used by some companies. FDDI is sometimes used as a backbone LAN interconnecting Ethernet or Token Ring LANs. WLAN using IEEE 802.11 technologies is rapidly becoming the new leading LAN technology for its mobility and easy to use features.

Local Area Network could be interconnected using Wide Area Network (WAN) or Metropolitan Area Network (MAN) technologies. The common WAN technologies include TCP/IP, ATM, Frame Relay, etc. The common MAN technologies include SMDS and 10 Gigabit Ethernet.

LANs are traditionally used to connect a group of people who are in the same local area. However, the working group are becoming more geographically distributed in today's working environment. The virtual LAN (VLAN) technologies are defined for people in different places to share the same networking resource.

Local Area Network protocols are mostly used at data link layer (layer 2). IEEE is the leading organization defining most of the LAN protocols.

Protocol Structure - Local Area Network and LAN Protocols :

The key LAN protocols are listed as follows :

LAN - Local Area Network Protocols	
Ethernet	Ethernet LAN protocols as defined in IEEE 802.3 suite
	Fast Ethernet : Ethernet LAN at data rate 100Mbps (IEEE 802.3u)
	Gigabit Ethernet : Ethernet at data rate 1000Mbps (IEEE 802.3z, 802.3ab)
	10Gigabit Ethernet : Ethernet at data rate 10 Gbps (IEEE 802.3ae)
WLAN	Wireless LAN in IEEE 802.11, 802,11a, 802.11b, 802.11g and 802.11n
	IEEE 802.11i : WLAN Security Standards
	IEEE 802.1X : WLAN Authentication & Key Management
	IEEE 802.15 : Bluetooth for Wireless Personal Area Network (WPAN)
VLAN	IEEE 802.1Q : Virtual LAN Bridging Switching Protocol
	GARP : Generic Attribute Registration Protocol (802.1P)
	GMRP : GARP Multicast Registration Protocol (802.1P)
	GVRP : GARP VLAN Registration Protocol (802.1P, 802.1Q)
Token Bus	IEEE 802.4 : LAN Protocol
Token Ring	IEEE 802.5 LAN protocol
FDDI	Fiber Distributed Data Interface
Others	LLC : Logic Link Control (IEEE 802.2)
	SNAP : SubNetwork Access Protocol
	STP : Spanning Tree Protocol (IEEE 802.1D)
	IEEE 802.1p : LAN Layer 2 QoS/CoS Protocol

8.5.1 Ethernet : IEEE 802.3 Local Area Network (LAN) Protocols

Ethernet protocols refer to the family of local-area network (LAN) covered by the IEEE 802.3. In the Ethernet standard, there are two modes of operation : half-duplex and full-duplex modes. In the half duplex mode, data are transmitted using the popular Carrier-Sense Multiple Access/Collision Detection (CSMA/CD) protocol on a shared medium. The main disadvantages of the half-duplex are the efficiency and distance limitation, in which the link distance is limited by the minimum MAC frame size. This restriction reduces the efficiency drastically for high-rate transmission. Therefore, the carrier extension technique is used to ensure the minimum frame size of 512 bytes in Gigabit Ethernet to achieve a reasonable link distance.

Four data rates are currently defined for operation over optical fiber and twisted-pair cables :

- 10 Mbps - 10Base-T Ethernet (IEEE 802.3)
- 100 Mbps - Fast Ethernet (IEEE 802.3u)
- 1000 Mbps - Gigabit Ethernet (IEEE 802.3z)
- 10-Gigabit - 10 Gbps Ethernet (IEEE 802.3ae).

The Ethernet system consists of three basic elements :

1. The physical medium used to carry Ethernet signals between computers,
2. A set of medium access control rules embedded in each Ethernet interface that allow multiple computers to fairly arbitrate access to the shared Ethernet channel, and
3. An Ethernet frame that consists of a standardized set of bits used to carry data over the system.

As with all IEEE 802 protocols, the ISO data link layer is divided into two IEEE 802 sublayers, the Media Access Control (MAC) sublayer and the MAC-client sublayer. The IEEE 802.3 physical layer corresponds to the ISO physical layer.

The MAC sub-layer has two primary responsibilities :

- Data encapsulation, including frame assembly before transmission, and frame parsing/error detection during and after reception.
- Media access control, including initiation of frame transmission and recovery from transmission failure.

The MAC-client sub-layer may be one of the following :

- Logical Link Control (LLC), which provides the interface between the Ethernet MAC and the upper layers in the protocol stack of the end station. The LLC sublayer is defined by IEEE 802.2 standards.
- Bridge entity, which provides LAN-to-LAN interfaces between LANs that use the same protocol (for example, Ethernet to Ethernet) and also between different protocols (for example, Ethernet to Token Ring). Bridge entities are defined by IEEE 802.1 standards.

Each Ethernet-equipped computer operates independently of all other stations on the network : there is no central controller. All stations attached to an Ethernet are connected to a shared signaling system, also called the medium. To send data a station first listens to the channel, and when the channel is idle the station transmits its data in the form of an Ethernet frame, or packet. After each frame transmission, all stations on the network must contend equally for the next frame transmission opportunity. Access to the shared channel is determined by the Medium Access Control (MAC) mechanism embedded in the Ethernet interface located in each station. The medium access control mechanism is based on a system called Carrier Sense Multiple Access with Collision Detection (CSMA/CD).

As each Ethernet frame is sent onto the shared signal channel, all Ethernet interfaces look at the destination address. If the destination address of the frame matches with the interface address, the frame will be read entirely and be delivered to the networking software running on that computer. All other network interfaces will stop reading the frame when they discover that the destination address does not match their own address.

When it comes to how signals flow over the set of media segments that make up an Ethernet system, it helps to understand the topology of the system. The signal topology of the Ethernet is also known as the logical topology, to distinguish it from the actual physical layout of the media cables. The logical topology of an Ethernet provides a single channel (or bus) that carries Ethernet signals to all stations. Multiple Ethernet segments can be linked together to form a larger Ethernet LAN using a signal amplifying and retiming device called a repeater. Through the use of repeaters, a given Ethernet system of multiple segments can grow as a "non-rooted branching tree". "Non-rooted" means that the resulting system of linked segments may grow in any direction, and does not have a specific root segment. Most importantly, segments must never be connected in a loop. Every segment in the system must have two ends, since the Ethernet system will not operate correctly in the presence of loop paths. Even though the media segments may be physically connected in a star pattern, with multiple segments attached to a repeater, the logical topology is still that of a single Ethernet channel that carries signals to all stations.

8.5.2 Standard Ethernet

MAC Layer : In standard Ethernet MAC layer performs two functions :

1. Controls the access.
2. Data received from network layer is used for preparation of frame to pass it to physical layer.

Ethernet MAC Data Frame for 10/100 Mbps Ethernet

Number of bytes	7	1	2/6	2/6	2	46-1500bytes	4
Name of field	Pre	SFD	DA	SA	Length/Type	Data unit + pad	FCS

- **Preamble (PRE)** - 7 bytes. The PRE is an alternating pattern of ones and zeros that tells receiving stations that a frame is coming, and that provides a means to synchronize the frame-reception portions of receiving physical layers with the incoming bit stream.

- **Start-of-Frame Delimiter (SFD)** - 1 byte. The SFD is an alternating pattern of ones and zeros, ending with two consecutive 1-bits indicating that the next bit is the leftmost bit in the leftmost byte of the destination address.
- **Destination Address (DA)** - 6 bytes. The DA field identifies which station(s) should receive the frame.
- **Source Addresses (SA)** - 6 bytes. The SA field identifies the sending station.
- **Length/Type** - 2 bytes. This field indicates either the number of MAC-client data bytes that are contained in the data field of the frame, or the frame type ID if the frame is assembled using an optional format.
- **Data** - Is a sequence of n bytes ($46 \leq n \leq 1500$) of any value. (The total frame minimum is 64 bytes).
- **Frame Check Sequence (FCS)** - 4 bytes. This sequence contains a 32-bit Cyclic Redundancy Check (CRC) value, which is created by the sending MAC and is recalculated by the receiving MAC to check for damaged frames.

Physical Layer :

There are several physical layer implementations. Some of them are :
1. 10Base5 : Bus, thick coaxial.
2. 10Base2 : Bus thin coaxial.
3. 10Base7 : Star UTP.
4. 10BaseF : Star, fibre.

10Base5 : Thick Ethernet :

The first implementation is called 10Base5, thick Ethernet, or Thicknet. The nick name derives from the size of the cable, which is roughly the size of a garden hose and too stiff to bend with your hands. 10Base5 was the first Ethernet specification to use a bus topology with an external transceiver (transmitter/receiver) connected via to tap to a thick coaxial cable. Fig. 8.1 shows a schematic diagram of a 10Base5 implementation.

The transceiver is responsible for transmitting, receiving and detecting collisions. The transceiver is connected to the station via a transceiver cable that provides separate path for sending and receiving. This means that collision can only happen in the coaxial cable.

The maximum length of the coaxial cable must not exceed 500 m, otherwise, there is excessive degradation of the signal. If a length of more than 500 m is needed, upto five segments, each a maximum of 500 meter, can be connected using repeaters.

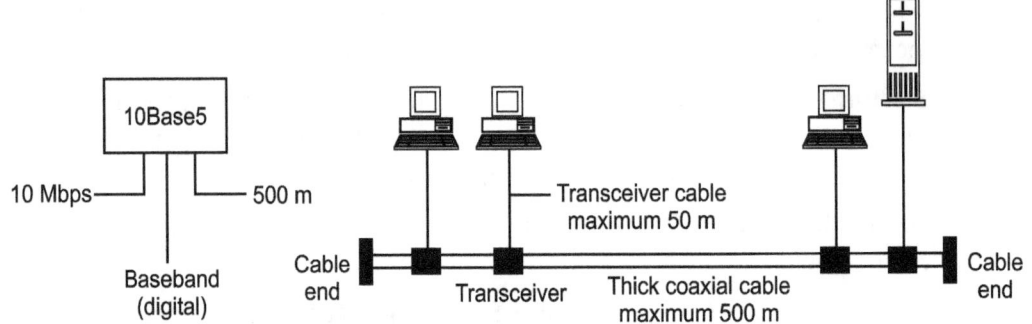

Fig. 8.1 : 10Base5 Implementation

10Base2 : Thin Ethernet :

The second implementation is called 10Base2, thin Ethernet, or Cheapernet, 10Base2 also uses a bus topology, but the cable is much thinner and more flexible. The cable can be bent to pass very close to the stations.

In this case, the transceiver is normally part of the Network Interface Card (NIC), which is installed inside the station. Fig. 8.2 shows the schematic diagram of a 10Base2 implementation.

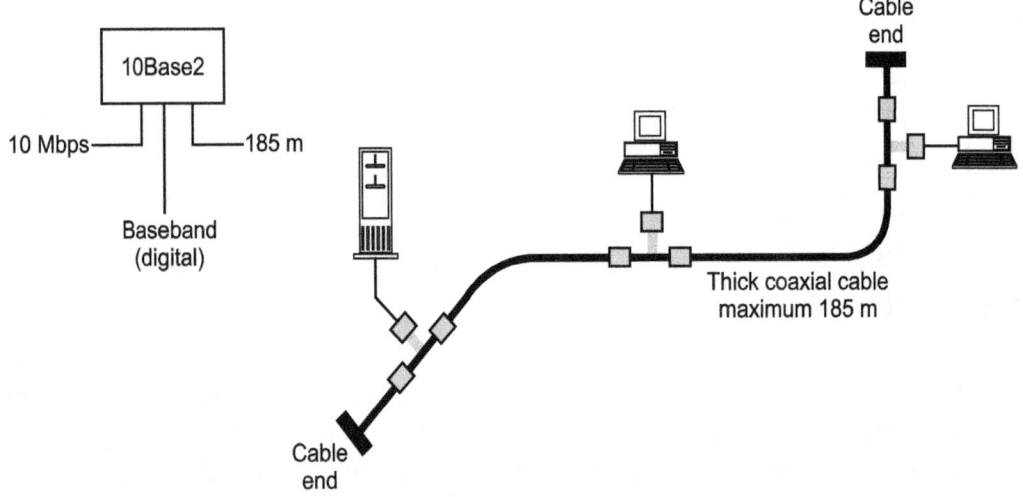

Fig. 8.2 : 10Base2 Implementation

Note that the collision here occurs in the thin coaxial cable. This implementation is more cost effective than 10Base5 because thin coaxial cable is less expensive than thick coaxial and the tee connections are much cheaper than taps. Installation is simpler because the thin coaxial cable is very flexible. However, the length of each segment cannot exceed 185 m (close to 200 m) due to the high level of attenuation in thin coaxial cable.

10Base-T : Twisted-Pair Ethernet :

The third implementation is called 10Base-T or twisted-pair Ethernet. 10Base-T uses a physical star topology. The stations are connected to a hub via two pairs of twisted cable, as shown in Fig. 8.3.

Note that two pairs of twisted cable create two paths (one for sending and one for receiving) between the station and the hub. Any collision here happens in the hub. Compared to 10Base5 or 10Base2, we can see that the hub actually replaces the coaxial cable as far as collision is concerned. The maximum length of the twisted cable here is defined as 100 m, to minimize the effect of attenuation in the twisted cable.

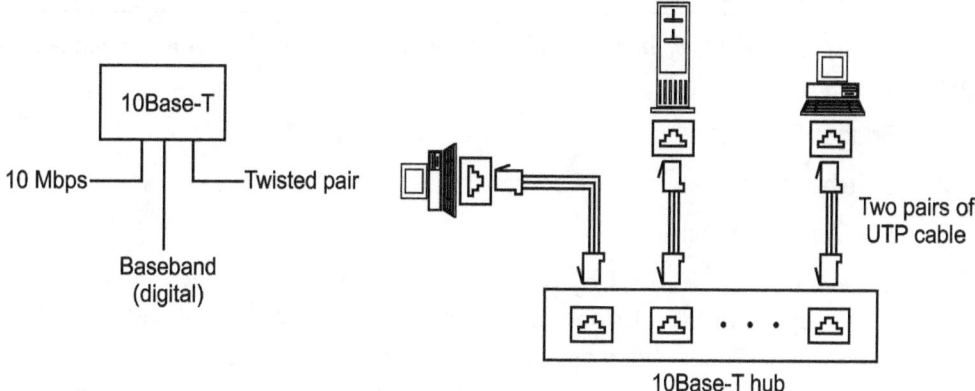

Fig. 8.3 : 10Base-T Implementation

10Base-F : Fiber Ethernet :

Although there are several types of optical fiber 10 Mbps Ethernet, the most common is called 10Base-F. 10Base-F uses a star topology to connect stations to a hub. The stations are connected to the hub using two fiber-optic cables, as shown in Fig. 8.4.

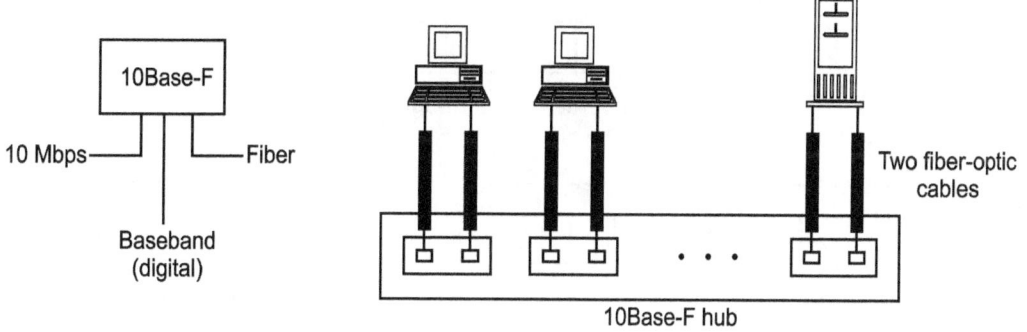

Fig. 8.4 : 10Base-F Implementation

Following table gives Comparison of Physical Layer Implementation of Ethernet.

Table 8.1 : Summary of Standard Ethernet Implementations

Characteristics	10Base5	10Base2	10Base-T	10Base-F
Media used	Thick coaxial cable	Thin coaxial cable	2 UTP	2 Fiber
Length	< 500 m	< 185 m	< 100 m	< 2000 m
Line coding technique	Split phase Manchester	Split phase Manchester	Split phase Manchester	Split phase Manchester

8.5.3 Bridged Ethernet

In order to have compatibility between 10 Mbps and 100 Mbps LANs, some changes were required. They are :

1. Bridged Ethernet.
2. Switched Ethernet.
3. Full Duplex Ethernet.

The bridged ethernet divides LAN by bridges because of which there is improvement in bandwidth and separation of collision domains. If we have 10 Mbps LAN and 10 nodes are there, the bandwidth will be divided among these nodes depending on need. e.g. if only one station wants to transmit entire bandwidth will be available to it. But if all of them want to transmit each one will have 1 Mbps bandwidth. We can improve the bandwidth efficiency by using a bridge. If 10 nodes are divided into 2 groups of 5 each, each group will have an average bandwidth of 10/5 = 2 Mbps instead of 1 Mbps.

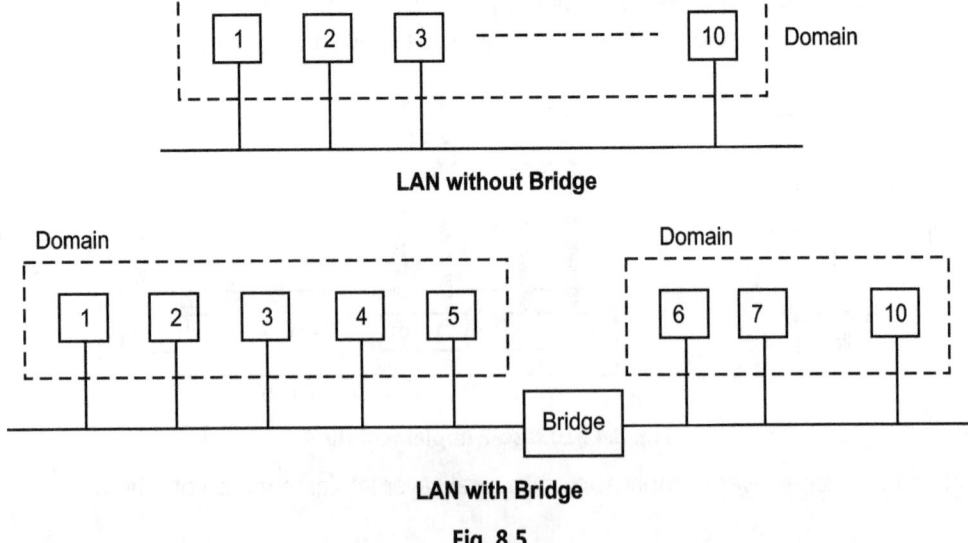

Fig. 8.5

Another advantage is number of nodes in collision domain are reduced and hence probability of collision reduces by 50%.

8.5.4 Switched Ethernet

If we divide the number of nodes in the LAN, there is improvement in bandwidth efficiency. We can have only single node in each network. If there are N nodes in LAN, there will be N networks. It is called switched LAN as shown below. The collision domain is also divided into N domains.

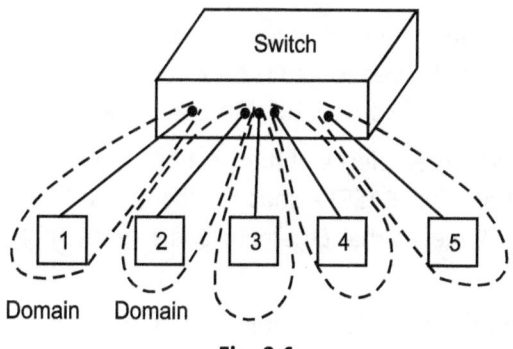

Fig. 8.6

The bandwidth will be shared between station and the switch (i.e. 5 Mbps each).

Full Duplex Ethernet :

In half duplex a station can either send or receive. In full duplex mode Ethernet, send and receive operations can be done simultaneously. The capacity of each domain is doubled because of this. Two links will be used in such configuration.

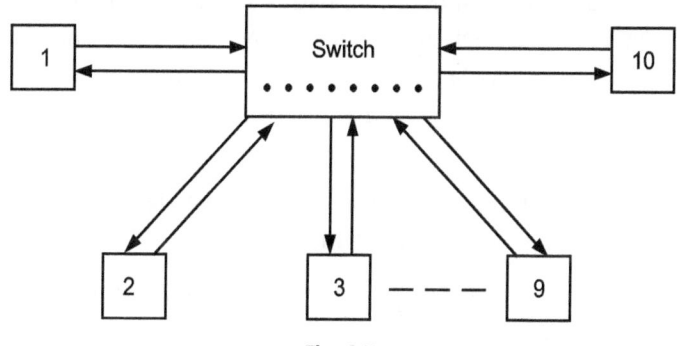

Fig. 8.7

In this mode, there is node of CSMA/CD, since each station is independent.

8.5.5 Fast Ethernet : 100 Mbps Ethernet

Fast Ethernet (100BASE-T) offers a speed increase ten times that of the 10BaseT Ethernet specification, while preserving such qualities as frame format, MAC mechanisms, and MTU.

Such similarities allow the use of existing 10BaseT applications and network management tools on Fast Ethernet networks. Officially, the 100BASE-T standard is IEEE 802.3u.

Like Ethernet, 100BASE-T is based on the CSMA/CD LAN access method. There are several different cabling schemes that can be used with 100BASE-T, including :

- 100BASE-TX : Two pairs of high-quality twisted-pair wires.
- 100BASE-T4 : Four pairs of normal-quality twisted-pair wires.
- 100BASE-FX : Fiber optic cables.

The Fast Ethernet specifications include mechanisms for Auto-Negotiation of the media speed. This makes it possible for vendors to provide dual-speed Ethernet interfaces that can be installed and run at either 10-Mbps or 100-Mbps automatically.

The IEEE identifiers include three pieces of information. The first item, "100", stands for the media speed of 100-Mbps. The "BASE" stands for "baseband," which is a type of signaling. Baseband signaling simply means that Ethernet signals are the only signals carried over the media system.

The third part of the identifier provides an indication of the segment type. The "T4" segment type is a twisted-pair segment that uses four pairs of telephone-grade twisted-pair wire. The "TX" segment type is a twisted-pair segment that uses two pairs of wires and is based on the data grade twisted-pair physical medium standard developed by ANSI. The "FX" segment type is a fiber optic link segment based on the fiber optic physical medium standard developed by ANSI and that uses two strands of fiber cable. The TX and FX medium standards are collectively known as 100BASE-X.

The 100BASE-TX and 100BASE-FX media standards used in Fast Ethernet are both adopted from physical media standards first developed by ANSI, the American National Standards Institute. The ANSI physical media standards were originally developed for the Fiber Distributed Data Interface (FDDI) LAN standard (ANSI standard X3T9.5), and are widely used in FDDI LANs.

Protocol Structure - Fast Ethernet : 100 Mbps Ethernet (IEEE 802.3u) The basic IEEE 802.3 Ethernet MAC Data Frame for 10/100 Mbps Ethernet

Number of bytes	7	1	2/6	2/6	2	612 <= n <= 1500	4 bytes
Name of field	Pre	SFD	DA	SA	Length/Type	Data unit + pad	FCS

- **Preamble (PRE)** - 7 bytes. The PRE is an alternating pattern of ones and zeros that tells receiving stations that a frame is coming, and that provides a means to synchronize the frame-reception portions of receiving physical layers with the incoming bit stream.

- **Start-of-Frame Delimiter (SFD)** - 1 byte. The SFD is an alternating pattern of ones and zeros, ending with two consecutive 1-bits indicating that the next bit is the left-most bit in the left-most byte of the destination address.
- **Destination Address (DA)** - 6 bytes. The DA field identifies which station(s) should receive the frame.
- **Source Addresses (SA)** - 6 bytes. The SA field identifies the sending station.
- **Length/Type** - 2 bytes. This field indicates either the number of MAC-client data bytes that are contained in the data field of the frame, or the frame type ID if the frame is assembled using an optional format.
- **Data** - Is a sequence of n bytes ($612 \leq n \leq 1500$) of any value. Note that since transmission speed has increased from 10 Mbps to 100 Mbps, frame transmission time reduces by factor of 10. Hence, minimum frame size increases by a factor of 10 to 640.
- **Frame Check Sequence (FCS)** - 4 bytes. This sequence contains a 32-bit Cyclic Redundancy Check (CRC) value, which is created by the sending MAC and is recalculated by the receiving MAC to check for damaged frames.

Gigabit (1000 Mbps) Ethernet :

Ethernet protocols refer to the family of Local-Area Network (LAN) covered by the IEEE 802.3 standard. The Gigabit Ethernet is based on the Ethernet protocol, but increased speed tenfold over the fast Ethernet, using shorter frames with carrier extension. It is published as the IEEE 802.3z and 802.3ab, supplement to the IEEE 802.3 base standards. The Gigabit Ethernet standards are fully compatible with Ethernet and Fast Ethernet installations. It retains Carrier Sense Multiple Access/Collision Detection (CSMA/CD) as the access method. It supports full-duplex as well as half duplex modes of operation. Single-mode and multi mode fiber and short-haul coaxial cable, and twisted pair cables are supported. The Gigabit Ethernet architecture is displayed in Fig. 8.8.

The IEEE 802.3z defines the Gigabit Ethernet over fiber and cable, which has a physical media standard 1000Base-X (1000BaseSX - short wave covers up to 500 m, and 1000BaseLX - long wave covers up to 5 km). The IEEE 802.3ab defines the Gigabit Ethernet over the unshielded twisted pair wire (1000Base-T covers up to 75m).

The Gigabit interface converter (GBIC) allows network managers to configure each gigabit port on a port-by-port basis for short-wave (SX), long-wave (LX), long-haul (LH), and copper physical interfaces (CX). LH GBICs extended the single-mode fiber distance from the standard 5 km to 10 km.

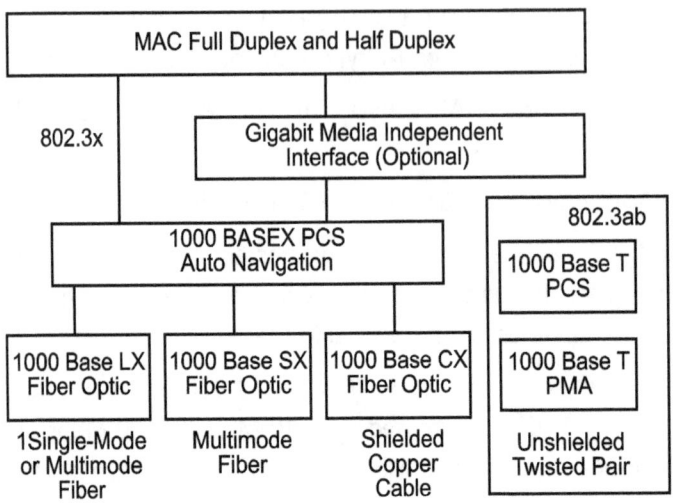

Fig. 8.8

Protocol Structure - Gigabit (1000 Mbps) Ethernet :

1000Base-X has a minimum frame size of 416 bytes, and 1000Base-T has a minimum frame size of 520 bytes. An extension field is used to fill the frames that are shorter than the minimum length.

Number of bytes	7	1	6	6	2	494 <= n <=1500	4	Variable
Name of field	Pre	SFD	DA	SA	Length/Type	Data unit + pad	FCS	Ext

- **Preamble (PRE)** - 7 bytes. The PRE is an alternating pattern of ones and zeros that tells receiving stations that a frame is coming, and that provides a means to synchronize the frame-reception portions of receiving physical layers with the incoming bit stream.

- **Start-of-Frame Delimiter (SFD)** - 1 byte. The SFD is an alternating pattern of ones and zeros, ending with two consecutive 1-bits indicating that the next bit is the left-most bit in the left-most byte of the destination address.

- **Destination Address (DA)** - 6 bytes. The DA field identifies which station(s) should receive the frame.

- **Source Addresses (SA)** - 6 bytes. The SA field identifies the sending station.

- **Length/Type** - 2 bytes. This field indicates either the number of MAC-Client Data Bytes that are contained in the data field of the frame, or the frame type ID if the frame is assembled using an optional format.

- **Data** - Is a sequence of n bytes (494 <= n <=1500) of any value.

- **Frame Check Sequence (FCS)** - 4 bytes. This sequence contains a 32-bit cyclic redundancy check (CRC) value, which is created by the sending MAC and is recalculated by the receiving MAC to check for damaged frames.
- **Ext** - extension, which is an non-data variable extension field for frames that are shorter than the minimum length.

8.5.6 Ten-Gigabit Ethernet

It is the fastest Ethernet which use optical fibre cable. It is specified as IEEE 802.3ae standard.

The goals of Ten-Gigabit Ethernet are :

- Upgradation of data rate to 10 Gbps.
- Make it compatible with other Ethernet standards.
- Use 48 bit address.
- Use same frame format.
- Make it compatible with other technologies such as ATM and frame relay.
- Keep same frame lengths (maximum and minimum).
- Allow existing LANs in WAN and MAN.

The specifications of MAC sublayer are full duplex mode of operation. Hence no contention. No need of CSMA/CD.

The physical layer specifications are :

- Fibre optic cables over long distance.
- Three different layers are :

    10GBase-S : Uses (300 m) short wave 850 nm multimode fibre.

    10GBase-L : Uses (10 km) long wave 1310 nm singlemode fibre.

    10GBase-E : Uses (40 km) extended 1550 nm single mode fibre.

8.2 TOKEN BUS

IEEE 802.4 Token Bus :

In token bus Computer network station must have possession of a token before it can transmit on the computer network. The IEEE 802.4 Committee has defined **token bus** standards as broadband computer networks, as opposed to Ethernet's baseband transmission technique. Physically, the token bus is a linear or tree-shape cable to which the stations are attached.

The topology of the computer network can include groups of workstations connected by long trunk cables. Logically, the stations are organized into a ring. These workstations branch from hubs in a star configuration, so the network has both a bus and star topology. Token bus topology is well suited to groups of users that are separated by some distance. IEEE 802.4 token bus networks are constructed with 75-ohm coaxial cable using a bus topology. The broadband characteristics of the 802.4 standard support transmission over several different channels simultaneously.

When the logical ring is initialized, the highest numbered station may send the first frame. The token and frames of data are passed from one station to another following the numeric sequence of the station addresses. Thus, the token follows a logical ring rather than a physical ring. The last station in numeric order passes the token back to the first station. The token does not follow the physical ordering of workstation attachment to the cable. Station 1 might be at one end of the cable and station 2 might be at the other, with station 3 in the middle. In such a case, there is no collision as only one station possesses a token at any given time. In token bus, each station receives each frame; the station whose address is specified in the frame processes it and the other stations discard the frame.

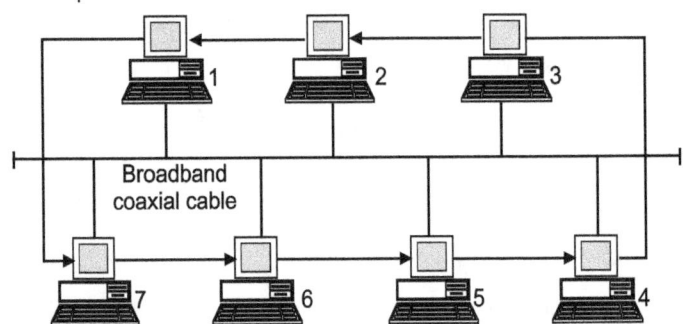

Fig. 8.9 token bus

MAC Sublayer Function

- When the ring is initialized, stations are inserted into it in order of station address, from highest to lowest.
- Token passing is done from high to low address.
- Whenever a station acquires the token, it can transmit frames for a specific amount of time.
- If a station has no data, it passes the token immediately upon receiving it.
- The token bus defines four priority classes, 0, 2, 4, and 6 for traffic, with 0 the lowest and 6 the highest.
- Each station is internally divided into four substations, one at each priority level i.e. 0, 2, 4 and 6.

- As input comes in to the MAC sublayer from above, the data are checked for priority and routed to one of the four substations.
- Thus each station maintains its own queue of frames to be transmitted.
- When a token comes into the station over the cable, it is passed internally to the priority 6 substation, which can begin transmitting its frames, if it has any.
- When it is done or when its time expires, the token is passed to the priority 4 substation, which can then transmit frames until its timer expires. After this the token is then passed internally to priority 2 substation.
- This process continues until either the priority 0 substation has sent all its frames or its time expires.
- After this the token is passed to the next station in the ring.

Frame format of Token Bus

The various fields present in the frame format are

1. Preamble : This. Field is at least 1 byte long. It is used for bit synchronization.

1byte	1byte	1byte	2-6byte	2-6 byte	0-8182	4byte	1byte
Preamble	Start delimiter	Frame control	Destination address	Source address	Data	Checksum	End delimiter

Fig. 8.10

2. Start Delimiter : This one byte field marks the beginning of frame.

3. Frame Control : This one byte field specifies the type of frame. It distinguishes data frame from control frames. For data frames it carries frame's priority. For control frames, it specifies the frame type. The control frame types include. token passing and various ring maintenance frames, including the mechanism for letting new station enter the ring, the mechanism for allowing stations to leave the ring.

4. Destination Address : It specifies 2 to 6 bytes destination address.

5. Source Address : It specifies 2 to 6 bytes source address.

6. Data : This field may be upto 8182 bytes long when 2 bytes addresses are used & upto 8174 bytes long when 6 bytes address is used.

7. Checksum : This 4 byte field detects transmission errors.

8. End Delimiter : This one byte field marks the end of frame.

The various control frames used in token bus are:

Frame Control Field	Name	Meaning
00000000	Claim_token	Claim token during ring initialization
00000001	Solicit_successor_1	Allow station to enter the ring
00000010	Solicit_successor_2	Allow stations to enter the ring
00000011	Who_follows	Recover from lost token
00000100	Resolve_contention	Used when multiple stations want to enter
00001000	Token	Pass the token
00001100	Set_successor	Allow station to leave the ring

8.3 TOKEN RING

Token Ring is formed by the nodes connected in ring format as shown in the diagram below. The principle used in the token ring network is that a token is circulating in the ring and whichever node grabs that token will have right to transmit the data.

Whenever a station wants to transmit a frame it inverts a single bit of the 3-byte token which instantaneously changes it into a normal data packet. Because there is only one token, there can at most be one transmission at a time. Since the token rotates in the ring it is guaranteed that every node gets the token with in some specified time. So there is an upper bound on the time of waiting to grab the token so that starvation is avoided. There is also an upper limit of 250 on the number of nodes in the network. To distinguish the normal data packets from token (control packet) a special sequence is assigned to the token packet. When any node gets the token it first sends the data it wants to send, then recirculates the token.

If a node transmits the token and nobody wants to send the data the token comes back to the sender. If the first bit of the token reaches the sender before the transmission of the last bit, then error situation araises. So to avoid this we should have: propogation delay + transmission of n-bits (1-bit delay in each node) > transmission of the token time. A station may hold the token for the token-holding time. which is 10 ms unless the installation sets a different value. If there is enough time left after the first frame has been transmitted to send more frames, then these frames may be sent as well. After all pending frames have been transmitted or the transmission frame would exceed the token-holding time, the station regenerates the 3-byte token frame and puts it back on the ring.

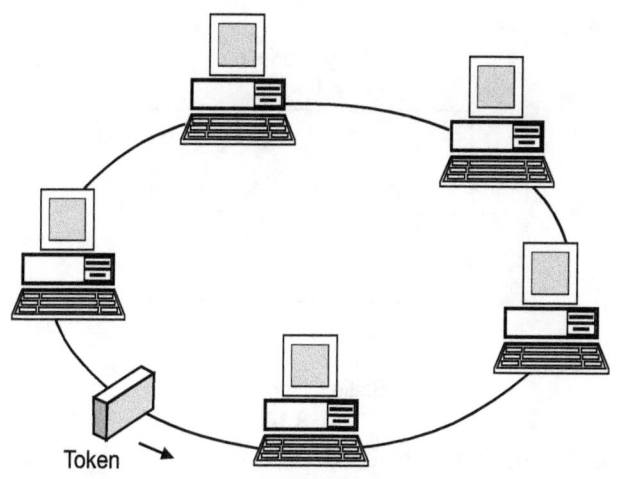

Fig. 8.11 : Token Ring

	IBM Token Ring Network	IEEE 802.5
Data Rates	4.16 Mbps	4.16 Mbps
Stations /segment	260 (shielded twisted pair) 72 (unshielded twisted pair)	250
Topology	Star	Not specified
Media	Twisted pair	Not specified
Signaling	Baseband	Baseband
Access method	Token passing	Token passing
Encoding	Differential Manchester	Differential Manchester

Fig. 8.12 : Although Dissimilar in Some Respects, IBM's Token Ring Network and IEEE 802.5 Are Generally Compatible

Modes of Operation :

1. **Listen Mode**: In this mode the node listens to the data and transmits the data to the next node. In this mode there is a one-bit delay associated with the transmission.

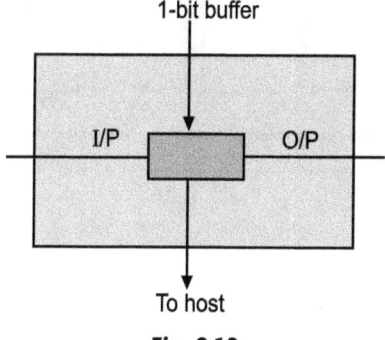

Fig. 8.13

2. **Transmit Mode:** In this mode the node just discards the any data and puts the data onto the network.

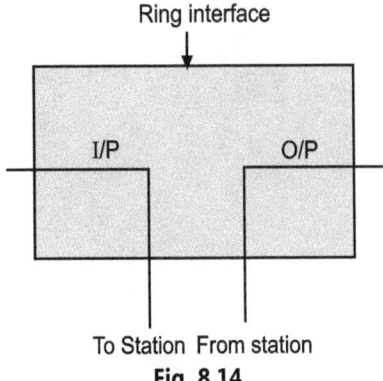

Fig. 8.14

3. **By-pass Mode:** In this mode reached when the node is down. Any data is just bypassed. There is no one-bit delay in this mode.

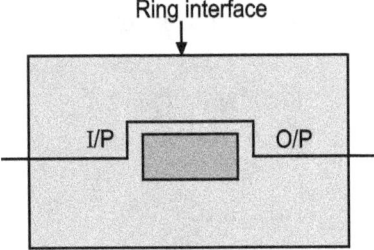

Fig. 8.15

Token Ring Using Ring Concentrator

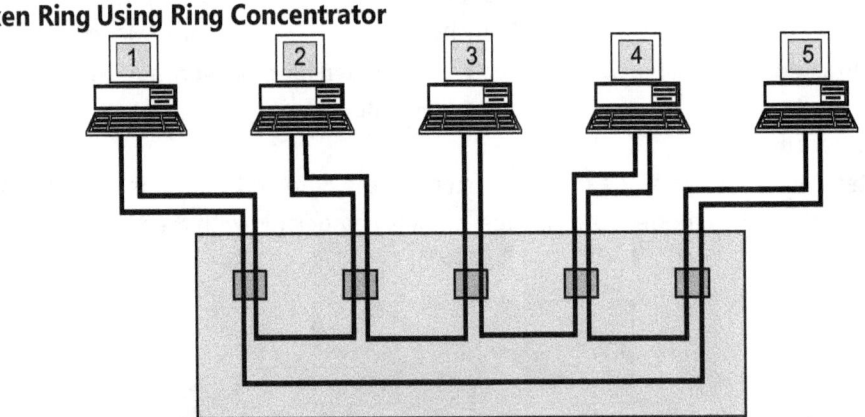

Fig. 8.16

One problem with a ring network is that if the cable breaks somewhere, the ring dies. This problem is elegantly addressed by using a ring concentrator. A Token Ring concentrator simply changes the topology from a physical ring to a star wired ring. But the network still remains a ring logically. Physically, each station is connected to the ring concentrator (wire center) by a cable containing at least two twisted pairs, one for data to the station and one for data from the station. The Token still circulates around the network and is still controlled in the same manner, however, using a hub or a switch greatly improves reliability because the hub can automatically bypass any ports that are disconnected or have a cabling fault. This is done by having bypass relays inside the concentrator that are energized by current from the stations. If the ring breaks or station goes down, loss of the drive current will release the relay and bypass the station. The ring can then continue operation with the bad segment bypassed. Who should remove the packet from the ring?

There are 3 possibilities-

The source itself removes the packet after one full round in the ring. The destination removes it after accepting it: This has two potential problems. Firstly, the solution won't work for broadcast or multicast, and secondly, there would be no way to acknowledge the sender about the receipt of the packet. Have a specialized node only to discard packets: This is a bad solution as the specialized node would know that the packet has been received by the destination only when it receives the packet the second time and by that time the packet may have actually made about one and half (or almost two in the worst case) rounds in the ring. Thus the first solution is adopted with the source itself removing the packet from the ring after a full one round. With this scheme, broadcasting and multicasting can be handled as well as the destination can acknowledge the source about the receipt of the packet (or can tell the source about some error).

Frame Format :

Token Ring and IEEE 802.5 support two basic frame types: tokens and data/command frames. Tokens are 3 bytes in length and consist of a start delimiter, an access control byte, and an end delimiter. Data/command frames vary in size, depending on the size of the Information field. Data frames carry information for upper-layer protocols, while command frames contain control information and have no data for upper-layer protocols. Both formats are shown in Token Frame Fields.

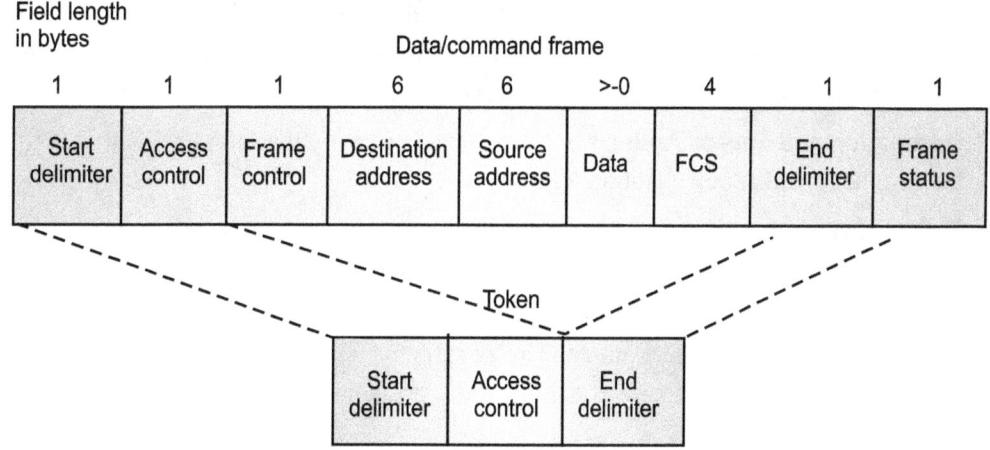

Fig. 8.17 : IEEE 802.5 and Token Ring Specify Tokens and Data/Command Frames.

The three token frame fields illustrated in Fig. 8.17 are summarized in the descriptions that follow:

Start Delimiter :

Alerts each station of the arrival of a token (or data/command frame). This field includes signals that distinguish the byte from the rest of the frame by violating the encoding scheme used elsewhere in the frame.

Access-Control Byte :

Contains the Priority field (the most significant 3 bits) and the Reservation field (the least significant 3 bits), as well as a token bit (used to differentiate a token from a data/command frame) and a monitor bit (used by the active monitor to determine whether a frame is circling the ring endlessly).

End Delimiter :

Signals the end of the token or data/command frame. This field also contains bits to indicate a damaged frame and identify the frame that is the last in a logical sequence.

Data/Command Frame Fields

Data/command frames have the same three fields as Token Frames, plus several others. The Data/command frame fields illustrated in Fig. 8.17 are described in the following summaries:

- **Start Delimiter :** Alerts each station of the arrival of a token (or data/command frame). This field includes signals that distinguish the byte from the rest of the frame by violating the encoding scheme used elsewhere in the frame.

- **Access-Control Byte :** Contains the Priority field (the most significant 3 bits) and the Reservation field (the least significant 3 bits), as well as a token bit (used to differentiate a token from a data/command frame) and a monitor bit (used by the active monitor to determine whether a frame is circling the ring endlessly).

- **Frame-Control Bytes :** Indicates whether the frame contains data or control information. In control frames, this byte specifies the type of control information.

- **Destination and Source Addresses :** Consists of two 6-byte address fields that identify the destination and source station addresses.

- **Data :** Indicates that the length of field is limited by the ring token holding time, which defines the maximum time a station can hold the token.

- **Frame-Check Sequence (FCS) :** Is filed by the source station with a calculated value dependent on the frame contents. The destination station recalculates the value to determine whether the frame was damaged in transit. If so, the frame is discarded.

- **End Delimiter :** Signals the end of the token or data/command frame. The end delimiter also contains bits to indicate a damaged frame and identify the frame that is the last in a logical sequence.

- **Frame Status :** Is a 1-byte field terminating a command/data frame. The Frame Status field includes the address-recognized indicator and frame-copied indicator.

8.4 COMPARISON OF 802.3, 802.4 AND 802.5

Sr. No.	Parameter of comparison	802.3 Ethernet	802.4 Token Bus	802.5 Token Ring
1	Physical topology	Linear	Linear	Ring
2	Logical topology	None	Ring	Ring
3	Contention	Random chance	By token	By token
4	Adding stations	A new station can be added almost anywhere on the cable at any time.	Distributed algorithms are needed to add new stations.	Must be added between two specified stations.
5	Performance	Stations often transmit immediately under light loads, but heavy traffic can reduce the effective data to nearly 0.	Stations must wait for the token even if no other station is transmitting. Under heavy load, token passing provides fair access to all stations.	Stations must wait for the token even if no other station is transmitting. Under heavy loads, token passing provides fair access to all stations.

6	Maximum delay before transmitting	None	Bounded, depending on distance spanned and number of stations.	Bounded, depending on distance spanned and number of stations. However, if priorities are used, a low priority station may have no maximum delay.
7	Maintainence	No central maintenance	Distributed algorithm provide maintenance	a designated monitor station performs maintenance
8	Cable used	Twisted pair, co-axial fiber optic	co axial	Twisted pair and fiber optic.
9	Cable length	50 to 2000 m	200 to 500 m	50 to 2000 m
10	Frame	10Mbps to 100 Mbps	10Mbps	4 to 100Mbps
11	Structure	1500 bytes	8191 bytes	5000 bytes

8.5 802.6 (DQDB)

IEEE 802.6 is a standard governed by the ANSI for Metropolitan Area Networks (MAN). It is an improvement of an older standard (also created by ANSI) which used the Fiber distributed data interface (FDDI) network structure. The FDDI-based standard failed due to its expensive implementation and lack of compatibility with current LAN standards. The IEEE 802.6 standard uses the Distributed Queue Dual Bus (DQDB) network form. This form supports 150 Mbit/s transfer rates. It consists of two unconnected unidirectional buses. DQDB is rated for a maximum of 160 km before significant signal degradation over fiberoptic cable with an optical wavelength of 1310 nm.

This standard has also failed, mostly due to the same reasons that the FDDI standard failed. Most MANs now use Synchronous Optical Network (SONET) or Asynchronous Transfer Mode (ATM) network designs, with recent designs using native Ethernet or MPLS.

IEEE 802.3 to 802.5 protocols are only suited for "small" LANs. They cannot be used for very large but non-wide area networks. IEEE 802.6 DQDB is designed for MANs

- It can cover an entire city, up to 160 km at a rate of 44.736 Mbps

Basic rule: if you want to send something to one of your right- hand neighbours, use upper A; otherwise, lower bus B Direction of flow on a bus points to downstream. Fixed-size 53-byte cells with 44-byte payload are used, similar to ATM – Stream of cells flows down on a bus. Each cell has a busy (B) bit and request (R) bit. If a cell is occupied, its B bit is 1. You make a request by setting a cell's R bit (if it is zero) to 1

- Unlike 802.3 to 802.5 where a user transmits at first chance, DQDB MAC is non greedy
- Users queue up in the order they became ready to send and transmit in FIFO order
- This is achieved without a central queue control, hence called distributed queue
- The key of this MAC protocol is: be polite to your downstream stations, and let them have go first if they requested before yours

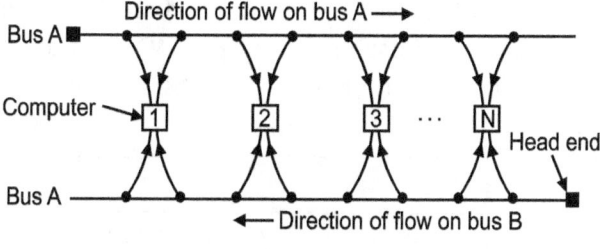

Fig. 8.18

How the MAC works :

consider transmission on bus A (on bus B is similar), each user has

– A RC that counts number of requests from its downstream stations

– A CD that counts number of outstanding requests issued before its own request

– Note that the downstream requests come from bus B, as you becomes "downstream" on bus B If a user wants to send something to its downstream (on bus A), it sets first available request bit in a cell on bus B to 1, and copies RC to CD

- Assume that the value of CD at this moment is x. Then there are x requests from the station's

downstream, and it has to let x free cells pass to the downstream

- Also, the user must let its upstream stations on bus A know its request, that is why it uses bus B to make a reservation

- Each time a non-busy cell passes by, CD is reduced by 1. When CD drops to zero, the user can take the next non-busy cell on bus A to transmit

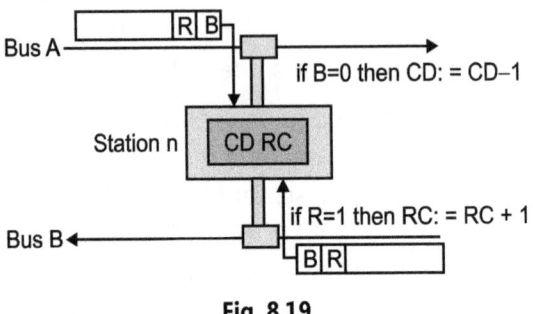

Fig. 8.19

Broadband Wireless

- IEEE 802.16 air interface for fixed broadband wireless access systems, also called wireless MAN or wireless local loop, has protocol stack:

It provides multimegabits wireless services for voice, Internet, movies on demand, etc.

- Physical layer operates in 10 to 66 GHz range, and base has multiple antennas, each pointing at a separate sector For close-in subscribers, 64QAM is used, so typical 25 MHz spectrum offers 150 Mbps; for medium-distance subscribers, 16QAM is used; and for distant subscribers QPSK is used

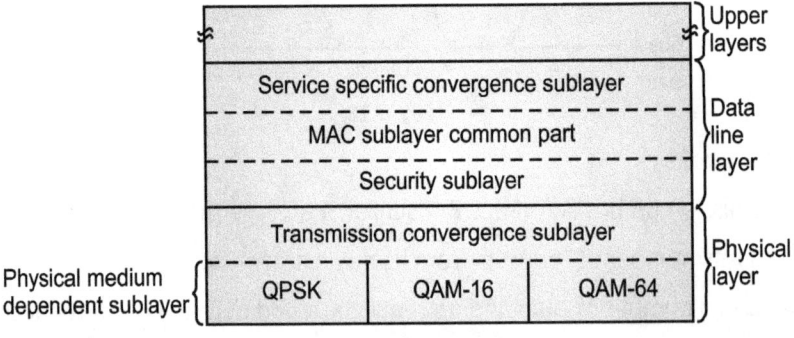

Fig. 8.20

- Data link layer consists of three sublayers

- Security sublayer manages encryption, decryption, and key management, crucial for privacy and security

- Service-specific convergence replaces logical link control, providing seamlessly interface for network layer that may have both datagram protocols and ATM

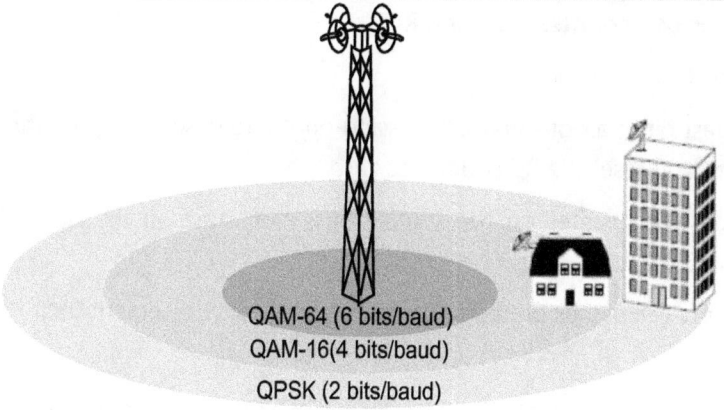

Fig. 8.21

802.16 MAC Sublayer Protocol

- 802.16 MAC sublayer is completely connection oriented to provide quality-of-service guarantees for telephony and multimedia, and MAC frames occupy integral number of physical layer time slots. Each frame is composed of subframes, and the first two are downstream and upstream maps

- These two maps tell what is in which time slot and which time slots are free

- Downstream map also contains system parameters to inform new users as they come on-line

- Downstream channel: base simply decides what to put in which subframe

- Upstream channel: there are competing subscribers and its allocation is tied to class of service.

- Constant bit rate: dedicate certain time slots to each connection and bandwidth is fixed through the connection, providing typical telephone channel service

- Real-time variable bit rate: for compressed multimedia and other soft real-time applications in which bandwidth needed each instant may vary Base polls subscriber at fixed interval to ask how much bandwidth is needed this time

- Non-real-time variable bit rate: for non-real-time heavy transmissions such as large file transfers Base polls subscribers often at non rigidly defined intervals to see who needs this service

- Best-efforts: no polling and subscriber contends for bandwidth with others

Requests for bandwidth are done in time slots marked in upstream map as available for contention.

Successful request will be noted in next downstream map, and unsuccessful subscriber has to wait a random period of time before try again

Each host keeps two counters, CD and RC

- Procedure for sending a cell:

- Set the request bit in a non-busy cell passing on the reverse bus. Copy the RC counter to the CD counter, and reset the RC counter to zero.

- As the request cell passes on the reverse bus, each host on the path observes it and increments its RC counter

- When an empty cell passes on the forward bus, the hosts decrement their RC counters and CD counters

- If RC and CD equal zero when an empty cell passes on the forward bus, it may be used to send the message

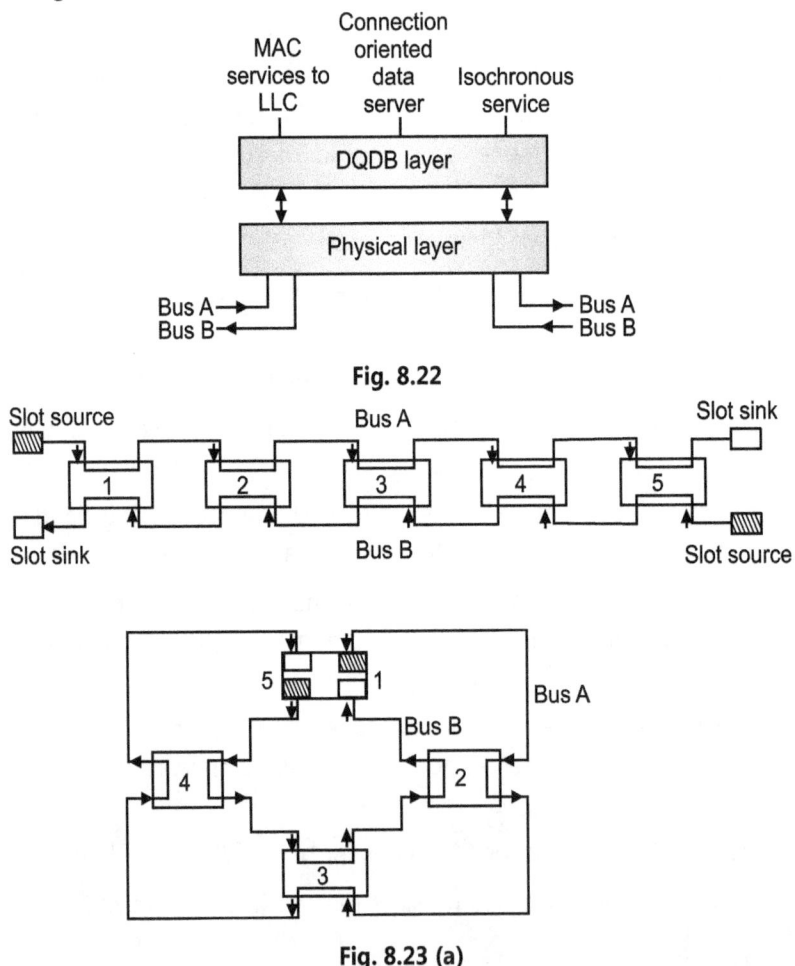

Fig. 8.22

Fig. 8.23 (a)

Transmitting Data

- Node acquires slot
- Sets header
- Copies data into slot
- Cells propagate to end of bus

(absorbed by sink)

- Copied by intended destination on way

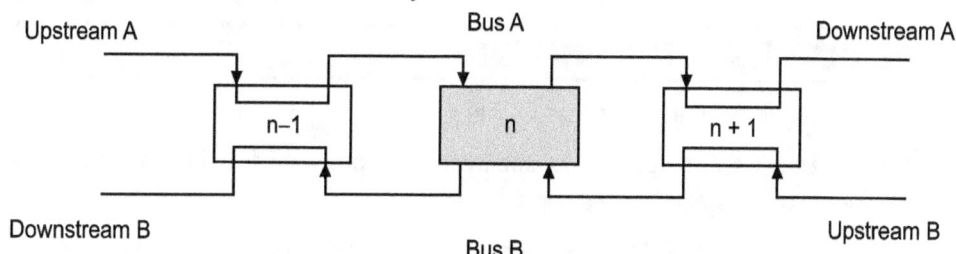

Fig. 8.23 (b) : A fragment of a DQDB network

802.16 Frame Structure

Generic frame (a) and bandwidth request (a control) frame (b):

Header is followed by an optional payload and an optional frame CRC

Control frames have no payload Generic frame starts with a bit 0

- EC bit: tells whether payload is encrypted
- Type: identifies frame type, telling whether packing and fragmentation are presented
- CI: indicates presence or absence of final checksum
- EK: tells which encryption keys is used (if any)
- Length: gives complete length of frame, including header
- Connection identifier: tells which connection this frame belongs to
- Header CRC: checksum over header only, using $x^8 + x^2 + x + 1$
- Control frame starts with a bit 1: 2nd and 3rd bytes form a 16-bit number telling how much bandwidth is needed to carry specific number of bytes
- Why optional frame CRC: no attempt is made to retransmit real-time frames ! Why bother with a CRC if no retransmission? Also error correction is present in physical layer (channel coding).

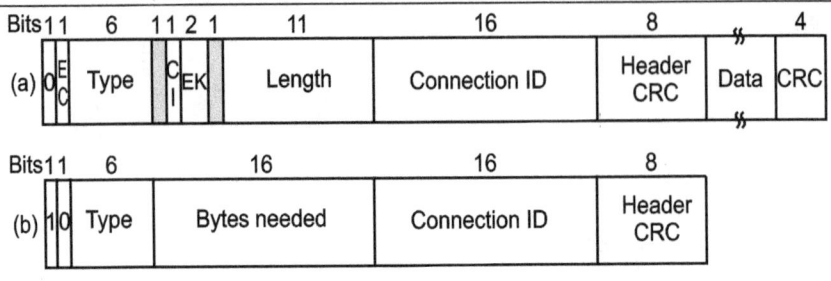

Fig. 8.24 (b)

8.6 802.2 LOGICAL LINK CONTROL

This Data Link Layer is divided into two sublayers:

- Logical Link Control (LLC). This sublayer is responsible for the data transmission between computers or devices on a network.

- Media Access Control (MAC). On a network, the network interface card (NIC) has an unique hardware address which identifies a computer or device. The physical address is utilized for the MAC sublayer addressing.

The function of the Logical Link Control (LLC) is to manage and ensure the integrity of data transmissions. The LLC provides Data Link Layer links to services for the Network Layer protocols. This is accomplished by the LLC Service Access Points (SAPs) for the services residing on network computers. Also, there is a LLC Control field for delivery requests or services.

The Logical Link Control (LLC) has several service types:

- Service type 1, is a connectionless service with no establishment of a connection, and an unacknowledged delivery.
- Service type 2, is a connection logical service with an acknowledgement of delivery.
- Service type 3, is a connectionless service with an acknowledgement of delivery.

Service classes furthermore support sundry permutations of these LLC service types:

- Class I supports only service type 1.
- Class II supports both service type 1 and type 2.
- Class III support both service type 1 and type 3.
- Class IV support all three service types.

The SubNetwork Access Protocol (SNAP) is an augmentation of the IEEE 802.2 LLC header. SNAP provides a method by which to utilize non-IEEE protocols on IEEE 802 networks.

RFC 1042:

IEEE 802 networks may be used as IP networks of any class (A, B, or C). These systems use two Link Service Access Point (LSAP) fields of the LLC header in much the same way the ARPANET uses the "link" field. Further, there is an extension of the LLC header called the Sub-Network Access Protocol (SNAP).

IP datagrams are sent on IEEE 802 networks encapsulated within the 802.2 LLC and SNAP data link layers, and the 802.3, 802.4, or 802.5 physical networks layers. The SNAP is used with an Organization Code indicating that the following 16 bits specify the EtherType code.

Normally, all communication is performed using 802.2 type 1 communication. Consenting systems on the same IEEE 802 network may use 802.2 type 2 communication after verifying that it is supported by both nodes. This is accomplished using the 802.2 XID mechanism.

However, type 1 communication is the recommended method at this time and must be supported by all implementations. The rest of this specification assumes the use of type 1 communication. The IEEE 802 networks may have 16-bit or 48-bit physical addresses. This specification allows the use of either size of address within a given IEEE 802 network.

RFC 1042:

The mapping of 32-bit Internet addresses to 16-bit or 48-bit IEEE 802 addresses must be done via the dynamic discovery procedure of the Address Resolution Protocol (ARP). Internet addresses are assigned arbitrarily on Internet networks. Each host's implementation must know its own Internet address and respond to Address Resolution requests appropriately. It must also use ARP to translate Internet addresses to IEEE 802 addresses when needed.

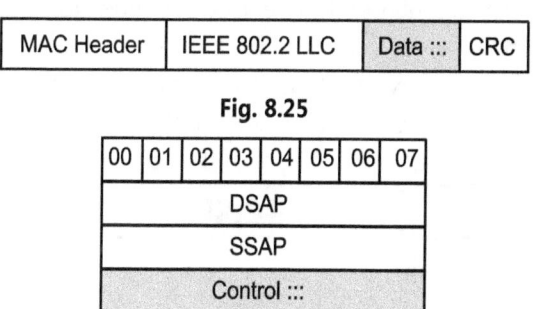

Fig. 8.25

Fig. 8.26 : IEEE 802.2 LLC packet format

DSAP, Destination Service Access Point. 8 bits:The LLC service access point address for the destination Service Access Point (SAP). SSAP, Source Service Access Point. 8 bits :The LLC service access point address for the source Service Access Point (SAP).

Control. 8 or 16 bits.

This field length depends upon whether the service has been requested or supplied.

Data : This field contains the encapsulated protocol. CRC, Cycle Redundancy Check. 4 bytes:Error checking.

| MAC Header | IEEE 802.2 LLC and SNAP | Data ::: | CRC |

Fig. 8.27 : Packet Header

Size (Bytes)	Value	Description	IEEE Types
1	AA		802.2 LLC
1	AA	SSAP, Source Service Access Point	802.2 LLC
1 or 2	03	Control	802.2 LLC
3		Organization Code.	802.2 SNAP
2		Ether Type	802.2 SNAP

IEEE_SNAP Frame format.

IEEE SNAP. Organization Code and EtherType fields follow the LLC fields. Organization Code. 3 bytes.:For the organization who assigned the EtherType field. EtherType. 2 bytes.:For the non-IEEE protocol. Data. Variable length.:This field contains the encapsulated protocol. CRC, Cycle Redundancy Check. 4 bytes.:Error checking.

Control Field :

Following the destination and source SAP fields is a control field. IEEE 802.2 was conceptually derived from HDLC, and has the same three types of PDUs:
- Unnumbered format PDUs, or U-format PDUs, with an 8-bit control field, which are intended for connectionless applications;
- Information transfer format PDUs, or I-format PDUs, with a 16-bit control and sequence numbering field, which are intended to be used in connection-oriented applications;
- Supervisory format PDUs, or S-format PDUs, with a 16-bit control field, which are intended to be used for supervisory functions at the LLC (Logical Link Control) layer.

Of these three formats, only the U-format is commonly used. The format of a PDU frame is identified by the lower two bits of the first byte of the control field.

EXERCISES

1. Explain the concept of Ethernet
2. Explain the 802.2 standard
3. Explain the 802.3 standard
4. Explain the 802.4 standard
5. Explain the 802.6 standard
6. Compare 802.2,802.3 and 802.4